The Long Twentieth Century

The Long Twentieth Century

Money, Power, and the Origins
of Our Times

GIOVANNI ARRIGHI

VERSO

London · New York

First published by Verso 1994
© Giovanni Arrighi 1994
All rights reserved

Reprinted 1996, 1999

Verso
UK: 6 Meard Street, London W1V 3HR
USA: 180 Varick Street, New York NY 10014-4606

Verso is the imprint of New Left Books

ISBN 1–85984–915–6
ISBN 1–85984–015–9 (pbk)

British Library Cataloguing in Publication Data
A catalogue record for this book is available from the British Library

Library of Congress Cataloging-in-Publication Data
Arrighi, Giovanni.
The long twentieth century: money, power, and the origins of our
times / Giovanni Arrighi.
p.   cm.
Includes bibliographical references and index.
ISBN 1–85984–915–6. – ISBN 1–85984–015–9 (pbk.)
1. Capitalism–History. 2. Economic history. I. Title.
HB501.A75 1994   94–25092
330.9′04–dc20   CIP

Typeset by Solidus (Bristol) Limited
Printed and bound in Great Britain by
Biddles Ltd, Guildford and King's Lynn

Contents

To my graduate students
at SUNY-Binghamton, 1979–94

Preface and Acknowledgements

This book began almost fifteen years ago as a study of the world economic crisis of the 1970s. The crisis was conceptualized as the third and concluding moment of a single historical process defined by the rise, full expansion, and demise of the US system of capital accumulation on a world scale. The other two moments were the Great Depression of 1873–96 and the thirty-year crisis of 1914–45. The three moments taken together defined the long twentieth century as a particular epoch or stage of development of the capitalist world-economy.

As I originally conceived this book, the long twentieth century constituted its exclusive subject-matter. To be sure, I was aware from the start that the rise of the US system could only be understood in relation to the demise of the British system. But I felt no need or desire to take the analysis further back than the second half of the nineteenth century.

Over the years I changed my mind, and the book turned into a study of what have been called "the two interdependent master processes of the [modern] era: the creation of a system of national states and the formation of a worldwide capitalist system" (Tilly 1984: 147). This change was prompted by the very evolution of the world economic crisis in the 1980s. With the advent of the Reagan era, the "financialization" of capital, which had been one of several features of the world economic crisis of the 1970s, became the absolutely predominant feature of the crisis. As had happened eighty years earlier in the course of the demise of the British system, observers and scholars began once more hailing "finance capital" as the latest and highest stage of world capitalism.

It was in this intellectual atmosphere that I discovered in the second and third volumes of Fernand Braudel's trilogy, *Capitalism and Civilization*, the interpretative scheme that became the basis of this book. In this interpretative scheme, finance capital is not a particular stage of world capitalism, let alone its latest and highest stage. Rather, it is a recurrent phenomenon which has marked the capitalist era from its earliest beginnings in late medieval and early modern Europe. Throughout the capitalist era financial expansions have signalled the transition from one regime of accumulation on a world scale to another. They are integral aspects of the recurrent destruction of "old" regimes and the simultaneous creation of "new" ones.

In the light of this discovery, I reconceptualized the long twentieth century as consisting of three phases: (1) the financial expansion of the late nineteenth and early twentieth centuries, in the course of which the structures of the "old" British regime were destroyed and those of the "new" US regime were created; (2) the material expansion of the 1950s and 1960s, during which the dominance of the "new" US regime translated in a world-wide expansion of trade and production; and (3) the current financial expansion, in the course of which the structures of the now "old" US regime are being destroyed and those of a "new" regime are presumably being created. More importantly, in the interpretative scheme which I derived from Braudel, the long twentieth century now appeared as the latest of four similarly structured long centuries, each constituting a particular stage of development of the modern capitalist world system. It became clear to me that a comparative analysis of these successive long centuries could reveal more about the dynamic and likely future outcome of the present crisis than an in-depth analysis of the long twentieth century as such.

This recasting of the investigation in a much longer time frame has resulted in a contraction of the space taken up by the overt discussion of the long twentieth century to about one third of the book. I have none the less decided to retain the original title of the book to underscore the strictly instrumental nature of my excursions into the past. That is to say, the only purpose of reconstructing the financial expansions of earlier centuries has been to deepen our understanding of the current financial expansion as the concluding moment of a particular stage of development of the capitalist world system – the stage encompassed by the long twentieth century.

These excursions into the past brought me onto the treacherous terrain of world historical analysis. Commenting on Braudel's *magnum opus* from which I have drawn inspiration, Charles Tilly has wisely warned us against the dangers of venturing on this terrain:

If consistency be a hobgoblin of little minds, Braudel has no trouble escaping the demon. When Braudel is not bedeviling us with our demands for consistency, he parades ... indecision. Throughout the second volume of *Civilisation matérielle*, he repeatedly begins to treat the relationship between capitalists and statemakers, then veers away.... Precisely because the conversation ranges so widely, a look back over the third volume's subject matter brings astonishment: The grand themes of the first volume – population, food,

clothing, technology – have almost entirely disappeared!... Should we have
expected anything else from a man of Braudel's temper? He approaches a
problem by enumerating its elements; fondling its ironies, contradictions, and
complexities; confronting the various theories scholars have proposed; and
giving each theory its historical due. The sum of all theories is, alas, no
theory.... If Braudel could not bring off the coup, who could? Perhaps
someone else will succeed in writing a "total history" that accounts for the
entire development of capitalism and the full growth of the European state
system. At least for the time being, we are better off treating Braudel's giant
essay as a source of inspiration rather than a model of analysis. Except with
a Braudel lending it extra power, a vessel so large and complex seems destined
to sink before it reaches the far shore. (Tilly 1984: 70–1, 73–4)

Tilly's recommendation is that we deal with more manageable units of
analysis than entire world systems. The more manageable units he prefers
are the components of particular world systems, such as networks of
coercion that cluster in states, and networks of exchange that cluster in
regional modes of production. By systematically comparing these components, we may be able "to fix accounts of specific structures and processes
within particular world systems to historically grounded generalizations
concerning those world systems" (Tilly 1984: 63, 74).

In this book I have sought another way out of the difficulties involved
in accounting for the full development of world capitalism and of the
modern inter-state system. Instead of jumping off Braudel's vessel of
world historical analysis, I stayed on it to do the kinds of thing that were
not in the captain's intellectual temperament to do but were within the
reach of my weaker eyes and shakier legs. I let Braudel plow for me the
high seas of world historical fact, and chose for myself the smaller task
of processing his overabundant supply of conjectures and interpretations
into an economical, consistent, and plausible explanation of the rise and
full expansion of the capitalist world system.

It so happens that Braudel's notion of financial expansions as closing
phases of major capitalist developments has enabled me to break down
the entire lifetime of the capitalist world system (Braudel's *longue durée*)
into more manageable units of analysis, which I have called systemic
cycles of accumulation. Although I have named these cycles after
particular components of the system (Genoa, Holland, Britain, and the
United States), the cycles themselves refer to the system as a whole and
not to its components. What is compared in this book are the structures
and processes of the capitalist world system as a whole at different stages
of its development. Our focus on the strategies and structures of Genoese,
Dutch, British, and US governmental and business agencies is due
exclusively to their successive centrality in the formation of these stages.

This is admittedly a very narrow focus. As I explain in the Introduction, systemic cycles of accumulation are processes of the "commanding heights" of the capitalist world-economy – Braudel's "real home of capitalism." Thanks to this narrow focus, I have been able to add to Braudel's survey of world capitalism some logical consistency and some extra mileage – the two centuries that separate us from 1800, where Braudel ended his journey. But the narrowing of the focus also has great costs. Class struggle and the polarization of the world-economy in core and peripheral locales – both of which played a prominent role in my original conception of the long twentieth century – have almost completely dropped out of the picture.

Many readers will be puzzled or even shocked by these and other omissions. All I can tell them is that the construction presented here is only one of several equally valid, though not necessarily equally relevant, accounts of the long twentieth century. I have presented elsewhere an interpretation of the long twentieth century which focuses on class struggle and core–periphery relations (see Arrighi 1990b). Having completed this book, there are many new insights that I would like to *add* to that earlier interpretation. Nevertheless, there are very few things that I would *change*. As far as I can tell, that account still stands from its own angle of vision. But the account presented in this book, as indicated by its subtitle, is the more relevant to an understanding of the relationship between money and power in the making of our times.

In order to bring my leaner version of Braudel's vessel to the far shores of the late twentieth century, I had to vow to keep out of the debates and polemics that raged in the islands of specialized knowledge that I visited and raided. Like Arno Mayer (1981: x), "I freely admit to being an ardent 'lumper' and master builder rather than an avid 'splitter' and wrecker." And like him, all I ask is " 'a patient hearing' and that [the] book be 'taken and judged as a *whole*' and not only in its discrete parts."

The idea that I should write a book about the long twentieth century was not mine but Perry Anderson's. After a heated discussion about one of the several long papers that I had written on the world economic crisis of the 1970s, he convinced me, as long ago as 1981, that only a full-length book was an adequate medium for the kind of construction I had in mind. He then kept a watchful eye on my wanderings through the centuries, always giving good advice on what to do and not to do.

If Perry Anderson is the main culprit for my involvement in this overambitious project, Immanuel Wallerstein is the main culprit for making the project even more ambitious than it originally was. In lengthening the time horizon of the investigation to encompass Braudel's *longue durée*, I was in fact following in his footsteps. His insistence in our daily work at the Fernand Braudel Center that the trends and conjunctures of my long twentieth century might reflect structures and processes that had been in place since the sixteenth century were sufficiently unsettling to make me check the validity of the claim. As I checked, I saw different things than he had; and even when I saw the same things, I gave them a different treatment and application than he has been doing in *The Modern World-System*. But in insisting that the *longue durée* of historical capitalism was the relevant time frame for the kind of construction I had in mind, he was absolutely right. Without his intellectual stimulus and provocation, I would not even have thought of writing this book in the way I did.

Between conceiving a book like this and actually writing it, there is a gulf that I would never have bridged were it not for the exceptional community of graduate students with whom I have been fortunate to work during my fifteen years at SUNY-Binghamton. Knowingly or unknowingly, the members of this community have provided me with most of the questions and many of the answers that constitute the substance of this work. Collectively, they are the giant on whose shoulders I have travelled. And to them the book is rightfully dedicated.

As mastermind of the Sociology Graduate Program at SUNY-Binghamton, Terence Hopkins is largely responsible for turning Binghamton into the only place where I could have written this book. He is also responsible for anything that is valuable in the methodology I have used. As the harshest of my critics and the strongest of my supporters, Beverly Silver has played a central role in the realization of this work. Without her intellectual guidance, I would have gone astray; without her moral support, I would have settled for far less than I eventually did.

An earlier version of chapter 1 was presented at the Second ESRC Conference on Structural Change in the West held at Emmanuel College, Cambridge, in September 1989, and was subsequently published in *Review* (Summer 1990) and reprinted in Gill (1993). Sections of chapters 2 and 3 were presented at the Third ESRC Conference on the same topic held at Emmanuel College in September 1990. Participation in these two conferences, as well as in the preceding one held in September 1988, added steam to my vessel at a time when it might otherwise have sunk. I am very grateful to Fred Halliday and Michael Mann for inviting me to the entire series of ESRC conferences, to John Hobson for organizing them effectively, and to all the other participants for the stimulating discussions we had.

Perry Anderson, Gopal Balakrishnan, Robin Blackburn, Terence Hopkins, Reşat Kasaba, Ravi Palat, Thomas Reifer, Beverly Silver, and Immanuel Wallerstein read and commented on the manuscript before the final round of revisions. Their different specializations and intellectual perspectives helped me enormously in fixing what could be fixed in the product of this hazardous enterprise. Thomas Reifer also helped me in a last-minute check of references and quotations. With greater reason than is customary, I take full responsibility for what remains unfixed and unchecked.

Finally, a special thanks goes to my son Andrea. When I began this work, he was about to enter high school. By the time I was writing the last draft, he had completed his *tesi di laurea* in philosophy at the Universita' Statale in Milan. Throughout, he was truly the best of sons. But as this work was drawing to a close, he had become also an invaluable editorial adviser. If the book finds any readership outside the historical and social science professions, I owe it largely to him.

GIOVANNI ARRIGHI
March 1994

Introduction

Over the last quarter of a century something fundamental seems to have changed in the way in which capitalism works. In the 1970s, many spoke of crisis. In the 1980s, most spoke of restructuring and reorganization. In the 1990s, we are no longer sure that the crisis of the 1970s was ever really resolved and the view has begun to spread that capitalist history might be at a decisive turning point.

Our thesis is that capitalist history is indeed in the midst of a decisive turning point, but that the situation is not as unprecedented as it may appear at first sight. Long periods of crisis, restructuring and reorganization, in short, of discontinuous change, have been far more typical of the history of the capitalist world-economy than those brief moments of generalized expansion along a definite developmental path like the one that occurred in the 1950s and 1960s. In the past, these long periods of discontinuous change ended in a reconstitution of the capitalist world-economy on new and enlarged foundations. Our investigation is aimed primarily at identifying the systemic conditions under which a new reconstitution of this kind may occur and, if it does occur, what it may look like.

Changes since about 1970 in the way capitalism functions locally and globally have been widely noted; though the precise nature of these changes is still a matter of some debate. But that they amount to something fundamental is the common theme of a rapidly growing literature.

There have been changes in the spatial configuration of processes of capital accumulation. In the 1970s the predominant tendency appeared to be towards a relocation of processes of capital accumulation from high-income to low-income countries and regions (Fröbel, Heinrichs, and Kreye 1980; Bluestone and Harrison 1982; Massey 1984; Walton 1985). In the 1980s, in contrast, the predominant tendency appeared to be towards the recentralization of capital in high-income countries and regions (Gordon 1988). But whatever the direction of the movement, the

1

tendency since 1970 has been towards greater geographical mobility of capital (Sassen 1988; Scott 1988; Storper and Walker 1989). This has been closely associated with changes in the organization of processes of production and exchange. Some authors have claimed that the crisis of "Fordist" mass production – based on systems of specialized machines, operating within the organizational domains of vertically integrated, bureaucratically managed, giant corporations – has created unique opportunities for a revival of systems of "flexible specialization" – based on small-batch craft production, carried out in small and medium-sized business units coordinated by market-like processes of exchange (Piore and Sable 1984; Sable and Zeitlin 1985; Hirst and Zeitlin 1991). Others have focused on the legal regulation of income-generating activities and have noted how the ever-increasing "formalization" of economic life – that is, the proliferation of legal constraints on the organization of processes of production and exchange – has called forth the opposite tendency towards "informalization" – that is, a proliferation of income-generating activities that bypass legal regulation through one kind or another of "personal" or "familial" entrepreneurialism (Lomnitz 1988; Portes, Castells, and Benton 1989; Feige 1990; Portes 1994).

Partly overlapping this literature, numerous studies have followed in the footsteps of the French "regulation school" and have interpreted current changes in the mode of operation of capitalism as a structural crisis of what they call the Fordist–Keynesian "regime of accumulation" (for a survey, see Boyer 1990; Jessop 1990; Tickell and Peck 1992). This regime is conceptualized as constituting a particular phase of capitalist development characterized by investments in fixed capital that create the potential for regular increases in productivity and mass consumption. For this potential to be realized, adequate governmental policies and actions, social institutions, norms and habits of behavior (the "mode of regulation") were required. "Keynesianism" is described as the mode of regulation that enabled the emergent Fordist regime fully to realize its potential. And this in turn is conceived of as the underlying cause of the crisis of the 1970s (Aglietta 1979b; De Vroey 1984; Lipietz 1987; 1988).

By and large, "regulationists" are agnostic as to what the successor of Fordism–Keynesianism might be, or indeed as to whether there will ever be another regime of accumulation with an appropriate mode of regulation. In a similar vein, but using a different conceptual apparatus, Claus Offe (1985) and, more explicitly, Scott Lash and John Urry (1987) have spoken of the end of "organized capitalism" and of the emergence of "disorganized capitalism." The central feature of "organized capitalism" – the administration and conscious regulation of national economies by managerial hierarchies and government officials – is seen as being jeopardized by an increasing spatial and functional deconcentration and decentralization of corporate powers, which leaves processes of capital accumulation in a state of seemingly irremediable "disorganization."

Taking issue with this emphasis on the disintegration rather than coherence of contemporary capitalism, David Harvey (1989) suggests that, in fact, capitalism may be in the midst of a "historical transition" from Fordism–Keynesianism to a new regime of accumulation, which he tentatively calls "flexible accumulation." Between 1965 and 1973, he argues, the difficulties met by Fordism and Keynesianism in containing the inherent contradictions of capitalism became more and more apparent: "On the surface, these difficulties could best be captured by one word: rigidity." There were problems with the rigidity of long-term and large-scale investments in mass production systems, with the rigidity of regulated labor markets and contracts, and with the rigidity of state commitments to entitlement and defense programs.

> Behind all these specific rigidities lay a rather unwieldy and seemingly fixed configuration of political power and reciprocal relations that bound big labor, big capital, and big government into what increasingly appeared as a dysfunctional embrace of such narrowly defined vested interests as to undermine rather than secure capital accumulation. (Harvey 1989: 142)

The US and British governments' attempt to maintain the momentum of the post-war economic boom through an extraordinarily loose monetary policy met with some success in the late 1960s but backfired in the early 1970s. Rigidities increased further, real growth ceased, inflationary tendencies got out of hand, and the system of fixed exchange rates, which had sustained and regulated the post-war expansion, collapsed. Since that time, all states have been at the mercy of financial discipline, either through the effects of capital flight or by direct institutional pressures. "There had, of course, always been a delicate balance between financial and state powers under capitalism, but the breakdown of Fordism–Keynesianism evidently meant a shift towards the empowerment of finance capital vis-à-vis the nation state" (Harvey 1989: 145, 168).

This shift, in turn, has led to an "explosion in new financial instruments and markets, coupled with the rise of highly sophisticated systems of financial coordination on a global scale." It is this "extraordinary efflorescence and transformation in financial markets" that Harvey, not without hesitation, takes as the real novelty of capitalism in the 1970s and 1980s and the key feature of the emerging regime of "flexible accumulation." The spatial reshuffling of processes of production and accumulation, the resurgence of craft production and of personal/familial business networks, the spread of market-like coordinations at the expense of corporate and governmental planning – all, in Harvey's view, are different facets of the passage to the new regime of flexible accumulation. However, he is inclined to see them as expressions of the search for financial solutions to the crisis tendencies of capitalism (Harvey 1989: 191–4).

Harvey is fully aware of the difficulties involved in theorizing the transition to flexible accumulation – assuming that that is what capitalism is actually experiencing – and points to several "theoretical dilemmas."

> Can we grasp the logic, if not the necessity, of the transition? To what degree do past and present theoretical formulations of the dynamics of capitalism have to be modified in the light of the radical reorganizations and restructurings taking place in both the productive forces and social relations? And can we represent the current regime sufficiently well to get some grip on the probable course and implications of what appears to be an ongoing revolution? The transition from Fordism to flexible accumulation has ... posed serious difficulties for theories of any sort.... The only general point of agreement is that something significant has changed in the way capitalism has been working since about 1970. (Harvey 1989: 173)

The questions that have informed this study are similar to Harvey's. But the answers are sought in an investigation of current tendencies in the light of patterns of recurrence and evolution, which span the entire lifetime of historical capitalism as a world system. Once we stretch the space–time horizon of our observations and theoretical conjectures in this way, tendencies that seemed novel and unpredictable begin to look familiar.

More specifically, the starting point of our investigation has been Fernand Braudel's contention that the essential feature of historical capitalism over its *longue durée* – that is, over its entire lifetime – has been the "flexibility" and "eclecticism" of capital rather than the concrete forms assumed by the latter at different places and at different times:

> Let me emphasize the quality that seems to me to be an essential feature of the general history of capitalism: its unlimited flexibility, its capacity for change and *adaptation*. If there is, as I believe, a certain unity in capitalism, from thirteenth-century Italy to the present-day West, it is here above all that such unity must be located and observed. (Braudel 1982: 433; emphasis in the original)

In certain periods, even long periods, capitalism did seem to "specialize," as in the nineteenth century, when it "moved so spectacularly into the new

world of industry." This specialization has led "historians in general ...
to regard industry as the final flowering which gave capitalism its 'true'
identity." But this is a short-term view:

> [After] the initial boom of mechanization, the most advanced kind of
> capitalism reverted to eclecticism, to an indivisibility of interests so to speak,
> as if the characteristic advantage of standing at the commanding heights of the
> economy, today just as much as in the days of Jacques Coeur (the fourteenth-
> century tycoon) consisted precisely of *not* having to confine oneself to a single
> choice, of being eminently adaptable, hence non-specialized. (Braudel 1982:
> 381; emphasis in the original; translation amended as indicated in Wallerstein
> 1991: 213)

It seems to me that these passages can be read as a restatement of Karl
Marx's general formula of capital: MCM'. Money capital (M) means
liquidity, flexibility, freedom of choice. Commodity capital (C) means
capital invested in a particular input–output combination in view of a
profit. Hence, it means concreteness, rigidity, and a narrowing down or
closing of options. M' means *expanded* liquidity, flexibility, and freedom
of choice.

Thus understood, Marx's formula tells us that capitalist agencies do
not invest money in particular input–output combinations, with all the
attendant loss of flexibility and freedom of choice, as an end in itself.
Rather, they do so as a *means* towards the end of securing an even greater
flexibility and freedom of choice at some future point. Marx's formula
also tells us that if there is no expectation on the part of capitalist agencies
that their freedom of choice will increase, or if this expectation is
systematically unfulfilled, capital *tends* to revert to more flexible forms of
investment – above all, to its money form. In other words, capitalist
agencies "prefer" liquidity, and an unusually large share of their cash flow
tends to remain in liquid form.

This second reading is implicit in Braudel's characterization of "financial expansion" as a symptom of maturity of a particular capitalist
development. In discussing the withdrawal of the Dutch from commerce
in the middle of the eighteenth century to become "the bankers of
Europe," Braudel suggests that such a withdrawal is a recurrent world-
systemic tendency. The same tendency had earlier been in evidence in
fifteenth-century Italy, when the Genoese capitalist oligarchy switched
from commodities to banking, and in the latter half of the sixteenth
century, when the Genoese *nobili vecchi*, the official lenders to the king
of Spain, gradually withdrew from commerce. Following the Dutch, the
tendency was replicated by the English in the late nineteenth and early
twentieth centuries, when the end of "the fantastic venture of the

industrial revolution" created an oversupply of money capital (Braudel 1984: 242–3, 246).

After the equally fantastic venture of so-called Fordism–Keynesianism, US capital followed a similar path in the 1970s and 1980s. Braudel does not discuss the financial expansion of our day, which gained momentum after he had completed his trilogy on *Civilization and Capitalism*. Nevertheless, we can readily recognize in this latest "rebirth" of finance capital yet another instance of that reversal to "eclecticism" which in the past has been associated with the maturing of a major capitalist development: "[Every] capitalist development of this order seems, by reaching the stage of financial expansion, to have in some sense announced its maturity: it [is] *a sign of autumn*" (Braudel 1984: 246; emphasis added).

Marx's general formula of capital (MCM') can therefore be interpreted as depicting not just the logic of individual capitalist investments, but also a recurrent pattern of historical capitalism as world system. The central aspect of this pattern is the alternation of epochs of material expansion (MC phases of capital accumulation) with phases of financial rebirth and expansion (CM' phases). In phases of material expansion money capital "sets in motion" an increasing mass of commodities (including commoditized labor-power and gifts of nature); and in phases of financial expansion an increasing mass of money capital "sets itself free" from its commodity form, and accumulation proceeds through financial deals (as in Marx's abridged formula MM'). Together, the two epochs or phases constitute a full *systemic cycle of accumulation* (MCM').

Our investigation is essentially a comparative analysis of successive systemic cycles of accumulation in an attempt to identify (1) patterns of recurrence and evolution, which are reproduced in the current phase of financial expansion and of systemic restructuring; and (2) the anomalies of this current phase of financial expansion, which may lead to a break with past patterns of recurrence and evolution. Four systemic cycles of accumulation will be identified, each characterized by a fundamental unity of the primary agency and structure of world-scale processes of capital accumulation: a Genoese cycle, from the fifteenth to the early seventeenth centuries; a Dutch cycle, from the late sixteenth century through most of the eighteenth century; a British cycle, from the latter half of the eighteenth century through the early twentieth century; and a US cycle, which began in the late nineteenth century and has continued into the current phase of financial expansion. As this approximate and preliminary periodization implies, consecutive systemic cycles of accumulation overlap, and although they become progressively shorter in duration, they all last longer than a century: hence the notion of the "long century," which will be taken as the basic temporal unit in the analysis of world-scale processes of capital accumulation.

These cycles are altogether different from the "secular cycles" (or price logistics) and the shorter Kondratieff cycles to which Braudel has attached so much importance. Secular and Kondratieff cycles are both empirical constructs of uncertain theoretical standing derived from observed long-term fluctuations in commodity prices (for surveys of the relevant literature, see Barr 1979; Goldstein 1988). Secular cycles bear some striking similarities to our systemic cycles. They are four in number; they all last longer than a century; and they become progressively shorter (Braudel 1984: 78). However, secular price cycles and systemic cycles of accumulation are completely out of synchrony with one another. A financial expansion is equally likely to come at the beginning, middle, or end of a secular (price) cycle (see figure 10, this volume).

Braudel does not attempt to reconcile this discrepancy between his dating of financial expansions – on which our periodization of systemic cycles of accumulation is based – and his dating of secular (price) cycles. And nor shall we. Faced with a choice between these two kinds of cycles, we have opted for systemic cycles because they are far more valid and reliable indicators of what is specifically capitalist in the modern world system than secular or Kondratieff cycles.

Indeed, there is no agreement in the literature on what long-term fluctuations in prices – whether of the logistic or the Kondratieff kind – indicate. They are certainly not reliable indicators of the contractions and expansions of whatever is specifically capitalist in the modern world system. Profitability and the command of capital over human and natural resources can decrease or increase just as much in a downswing as in an upswing. It all depends on whose competition is driving prices up or down. If it is the "capitalists" themselves, however defined, that are competing more (less) intensely than their "non-capitalist" suppliers and customers, profitability will fall (rise) and the command of capital over resources will decrease (increase), regardless of whether the overall tendency of prices is to rise or fall.

Nor do price logistics and Kondratieffs seem to be specifically capitalist phenomena. It is interesting to note that in Joshua Goldstein's synthesis of the empirical findings and theoretical underpinnings of long-wave studies, the notion of "capitalism" plays no role at all. Statistically, he finds that long waves in prices and production are "explained" primarily by the severity of what he calls "great power wars." As for capitalism, the issue of its emergence and expansion is put squarely outside the scope of his investigation (Goldstein 1988: 258–74, 286).

The issue of the relationship between the rise of capitalism and long-term price fluctuations has troubled world system studies right from the start. Nicole Bousquet (1979: 503) considered it "embarrassing" that price logistics long pre-dated 1500. For the same reason, Albert Bergesen (1983: 78) wondered whether price logistics "represent the dynamics of feudalism or capitalism, or both." Even Imperial China seems to have experienced wave-like phenomena of the same kind as Europe (Hartwell 1982; Skinner 1985). Most unsettling of all, Barry Gills and André Gunder Frank (1992: 621–2) have maintained that "the fundamental cyclical rhythms and secular trends of the world system should be recognized as having existed for some 5000 years, rather than the 500 years that has been conventional in the world system and long wave approaches."

In short, the connection between Braudel's secular cycles and the *capitalist* accumulation of capital has no clear logical or historical foundation. The notion of systemic cycles of accumulation, in contrast, derives directly from Braudel's notion of capitalism as the "non-specialized" top layer in the hierarchy of the world of trade. This top layer is where "large-scale profits" are made. Here the profits are large, not just because the capitalist stratum "monopolizes" the most profitable lines of business; even more important is the fact that the capitalist stratum has the flexibility needed to switch its investments continually from the lines of business that face diminishing returns to the lines that do not (Braudel 1982: 22, 231, 428–30).

As in Marx's *general* formula of capital (MCM'), so in Braudel's definition of capitalism what makes an agency or social stratum capitalist is not its predisposition to invest in a particular commodity (e.g. labor-power) or sphere of activity (e.g. industry). An agency is capitalist in virtue of the fact that its money is endowed with the "power of breeding" (Marx's expression) systematically and persistently, regardless of the nature of the particular commodities and activities that are incidentally the medium at any given time. The notion of systemic cycles of accumulation which we have derived from Braudel's historical observation of recurrent financial expansions follows logically from this strictly instrumental relationship of capitalism to the world of trade and production, and emphasizes it. That is to say, financial expansions are taken to be symptomatic of a situation in which the investment of money in the expansion of trade and production no longer serves the purpose of increasing the cash flow to the capitalist stratum as effectively as pure financial deals can. In such a situation, capital invested in trade and production tends to revert to its money form and accumulate more directly, as in Marx's abridged formula MM'.

Systemic cycles of accumulation, unlike price logistics and Kon-dratieffs, are thus inherently capitalist phenomena. They point to a fundamental continuity in world-scale processes of capital accumulation in modern times. But they also constitute fundamental breaks in the strategies and structures that have shaped these processes over the centuries. Like some conceptualizations of Kondratieffs, such as Gerhard Mensch's (1979), David Gordon's (1980), and Carlota Perez's (1983), our cycles highlight the alternation of phases of continuous change with phases of discontinuous change.

Thus, our sequence of partly overlapping systemic cycles bears a close formal resemblance to Mensch's "metamorphosis model" of socio-economic development. Mensch (1979: 73) abandons "the notion that the economy has developed in waves in favor of the theory that it has evolved through a series of intermittent innovative impulses that take the form of successive S-shaped cycles" (see figure 1). His model depicts phases of stable growth along a well-defined path alternating with phases of crisis, restructuring, and turbulence, which eventually recreate the conditions of stable growth.

Mensch's model refers primarily to growth and innovations in partic-ular industries or in particular national economies, and as such has no immediate relevance to our investigation. Nevertheless, the idea of cycles consisting of phases of continuous change along a single path alternating with phases of discontinuous change from one path to another underlies our sequence of systemic cycles of accumulation. The difference is that what "develops" in our model is not a particular industry or national economy but the capitalist world-economy as a whole over its entire lifetime. Thus, (MC) phases of material expansion will be shown to consist of phases of continuous change, during which the capitalist world-economy grows along a single developmental path. And (CM') phases of financial expansion will be shown to consist of phases of discontinuous change during which growth along the established path has attained or is attaining its limits, and the capitalist world-economy "shifts" through radical restructurings and reorganizations onto another path.

Historically, growth along a single developmental path and shifts from one path to another have not been simply the unintended outcome of the innumerable actions undertaken autonomously at any given time by individuals and the multiple communities into which the world-economy is divided. Rather, the recurrent expansions and restructurings of the capitalist world-economy have occurred under the leadership of partic-ular communities and blocs of governmental and business agencies which were uniquely well placed to turn to their own advantage the unintended consequences of the actions of other agencies. The strategies and structures through which these leading agencies have promoted, orga-nized, and regulated the expansion or the restructuring of the capitalist world-economy is what we shall understand by regime of accumulation on a world scale. The main purpose of the concept of systemic cycles is to describe and elucidate the formation, consolidation, and disintegration of the successive regimes through which the capitalist world-economy has expanded from its late medieval sub-systemic embryo to its present global dimension.

The entire construction rests on Braudel's unconventional view of the relationship that links the formation and enlarged reproduction of historical capitalism as world system to processes of state formation on the one side, and of market formation on the other. The conventional view in the social sciences, in political discourse, and in the mass media is that capitalism and the market economy are more or less the same thing, and that state power is antithetical to both. Braudel, in contrast, sees capitalism as being absolutely dependent for its emergence and expansion on state power and as constituting the antithesis of the market economy (cf. Wallerstein 1991: chs 14–15).

More specifically, Braudel conceived of capitalism as the top layer of a three-tiered structure – a structure in which, "as in all hierarchies, the upper [layers] could not exist without the lower stages on which they depend." The lowest and until very recently broadest layer is that of an extremely elementary and mostly self-sufficient economy. For want of a better expression, he called this the layer of *material life*, "the stratum of the non-economy, the soil into which capitalism thrusts its roots but which it can never really penetrate" (Braudel 1982: 21–2, 229):

> Above [this lowest layer], comes the favoured terrain of the *market economy*, with its many horizontal communications between the different markets: here a degree of automatic coordination usually links supply, demand and prices. Then alongside, or rather above this layer, comes the zone of the *anti-market*, where the great predators roam and the law of the jungle operates. This – today as in the past, before and after the industrial revolution – is the real home of *capitalism*. (Braudel 1982: 229–30; emphasis added)

A *world* market economy, in the sense of many horizontal communications between different markets, emerged from the depth of the underlying layer of material life long before capitalism-as-world-system rose above the layer of the market economy. As Janet Abu-Lughod (1989) has shown, a loose but none the less clearly recognizable system of horizontal communications between the principal markets of Eurasia and Africa was already in place in the thirteenth century. And for all we know, Gills and Frank may well be right in their claim that this system of horizontal communications actually emerged several millennia earlier.

Be that as it may, the question that bears directly on our research is not when and how a world market economy rose above the primordial structures of everyday life; it is when and how capitalism rose above the structures of the pre-existing world market economy and, over time, acquired its power to reshape the markets and lives of the entire world. As Braudel (1984: 92) points out, the metamorphosis of Europe into the "monstrous shaper of world history" that it became after 1500 was not a simple transition. Rather, it was "a series of stages and transitions, the earliest dating from well before what is usually known as 'the' Renaissance of the late fifteenth century."

The most decisive moment of this series of transitions was not the proliferation of elements of capitalist enterprise across Europe. Elements of this kind had occurred throughout the Eurasian trading system and were by no means peculiar to the West:

> Everywhere, from Egypt to Japan, we shall find genuine capitalists, wholesalers, the rentiers of trade, and their thousands of auxiliaries – the commission agents, brokers, money-changers and bankers. As for the techniques, possibilities or guarantees of exchange, any of these groups of merchants would stand comparison with its western equivalents. Both inside and outside India, Tamil, Bengali, and Gujerati merchants formed close-knit partnerships with business and contracts passing in turn from one group to another, just as they would in Europe from the Florentines to the Lucchese, the Genoese, the South Germans or the English. There were even, in medieval times, merchant kings in Cairo, Aden and the Persian Gulf ports. (Braudel 1984: 486)

Nowhere, except in Europe, did these elements of capitalism coalesce into the powerful mix that propelled European states towards the territorial conquest of the world and the formation of an all-powerful and truly global capitalist world-economy. From this perspective, the really important transition that needs to be elucidated is not that from feudalism to capitalism but from scattered to concentrated capitalist power. And the most important aspect of this much neglected transition is the unique fusion of state and capital, which was realized nowhere more favorably for capitalism than in Europe:

> Capitalism only triumphs when it becomes identified with the state, *when it is the state*. In its first great phase, that of the Italian city-states of Venice, Genoa, and Florence, power lay in the hands of the moneyed elite. In seventeenth-century Holland the aristocracy of the Regents governed for the benefit and even according to the directives of the businessmen, merchants, and moneylenders. Likewise, in England the Glorious Revolution of 1688 marked the accession of business similar to that in Holland. (Braudel 1977: 64–5; emphasis added)

The obverse of this process has been inter-state competition for mobile capital. As Max Weber pointed out in his *General Economic History*, in antiquity, as in the late Middle Ages, European cities had been the seedbeds of "political capitalism." In both periods the autonomy of these cities was progressively eroded by larger political structures. Nevertheless, while in antiquity this loss of autonomy meant the end of political capitalism, in early modern times it meant the expansion of capitalism into a new kind of world system:)

> In antiquity the freedom of the cities was swept away by a bureaucratically organized world empire within which there was no longer a place for political capitalism.... [In] contrast with antiquity [in the modern era the cities] came under the power of competing national states in a condition of perpetual struggle for power in peace or war. This competitive struggle created the largest opportunities for modern western capitalism. *The separate states had to compete for mobile capital, which dictated to them the conditions under which it would assist them to power....* Hence it is the closed national state which afforded to capitalism its chance for development – and as long as the national state does not give place to a world empire capitalism also will endure. (Weber 1961: 247–9; emphasis added)

In making the same point in *Economy and Society*, Weber (1978: 353–4) further suggested that this competition for mobile capital among "large, approximately equal and purely political structures" resulted

> in that memorable alliance between the rising states and the sought-after and privileged capitalist powers that was a major factor in creating modern capitalism.... Neither the trade nor the monetary policies of the modern states ... can be understood without this peculiar political competition and "equilibrium" among the European states during the last five hundred years.

Our analysis will substantiate these remarks by showing that inter-state competition has been a critical component of each and every phase of financial expansion and a major factor in the formation of those blocs of governmental and business organizations that have led the capitalist world-economy through its successive phases of material expansion. But in partial qualification of Weber's thesis, our analysis will also show that the *concentration* of power in the hands of particular blocs of governmental and business agencies has been as essential to the recurrent *material* expansions of the capitalist world-economy as the competition among "approximately equal" political structures. As a rule, major material expansions have occurred only when a new dominant bloc accrued sufficient world power to be in a position not just to bypass or rise above inter-state competition, but to bring it under control and ensure minimal inter-state cooperation. What has propelled the prodigious expansion of the capitalist world-economy over the last five hundred years, in other words, has not been inter-state competition as such, but inter-state competition in combination with an ever-increasing concentration of capitalist power in the world system at large.

The idea of an ever-increasing concentration of capitalist power in the modern world system is implicit in a pattern noted by Karl Marx in *Capital*. Like Weber, Marx attributed great importance to the role played by the system of national debts pioneered by Genoa and Venice in the late Middle Ages in propelling the initial expansion of modern capitalism:

> National debts, i.e., the alienation of the state – whether despotic, constitutional or republican – marked with its stamp the capitalistic era.... As with the stroke of an enchanter's wand, [the public debt] endows barren money with the power of breeding and thus turns it into capital, without the necessity of its exposing itself to the troubles and risks inseparable from its employment in industry or even in usury. The state-creditors actually give nothing away, for the sum lent is transformed into public bonds, easily negotiable, which can go on functioning in their hands just as so much hard cash would. (Marx 1959: 754–5)

Marx's focus on the domestic aspects of capital accumulation prevented him from appreciating the continuing significance of national debts in a system of states in constant competion with one another for assistance from capitalists for their power pursuits. For Marx, the alienation of the assets and future revenues of states was simply an aspect of "primitive accumulation" – Adam Smith's "previous accumulation," "an accumulation not the result of the capitalist mode of production, but its starting point" (Marx 1959: 713). Nevertheless, Marx did acknowledge the continuing significance of national debts, not as the expression of inter-state competition, but as means of an "invisible" inter-capitalist cooperation which "started" capital accumulation over and over again across the space–time of the capitalist world-economy from its inception through his own day:

> With the national debt arose an international credit system, which often conceals one of the sources of primitive accumulation in this or that people. Thus the villainies of the Venetian thieving system formed one of the secret bases of the capital-wealth of Holland to whom Venice in her decadence lent large sums of money. So was it with Holland and England. By the beginning of the 18th century ... Holland had ceased to be the nation preponderant in commerce and industry. One of its main lines of business, therefore, [became] the lending out of enormous amounts of capital, especially to its great rival England. [And the] same thing is going on to-day between England and the United States. (Marx 1959: 755–6)

Marx, however, failed to notice that the sequence of leading capitalist states outlined in this passage consists of units of increasing size, resources, and world power. All four states – Venice, the United Provinces, the United Kingdom, and the United States – have been great powers of the successive epochs during which their ruling groups simultaneously played the role of leader in processes of state formation and of capital accumulation. Seen sequentially, however, the four states appear to have been great powers of a very different and increasing order. As we shall detail in the course of this study, the metropolitan domains of each state in this sequence encompass a larger territory and a greater variety of resources than those of its predecessor. More importantly, the networks of power and accumulation that enabled the states in question to reorganize and control the world system within which they operated grew in scale and scope as the sequence progresses.

It can thus be seen that the expansion of capitalist power over the last five hundred years has been associated not just with inter-state competition for mobile capital, as underscored by Weber, but also with the formation of political structures endowed with ever-more extensive and complex organizational capabilities to control the social and political environment of capital accumulation on a world scale. Over the last five hundred years these two underlying conditions of capitalist expansion have been continually recreated in parallel with one another. Whenever world-scale processes of capital accumulation as instituted at any given time attained their limits, long periods of inter-state struggle ensued, during which the state that controlled or came to control the most abundant sources of surplus capital tended also to acquire the organizational capabilities needed to promote, organize, and regulate a new phase of capitalist expansion of greater scale and scope than the preceding one.

As a rule, acquiring these organizational capabilities was far more the result of positional advantages in the changing spatial configuration of the capitalist world-economy than of innovation as such. Braudel (1977: 66–7) goes as far as saying that innovation played no role whatsoever in the successive spatial shifts of the center of systemic processes of accumulation: "Amsterdam copied Venice, as London would subsequently copy Amsterdam, and as New York would one day copy London." As we shall see, this process of imitation was far more complex than the simple sequence outlined here implies. Each shift will be shown to have been associated with a true "organizational revolution" in the strategies and structures of the leading agency of capitalist expansion. Nevertheless, Braudel's contention that the shifts reflected "the victory of a new region over an old one" combined with "a vast change of scale" will stand.

The flows of capital from declining to rising centers that Marx noted

were the instrument of attempts on the part of declining centers to lay
some claim to the large-scale surpluses that accrued to the new centers.
Flows of this kind have characterized all past financial expansions. The
current financial expansion, in contrast, is said to diverge from this
pattern.

As we shall document in the Epilogue, the current financial expansion
has witnessed the explosive growth of Japan and lesser East Asian states
to a new center of world-scale processes of capital accumulation. And yet
there was little evidence in the 1980s of a major flow of capital from the
declining center to this emergent center. On the contrary, as Joel Kotkin
and Yoriko Kishimoto (1988: 123) have pointed out, after quoting from
the passage in which Marx describes the "secret" support that declining
leaders of processes of capital accumulation have accorded to their
successors, "in a stunning reversal of Marx's dictum, the United States is
not following the pattern of other capital-exporting empires (Venice,
Holland and Great Britain), but now is attracting a new wave of overseas
investment." In their view, this reversal is due primarily to the pull
exercised on foreign capital by the United States' relative lack of control
over foreign business activity, expanding population, physical expanse,
vast resources, and "status as the world's richest and most developed
continental power." In partial support of this contention, they report the
view of the chief economist of a Japanese bank and "well-known
economic nationalist" Hiroshi Takeuchi, according to whom the United
States has the scale and resources that Japan will never possess. As a
result, Japanese surpluses flowed to the United States just as British
surpluses did in the late nineteenth century. "The Japanese role will be to
assist the United States by exporting our money to rebuild your economy.
This is the evidence that our economy is fundamentally weak. The money
goes to America because you are fundamentally strong" (quoted in
Kotkin and Kishimoto 1988: 122–3).

Takeuchi's view of Japanese power relative to US power is basically the
same as that expressed by Samuel Huntington at a Harvard seminar on
Japan held in 1979. As Bruce Cumings (1987: 64) reports, when Ezra
Vogel opened the seminar by saying: "I am really very troubled when I
think through the consequences of the rise of Japanese power," Huntington's reply was that Japan was in fact "an extraordinarily weak country."
Its most fundamental weaknesses were "energy, food, and military
security."

This assessment is based on the conventional view of inter-state power
as consisting primarily of relative size, self-sufficiency, and military forces.
Such a view entirely overlooks the fact that the "technology of power" of
capitalism – to borrow an expression from Michael Mann (1986) – has
been quite different from territorialism. As Weber underscores in the

passages quoted above, and as our investigation will substantiate, competition for mobile capital among large but approximately equal political structures has been the most essential and enduring factor in the rise and expansion of capitalist power in the modern era. Unless we take into account the effects of this competition on the power of the competing states and on the power of the statal and non-statal organizations that assist them economically in the struggle, our assessments of relationships of forces in the world system are bound to be fundamentally flawed. The capabilities of some Italian city-states over several centuries to keep at bay militarily and to influence politically the great territorial powers of late medieval and early modern Europe would be as incomprehensible as the sudden collapse and disintegration in the late 1980s and early 1990s of the largest, most self-sufficient, and second greatest military power of our times: the USSR.

It is no accident that the seeming reversal of Marx's dictum noted by Kotkin and Kishimoto occurred in the midst of a sudden escalation of the armaments race and political–ideological struggle between the United States and the USSR – Fred Halliday's (1986) Second Cold War. Nor is it by chance that the financial expansion of the 1970s and 1980s attained its moment of greatest splendor precisely at the time of this sudden escalation. To paraphrase Marx, it was at this time that the alienation of the US state proceeded faster than ever before; and to paraphrase Weber, it was at this time that the competition for mobile capital between the two largest political structures in the world created for capitalism an extraordinary new opportunity for self-expansion.

The flow of capital from Japan to the United States in the early 1980s must be seen in this context. Political considerations inspired by Japan's dependence on, and subordination to, US world power no doubt played a critical role in prompting Japanese capital to assist the United States in the escalation of the power struggle, as Takeuchi seems to imply. Nevertheless, as subsequent events have shown, political considerations were inseparable from considerations of profit.

In this respect, the flow of capital from Japan to the United States was not as anomalous as Kotkin and Kishimoto thought. It was somewhat analogous to the financial assistance that the rising capitalist power (the United States) gave the declining capitalist power (the United Kingdom) in the two world wars. The Anglo-German confrontations, unlike the US–Soviet confrontation of the 1980s, were, of course, "hot" rather than "cold." But the financial requirements of the two confrontations and the profits that could be expected from "backing" the winner were none the less comparable.

The main difference between US financial assistance to Britain in the two world wars and Japanese financial assistance to the United States in the Second Cold War lies in the outcomes. Whereas the United States reaped enormous benefits, Japan did not. As we shall see in chapter 4, the two world wars and their aftermath were decisive moments in the redistribution of assets from Britain to the United States which hastened the change of leadership in systemic processes of capital accumulation. During and after the Second Cold War, in contrast, there was no comparable redistribution. In fact, Japan probably never got its money back.

The greatest losses were suffered as a consequence of the fall in the value of the US dollar after 1985. This meant that money borrowed in greatly overvalued dollars was serviced and repaid in undervalued dollars. The losses inflicted on Japanese capital by the devaluation were such that Japanese business and the Japanese government withdrew their previously unconditional financial support for the US government. In mid-1987 Japanese private investors reversed their export of capital to the United States for the first time since the early 1980s. And after the stock market crash of October 1987, the Japanese Ministry of Finance did nothing to encourage financial intermediaries to support the important auction of US government debt held in November 1987 (Helleiner 1992: 434).

The difficulties Japan met in wielding its increasing command over surplus capital in order to redistribute assets from US to Japanese control were not simply the result of the historically unprecedented power of US public and private agencies, acting in concert, to manipulate demand and supply, interest rates, and rates of exchange in world financial markets. The acquisition of material assets in the United States presented difficulties of its own. As far as Japanese capital was concerned, the world's richest and most developed continental power proved to be not as devoid of control over foreign business as Kotkin and Kishimoto thought.

This "control" has been more informal than formal, but is no less real for all that. There have been cultural barriers of the kind best epitomized by the hysterical reaction triggered in and by the US media when Japanese capital bought the Rockefeller Center in New York City. Since Japanese purchases of US real estate paled in comparison with European, Canadian, and Australian purchases, the reaction sent the message to buyers and sellers alike that Japanese money did not have quite the same "right" to acquire US assets as did the money of foreigners of European stock.

If the mass media have been the chief protagonists in erecting cultural barriers to the transfer of US assets to Japanese capital, the US government has played its part by erecting political barriers. It welcomed Japanese money to finance its deficit and public debt and to establish production facilities that created jobs in the United States and reduced the US balance of payments deficit. But it strongly discouraged that same money from taking over profitable but strategically sensitive enterprises. Thus, in March 1987 protests from the Secretary of Defense, Caspar Weinberger, and Secretary of Commerce, Malcom Baldridge, convinced Fujitsu that it would be prudent to withdraw its attempt to take over the Fairchild Semiconductor Corporation. Yet, as Stephen Krasner (1988: 29) remarked: "Fairchild was owned by the French company Schlumberger, so the issue was not simply one of foreign ownership."

What cultural and political barriers could not stop, the barriers to entry built into the very structure of US corporate capitalism did. The complexities of US corporate life proved to be more insurmountable barriers to entry for Japanese money than cultural hostility and political mistrust. The biggest ever Japanese takeovers in the United States – Sony's takeover of Columbia Pictures in 1989, and Matsushita's takeover of MCA the following year – failed completely in their objective. When the Sony deal was struck, the media over-reacted and *Newsweek*'s cover talked of Japan's "invasion" of Hollywood. And yet, as Bill Emmott wrote in the op-ed page of the *New York Times* (26 November 1993: A19),

> less than two years passed before it became clear that the scares and hyperbole had got it wrong.... [T]he Japanese "invasion" of U.S. business has been no such thing. Even the best Japanese companies have made spectacular and costly mistakes and have not taken control even of the businesses they purchased, let alone of culture and technology. (see also Emmott 1993)

In short, the real anomaly of US–Japanese relations during the current financial expansion is not that Japanese capital flowed to the United States in the early 1980s; rather, it is that Japanese capital benefited so little from assisting the United States economically in the final escalation of the Cold War with the former USSR. Is this anomaly symptomatic of a fundamental change in the mechanisms of inter-state competition for mobile capital which have propelled and sustained the expansion of capitalist power over the last six hundred years?

These mechanisms have a clear built-in limit. Capitalist power in the world system cannot expand indefinitely without undermining inter-state competition for mobile capital on which the expansion rests. Sooner or later a point will be reached where the alliances between the powers of state and capital that are formed in response to this competition become so formidable that they eliminate the competition itself and, therefore, the possibility for new capitalist powers of a higher order to emerge. Are the difficulties met by the emerging structures of Japanese capitalism in profiting from inter-state competition for mobile capital a symptom of the fact that this point has been reached, or is about to be reached? Or, to rephrase it, do the structures of US capitalism constitute the ultimate limit of the six centuries-long process through which capitalist power has attained its present, seemingly all-encompassing scale and scope?

In seeking plausible answers to these questions, the complementary insights of Weber and Marx concerning the role of high finance in the modern era must be supplemented by Adam Smith's insights concerning the process of world market formation. Like Marx after him, Smith saw in the European "discoveries" of America and of a passage to the East Indies via the Cape of Good Hope a decisive turning point in world history. He was none the less far less sanguine than Marx about the ultimate benefits of these events for humanity:

> Their consequences have already been great; but, in the short period of between two and three centuries which has elapsed since these discoveries were made, it is impossible that the whole extent of their consequences can have been seen. What benefits, or what misfortunes to mankind may hereafter result from these events, no human wisdom can foresee. By uniting, in some measure, the most distant parts of the world, by enabling them to relieve one another's wants, to increase one another's enjoyments, and to encourage one another's industry, their general tendency would seem to be beneficial. To the natives, however, both of the East and West Indies, all the commercial benefits which can have resulted from these events have been sunk and lost in the dreadful misfortunes which they have occasioned. These misfortunes, however, seem to have arisen rather from accident than from any thing in the nature of those events themselves. At the particular time when these discoveries were made, the *superiority of force* happened to be so great on the side of the Europeans, that they were enabled to commit with impunity every sort of injustice in those remote countries. Hereafter, perhaps, the natives of those countries may grow stronger, or those of Europe may grow weaker, and the inhabitants of all the different quarters of the world may arrive at that equality of courage and force which, by inspiring mutual fear, can alone overawe the injustice of independent nations into some sort of respect for the rights of one another. But nothing seems more likely to establish this equality of force than that mutual communication of knowledge and of all sorts of improvements which an extensive commerce from all countries to all countries naturally, or rather necessarily, carries along with it. (Smith 1961: II, 141; emphasis added)

The process sketched in this passage presents some striking similarities with Braudel's view of the formation of a capitalist world-economy: the fortunes of the conquering West and the misfortunes of the conquered non-West as joint outcomes of a single historical process; the long time-horizon needed to describe and assess the consequences of this single historical process; and most important for our present purposes, the centrality of "force" in determining the distribution of costs and benefits among participants in the market economy.

Smith, of course, did not use the term "capitalism" – a term introduced in the vocabulary of the social sciences only in the twentieth century. Yet, his assessment that "superiority of force" was the most important factor in enabling the conquering West to appropriate most of the benefits – and to impose on the conquered non-West most of the costs – of the wider market economy established as a result of the so-called Discoveries, parallels Braudel's assessment that the fusion of state and capital was the vital ingredient in the emergence of a distinctly capitalist layer on top of, and in antithesis to, the layer of market economy. As we shall see in chapter 3, in Smith's scheme of things large-scale profits can be maintained for any length of time only through restrictive practices, buttressed by state power, which constrain and disrupt the "natural" operation of the market economy. In this scheme of things, as in Braudel's, the upper layer of merchants and manufacturers "who commonly employ the largest capitals, and who by their wealth draw to themselves the greatest share of the public consideration" (Smith 1961: I, 278) is truly the "anti-market," Braudel's *contre-marché*.

However, Braudel's and Smith's conceptions of the relationship between the market economy and its capitalist antithesis differ in one important respect. For Braudel the relationship is fundamentally static. He neither sees nor foresees any synthesis emerging from the struggle between "thesis" and "antithesis." Smith, in contrast, does see such a synthesis emerging out of the withering away of inequality of force under the impact of the very process of world market formation. As the last sentence of the passage quoted above indicates, Smith thought that the widening and deepening of exchanges in the world market economy would act as an unstoppable equalizer of relationships of force between the West and the non-West.

A more dialectical conception of historical processes is not necessarily more accurate than a less dialectical one. As it turned out, for more than 150 years after Smith advanced the thesis of the corrosive impact of processes of world market formation on the superiority of force of the West, the inequality of force between West and non-West increased rather than decreased. World market formation and the military conquest of the non-West proceeded in tandem. By the 1930s, only Japan had fully escaped the misfortunes of Western conquest, but only by itself becoming an honorary member of the conquering West.

Then, during and after the Second World War, the wheel turned. Throughout Asia and Africa old sovereignties were re-established and scores of new ones were created. To be sure, massive decolonization was accompanied by the establishment of the most extensive and potentially destructive apparatus of Western force the world had ever seen. The far-flung network of quasi-permanent overseas military bases put in place by the United States during and after the Second World War, Krasner (1988: 21) notes, "was without historical precedent; no state had previously based its own troops on the sovereign territory of other states in such extensive numbers for so long a peacetime period." And yet, on the battlefields of Indochina, this world-encompassing military apparatus proved to be wholly inadequate to the task of coercing one of the poorest nations on earth to its will.

The successful resistance of the Vietnamese people marked the apogee of a process initiated by the Russian Revolution of 1917, whereby the West and non-West were reshuffled into a tripartite grouping consisting of a First, Second, and Third World. While the historical non-West came to be grouped almost entirely in the Third World, the historical West split into three distinct components. Its more prosperous components (North America, Western Europe, and Australia) joined by Japan, came to constitute the First World. One of its less prosperous components (the USSR and Eastern Europe) came to constitute the Second World, and another (Latin America) joined the non-West to constitute the Third World. Partly a cause and partly an effect of this tripartite fission of the historical West, the fortunes of the non-West from the end of the Second World War to the Vietnam War seemed to be in the ascendant.

Writing for the bicentenary of the publication of the *Wealth of Nations*, and shortly after the United States had decided to withdraw from Vietnam, Paolo Sylos-Labini (1976: 230–2) speculated on whether Smith's vision was about to be realized – whether the time had finally come when "the inhabitants of all the different quarters of the world ... arrive at that equality of courage and force which, by inspiring mutual fear, can alone overawe the injustice of independent nations into some sort of respect for the rights of one another." The economic conjuncture also seemed to signal that some equalization of relationship of forces in the world system at large was imminent. The natural resources of Third World countries were in great demand, as was their abundant and cheap labor. Agents of First World bankers were queuing up in the ante-chambers of Third (and Second) World governments offering at bargain prices the overabundant capital that could not find profitable investment in their home countries. Terms of trade had turned sharply against the capitalist West, and the income gap between First and Third World countries seemed to be narrowing.

Within six years, though, it had become clear that any hope (or fear) of an imminent equalization of the opportunities of the peoples of the world to benefit from the continuing process of world market formation was, to say the least, premature. US competition for mobile capital in world money markets to finance both the Second Cold War and the "buying" of electoral votes at home through tax cuts, suddenly dried up the supply of funds to Third and Second World countries and triggered a major contraction in world purchasing power. Terms of trade swung back in favor of the capitalist West as fast and as sharply as they had swung against it in the 1970s, and the income gap between the capitalist West and the rest of the world became wider than ever (Arrighi 1991).

Nevertheless, the backlash did not restore the status quo ante. On the one hand, the superiority of force of the capitalist West seemed to have become greater than ever. Disoriented and disorganized by the increasing turbulence of the world-economy, and hard-pressed by the Second Cold War, the USSR was squeezed out of the "superpower business." Instead of having two superpowers to play off against one another, Third World countries now had to compete with the fragments of the Soviet empire in gaining access to the markets and resources of the capitalist West. And the capitalist West, under US leadership, moved quickly to take advantage of the situation to tighten its *de facto* global "monopoly" of the legitimate use of violence.

On the other hand, superiority of force and the capitalist accumulation of capital seemed to diverge geopolitically as never before. The decline of Soviet power was matched by the emergence of what Bruce Cumings (1993: 25–6) has aptly called the "capitalist archipelago" of East and Southeast Asia. This archipelago consists of several "islands" of capitalism, which rise above a "sea" of horizontal exchanges among local and world markets through the centralization within their domains of large-scale profits and high value-added activities. Below this sea lie the huge, low-cost, and highly industrious laboring masses of the entire East and Southeast Asian regions, into which the capitalist "islands" thrust their roots but without providing them with the means needed to rise to or above "sea level."

Japan is by far the largest among these capitalist "islands." Lesser "islands" of the capitalist archipelago are the city-states of Singapore and Hong Kong, the garrison state of Taiwan, and the half nation-state of South Korea. None of these states is powerful by conventional standards. Hong Kong has not even attained – nor probably will ever attain – full sovereignty. The three bigger states – Japan, South Korea, and Taiwan – are wholly dependent on the United States not just for military protection but also for much of their energy and food supplies as well as for the profitable disposal of their manufactures. Yet, collectively, the competitiveness of the East and Southeast Asian capitalist archipelago as the new "workshop of the world" is the single most important factor forcing the traditional centers of capitalist power – Western Europe and North America – to restructure and reorganize their own industries, their own economies, and their own ways of life.

What kind of power is this that even an expert eye can hardly discern?

Is it a new kind of "superiority of force" or, rather, the beginning of the end of the superiority of force on which, over the last five hundred years, the capitalist fortunes of the West have been built? Is capitalist history about to end through the formation of a truly global world empire based on the enduring superiority of force of the West as Max Weber seemed to envisage, or is it going to end through the formation of a world market economy in which the superiority of force of the West withers away as Adam Smith seemed to envisage?

In seeking plausible answers to these questions we shall proceed by successive approximations. Chapter 1 focuses on the process of formation and expansion of the modern inter-state system as the primary locus of world power. The earliest beginnings of this process will be traced to the formation in late medieval Europe of a northern Italian sub-system of capitalist city-states. This sub-system was and remained an enclave of the disintegrating mode of rule of medieval Europe – a form of warlordism subjected to and held together by the dual systemic power of pope and emperor. It none the less prefigured, and unintentionally created the conditions for, the emergence two centuries later of the larger Westphalia system of nation-states.

The global expansion of this system will then be described as consisting of a series of transitions, in the course of which the system as previously instituted broke down, only to be reconstituted on wider social foundations. This preliminary analysis ends with the late twentieth-century crisis of the enlarged and thoroughly transformed Westphalia System. In diagnosing the symptoms of the present crisis, a new research agenda will be formulated which focuses more directly on the "space-of-flows" of business organizations than on the "space-of-places" of governments. It is at this point that our construction and comparison of systemic cycles of accumulation will begin.

The comparative analysis through which systemic cycles of accumulation will be constructed follows the procedure that Philip McMichael (1990) has called "incorporating comparison." The cycles are not presumed but constructed, both factually and theoretically, with the explicit purpose of gaining some understanding of the logic and likely outcome of the present financial expansion. The comparison is *incorporated* into the very definition of the research problem: it constitutes the substance rather than the framework of the inquiry. The cycles that emerge from the inquiry are neither subordinated parts of a preconceived whole, nor independent instances of a condition; they are interconnected instances of a *single* historical process of capitalist expansion which they themselves constitute and modify.

Chapter 2 constructs the first two instances of this single historical process of capitalist expansion: the Genoese and the Dutch cycles.

Chapter 3 adds a new stage to the process by defining the third (British) cycle and comparing it with the first two. The concluding section of the chapter makes explicit and seeks some plausible explanation for the pattern of recurrence and evolution revealed by the comparative analysis of the first three cycles. The stage is thus set for the construction in chapter 4 of the fourth (US) systemic cycle of accumulation, portrayed as an outgrowth of the preceding cycles and the matrix of our times. In the Epilogue we shall return to the questions that we have raised in this Introduction.

This reconstruction of capitalist history has its own limitation. The notion of systemic cycle of accumulation, we have noted, derives directly from Braudel's notion of capitalism as the top layer of the hierarchy of the world of trade. Our analytical construct, therefore, focuses on that top layer and offers a limited view of what goes on in the middle layer of market economy and the bottom layer of material life. This is simultaneously the main strength and the main weakness of the construct. It is its main strength because the top layer is "the real home of capitalism" and at the same time it is less transparent and less explored than the intermediate layer of the market economy. The transparency of the activities that constitute the layer of market economy and the wealth of data (particularly quantitative data) that these activities generate, have made this intermediate layer the "privileged arena" of historical social science and economics. The layers below and above the market economy are instead "shadowy zones" (zones d'opacité). The bottom layer of material life is "hard to see for lack of adequate historical documents." The upper layer, in contrast, is hard to see because of the actual invisibility or the complexity of the activities that constitute it (Braudel 1981: 23–4; Wallerstein 1991: 208–9):

At this exalted level, a few wealthy merchants in eighteenth-century Amsterdam or sixteenth-century Genoa could throw whole sectors of the European or even world economy into confusion, from a distance. Certain groups of privileged actors are engaged in circuits and calculations that ordinary people knew nothing of. Foreign exchange, for example, which was tied to distant trade movements and to the complicated arrangements for credit, was a sophisticated art open only to a few initiates at most. To me, this second shadowy zone, hovering above the sunlit world of the market economy and constituting its upper limit so to speak, represents the favored domain of capitalism.... Without this zone, capitalism is unthinkable: this is where it takes up residence and prospers. (Braudel 1981: 24)

Systemic cycles of accumulation are meant to throw some light on this shadowy zone without which "capitalism is unthinkable." They are not meant to tell us what goes on in the lower layers, except for what is directly relevant to the dynamic of the systemic cycles themselves. This, of course, leaves much out of sight or in the dark, including the privileged arenas of world systems studies: core–periphery and labor–capital relations. But we cannot do everything at once.

Marx (1959: 176) invited us to "take leave for a time of [the] noisy sphere [of circulation], where everything takes place on the surface and in view of all men, and follow [the possessor of money and the possessor of labor-power] into the hidden abode of production, on whose threshold there stares us in the face 'No admittance except on business.'" Here, he promised, "[w]e shall at last force the secret of profit making." Braudel also invited us to take leave for a time of the noisy and transparent sphere of the market economy, and follow the possessor of money into another hidden abode, where admittance is only on business but which is one floor above, rather than one floor below the marketplace. Here, the possessor of money meets the possessor, not of labor-power, but of political power. And here, promised Braudel, we shall force the secret of making those large and regular profits that has enabled capitalism to prosper and expand "endlessly" over the last five to six hundred years, before and after its ventures into the hidden abodes of production.

These are complementary projects, not alternative ones. However, we cannot go to the top and the bottom floors at the same time. Generations of historians and social scientists have taken up Marx's invitation and have extensively explored the bottom floor. In so doing, they may not have discovered "the" secret of profit-making in the industrial phase of capitalism, but they have certainly discovered many of its secrets. Then dependency and world system theorists and practitioners have invited us to have another look at the middle floor of market economy to see how its "laws" tend to polarize the hidden abodes of production into core and peripheral locales. In this way more of the secrets of profit-making have been exposed. But few have ventured to the top floor of the "anti-market" where, in the words of Braudel's hyperbole, "the great predators roam and the law of the jungle operates" and where the secrets of the *longue durée* of historical capitalism are said to be hidden.

Today – when world capitalism seems to be prospering, not by thrusting its roots more deeply into the lower layers of material life and market economy, but by pulling them out – is as good a time as any to take up Braudel's invitation and explore the real home of capitalism on the top floor of the house of trade. That and that only is what we are about to undertake.

It follows that our construction is both partial and somewhat indeterminate. Partial because it seeks some understanding of the logic of the present financial expansion abstracting from the movements that go on under their own steam and laws at the levels of the world's market economies and of the world's material civilizations. It is somewhat indeterminate for the same reason. The logic of the top layer is only relatively autonomous from the logics of the lower layers and can be fully understood only in relation to these other logics.

Certainly, as our construction proceeds, what initially may appear to be mere historical contingency will begin to appear to reflect a structural logic. Nevertheless, the tension between the two kinds of appearance cannot be fully resolved within the limits of our research agenda. A full resolution of the tension – if that is possible – requires that we descend again to explore the lower layers of market economy and material life with the knowledge and questions brought back from the journey into the top layer which this book undertakes.

The Three Hegemonies of Historical Capitalism

Hegemony, Capitalism, and Territorialism

The decline of US world power since about 1970 has occasioned a wave of studies on the rise and decline of "hegemonies" (Hopkins and Wallerstein 1979; Bousquet 1979; 1980; Wallerstein1984), "core hegemonic states" (Chase-Dunn 1989), "world or global powers" (Modelski 1978; 1981; 1987; Modelski and Thompson 1988; Thompson 1988; 1992), "cores" (Gilpin 1975), and "great powers" (Kennedy 1987). These studies differ considerably in their object of study, methodology, and conclusions but they have two characteristics in common. First, if and when they use the term "hegemony," they mean "dominance" (cf. Rapkin 1990) and, second, their focus and emphasis is on an alleged basic invariance of the system within which the power of a state rises and declines.

Most of these studies rely on some notion of "innovation" and "leadership" in defining the relative capabilities of states. For Modelski, systemic innovations and leadership in carrying them out are assumed to be the main sources of "world power." But in all these studies, including Modelski's, systemic innovations do not change the basic mechanisms through which power in the inter-state system rises and declines. In fact, the invariance of these mechanisms is generally held to be one of the central features of the inter-state system.

The concept of "world hegemony" adopted here, in contrast, refers specifically to the power of a state to exercise functions of leadership and governance over a system of sovereign states. In principle, this power may involve just the ordinary management of such a system as instituted at a given time. Historically, however, the government of a system of sovereign states has always involved some kind of transformative action, which changed the mode of operation of the system in a fundamental way.

This power is something more and different from "dominance" pure

27

and simple. It is the power associated with dominance expanded by the exercise of "intellectual and moral leadership." As Antonio Gramsci emphasized, with reference to hegemony at the national level,

> the supremacy of a social group manifests itself in two ways, as "domination" and as "intellectual and moral leadership". A social group dominates antagonistic groups, which it tends to "liquidate", or to subjugate perhaps even by armed force; it leads kindred or allied groups. A social group can, and indeed must, already exercise "leadership" before winning governmental power (this indeed is one of the principal conditions for winning such power); it subsequently becomes dominant when it exercises power, but even if it holds it firmly in its grasp, it must continue to "lead" as well. (Gramsci 1971: 57–8)

This is a reformulation of Machiavelli's conception of power as a combination of consent and coercion. Coercion implies the use of force, or a credible threat of force; consent implies moral leadership. In this dichotomy there is no room for the most distinctive instrument of capitalist power: control over means of payment. In Gramsci's conceptualization of power the grey area that lies between coercion and consent is occupied by "corruption" and "fraud":

> Between consent and force stands corruption/fraud (which is characteristic of certain situations when it is hard to exercise the hegemonic function, and when the use of force is too risky). This consists in procuring the demoralization and paralysis of the antagonist (or antagonists) by buying its leaders – either covertly, or, in case of imminent danger, openly – in order to sow disarray and confusion in its ranks. (Gramsci 1971: 80n)

In our scheme of things, much more than mere corruption and fraud stands in the grey area between coercion and consent. But until we turn to explore this area through the construction of systemic cycles of accumulation, we shall assume that no autonomous source of world power lies between coercion and consent. Whereas dominance will be conceived of as resting primarily on coercion, hegemony will be understood as the *additional* power that accrues to a dominant group by virtue of its capacity to place all the issues around which conflict rages on a "universal" plane.

> It is true that the State is seen as the organ of one particular group, destined to create favorable conditions for the latter's maximum expansion. But the development and expansion of the particular group are conceived of, and presented, as being the motor force of a universal expansion, a development of all the "national" energies. (Gramsci 1971: 181–2)

The claim of the dominant group to represent the general interest is always more or less fraudulent. Nevertheless, following Gramsci, we shall speak of hegemony only when the claim is at least partly true and adds something to the power of the dominant group. A situation in which the claim of the dominant group to represent the general interest is purely fraudulent will be defined as a situation not of hegemony but of the failure of hegemony.

Since the word hegemony, in its etymological sense of "leadership" and in its derived sense of "dominance," normally refers to relations between states, it is entirely possible that Gramsci was using the term metaphorically to clarify relations between social groups through an analogy with relations between states. In transposing Gramsci's concept of social hegemony from intra-state relations to inter-state relations – as Arrighi (1982), Cox (1983; 1987), Keohane (1984a), Gill (1986; 1993), and Gill and Law (1988) among others do explicitly or implicitly – we may simply be retracing in reverse Gramsci's mental process. In so doing we are faced with two problems.

The first concerns the double meaning of "leadership," particularly when applied to relations between states. A dominant state exercises a hegemonic function if it leads the *system* of states in a desired direction and, in so doing, is perceived as pursuing a general interest. It is this kind of leadership that makes the dominant state hegemonic. But a dominant state may lead also in the sense that it draws other states onto its own path of development. Borrowing an expression from Joseph Schumpeter (1963: 89), this second kind of leadership can be designated as "leadership against one's own will" because, over time, it enhances competition for power rather than the power of the hegemon. These two kinds of leadership may coexist – at least for a time. But it is only leadership in the first sense that defines a situation as hegemonic.

The second problem concerns the fact that it is more difficult to define a general interest at the level of the inter-state system than it is at the level of individual states. At the level of individual states, an increase in the power of the state *vis-à-vis* other states is an important component and in itself a measure of the successful pursuit of a general (that is, national) interest. But power in this sense cannot increase for the system of states as a whole, by definition. It can, of course, increase for a particular group of states at the expense of all other states, but the hegemony of the leader of that group is at best "regional" or "coalitional," not a true world hegemony.

World hegemonies as understood here can only arise if the pursuit of power by states in relation to one another is not the only objective of state action. In fact, the pursuit of power in the inter-state system is only one side of the coin that jointly defines the strategy and structure of states *qua* organizations. The other side is the maximization of power *vis-à-vis* subjects. A state may therefore become world hegemonic because it can credibly claim to be the motor force of a general expansion of the *collective* power of rulers *vis-à-vis* subjects. Or conversely, a state may become world hegemonic because it can credibly claim that the expansion of its power relative to some or even all other states is in the general interest of the subjects of all states.

Claims of this kind are most likely to be truthful and credible in conditions of "systemic chaos." "Chaos" is not the same thing as "anarchy." Although the two terms are often used interchangeably, an understanding of the systemic origins of world hegemonies requires that we distinguish between the two.

"Anarchy" designates "absence of central rule." In this sense, the modern system of sovereign states as well as the system of rule of medieval Europe out of which the latter emerged, qualify as anarchic systems. Yet, each of these two systems had or has its own implicit and explicit principles, norms, rules, and procedures which justify our referring to them as "ordered anarchies" or "anarchic orders."

The concept of "ordered anarchy" was first introduced by anthropologists seeking to explicate the observed tendency of "tribal" systems to generate order out of conflict (Evans-Pritchard 1940; Gluckman 1963: ch. 1). This tendency has been at work in the medieval and modern systems of rule as well, because in these systems too the "absence of central rule" has not meant lack of organization and, within limits, conflict has tended to generate order.

"Chaos" and "systemic chaos," in contrast, refer to a situation of total and apparently irremediable lack of organization. It is a situation that arises because conflict escalates beyond the threshold within which it calls forth powerful countervailing tendencies, or because a new set of rules and norms of behavior is imposed on, or grows from within, an older set of rules and norms without displacing it, or because of a combination of these two circumstances. As systemic chaos increases, the demand for "order" – the old order, a new order, any order! – tends to become more and more general among rulers, or among subjects, or both. Whichever state or group of states is in a position to satisfy this system-wide demand for order is thus presented with the opportunity of becoming world hegemonic.

Historically, the states that have successfully seized this opportunity did so by reconstituting the world system on new and enlarged foundations thereby restoring some measure of inter-state cooperation. In other words, world hegemonies have not "risen" and "declined" in a world system that expanded independently on the basis of an invariant structure, however defined. Rather, the modern world system itself has been formed by, and has expanded on the basis of, recurrent fundamental restructurings led and governed by successive hegemonic states.

These restructurings are a characteristic phenomenon of the modern system of rule which emerged out of the decay and eventual disintegration of the medieval European system of rule. As John Ruggie has argued, there is a fundamental difference between the modern and the medieval (European) systems of rule. Both can be characterized as "anarchic," but anarchy, in the sense of "absence of central rule," means different things, according to the principles on the basis of which the units of the system are separated from one another: "If anarchy tells us *that* the political system is a segmental realm, differentiation tells us *on what basis* the segments are determined" (Ruggie 1983: 274; emphasis in the original).

The medieval system of rule consisted of chains of lord–vassal relationships, based on an amalgam of conditional property and private authority. As a result, "different juridical instances were geographically interwoven and stratified, and plural allegiances, asymmetrical suzerainties and anomalous enclaves abounded" (Anderson 1974: 37–8). In addition, ruling elites were extremely mobile *across* the space of these overlapping political jurisdictions, being able "to travel and assume governance from one end of the continent to the other without hesitation or difficulty." Finally, this system of rule was "legitimated by common bodies of law, religion, and custom that expressed inclusive natural rights pertaining to the social totality formed by the constituent units" (Ruggie 1983: 275):

> In sum, this was quintessentially a system of segmental rule; it was anarchy. But it was a form of segmental territorial rule that had none of the connotations of possessiveness and exclusiveness conveyed by the modern concept of sovereignty. It represented a heteronomous organization of territorial rights and claims – of political space. (Ruggie 1983: 275)

In contrast to the medieval system, "the modern system of rule consists of the institutionalization of public authority within mutually exclusive jurisdictional domains" (Ruggie 1983: 275). Rights of private property and rights of public government become absolute and discrete; political jurisdictions become exclusive and are clearly demarcated by boundaries; the mobility of ruling elites across political jurisdictions slows down and eventually ceases; law, religion, and custom become "national," that is, subject to no political authority other than that of the sovereign. As Etienne Balibar (1990: 337) has put it:

> the correspondence between the nation form and all other phenomena toward which it tends has as its prerequisite a complete (no "omissions") and

nonoverlapping divisioning of the world's territory and populations (and therefore resources) among the political entities.... To each individual a nation, and to each nation its "nationals."

This "becoming" of the modern system of rule has been closely associated with the development of capitalism as a system of accumulation on a world scale, as underscored in Immanuel Wallerstein's conceptualization of the modern world system as a capitalist world-economy. In his analysis, the rise and expansion of the modern inter-state system is both the main cause and an effect of the endless accumulation of capital: "Capitalism has been able to flourish precisely because the world-economy has had within its bounds not one but a multiplicity of political systems" (Wallerstein 1974a: 348). At the same time, the tendency of capitalist groups to mobilize their respective states in order to enhance their competitive position in the world-economy has continually reproduced the segmentation of the political realm into separate jurisdictions (Wallerstein 1974b: 402).

In the scheme of things proposed here, the close historical tie between capitalism and the modern inter-state system is just as much one of contradiction as it is one of unity. We must take into account the fact that "capitalism and national states grew up together, and presumably depended on each other in some way, yet capitalists and centers of capital accumulation often offered concerted resistance to the extension of state power" (Tilly 1984: 140). In our account, the division of the world-economy into competing political jurisdictions does not necessarily benefit the capitalist accumulation of capital. Whether it does or not depends largely on the form and intensity of competition.

 Thus, if inter-state competition takes the form of intense and long-drawn-out armed struggles, there is no reason why the costs of inter-state competition to capitalist enterprises should not exceed the costs of centralized rule they would have to bear in a world empire. On the contrary, under such circumstances the profitability of capitalist enterprise might very well be undermined and eventually destroyed by an ever-increasing diversion of resources to military enterprise and/or by an ever-increasing disruption of the networks of production and exchange through which capitalist enterprises appropriate surpluses and transform such surpluses into profits.

At the same time, competition among capitalist enterprises does not necessarily promote the continual segmentation of the political realm into separate jurisdictions. Again, it largely depends on the form and intensity of competition, in this case among capitalist enterprises. If these enterprises are enmeshed in dense trans-statal networks of production and exchange, the segmentation of these networks into discrete political jurisdictions may have a detrimental bearing on the competitive position of each and every capitalist enterprise relative to non-capitalist institutions. In these circumstances, capitalist enterprises may well mobilize governments to reduce rather than increase or reproduce the political division of the world-economy.

In other words, inter-state and inter-enterprise competition can take different forms, and the form they take has important consequences for the way in which the modern world system – as mode of rule and as mode of accumulation – functions or does not function. It is not enough to emphasize the historical connection between inter-state and inter-enterprise competition. We must also specify the form which they take and how they change over time. Only in this way can we fully appreciate the evolutionary nature of the modern world system and the role played by successive world hegemonies in making and remaking the system in order to resolve the recurrent contradiction between an "endless" accumulation of capital and a comparatively stable organization of political space.

Central to such an understanding is the definition of "capitalism" and "territorialism" as opposite modes of rule or logics of power. Territorialist rulers identify power with the extent and populousness of their domains, and conceive of wealth/capital as a means or a by-product of the pursuit of territorial expansion. Capitalist rulers, in contrast, identify power with the extent of their command over scarce resources and consider territorial acquisitions as a means and a by-product of the accumulation of capital.

Paraphrasing Marx's general formula of capitalist production (MCM'), we may render the difference between the two logics of power by the formulas TMT' and MTM', respectively. According to the first formula, abstract economic command or money (M) is a means or intermediate link in a process aimed at the acquisition of additional territories (T' minus T = + ΔT). According to the second formula, territory (T) is a means or an intermediate link in a process aimed at the acquisition of additional means of payments (M' minus M = + ΔM).

The difference between these two logics can also be expressed by the metaphor that defines states as "containers of power" (Giddens 1987). Territorialist rulers tend to increase their power by expanding the size of their container. Capitalist rulers, in contrast, tend to increase their power by piling up wealth within a small container and increase the size of the container only if it is justified by the requirements of the accumulation of capital.

The antinomy between a capitalist and a territorialist logic of power should not be confused with Charles Tilly's distinction between a "coercion-intensive," a "capital-intensive," and an intermediate "capitalized coercion" mode of state- and war-making. These modes, as Tilly (1990: 30) explains, do not represent alternative "strategies" of power. Rather they represent different combinations of coercion and capital in processes of state-making and war-making which may be oriented towards the same objective as far as gaining control over territory/population or means of payments is concerned. The "modes" are neutral as to the purpose of the process of state-making to which they contribute.

Capitalism and territorialism as defined here, in contrast, do represent alternative strategies of state formation. In the territorialist strategy control over territory and population is the objective, and control over mobile capital the means, of state- and war-making. In the capitalist strategy, the relationship between ends and means is turned upside down: control over mobile capital is the objective, and control over territory and population the means. This antinomy implies nothing concerning the intensity of coercion employed in the pursuit of power through either strategy. As we shall see, at the height of its power the Venetian republic was simultaneously the clearest embodiment of a capitalist logic of power and of a coercion-intensive path to state formation. What the antinomy does imply is that the truly innovative aspect of the process of formation of the Venetian state and of the system of city-states to which Venice belonged was not the extent to which the process relied on coercion but the extent to which it was oriented towards the accumulation of capital rather than the incorporation of territory and population.

The logical structure of state action with regard to territorial acquisition and capital accumulation should not be confused with actual outcomes. Historically, the capitalist and the territorialist logics of power have not operated in isolation from one another but in relation to one another, within a given spatio-temporal context. As a result, actual outcomes have departed significantly, even diametrically, from what is implicit in each logic conceived abstractly.

Thus, historically, the strongest tendency towards territorial expansion has arisen out of the seedbed of political capitalism (Europe) rather than out of the seat of the most developed and best established territorialist empire (China). This discrepancy was not due to initial differences in capabilities. "From what historians and archeologists can tell us of the size, power, and seaworthiness of Cheng Ho's navy," notes Paul Kennedy (1987: 7), "[the Chinese] might well have been able to sail around Africa and 'discover' Portugal several decades before Henry the Navigator's expeditions began earnestly to push south of Ceuta." After the successful expeditions of Admiral Cheng Ho in the Indian Ocean, however, Ming China withdrew its fleet, restricted maritime trade, and terminated relations with foreign powers. According to Janet Abu-Lughod, why

Ming China should have decided to do so, instead of taking the final steps to become truly hegemonic in the Eurasian world system, "has perplexed – indeed caused despair among – serious scholars for at least the past one hundred years." More specifically, having come

> [c]lose to exercise domination over a significant portion of the globe and enjoying a technological advantage not only in peaceful production but in naval and military might as well ... why did [China] turn her back, withdraw her fleet, and thus leave an enormous vacuum of power that Muslim merchantmen, unbacked by state sea power, were totally unprepared to fill, but which their European counterparts would be more than willing and able to – after a hiatus of some 70 years? (Abu-Lughod 1989: 321–2)

Why Ming China purposefully abstained from undertaking the kind of "discovery" and conquest of the world into which successive European states soon afterwards began concentrating their energies and resources in fact has a rather simple answer. As Eric Wolf has pointed out, ever since Roman times Asia had been a purveyor of valued goods for the tribute-taking classes of Europe and had thereby exercised a powerful pull on Europe's precious metals. This structural imbalance of European trade with the East created strong incentives for European governments and businesses to seek ways and means, through trade or conquest, to retrieve the purchasing power that relentlessly drained from West to East. As Charles Davenant was to observe in the seventeenth century, whoever controlled the Asian trade would be in a position to "give law to all the commercial world" (Wolf 1982: 125).

It follows that the expected benefits for Portugal and other European states of discovering and controlling a direct route to the East were incomparably greater than the expected benefits of discovering and controlling a direct route to the West were for the Chinese state. Christopher Columbus stumbled on the Americas because he and his Castillian sponsors had treasure to retrieve in the East. Cheng Ho was not so lucky because there was no treasure to retrieve in the West.

In other words, the decision not to do what the Europeans would do later is perfectly understandable in terms of a territorialist logic of power that weighed carefully the prospective benefits, costs, and risks of the additional commitment of resources to state- and war-making involved in the territorial and commercial expansion of empire. In this connection we should note that Joseph Schumpeter's (1955: 64–5) thesis that pre-capitalist state formations have been characterized by strong "objectless" tendencies "toward forcible expansion, without definite, utilitarian limits – that is, non-rational and irrational, purely instinctual inclinations toward war and conquest " – holds no water in the case of Imperial

China. *Pace* Schumpeter, a strictly territorialist logic of power as conceptualized here, and typified ideally by Imperial China in the premodern and modern eras, is neither more nor less "rational" than a strictly capitalist logic of power. It is rather a different logic – one in which control over territory and population is in itself the objective of state- and war-making activities rather than mere means in the pursuit of pecuniary profit. The fact that such a control is pursued as an end in itself does not mean that its expansion is not subject to "definite, utilitarian limits." Nor does it mean that expansion is undertaken mindlessly beyond the point at which its prospective benefits in terms of power are either negative or positive but insufficient to warrant the risks involved in one kind or another of "imperial overstretch."

In fact, the Chinese imperial state constitutes the clearest historical instance of a territorialist organization that never fell into the trap of the kind of overstretch to which Paul Kennedy (1987) attributes the eventual downfall of successive Western great powers. What is most puzzling in terms of a strictly territorialist logic of power is not the lack of an expansionist drive in Ming China but the seemingly unbounded expansionism of European states since the latter half of the fifteenth century. The extraordinary benefits that European governments and businesses could reap by seizing control of trade in and with Asia provide part of the explanation. They none the less provide no answer to three closely related questions: (1) why this unprecedented expansionism began when it did; (2) why it proceeded unimpeded by the fall of one Western power after another, until almost the entire land surface of the earth had been conquered by peoples of European descent; and (3) whether and how the phenomenon has been related to the contemporaneous formation and equally explosive expansion of capitalism as world system of accumulation and rule.

The Origins of the Modern Inter-state System

Preliminary answers to these questions can be sought and found in an investigation of the origins, structure, and evolution of the modern inter-state system. The critical feature of this system has been the constant opposition of the capitalist and territorialist logics of power and the recurrent resolution of their contradictions through the reorganization of world political–economic space by the leading capitalist state of the epoch. This dialectic between capitalism and territorialism antedates the establishment in the seventeenth century of a pan-European inter-state system. Its origins lie in the formation within the medieval system of rule of a regional sub-system of capitalist city-states in northern Italy.

Initially, the regional sub-system of capitalist city-states that emerged in northern Italy was no more than one of the "anomalous enclaves" that abounded in the political space of the medieval system of rule, as Perry Anderson reminds us in the passage quoted earlier. But as the decay of the medieval system of rule gathered pace, the northern Italian capitalist enclave became organized into a sub-system of separate and independent political jurisdictions, held together by the principle of the balance of power and by dense and extensive networks of residential diplomacy. As Mattingly (1988), Cox (1959), Lane (1966; 1979), Braudel (1984: ch. 2), and McNeill (1984: ch. 3) emphasize in different but complementary ways, this sub-system of city-states, centered on Venice, Florence, Genoa, and Milan – the "big four" as Robert Lopez (1976: 99) has called them – anticipated by two centuries or more many of the key features of the modern inter-state system. As Ruggie (1993: 166) put it, the Europeans invented the modern state not once but twice, "once in the leading cities of the Italian Renaissance and once again in the kingdoms north of the Alps sometime thereafter."

Four main features of this system were prefigured in the northern Italian sub-system of city-states. First, this sub-system constituted a quintessentially capitalist system of war- and state-making. The most powerful state in the sub-system, Venice, is the true prototype of the capitalist state, in the double sense of "perfect example" and "model for future instances" of such a state. A merchant capitalist oligarchy firmly held state power in its grip. Territorial acquisitions were subjected to careful cost–benefit analyses and, as a rule, were undertaken only as the means to the end of increasing the profitability of the traffics of the capitalist oligarchy that exercised state power (Cox 1959: chs 2–5; Lane 1966: 57; Braudel 1984: 120–1; Modelski and Modelski 1988: 19–32).

Pace Sombart, if there has ever been a state whose executive met the *Communist Manifesto*'s standards of the capitalist state ("but a committee for managing the common affairs of the whole bourgeoisie" – Marx and Engels 1967: 82), it was fifteenth-century Venice. From this standpoint, the leading capitalist states of future epochs (the United Provinces, the United Kingdom, the United States) appear as increasingly diluted versions of the ideotypical standards realized by Venice centuries earlier.

Second, the operation of the "balance of power" played a crucial role at three different levels in fostering the development of this enclave of capitalist rule within the medieval system. The balance of power between the central authorities of the medieval system (pope and emperor) was instrumental in the emergence of an organized capitalist enclave in northern Italy – the geopolitical locus of that balance. The balance of power between the northern Italian city-states themselves was instrumental in preserving their mutual separateness and autonomy. And the balance of power between the emerging dynastic states of Western Europe was instrumental in preventing the logic of territorialism from nipping in the bud the rise of a capitalist logic within the European system of rule (cf. Mattingly 1988; McNeill 1984: ch. 3).

The balance of power was thus always integral to the development of capitalism as mode of rule. In fact, the balance of power can be interpreted as a mechanism by means of which capitalist states can, separately or jointly, reduce protection costs both absolutely and relative to their competitors and rivals. For the balance of power to be or become such a mechanism, however, the capitalist state(s) must be in a position to manipulate the balance to its (their) advantage instead of being cog(s) in a mechanism which no one or someone else controls. If the balance of power can be maintained only through repeated and costly wars, then participation in its working defeats the purpose of the capitalist state(s), because the pecuniary costs of such wars inevitably tend to exceed their pecuniary benefits. The secret of capitalist success is to have one's wars fought by others, if feasible costlessly and, if not, at the least possible cost.

Third, by developing wage-labor relations in what Frederic Lane (1979) has aptly called the "protection-producing industry," that is, war-making and state-making, the Italian city-states managed to transform at least part of their protection costs into revenues, and thus make wars pay for themselves:

> [Enough] money circulated in the richer Italian towns to make it possible for citizens to tax themselves and use the proceeds to buy the services of armed strangers. Then, simply by spending their pay, the hired soldiers put these monies back in circulation. Thereby, they intensified the market exchanges that allowed such towns to commercialize armed violence in the first place. The emergent system thus tended to become self-sustaining. (McNeill 1984: 74)

Indeed, the emergent system could become self-sustaining only up to a point. According to this characterization, the Italian city-states were practicing a kind of small-scale "military Keynesianism" – the practice through which military expenditures boost the incomes of the citizens of the state that has made the expenditures, thereby increasing tax revenues and the capacity to finance new rounds of military expenditures. As in all subsequent kinds of military Keynesianism, however, the "self-expansion" of military expenditures was strictly limited by permanent leakages of effective demand to other jurisdictions, by cost inflation, and by other redistributive effects of ever-increasing military expenditures which drove down the willingness of capitalist strata to tax themselves or be taxed for the purpose.

Fourth and last, the capitalist rulers of the northern Italian city-states (again, Venice in the first place) took the lead in developing dense and extensive networks of residential diplomacy. Through these networks they acquired the knowledge and the information concerning the ambitions and capabilities of other rulers (including the territorialist rulers of the wider medieval system of rule within which they operated) which were necessary to manipulate the balance of power in order to minimize protection costs. Just as the profitability of long-distance trade depended crucially on a quasi-monopolistic control of information over the largest economic space possible (Braudel 1982), so the capacity of capitalist rulers to manage the balance of power to their own advantage depended crucially on a quasi-monopolistic knowledge of, and capacity to monitor, the decision-making processes of other rulers.

This was the function of residential diplomacy. In comparison with territorialist rulers, capitalist rulers had both stronger motivations and greater opportunities to promote its development: stronger motivations because superior knowledge concerning the ambitions and capabilities of rulers was essential to the management of the balance of power which, in turn, was central to economizing in state-making and war-making; but greater opportunities, because the networks of long-distance trade controlled by the capitalist oligarchies provided a ready-made and self-financing foundation on which to build diplomatic networks (Mattingly 1988: 58–60). Be that as it may, the achievements of diplomacy in the consolidation of the northern Italian system of city-states – most notably the Peace of Lodi (1454) – provided a model for the formation two centuries later of the European system of nation-states (Mattingly 1988: 178).

The accumulation of capital from long-distance trade and high finance, the management of the balance of power, the commercialization of war, and the development of residential diplomacy thus complemented one another and, for a century or more, promoted an extraordinary concentration of wealth and power in the hands of the oligarchies that ruled the northern Italian city-states. By about 1420 the leading Italian city-states not only functioned as great powers in European politics (McNeill 1984: 78), but had revenues that compared very favorably with the revenues of the most successful dynastic states of western and northwestern Europe (Braudel 1984: 120). They thereby showed that even small territories could become huge containers of power by pursuing onesidedly the accumulation of riches rather than the acquisition of territories and subjects. Henceforth, "considerations of plenty" would become central to "considerations of power" throughout Europe.

The Italian city-states, however, never attempted individually or collectively a purposive transformation of the medieval system of rule.

For reasons that will become evident later, they had neither the desire nor the capabilities to undertake such a transformative action. Two more centuries had to elapse – from about 1450 to about 1650 (Braudel's "long" sixteenth century) – before a new kind of capitalist state, the United Provinces, would be presented with, and seize, the opportunity to transform the European system of rule to suit the requirements of the accumulation of capital on a world scale.

This new situation arose as a result of a quantum leap in the European power struggle, precipitated by the attempts of territorialist rulers to incorporate within their domains, or to prevent others from incorporating, the wealth and power of the Italian city-states. As it turned out, outright conquest proved impossible, primarily because of competition between the territorialist rulers themselves. In this struggle for the impossible, however, select territorial states – Spain and France in particular – developed new war-making techniques (the Spanish *tercios*, professional standing armies, mobile siege cannons, new fortification systems, and so on), which gave them a decisive power advantage vis-à-vis other rulers, including the suprastatal and substatal authorities of the medieval system of rule (cf. McNeill 1984: 79–95).

The intensification of the European power struggle was soon followed by its geographical expansion, because some territorialist rulers sought more roundabout ways to incorporate within their domains the wealth and power of the Italian city-states. Instead of, or in addition to, seeking the annexation of the city-states, these rulers tried to conquer the very sources of their wealth and power: the circuits of long-distance trade.

More specifically, the fortunes of the Italian city-states in general and of Venice in particular rested above all on monopolistic control over a crucial link in the chain of commercial exchanges that connected Western Europe to India and China via the world of Islam. No territorial state was powerful enough to take over that monopoly, but select territorialist rulers could and did attempt to establish a more direct link between Western Europe and India and China in order to divert money flows and supplies from the Venetian to their own trade circuits. Portugal and Spain, led and assisted by Genoese capitalist agencies crowded out by Venice from the most profitable traffics of the Mediterranean, took the lead. While Portugal succeeded, Spain failed but stumbled across an entirely new source of wealth and power: the Americas.

The intensification and global expansion of the European power struggle fed on one another and thereby engendered a vicious/virtuous circle – vicious for its victims, virtuous for its beneficiaries – of more and more massive resources and of increasingly sophisticated and costly techniques of state- and war-making deployed in the power struggle. Techniques which had been developed in the struggle within Europe were deployed to subjugate extra-European territories and communities; and the wealth and power originating from the subjugation of extra-European territories and communities were deployed in the struggle within Europe (McNeill 1984: 94–5, 100ff).

The state that initially benefited most from this vicious/virtuous circle was Spain, the only state that was simultaneously a protagonist of the power struggle on the European and on the extra-European fronts. Throughout the sixteenth century, the power of Spain exceeded that of all other European states by a good margin. This power, however, far from being used to oversee a smooth transition to the modern system of rule, became an instrument of the Habsburg Imperial House and of the papacy to save what could be saved of the disintegrating medieval system of rule.

In reality, little or nothing could be saved because the quantum leap in the European power struggle since the middle of the fifteenth century had taken the disintegration of the medieval system beyond the point of no return. Out of that struggle new realities of power had emerged in northwestern Europe which, to varying degrees, had subsumed the capitalist logic of power within the territorialist logic. The result was the formation of compact mini-empires, best exemplified by the French, English, and Swedish dynastic states, which, individually, could not match the power of Spain but, collectively, could not be subordinated to any old or new central political authority. The attempt of Spain, in conjunction with the papacy and the Habsburg Imperial House, to unmake or subordinate these new realities of power not only failed, but translated into a situation of systemic chaos which created the conditions for the rise of Dutch hegemony and the final liquidation of the medieval system of rule.

For conflict quickly escalated beyond the regulative capacities of the medieval system of rule and turned its institutions into so many new causes of conflict. As a consequence, the European power struggle became an ever-more negative-sum game in which all or most of the European rulers began to realize that they had nothing to gain and everything to lose from its continuation. The most important factor here was the sudden escalation of system-wide social conflict into a serious threat to the collective power of European rulers.

As Marc Bloch once wrote, "[the] peasant revolt was as common in early modern Europe as strikes are in industrial societies today" (cited in Parker and Smith 1985). But in the late sixteenth century and, above all, in the first half of the seventeenth century, this rural unrest was compounded by urban revolts on an unprecedented scale – revolts that were directed not against the "employers" but against the state itself. The Puritan Revolution in England was the most dramatic episode of this explosive combination of rural and urban revolts, but almost all

European rulers were directly affected or felt seriously threatened by the social upheaval (Parker and Smith 1985:12ff).

This system-wide intensification of social conflict was a direct result of the previous and contemporaneous escalation of armed conflicts among rulers. From about 1550 to about 1640, the number of soldiers mobilized by the great powers of Europe more than doubled, while from 1530 to 1630 the cost of putting each of these soldiers in the field increased on average by a factor of 5 (Parker and Smith 1985: 14). This escalation of protection costs led to a sharp increase in the fiscal pressure on subjects which, in turn, triggered many of the seventeenth-century revolts (Steensgaard 1985: 42–4).

Alongside this escalation in protection costs, an escalation in the ideological struggle occurred. The progressive breakdown of the medieval system of rule had led to a mixture of religious innovations and religious restorations from above, following the principle *cuius regio eius religio*, which provoked popular resentment and rebellions against both (Parker and Smith 1985: 15–18). As rulers turned religion into an instrument of their mutual power struggles, subjects followed their lead and turned religion into an instrument of insurrection against rulers.

Last but not least, the escalation of armed conflicts between rulers disrupted the trans-European networks of trade on which they depended to obtain means of war and subjects depended for their livelihood. The costs and risks of moving goods across political jurisdictions increased dramatically, and supplies were diverted from the provision of means of livelihood to the provision of means of war. It is plausible to suppose that this disruption and diversion of trade flows contributed far more decisively than demographic and climatic factors to the sudden worsening problem of vagrancy and to the "subsistence crisis" which constitute the social and economic backdrop of the general crisis of legitimacy of the seventeenth century (cf. Braudel and Spooner 1967; Romano 1985; Goldstone 1991).

Whatever the tendencies that caused popular insurgency, the result was a heightened consciousness among European rulers of their common power interest *vis-à-vis* their subjects. As James I put it at an early stage of the general crisis, there existed "an implicit tie amongst kings which obligeth them, though there may be no other interest or particular engagement, to stick unto and right one another upon insurrection of subjects" (quoted in Hill 1958: 126). Under normal circumstances, this "implicit tie" had little or no influence on the conduct of rulers. But on those occasions in which the authority of all or most rulers was seriously challenged by their subjects – as it was in the middle of the seventeenth century – the general interest of rulers in preserving their collective power over their subjects overshadowed their quarrels and mutual antagonisms.

It was under these circumstances that the United Provinces became hegemonic by leading a large and powerful coalition of dynastic states towards the liquidation of the medieval system of rule and the establishment of the modern inter-state system. In the course of their earlier struggle for national independence from Spain, the Dutch had already established a strong intellectual and moral leadership over the dynastic states of northwestern Europe, which were among the main beneficiaries of the disintegration of the medieval system of rule. As systemic chaos increased during the Thirty Years War, "[t]he threads of diplomacy [came to be] woven and unwoven at the Hague" (Braudel 1984: 203) and Dutch proposals for a major reorganization of the pan-European system of rule found more and more supporters among European rulers until Spain was completely isolated.

With the Peace of Westphalia of 1648, a new world system of rule thus emerged:

> The idea of an authority or organization above sovereign states is no longer. What takes its place is the notion that all states form a world-wide political system or that, at any rate, the states of Western Europe form a single political system. This new system rests on international law and the balance of power, a law operating between rather than above states and a power operating between rather than above states. (Gross 1968: 54–5)

The world system of rule created at Westphalia had a social purpose as well. As rulers legitimated their respective absolute rights of government over mutually exclusive territories, the principle was established that civilians were not party to the quarrels between sovereigns. The most important application of this principle was in the field of commerce. In the treaties that followed the Settlement of Westphalia a clause was inserted that aimed at restoring freedom of commerce by abolishing barriers to trade which had developed in the course of the Thirty Years War. Subsequent agreements introduced rules to protect the property and commerce of non-combatants. The limitation of reprisals in the interest of trade typical of the northern Italian system of city-states (Sereni 1943: 43–9) thus found its way into the norms and rules of the European system of nation-states.

An inter-statal regime was thus established in which the effects of war-making between sovereigns on the everyday life of subjects were minimized:

> The 18th century witnessed many. wars; but in respect of the freedom and friendliness of intercourse between the educated classes in the principal European countries, with French as the recognized common language, it was

the most "international" period of modern history, and civilians could pass to and fro and transact their business freely with one another while their respective sovereigns were at war. (Carr 1945: 4)

The systemic chaos of the early seventeenth century was thus transformed into a new anarchic order. The considerable freedom granted to private enterprise to organize commerce peacefully across political jurisdictions even in wartime reflected not only the general interest of rulers and subjects in dependable supplies of means of war and means of livelihood, but the particular interests of the Dutch capitalist oligarchy in an unfettered accumulation of capital. This reorganization of political space in the interest of capital accumulation marks the birth not just of the modern inter-state system, but also of capitalism as world system. The reasons why it took place in the seventeenth century under Dutch leadership instead of in the fifteenth century under Venetian leadership are not far to seek.

The most important reason, which encompasses all the others, is that in the fifteenth century systemic chaos had not attained the scale and intensity that two centuries later induced European rulers to recognize their general interest in the liquidation of the medieval system of rule. The Venetian capitalist oligarchy had itself been doing so well within that system that it had no interest whatsoever in its liquidation. In any event, the Italian city-state system was a regional sub-system continually torn apart by the greater and lesser powers of the wider world system to which it belonged. Political rivalries and diplomatic alliances could not be confined to the sub-system. They systematically brought into play territorialist rulers who kept the capitalist oligarchies of northern Italy permanently on the defensive.

By the early seventeenth century, in contrast, the resurgence of systemic chaos created both a general interest in a major rationalization of the power struggle on the part of European rulers and a capitalist oligarchy with the motivations and the capabilities necessary to take the lead in serving that general interest. The Dutch capitalist oligarchy was in important respects a replica of the Venetian capitalist oligarchy. Like the latter, it was the bearer of a capitalist logic of power, and as such a leader in the management of the balance of power and in diplomatic initiatives and innovations. Unlike the latter, however, it was a product rather than a factor of the quantum leap in the European power struggle prompted by the emergence of capitalist states in northern Italy. This difference had several important implications.

First, the scale of operation, and hence the power, of the Dutch capitalist oligarchy in European and world politics was much greater than that of Venice. Venice's wealth and power rested on a circuit of trade, which was itself a link in a much longer circuit, which Venice itself did not control. As we have seen, this local link could be and was superseded by more roundabout circuits of trade. The wealth and power of Holland, in contrast, were based on commercial and financial networks which the Dutch capitalist oligarchy had carved out of the seaborne and colonial empires through which the territorialist rulers of Portugal and Spain, in alliance with the Genoese capitalist oligarchy, had superseded the wealth and power of Venice.

These networks encircled the world and could not easily be bypassed or superseded. In fact, the wealth and power of the Dutch capitalist oligarchy rested more on its control over world financial networks than on commercial networks. This meant that it was less vulnerable than the Venetian capitalist oligarchy to the establishment of competing trade routes or to increased competition on a given route. As competition in long-distance trade intensified, the Dutch oligarchs could recoup their losses and find a new field of profitable investment in financial specula-tion. The Dutch capitalist oligarchy therefore had the power to rise above the competition and turn it to its own advantage.

Second, the interests of the Dutch capitalist oligarchy clashed far more fundamentally with the interests of the central authorities of the medieval system of rule than the interests of the Venetian capitalist oligarchy ever did. As the history of the "long" sixteenth century demonstrated, the wealth and power of Venice were threatened more fundamentally by the increasing power of the dynastic states of south- and northwestern Europe which were emerging from the disintegration of the medieval system of rule than they were by the waning power of the papacy and the Imperial House.

The Dutch capitalist oligarchy, in contrast, had a strong common interest with the emerging dynastic states in the liquidation of the claims of pope and emperor to a suprastatal moral and political authority as embodied in the imperial pretensions of Spain. As a consequence of its eighty-year-long war of independence against Imperial Spain, the Dutch became a champion and organizer of the proto-nationalist aspirations of dynastic rulers. At the same time, they continuously sought ways and means to prevent conflict from escalating beyond the point where the commercial and financial foundations of their wealth and power would be seriously undermined. In pursuing its own interest, the Dutch capitalist oligarchy thus came to be perceived as the champion not just of independence from the central authorities of the medieval system of rule but also of a general interest in peace which the latter were no longer able to serve.

Third, the war-making capabilities of the Dutch capitalist oligarchy far surpassed those of the Venetian oligarchy. The capabilities of the latter were closely related to the geographical position of Venice and had little use outside that position, particularly after the great advances in war-making techniques of the "long" sixteenth century. The capabilities of the Dutch oligarchy, in contrast, were based on successful front-line partici-pation in that process. As a matter of fact, the Dutch were leaders not just in the accumulation of capital but also in the rationalization of military techniques.

By rediscovering and bringing to perfection long-forgotten Roman military techniques, Maurice of Nassau, Prince of Orange, achieved for the Dutch army in the early seventeenth century what scientific manage-ment would achieve for US industry two centuries later (cf. McNeill 1984: 127–39; vanDoorn 1975: 9ff). Siege techniques were transformed (1) to increase the efficiency of military labor-power, (2) to cut costs in terms of casualties, and (3) to facilitate the maintenance of discipline in the army's ranks. Marching and the loading and firing of guns were standardized, and drilling was made a regular activity. The army was divided into smaller tactical units, the numbers of commissioned and non-commissioned officers were increased, and lines of command ration-alized:

> In this way an army became an articulate organism with a central nervous system that allowed sensitive and more or less intelligent response to unforseen circumstances. Every movement attained a new level of exactitude and speed. The individual movements of soldiers when firing and marching as well as the movements of batallions across the battlefield could be controlled and predicted as never before. A well-drilled unit, by making every motion count, could increase the amount of lead projected against the enemy per minute of battle. The dexterity and resolution of individual infantry men scarcely mattered any more. Prowess and personal courage all but disappeared beneath an armor-plated routine.... Yet troops drilled in the Maurician fashion automatically exhibited superior effectiveness in battle. (McNeill 1984: 130)

The significance of this innovation is that it neutralized the advantages of scale enjoyed by Spain and thereby tended to equalize relative military capabilities within Europe. By actively encouraging the adoption of these new techniques by its allies, the United Provinces created the conditions of substantive equality among European states, which became the premiss of the future Westphalia System. And of course, by so doing, it strengthened its intellectual and moral leadership over the dynastic rulers who were seeking the legitimation of their absolute rights of government.

Fourth and last, the state-making capabilities of the Dutch capitalist oligarchy were far greater than those of the Venetian oligarchy. The exclusiveness of capitalist interests in the organization and management

of the Venetian state was the main source of its power but was also the
main limit of that power. For this exclusiveness kept the political horizon
of the Venetian oligarchy within the limits set by cost–benefit analysis and
double-entry bookkeeping. That is to say, it kept Venetian rulers aloof
from the political and social issues that were tearing apart the world
within which they operated.

The state-making capabilities of the Dutch capitalist oligarchy, in
contrast, had been forged in a long struggle of emancipation from Spanish
imperial rule. In order to succeed in this struggle, it had to forge an
alliance and share power with dynastic interests (the House of Orange)
and had to ride the tiger of popular rebellion (Calvinism). As a
consequence, the power of the capitalist oligarchy within the Dutch state
was far less absolute than it had been within the Venetian state. But for
this very reason the Dutch ruling group developed much greater capabilities than Venetian rulers ever had to pose and solve the problems around
which the European power struggle raged. The United Provinces thus
became hegemonic in virtue of being less rather than more capitalist than
Venice.

British Hegemony and Free-Trade Imperialism

The Dutch never governed the system that they had created. As soon as
the Westphalia System was in place, the United Provinces began losing its
recently acquired world-power status. For more than half a century the
Dutch continued to lead the states of the newly born Westphalia System
in a specific direction – most notably, in the direction of overseas
commercial expansion backed by naval power and the formation of joint-
stock chartered companies. But this leadership was typically what we
have called leadership against the leader's will since it undermined rather
than enhanced Dutch power. Dutch world hegemony was thus a highly
ephemeral formation which was unmade as soon as it was made.

In terms of world power, the principal beneficiaries of the new system
of rule were the United Provinces' former allies, France and England. For
the next century and a half – from the outbreak of the Anglo-Dutch Wars
in 1652 (a mere four years after the Settlement of Westphalia) to the end
of the Napoleonic Wars in 1815 – the inter-state system was dominated
by the struggle for world supremacy between these two great powers.

This long-drawn-out conflict developed in three partly overlapping
phases which replicated in some respects the phases of struggle of the
"long" sixteenth century. The first phase was once again characterized by
the attempts of territorialist rulers to incorporate within their domains
the leading capitalist state. Just as France and Spain had attempted to

conquer the northern Italian city-states in the late fifteenth century, so in the late seventeenth century England and above all France attempted to internalize within their own domains the networks of trade and power of the United Provinces.

As Colbert emphasized in his advice to Louis XIV, "[if] the king were to subjugate all the United Provinces to his authority, their commerce would become the commerce of the subjects of his majesty, and there would be nothing more to ask" (quoted in Anderson 1974: 36–7). The problem with this advice lies in the "if" clause. Even though the strategic capabilities of seventeenth-century France (or for that matter England) greatly exceeded the capabilities of their fifteenth-century counterparts, the strategic capabilities of the United Provinces exceeded those of the leading capitalist states of the fifteenth century by an even greater margin. Notwithstanding a short-lived joint effort, France and England failed to subjugate the Dutch. Once again, competition between the would-be conquerors proved an insuperable obstacle on the road to conquest.

As these attempts failed, the struggle entered a second phase, in which the efforts of the two rivals became increasingly focused on incorporating the sources of the wealth and power of the capitalist state rather than the capitalist state itself. Just as Portugal and Spain had struggled for control over the traffic with the East, so France and England struggled for control over the Atlantic. Differences between the two struggles, however, are as important as the analogies.

Both France and England were latecomers in the global power struggle. This lent them some advantages. The most important was that by the time France and England entered the business of territorial expansion in the extra-European world, the spread of Maurician "scientific management" to the European armies was beginning to turn their comparative advantage over the armies of extra-European rulers into an unbridgeable gulf. The power of the Ottoman empire had begun to decline irreversibly:

> Further East, the new style of training soldiers became important when European drill-masters began to create miniature armies by recruiting local manpower for the protection of French, Dutch, and English trading stations on the shores of the Indian Ocean. By the eighteenth century, such forces, however minuscule, exhibited a clear superiority over the unwieldy armies that local rulers were accustomed to bring into the field. (McNeill 1984: 135)

To be sure, it was not until the nineteenth century that this superiority became sufficiently overwhelming to translate into major territorial conquests in the Indian subcontinent and into the subordination of Imperial China to Western commands. But already in the eighteenth century the superiority was sufficient to enable the latecomers – and

Britain in particular – to conquer some of the most abundant sources of tribute of the collapsing Mughal empire – most notably Bengal – and thus go beyond the mere establishment of an Asian seaborne empire as the Portuguese and the Dutch had done. The emerging gulf between Western and non-Western military capabilities was none the less of little help to the latecomers in displacing the Portuguese, the Spaniards, and, above all, the Dutch from established positions at the crossroads of world commerce. In order to catch up with and overtake the early comers, the latecomers had radically to restructure the political geography of world commerce. This is precisely what was achieved by the new synthesis of capitalism and territorialism brought into being by French and British mercantilism in the eighteenth century.

This had three major and closely interrelated components: settler colonialism, capitalist slavery, and economic nationalism. All three components were essential to the reorganization of world political–economic space, but settler colonialism was probably the leading element in the combination. British rulers in particular relied heavily on the private initiative of their subjects in countering the advantages of early comers in overseas expansion:

> Although they could not match the Dutch in financial acumen and in the size and efficiency of their merchant fleet, the English believed in founding settlement colonies and not just ports of call en route to the Indies.... Besides joint-stock or chartered companies the English developed such expedients for colonization as the proprietory colony analogous to the Portuguese captaincies in Brazil, and Crown colonies nominally under direct royal control. What English colonies in America lacked in natural resources and uniformity they made up for in the number and industriousness of the colonists themselves. (Nadel and Curtis 1964: 9–10)

Capitalist slavery was partly a condition and partly a result of the success of settler colonialism. For the expansion in the number and industriousness of the colonists was continually limited by, and continually recreated, shortages of labor-power which could not be satisfied by relying exclusively, or even primarily, on the supplies engendered spontaneously from within the ranks of the settler populations or extracted forcibly from the indigenous populations. This chronic labor shortage enhanced the profitability of capitalist enterprises engaged in the procurement (primarily in Africa), transport, and productive use (primarily in the Americas) of slave labor. As Robin Blackburn (1988: 13) notes, "New World slavery solved the colonial labour problem at a time when no other solution was in sight." The solution of the colonial labor problem, in turn, became the leading factor in the expansion of the infrastructure and of the outlets necessary to sustain the settlers' productive efforts.

Settler colonialism and capitalist slavery were necessary but insufficient conditions of the success of French and British mercantilism in radically restructuring the global political economy. The third key ingredient, economic nationalism, had two main aspects. The first was the endless accumulation of monetary surpluses in colonial and inter-state commerce – an accumulation with which mercantilism is often identified. The second was national or, better, domestic economy-making. As underscored by Gustav von Schmoller, "in its inmost kernel [mercantilism was] nothing but state-making – not state-making in a narrow sense, but state-making and national-economy-making at the same time" (quoted in Wilson 1958: 6).

National economy-making brought to perfection on a greatly enlarged scale the practice of making wars pay for themselves by turning protection costs into revenues, which the Italian city-states had pioneered three centuries earlier. Partly through commands to state bureaucracies and partly through incentives to private enterprise, the rulers of France and of the United Kingdom internalized within their domains as many of the growing number of activities that, directly or indirectly, entered as inputs in war-making and state-making as was feasible. In this way they managed to turn into tax revenues a much larger share of protection costs than the Italian city-states, or for that matter the United Provinces, ever did or could have done. By spending these enhanced tax revenues within their domestic economies, they created new incentives and opportunities to establish ever new linkages between activities and thus make wars pay for themselves more and more.

What was happening, in fact, was not that wars were "paying for themselves," but that an increasing number of civilians were mobilized to sustain indirectly, and often unknowingly, the war-making and state-making efforts of rulers. War-making and state-making were becoming an increasingly roundabout business which involved an ever-growing number, range, and variety of seemingly unrelated activities. The capacity of mercantilist rulers to mobilize the energies of their civilian subjects in undertaking and carrying out these activities was not unlimited. On the contrary, it was strictly limited by their ability to appropriate the benefits of world commerce, of settler colonialism, and of capitalist slavery, and to turn these benefits into adequate rewards for the entrepreneurship and productive efforts of their metropolitan subjects (cf. Tilly 1990: 82–3).

In breaking out of these limits British rulers had a decisive comparative advantage over all their competitors, the French included. This was geopolitical, and resembled the comparative advantage of Venice at the height of its power:

Both in overseas trade and in naval strength, Britain gained supremacy, favored, like Venice, by two interacting factors: her island position and the new role which fell into her hands, the role of intermediary between two worlds. Unlike the continental powers, Britain could direct her undivided strength toward the sea; unlike her Dutch competitors, she did not have to man a land front. (Dehio 1962: 71)

As we shall see in chapter 3, England/Britain "became" a powerful island through a two-centuries-long and painful process of "learning" how to turn a fundamental geopolitical handicap in the continental power struggle *vis-à-vis* France and Spain into a decisive competitive advantage in the struggle for world commercial supremacy. By the mid-seventeenth century, however, this process was for all practical purposes complete. From then on, the channeling of British energies and resources towards overseas expansion, while the energies and resources of its European competitors were locked up in struggles close at home, generated a process of circular and cumulative causation. British successes in overseas expansion increased the pressure on the states of continental Europe to keep up with Britain's growing world power. But these successes also provided Britain with the means necessary to manage the balance of power in continental Europe in order to keep its rivals busy close to home. Over time, this virtuous/vicious circle put Britain in a position where it could eliminate all competitors from overseas expansion and, at the same time, become the undisputed master of the European balance of power.

When Britain won the Seven Years War (1756–63), the struggle with France for world supremacy was over. But it did not thereby become world-hegemonic. On the contrary, as soon as the struggle for world supremacy was over, conflict entered a third phase, characterized by increasing systemic chaos. Like the United Provinces in the early seventeenth century, Britain became hegemonic by creating a new world order out of this systemic chaos.

As in the early seventeenth century, systemic chaos was the result of the intrusion of social conflict into the power struggles of rulers. There were, however, important differences between the two situations. The most important is the much greater degree of autonomy and effectiveness demonstrated by the rebellious subjects in the late eighteenth and early nineteenth centuries in comparison with the early seventeenth century.

To be sure, the new wave of system-wide rebelliousness had its deeper origins in the struggle for the Atlantic, as we shall see. Yet once it exploded, rebellion created the conditions for a renewal of Anglo-French rivalry on entirely new foundations, and rebellion continued to rage for about thirty years after this new rivalry had ceased. Taking the period

848 as a whole, this second wave of rebelliousness resulted in a
[g]h transformation of ruler–subject relations throughout the Amer-
[d] in most of Europe and, second, in the establishment of an entirely
nd of world hegemony (British free-trade imperialism) which
thoroughly reorganized the inter-state system to accommodate that
transformation.

The deeper origins of this wave of rebelliousness can be traced to the
previous struggle for the Atlantic because its agents were precisely the
social forces that had been brought into being and forged into new
communities by that struggle: the colonial settlers, the plantation slaves,
and the metropolitan middle classes. Rebellion began in the colonies with
the American Declaration of Independence in 1776 and hit the United
Kingdom first. French rulers immediately seized the opportunity to
initiate a revanchist campaign. However, this quickly backfired with the
Revolution of 1789. The energies released by the revolution were
channeled under Napoleon into a redoubling of French revanchist efforts.
And these, in turn, led to a generalization of settler, slave, and middle-
class rebelliousness (cf. Hobsbawm 1962; Wallerstein 1988; Blackburn
1988; Schama 1989).

In the course of these inter-state and intra-state struggles widespread
violations of the principles, norms, and rules of the Westphalia System
occurred. Napoleonic France in particular trampled on the absolute
rights of government of European rulers both by fomenting revolt from
below and by imposing imperial commands from above. At the same
time, it encroached on the property rights and freedoms of commerce of
non-combatants through expropriations, blockades, and a command
economy spanning most of continental Europe.

The United Kingdom first became hegemonic by leading a vast alliance
of primarily dynastic forces in the struggle against these infringements on
their absolute rights of government and for the restoration of the
Westphalia System. This restoration was successfully accomplished with
the Settlement of Vienna of 1815 and the subsequent Congress of Aix-
la-Chapelle of 1818. Up to this point British hegemony was a replica of
Dutch hegemony. Just as the Dutch had successfully led the about-to-be-
born inter-state system in the struggle against the imperial pretensions of
Habsburg Spain, so the British successfully led the about-to-be-destroyed
inter-state system in the struggle against the imperial pretensions of
Napoleonic France (cf. Dehio 1962).

Unlike the United Provinces, however, the United Kingdom went on to
govern the inter-state system and, in doing so, it undertook a major
reorganization of that system aimed at accommodating the new realities
of power released by the continuing revolutionary upheaval. The system
that came into being is what John Gallagher and Ronald Robinson (1953)

called free-trade imperialism – a world-system of rule which both expanded and superseded the Westphalia System. This is noticeable at three different but interrelated levels of analysis.

First, a new group of states joined the group of dynastic and oligarchic states which had formed the original nucleus of the Westphalia System. This new group consisted primarily of states controlled by national communities of property-holders which had succeeded in gaining independence from old and new empires. Inter-state relations thus began to be governed not by the personal interests, ambitions, and emotions of monarchs but by the collective interests, ambitions, and emotions of these national communities (Carr 1945: 8).

This "democratization" of nationalism was accompanied by an unprecedented centralization of world power in the hands of a single state, the United Kingdom. In the expanded inter-state system that emerged out of the revolutionary upheaval of 1776–1848, only the United Kingdom was simultaneously involved in the politics of all the regions of the world and, more importantly, held a commanding position in most of them. For the first time, the objective of all previous capitalist states to be the master rather than the servant of the global balance of power was fully, if temporarily, realized by the leading capitalist state of the epoch.

In order to manage the global balance of power more effectively, the United Kingdom took the lead in tightening the loose system of consultation between the great powers of Europe which had been in operation since the Peace of Westphalia. The result was the Concert of Europe which, from the start, was primarily an instrument of British governance of the continental balance of power. For about thirty years after the Peace of Vienna the Concert of Europe played a secondary role in the politics of continental Europe relative to the "hierarchies of blood and grace" that had formed the Holy Alliance. But as the Alliance disintegrated under the rising pressure of democratic nationalism, the Concert quickly emerged as the main instrument of regulation of inter-state relations in Europe (cf. Polanyi 1957: 7–9).

Second, the disintegration of colonial empires in the Western world was accompanied and followed by their expansion in the non-Western world. At the beginning of the nineteenth century Western states claimed 55 per cent but actually held about 35 per cent of the earth's land surface. By 1878 the latter proportion had risen to 67 per cent, and by 1914 to 85 per cent (Magdoff 1978: 29, 35). "No other set of colonies in history was as large," notes Edward Said (1993: 8), "more so totally dominated, none so unequal in power to the Western metropolis."

Britain took the lion's share of this territorial conquest. In so doing, it resurrected imperial rule on a scale the world had never previously seen.

This resurgence of imperial rule is indeed the main reason for designating Britain's nineteenth-century world hegemony with the expression free-trade *imperialism* – an expression which we use to underscore not just Britain's governance of the world system through the practice and ideology of free trade, as Gallagher and Robinson do, but also and especially the imperial foundations of Britain's free trade regime of rule and accumulation on a world scale. No territorialist ruler had ever before incorporated within its domains so many, so populous, and so far-flung territories as the United Kingdom did in the nineteenth century. Nor had any territorialist ruler ever before forcibly extracted in so short a time so much tribute – in labor-power, in natural resources, and in means of payments – as the British state and its clients did in the Indian subcontinent in the course of the nineteenth century. Part of this tribute was used to buttress and expand the coercive apparatus through which more and more non-Western subjects were added to the British territorial empire. But another, equally conspicuous part was siphoned off in one form or another to London, to be recycled in the circuits of wealth through which British power in the Western world was continually reproduced and expanded. The territorialist and the capitalist logics of power (TMT' and MTM') thus cross-fertilized and sustained one another.

The recycling of imperial tribute extracted from the colonies into capital invested all over the world enhanced London's comparative advantage as a world financial center *vis-à-vis* competing centers such as Amsterdam and Paris (cf. Jenks 1938). This comparative advantage made London the natural home of *haute finance* – a closely knit body of cosmopolitan financiers whose global networks were turned into yet another instrument of British governance of the inter-state system:

> Finance ... acted as a powerful moderator in the councils and policies of a number of smaller sovereign states. Loans, and the renewal of loans, hinged upon credit, and credit upon good behavior. Since, under constitutional government (unconstitutional ones were severely frowned upon), behavior is reflected in the budget and the external value of the currency cannot be detached from appreciation of the budget, debtor governments were well advised to watch their exchanges carefully and to avoid policies which might reflect upon the soundness of the budgetary position. This useful maxim became a cogent rule of conduct once a country had adopted the gold standard, which limited permissible fluctuations to a minimum. Gold standard and constitutionalism were the instruments which made the voice of the City of London heard in many smaller countries which had adopted these symbols of adherence to the new international order. The Pax Britannica held its sway sometimes by the ominous poise of heavy ship's cannon, but more frequently it prevailed by the timely pull of a thread in the international monetary network. (Polanyi 1957: 14)

Finally, the expansion and supersession of the Westphalia System found expression in an entirely new instrument of world government. The Westphalia System was based on the principle that there was no authority operating above the inter-state system. Free-trade imperialism, in contrast, established the principle that the laws operating within and between states were subject to the higher authority of a new, metaphysical entity – a world market ruled by its own "laws" – allegedly endowed with supernatural powers greater than anything pope and emperor had ever mastered in the medieval system of rule. By presenting its world supremacy as the embodiment of this metaphysical entity, the United Kingdom succeeded in expanding its power in the inter-state system well beyond what was warranted by the extent and effectiveness of its coercive apparatus.

This power was the result of the United Kingdom's *unilateral* adoption of a free trade practice and ideology. A regime of multilateral free trade began only in 1860 with the signing of the Anglo-French Treaty of Commerce, and for all practical purposes ended in 1879 with the "new" German protectionism. But from the mid-1840s to 1931, Britain unilaterally kept its domestic market open to the products of the whole world (Bairoch 1976a). Combined with territorial expansion overseas and with the development of a capital goods industry at home, this policy became a powerful instrument of governance of the entire world-economy:

> The colonization of the empty spaces [sic], the development of the machine driven industry dependent on coal and the opening up of world-wide communications through railways and shipping services proceeded apace under British leadership, and stimulated everywhere the emergence and development of nations and national consciousness; and the counterpart of this "expansion of England" was the free market provided in Britain from the 1840s onwards for the natural products, foodstuffs and raw materials of the rest of the world. (Carr 1945: 13–14)

By opening up their domestic market, British rulers created world-wide networks of dependence on, and allegiance to, the expansion of wealth and power of the United Kingdom. This control over the world market, combined with mastery of the global balance of power and a close relationship of mutual instrumentality with *haute finance*, enabled the United Kingdom to govern the inter-state system as effectively as a world empire. The result was "a phenomenon unheard of in the annals of Western civilization, namely, a hundred years' [European] peace – 1815–1914" (Polanyi 1957: 5).

This reflected the unprecedented hegemonic capabilities of the United Kingdom. Its coercive apparatus – primarily its navy and colonial armies

.– and its island position no doubt endowed it with a decisive comparative advantage relative to all its rivals in the European and global power struggle. But, however great, this advantage cannot possibly account for the extraordinary capacity to restructure the world – not just the European inter-state system – to suit its national interests, which Britain demonstrated in the mid-nineteenth century.

This extraordinary capacity was a manifestation of hegemony – that is, of the capacity to claim with credibility that the expansion of UK power served not just UK national interest but a "universal" interest as well. Central to this hegemonic claim was a distinction between the power of rulers and the "wealth of nations" subtly drawn in the liberal ideology propagated by the British intelligentsia. In this ideology, the expansion of the power of British rulers relative to other rulers was presented as the motor force of a general expansion of the wealth of nations. Free trade might undermine the sovereignty of rulers, but it would at the same time expand the wealth of their subjects, or at least of their propertied subjects.

The appeal and credibility of this claim were based on systemic circumstances created by the revolutionary upheavals of 1776–1848. For the national communities that had risen to power in the Americas and in many parts of Europe in the course of these upheavals were primarily communities of property-holders, whose main concern was with the monetary value of their assets rather than with the autonomous power of their rulers. It was these communities that formed the "natural" constituency of British free trade hegemony.

At the same time, the revolutionary upheavals of 1776–1848 had promoted changes within the United Kingdom itself which enhanced the capacity of its rulers to satisfy this system-wide demand for "democratic" wealth. The most important of these changes was the industrial revolution, which took off under the impact of the French Revolutionary and Napoleonic Wars. For our present purposes, the main significance of this revolution was that it greatly enhanced the relationship of complementarity which linked the enterprises of British subjects to the enterprises of subjects of other states, particularly of the states that had emerged out of the settlers' rebellion against British rule in North America. As a result, British rulers began to realize that their lead in domestic economy-making gave them a considerable advantage in the use of subject–subject relations across political jurisdictions as invisible instruments of rule over other sovereign states. It was this realization more than anything else that persuaded British rulers after the Napoleonic Wars to sustain and protect the forces of democratic nationalism, first in the Americas, later in Europe, against the reactionary tendencies of its former dynastic allies (Aguilar 1968: 23). And as the national power of these forces increased, so did the capabilities of the British ruling groups to lead and govern the inter-state system in order to expand further their wealth, power, and prestige at home and abroad.

The world power achievements of nineteenth-century Britain were unprecedented. Nevertheless, the novelty of the developmental path that led to these achievements should not be exaggerated. For Britain's free-trade imperialism simply fused in a harmonious synthesis two seemingly divergent developmental paths which had been opened up long before by the ruling groups of other states. What was new was the combination of the paths, not the paths themselves.

One of these paths had been opened up by Venice centuries earlier. Indeed, to be the Venice of the nineteenth century was still the objective advocated for Britain by leading members of its business community at the end of the Napoleonic Wars. And the same analogy was evoked again – albeit with negative connotations – when the nineteenth-century expansion of British wealth and power began reaching its limits (Ingham 1984: 9).

If we focus on metropolitan domains and on relations between European states, then this is undoubtedly an apt analogy. Britain's comparatively small territory, its island position at the main intersection of world trade, its naval supremacy, the entrepôt-like structure of its domestic economy – all were traits that made it look like an enlarged replica of the Venetian Republic, or for that matter of the United Provinces, at the height of their respective power. Admittedly, Britain's metropolitan domains were larger, and enclosed much greater demographic and natural resources than the metropolitan domains of its Venetian and Dutch predecessors. But this difference could be taken as corresponding approximately to the increased size and resources of the capitalist world-economy in the nineteenth century, compared with the earlier epochs when Venetian and Dutch power rose and declined.

The second developmental path was altogether different, and can be perceived only by widening our angle of vision to encompass overseas domains and relations between political structures world-wide. From this wider angle of vision, nineteenth-century Britain appears to have followed in the footsteps not of Venice or the United Provinces, but of Imperial Spain. As Paul Kennedy (1987: 48) has observed, like the Habsburg bloc three centuries earlier, the nineteenth-century British empire "was a conglomeration of widely scattered territories, a political–dynastic tour de force which required enormous sustained resources of material and ingenuity to keep going."

As we shall detail in chapter 3, this similarity between the spatial configurations of the nineteenth-century British empire and the sixteenth-century Spanish empire was matched by a striking similarity between the strategies and structures of the cosmopolitan networks of long-distance trade and high finance which assisted the power pursuits of the ruling groups of the two imperial formations. Nor were these the only similarities. Even the notion of a free trade system encompassing multiple sovereign states seems to have originated in Imperial Spain (Nussbaum 1950: 59–62).

In short, the expansion and supersession of the Westphalia System which was realized by and through Britain's free trade imperialism did not involve simply a "progression" towards larger and more complex political structures along the developmental path opened up and pursued by the leading capitalist states of previous epochs. They also involved "regression" towards strategies and structures of world-scale rule and accumulation which seemed to have been made obsolete by earlier developments along that path. In particular, the creation in the nineteenth century of a part-capitalist and part-territorialist imperial structure, whose global power far surpassed anything the world had ever seen, shows that the formation and expansion of the capitalist world-economy has involved not so much a supersession as a continuation by other, more effective means of the imperial pursuits of pre-modern times.

For the capitalist world-economy as reconstituted under British hegemony in the nineteenth century was as much a "world empire" as it was a "world-economy" – an entirely new kind of world empire to be sure, but a world empire none the less. The most important and novel feature of this world empire *sui generis* was the extensive use by its ruling groups of a quasi-monopolistic control over universally accepted means of payments ("world money") to ensure compliance to their commands, not just within their widely scattered domains, but by the sovereigns and subjects of other political domains as well. The reproduction of this quasi-monopolistic control over world money was highly problematic and did not last very long – at least by the standards established by the most successful among pre-modern world empires. But as long as it lasted, it enabled the British government to rule with great effectiveness over a much larger political–economic space than any previous world empire ever did or could.

US Hegemony and the Rise of the Free Enterprise System

The United Kingdom exercised world governmental functions until the end of the nineteenth century. From the 1870s onwards, however, it began to lose control of the European balance of power and soon afterwards of the global balance of power as well. In both cases, the rise of Germany to world power status was the decisive development (Kennedy 1987: 209–13).

At the same time, the capacity of the United Kingdom to hold the center of the capitalist world-economy was being undermined by the emergence of a new national economy of greater wealth, size, and resources than its own. This was the United States, which developed into a sort of "black hole" with a power of attraction for the labor, capital, and entrepreneurship of Europe with which the United Kingdom, let alone less wealthy and powerful states, had few chances of competing. The German and US challenges to British world power strengthened one another, compromised the ability of Britain to govern the inter-state system, and eventually led to a new struggle for world supremacy of unprecedented violence and viciousness.

In the course of this struggle, conflict went through some, but not all, of the phases that had characterized the previous struggles for world supremacy. The initial phase, in which territorialist rulers attempted to incorporate the leading capitalist state, was ignored altogether. As a matter of fact, the fusion of the territorialist and capitalist logics of power had gone so far among the three main contenders (Britain, Germany, and the United States) for world supremacy that it is difficult to say which were the capitalist rulers and which the territorialist.

Throughout the confrontation, successive German rulers showed much stronger territorialist tendencies than the rulers of either of the other two contenders. But these stronger tendencies reflected their late arrival in the drive for territorial expansion. As we have seen, the United Kingdom had been all but parsimonious in its territorial acquisitions, and empire-building in the non-Western world had been integral to its world hegemony. As for the United States, its development into the main pole of attraction for the labor, capital, and entrepreneurial resources of the world-economy was closely tied to the continental scope attained by its domestic economy in the course of the nineteenth century. As Gareth Stedman Jones (1972: 216–17) has noted:

American historians who speak complacently of the absence of the settler-type colonialism characteristic of European powers merely conceal the fact that the whole *internal* history of United States imperialism was one vast process of territorial seizure and occupation. The absence of territorialism "abroad" was founded on an unprecedented territorialism "at home".

This unprecedented domestic territorialism was wholly internal to a capitalist logic of power. British territorialism and capitalism had cross-fertilized one another. But US capitalism and territorialism were indistinguishable from one another. This perfect harmony of territorialism and capitalism in the formation of the US state is best epitomized by their coexistence in Benjamin Franklin's thought.

Max Weber (1930: 48–55) has claimed that the ·capitalist spirit was present in Franklin's birthplace (Massachusetts) before a capitalistic order actually materialized, and supported this claim by quoting at length from a document in which Franklin upheld the virtues of relentless economizing with a view to earning more and more money as an end in itself. What Weber did not notice was that the capitalist spirit expressed in this document "in almost classical purity" was interwoven in Franklin's mind with an equally pronounced territorialist spirit. For in another document Franklin

> predicted that the population of the [North American] colonies would double every quarter century and admonished the British government to secure additional living space for these newcomers, on the grounds that a prince who "acquires new Territory, if he finds it vacant, or removes the Natives to give his own People Room" deserves the gratitude of posterity. (Lichteim 1974: 58)

The attempt of the British government following the defeat of the French in the Seven Years War to restrain the westward expansion of its Northern American colonies and to make them pay for the costs of empire together triggered the dissent that eventually led to the Revolution of 1776 (Wallerstein 1988: 202–3). But as soon as the Revolution had freed the settlers' hands, they set out to conquer as much of the North American continent as was profitable and to reorganize its space in a thoroughly capitalistic manner. Among other things this meant "removing the Natives" to make room for an ever-expanding immigrant population, just as Franklin had advocated. The result was a compact domestic territorial "empire" – a term that was used interchangeably with federal union in the vocabularies of Washington, Adams, Hamilton, and Jefferson (Van Alstyne 1960: 1–10) – characterized by substantially lower protection costs than Britain's far-flung overseas territorial empire.

Britain and America were the two models of "empire" that German rulers tried to reproduce with their late territorialism. Initially, they tried to follow Britain by seeking overseas colonies and by challenging British naval supremacy. But once the outcome of the First World War had demonstrated the futility of this goal, as well as the superiority of the American model, they tried to emulate the United States (Neumann 1942; Lichteim 1974: 67).

Neither Germany nor the United States ever tried to incorporate within their domain the leading capitalist state, as France and Spain had attempted in the fifteenth century and France and England in the seventeenth century. The world power of the leading capitalist state had grown so much in comparison to its forerunners and to its contemporary challengers that the struggle could only start with what had previously been the second phase – that is, the phase in which the challengers try to supersede the comparative wealth and power advantage of the leading capitalist state. Even though control over world commerce and finance continued to play an important role in determining relative capabilities in the inter-state system, in the course of the nineteenth century the decisive advantage in the struggle for world power had become the comparative size and growth potential of the domestic market. The larger and the more dynamic the domestic market of a state relative to all others, the better the chances of that state of ousting the United Kingdom from the center of the global networks of patron–client relations which constituted the world market (see chapter 4).

From this point of view, the United States was far better placed than Germany. Its continental dimension, its insularity, and its extremely favorable endowment of natural resources, as well as the policy consistently followed by its government of keeping the doors of the domestic market closed to foreign products but open to foreign capital, labor, and enterprise, had made it the main beneficiary of British free-trade imperialism. By the time the struggle for world supremacy began, the US domestic economy was well on its way to being the new center of the world-economy – a center connected to the rest of the world-economy not so much by trade flows as by more or less unilateral transfers of labor, capital, and entrepreneurship flowing from the rest of the world to its political jurisdiction.

Germany could not compete on this terrain. Its history and geographical position made it a tributary to rather than a beneficiary of these flows of labor, capital, and entrepreneurship, even though Prussia/ Germany's long involvement in the front line of the European power struggle gave its rulers a comparative advantage *vis-à-vis* all other European states – the United Kingdom included – in the creation of a powerful military–industrial complex. From the 1840s onwards, military and industrial innovations began to interact more and more closely within the geographical area that was in the process of becoming Germany. It was precisely this interaction that sustained both the spectacular industrialization and the ascent to world power status experienced by Germany in the second half of the nineteenth century (cf. McNeill 1984: chs 7–8; Kennedy 1987: 187, 210–11).

Nevertheless, the absolute and relative increase in its military–industrial capabilities did not fundamentally change Germany's tributary position in the circuits of wealth of the world-economy. On the contrary, tribute to the United Kingdom as the center of world commerce and finance was compounded by tribute to the United States in the form of outflows of labor, capital, and entrepreneurial resources. The growing obsession of German rulers with *Lebensraum* (literally "life space," that is, territory believed vital for national existence) had its systemic origins in this condition of powerlessness in turning rapidly increasing military–industrial capabilities into a commensurate increase in their command over world economic resources.

As we have said, this obsession drove German rulers to try first to follow in the British, and then in the US path of territorial expansion. However, their attempts triggered a sudden escalation of inter-state conflicts, which first undermined and then destroyed the foundations of British hegemony, but in the process inflicted even greater damage to the national wealth, power, and prestige of Germany itself. The state that benefited the most from the escalation of the inter-state power struggle was the United States, primarily because it had inherited Britain's position of insularity at the main intersection(s) of world trade:

> What the English Channel lacked in insularity by the time of World War II, the Atlantic Ocean still provided. The USA was remarkably sheltered from hegemonic war in 1914–45. Furthermore, as the world economy developed and technological innovation continued to overcome the limitations of distance, the world economy grew to encompass all parts of the world. The remote position of America, then, became less of a disadvantage commercially. Indeed, as the Pacific began to emerge as a rival economic zone to the Atlantic, the USA's position became central – a continent-sized island with unlimited access to both of the world's major oceans. (Goldstein and Rapkin 1991: 946)

Just as in the late seventeenth and early eighteenth centuries the hegemonic role had become too large for a state of the size and resources of the United Provinces, so in the early twentieth century that role had become too large for a state of the size and resources of the United Kingdom. In both instances, the hegemonic role fell on a state – the United Kingdom in the eighteenth century, the United States in the twentieth century – that had come to enjoy a substantial "protection rent," that is, exclusive cost advantages associated with absolute or relative geostrategic insularity from the main seat(s) of inter-state conflict on the one side, and with absolute or relative proximity to the main intersection(s) of world trade on the other (cf. Dehio 1962; Lane 1979: 12–13; Chase-Dunn 1989: 114, 118). But that state in both instances was also the bearer of sufficient weight in the capitalist world-economy to be able to shift the balance of power among the competing states in whatever direction it saw fit. And since the capitalist world-economy had expanded considerably in the nineteenth century, the territory and resources required to become hegemonic in the early twentieth century were much greater than in the eighteenth (cf. Chase-Dunn 1989: 65–6; Goldstein and Rapkin 1991; Thompson 1992).

The greater territorial size and resources of the United States in the early twentieth century, in comparison with those of the United Kingdom in the eighteenth century, are not the only differences between the struggles for world supremacy of the two epochs. As we have already noted, the early twentieth-century struggle ignored the phase in which contending territorialist powers seek to incorporate within their domains the leading capitalist state, as France and England had tried unsuccessfully to do in the late seventeenth and early eighteenth centuries. In addition, and more importantly, the escalation of inter-state conflict in the early twentieth century was followed almost immediately by increasing systemic chaos. In the previous struggle for world supremacy between France and England, it took more than a century of armed conflicts between the great powers before anarchy in inter-state relations turned into systemic chaos under the force of a major wave of popular rebellions. But in the early twentieth century anarchy turned into systemic chaos almost as soon as the great powers faced one another in an open confrontation.

Even before the outbreak of the First World War powerful social protest movements had begun to mobilize throughout the world. These movements were rooted in, and aimed at subverting, the double exclusion, of non-Western peoples on the one hand, and the propertyless masses of the West on the other, on which free-trade imperialism was based.

Under British hegemony, non-Western peoples did not qualify as national communities in the eyes of the hegemonic power and of its allies, clients, and followers. Dutch hegemony, through the Westphalia System, had already divided the world "into a favored Europe and a residual zone of alternative behaviors" (Taylor 1991: 21–2). While Europe had been instituted as a zone of "amity" and "civilized" behavior even in times of war, the realm beyond Europe had been instituted as a zone to which no standard of civilization applied and where rivals could simply be wiped out (Herz 1959: 67; Coplin 1968: 22; Taylor 1991: 21–2). Britain's free-trade imperialism carried this division one step further. While the zone of amity and civilized behavior was extended to include the newly independent settler states of the Americas, and the right of Western nations to pursue wealth was elevated above the absolute rights of government of their rulers, non-Western peoples were deprived both in principle and in practice of the most elementary rights to self-determination through despotic colonial rule and the invention of appropriate ideologies, such as "Orientalism" (cf. Said 1978).

At the same time, the nations that had become the constituent units of the inter-state system under British hegemony were as a rule communities of property-holders from which the propertyless were effectively excluded. The right of propertied subjects to pursue wealth was thus elevated not just above the absolute rights of government of rulers, but also above the age-old rights to a livelihood of the propertyless masses (cf. Polanyi 1957). Like Athenian democracy in the ancient world, nineteenth-century liberal democracy was an "egalitarian oligarchy," in which "a ruling class of citizens shared the rights and spoils of political control" (McIver 1932: 352).

Non-Western peoples and the propertyless masses of the West had always resisted those aspects of free-trade imperialism that most directly impinged on their traditional rights to self-determination and a live-lihood. By and large, however, their resistance had been ineffectual. This situation began to change at the end of the nineteenth century, as a direct result of the intensification of inter-state competition and of the spread of national economy-making as an instrument of that competition.

The process of socialization of war-making and state-making, which in the previous wave of struggle for world supremacy had led to the "democratization of nationalism," was carried a step further by the "industrialization of war" – the process, that is, through which an ever-increasing number, range and variety of machinofactured mechanical products were deployed in war-making activities (cf. Giddens 1987: 223–4). As a result, the productive efforts of the propertyless in general, and of the industrial proletariat in particular, became a central compo-nent of the state-making and war-making efforts of rulers. The social power of the propertyless increased correspondingly, as did the effective-ness of their struggles for state protection of their livelihoods (cf. Carr 1945: 19).

Under these circumstances, the outbreak of war between the great powers was bound to have a contradictory impact on ruler–subject relations. On the one hand, it enhanced the social power of the propertyless directly or indirectly involved in the military–industrial efforts of rulers; on the other, it curtailed the means available to the latter to accommodate that power. This contradiction became evident in the course of the First World War, when a few years of open hostilities were sufficient to release the most serious wave of popular protest and rebellion hitherto experienced by the capitalist world-economy (Silver 1992; 1995).

The Russian Revolution of 1917 soon became the focal point of this wave of rebellion. By upholding the right of all peoples to self-determination ("anti-imperialism") and the primacy of rights to live-lihood over rights of property and rights of government ("proletarian internationalism"), the leaders of the Russian Revolution raised the specter of a far more radical involvement in the operation of the inter-state system than anything previously experienced. Initially, the impact of the 1917 Revolution was similar to that of the American Revolution of 1776. That is to say, it fostered the revanchism of the great power that had just been defeated in the struggle for world supremacy (Germany, in this instance) and thereby led to a new round of open conflict between the great powers.

The inter-state system came to be polarized into two opposite and antagonistic factions. The dominant faction, headed by the United Kingdom and France, was conservative, that is, oriented towards the preservation of free-trade imperialism. In opposition to this, upstarts in the struggle for world power, who had neither a respectable colonial empire nor the right connections in the networks of world commerce and finance, coalesced in a reactionary faction led by Nazi Germany. This faction presented itself as the champion of the annihilation of Soviet power, which directly or indirectly stood in the way of its expansionist ambitions – be it German *Lebensraum*, Japanese *tairiku*, or Italian *mare nostrum*. It none the less calculated that its counter-revolutionary objectives were best served by a preliminary or contemporaneous confrontation with the conservative faction.

This confrontation culminated in the complete disintegration of the world market and in unprecedented violations of the principles, norms, and rules of the Westphalia System. What is more, like the Napoleonic Wars 150 years earlier, the Second World War acted as a powerful transmission belt for social revolution which, during and after the war, spread to the entire non-Western world in the form of national liberation movements. Under the joint impact of war and revolution the last remnants of the nineteenth-century world order were swept away and world society appeared once again to be in a state of irremediable disorganization. By 1945, Franz Schurmann (1974: 44) notes, many US government officials "had come to believe that a new world order was the only guarantee against chaos followed by revolution."

Like the United Kingdom in the early nineteenth century, the United States first became hegemonic by leading the inter-state system towards the restoration of the principles, norms, and rules of the Westphalia System, and then went on to govern and remake the system it had restored. Once again, this capability to remake the inter-state system was based on a widespread perception among the rulers and subjects of the system that the national interests of the hegemonic power embodied a general interest. This perception was fostered by the capacity of US rulers to pose and provide a solution to the problems around which the power struggle among revolutionary, reactionary, and conservative forces had raged since 1917. (See Mayer 1971: ch. 2 on the distinction between these three kinds of forces in the period under discussion.)

Right from the start, the most enlightened factions of the US ruling elite showed a much greater awareness than the ruling elites of the conservative and reactionary great powers of what these issues were:

> In many ways the most significant feature both of Wilson's programme and of Lenin's is that they were not European-centred but world-embracing: that is to say, both set out to appeal to all peoples of the world.... Both implied a negation of the preceding European system, whether it was confined to Europe or whether it spread ... over the whole world.... Lenin's summons to world revolution called forth, as a deliberate counter-stroke, Wilson's Fourteen Points, the solidarity of the proletariat and the revolt against imperialism were matched by self-determination and the century of the common man. (Barraclough 1967: 121; see also Mayer 1959: 33–4, 290)

This reformist response to the challenges posed by the Soviet Revolution was well ahead of its times. But once the struggle between the conservative and the reactionary forces of world politics had run its course, resulting in a massive increase in the world power of both the United States and the USSR, the stage was set for the remaking of the inter-state system to accommodate the demands of non-Western peoples and of the propertyless.

After the Second World War, every people, whether "Western" or "non-Western," was granted the right to self-determination, that is to say, to constitute itself into a national community and, once so constituted, to be accepted as a full member of the inter-state system. In this respect, global "decolonization" and the formation of the United Nations, whose General Assembly brought together all nations on an equal footing, have been the most significant correlates of US hegemony.

At the same time, the provision of a livelihood to all subjects became the key objective for the members of the inter-state system to pursue. Just as the liberal ideology of British hegemony had elevated the pursuit of wealth by propertied subjects above the absolute rights of government of rulers, so the ideology of US hegemony has elevated the welfare of all the subjects ("high mass consumption") above the absolute rights of property and the absolute rights of government. If British hegemony had expanded the inter-state system in order to accommodate the "democratization" of nationalism, US hegemony carried the expansion further by selectively accommodating the "proletarianization" of nationalism.

Once again, expansion had involved supersession. The supersession of the Westphalia System by free-trade imperialism was real but partial. The principles, norms, and rules of behavior restored by the Congress of Vienna left considerable leeway to the members of the inter-state system on how to organize their domestic and international relations. Free trade impinged on the sovereignty of rulers, but the latter's ability to "delink" from the trade and power networks of the hegemonic state if they so chose remained considerable. Above all, war and territorial expansion remained legitimate means to which the members of the inter-state system could resort in the pursuit of their ends.

Moreover, under British hegemony there were no organizations with capabilities autonomous from state power to rule over the inter-state system. International law and the balance of power continued to operate, as they had done since 1650, between rather than above states. As we have seen, the Concert of Europe, *haute finance*, and the world market all operated over the heads of most states. Nevertheless, they had little organizational autonomy from the world power of the United Kingdom. They were instruments of governance of a particular state over the inter-state system, rather than autonomous organizations overruling the inter-state system.

In comparison with free-trade imperialism, the institutions of US hegemony have considerably restricted the rights and powers of sovereign states to organize relations with other states and with their own subjects as they see fit. National governments have been far less free than ever before to pursue their ends by means of war, territorial expansion, and to a lesser but none the less significant extent, violations of their subjects' civil and human rights. In Franklin Roosevelt's original vision of the post-war world order these restrictions amounted to nothing less than a complete supersession of the very notion of state sovereignty.

The crucial feature of Roosevelt's vision

> was that security for the world had to be based on American power exercised through international systems. But for such a scheme to have a broad ideological appeal to the suffering peoples of the world, it had to emanate from an institution less esoteric than an international monetary system and less crude than a set of military alliances or bases. (Schurmann 1974: 68)

This institution was to be the United Nations with its appeal to the universal desire for peace on the one side, and to the desire of poor nations for independence, progress, and eventual equality with the rich nations on the other. The political implications of this vision were truly revolutionary:

> For the first time in world history, there was a concrete institutionalization of the idea of world government. Whereas the League of Nations was guided by an essentially nineteenth-century spirit of a congress of nations, the United Nations was openly guided by American political ideas. . . . There was nothing

revolutionary about the kind of world system Britain created through its empire. There was something revolutionary about the world market system that flowed out of Britain in the eighteenth century and created international capitalism.... Britain's true imperial greatness was economic, not political. The United Nations, however, was and remains a political idea. The American Revolution had proven that nations could be constructed through the conscious and deliberate actions of men. Until then it was assumed that they only grew naturally over long periods of time.... Since the American Revolution, many new nations have been created.... What Roosevelt had the audacity to conceive and implement was the extension of this process of government-building to the world as a whole. The power of that vision must not be underestimated, even as one looks at the shoddy reality that began to emerge even before the San Francisco Conference. (Schurmann 1974: 71)

Reality became even shoddier after the formation of the United Nations when Roosevelt's vision was reduced by the Truman Doctrine to the more realistic political project that came to be embodied in the Cold War world order. Roosevelt's "one worldism" – which included the USSR among the poor nations of the world to be incorporated into the evolving Pax Americana for the benefit and security of all – became "free worldism," which turned the containment of Soviet power into the main organizing principle of US hegemony. Roosevelt's revolutionary idealism, which saw in the institutionalization of the idea of world government the primary instrument through which the US New Deal would be extended to the world as a whole, was displaced by the reformist realism of his successors, who institutionalized US control over world money and over global military power as the primary instruments of US hegemony (cf. Schurmann 1974: 5, 67, 77).

As these more traditional instruments of power came to be deployed in the protection and reorganization of the "free world," the Bretton Woods organizations (the IMF and the World Bank) and the United Nations either became supplementary instruments wielded by the US government in the exercise of its world hegemonic functions or, if they could not be used in this way, were impeded in the exercise of their own institutional functions. Thus, throughout the 1950s and 1960s the International Monetary Fund (IMF) and the World Bank played little or no role in the regulation of world money in comparison with, and in relation to, a select ensemble of national central banks, led by the US Federal Reserve System. It was only with the crisis of US hegemony in the 1970s and, above all, in the 1980s that for the first time the Bretton Woods organizations rose to prominence in global monetary regulation. Similarly, in the early 1950s the UN Security Council and General Assembly were used instrumentally by the US government to legitimate its intervention in the Korean civil war, and subsequently lost all centrality in the regulation of inter-state conflicts until their revitalization in the late 1980s and early 1990s. We shall return to the significance of this recent resurgence of the Bretton Woods and UN organizations. But for now let us emphasize that the instrumental use and partial atrophy of these organizations at the moment of maximum expansion of US world hegemony did not involve a return to the strategies and structures of British world hegemony. Quite apart from the fact that simply by remaining in place the Bretton Woods and UN organizations retained much of their ideological value in the legitimation of US hegemony – in sharp contrast to the absence of trans-statal and inter-statal organizations of comparable visibility, permanence, and legitimacy in the establishment and reproduction of British hegemony – US "free worldism" was as much a negation as it was a continuation of British free-trade imperialism. A continuation because, like the latter, it re-established and expanded the Westphalia System after a period of increasing chaos in both inter- and intra-state relations. But a negation because it was neither "imperialist" nor "free tradist," at least not in the sense in which British free-trade imperialism was.

The reductive operationalization of Roosevelt's vision through the establishment of the Cold War world order, far from lessening, strengthened the "anti-imperialist" and "anti-free-tradist" thrust of US hegemony. This reductive operationalization simply institutionalized the ideological competition between the United States and the USSR which first took shape when Lenin's summons to world revolution called forth Wilson's proclamation of the rights of all peoples to self-determination and of the "common man" to a decent livelihood. And while the institutionalization of this competition narrowed considerably the parameters within which US hegemony legitimated the demands for advancement of non-Western peoples and of the propertyless classes of the world, it also speeded up the process of reorganization of the capitalist world-economy to satisfy those demands to the best of the US government's capabilities.

Thus, there can be little doubt that the process of decolonization of the non-Western world would have been far more problematic than it actually was, or would have taken much longer to run its course than it actually did, were it not for the intense ideological and political competition that pitted the United States and the USSR against one another in the late 1940s and early 1950s. To be sure, this same intense competition led the US government to trample on the right of the Korean and, later, of the Vietnamese to settle, without outside interference, the quarrel that had driven the governments of their northern and southern territories to wage war on one another. But this trampling on the customary rights of sovereign states was nothing other than an aspect of the expansion of the Westphalia System under US hegemony through the introduction of unprecedented restrictions on the freedom of sovereign states to organize relations with other states and with their own subjects as they pleased.

Thus, at the height of its world hegemony the British government did not come to the assistance of the free-tradist Confederacy against the fiercely protectionist Union in the American Civil War. Rather, it left its former colonists free to massacre one another in the bloodiest war fought under British hegemony, and concentrated instead on consolidating its control over the Indian Empire and on laying the foundations of the greatest wave of colonization the world had ever seen. At the height of its hegemony, in contrast, the US government substituted itself for the "free worldist" regimes of South Korea and South Vietnam in their respective wars against the communist regimes of North Korea and North Vietnam. At the same time, however, it actively encouraged the greatest wave of decolonization the world had ever seen. (On waves of colonization and decolonization, see Bergesen and Schoenberg 1980: 234–5.) These contrasting tendencies at the height of the British and US governments' respective world hegemonies provide a vivid illustration of the divergent thrusts of the two hegemonies. If we designate the main thrust of British hegemony as "imperialist," then we have no choice but to designate the main thrust of US hegemony as "anti-imperialist" (cf. Arrighi 1983).

This opposite thrust of US hegemony relative to British hegemony reproduced the pattern of "regression" already in evidence in the development of British hegemony. Just as the expansion and supersession of the Westphalia System under British hegemony were based on strategies and structures of world-scale rule and accumulation which were more like those of Imperial Spain in the sixteenth century than those of Dutch hegemony, so the expansion and supersession of that same system under US hegemony has involved a "regression" towards strategies and structures of world-scale rule and accumulation which resemble more closely those of Dutch than those of British hegemony. "Anti-imperialism," so defined, is one such similarity. Although the United States was formed through an unprecedented "domestic" territorialism, neither Dutch nor US hegemony was based on the kind of territorial "world empire" on which British hegemony was based. And conversely, Dutch and US hegemony were both based on leadership of movements of national self-determination – a strictly European movement in the case of the Dutch, a universal movement in the case of the United States – in a way in which British hegemony never was. Britain did lead the states that emerged out of the American wave of national self-determination towards a free trade world order. But that order was based on the full realization of Britain's "imperialist" dispositions in Asia and in Africa. By abandoning Britain's imperial developmental path in favor of a strictly domestic territorialism, the United States reproduced on an incomparably larger scale the national developmental path of Dutch hegemony.

Similar considerations apply to the "anti-free-tradist" thrust of US hegemony. The departure of US hegemony from the principles and practices of nineteenth-century liberalism in favor of greater governmental responsibility for economic regulation and for the welfare of subjects has been widely noted (see, for example, Ruggie 1982; Lipson 1982; Keohane 1984b; Ikenberry 1989; Mjoset 1990). Nevertheless, emphasis on the "liberalism" of the two hegemonic orders in comparison with the "mercantilism" of the intervening period of hegemonic struggle has tended to obscure the fundamental departure of the US Cold War world order from the free-trade policies and ideology of nineteenth-century Britain. The truth of the matter is that the US government never even considered adopting the kind of *unilateral* free trade that Britain practiced from the 1840s right up to 1931. The free trade ideologized and practiced by the US government throughout the period of its hegemonic ascendancy has been, rather, a strategy of bilateral and multilateral intergovernmental negotiation of trade liberalization, aimed primarily at opening up other states to US commodities and enterprise. Nineteenth-century beliefs in the "self-regulating market" – in Polanyi's (1957) sense – became the official ideology of the US government only in the 1980s under the Reagan and Bush administrations in response to the hegemonic crisis of the 1970s. Even then, however, the unilateral measures of trade liberalization actually undertaken by the US government were very limited.

In any event, free trade played no role in the formation of the Cold War world order. Far from being the policy that brought the US and Western Europe together,

[free trade] was the issue that divided them.... [T]he post-war Atlantic Community came into being only after the United States, prompted by its fear of Russian and domestic European communism, suppressed its liberal scruples in the interest of "mutual security" and Europe's rapid recovery.... Economics was subordinated to politics. Trade took directions from the flag. And America's hegemony over Europe took a more visible form than free-trade imperialism, and also a form more useful and acceptable to the Europeans. (Calleo and Rowland 1973: 43)

This more useful and acceptable form of hegemony departed from the nineteenth-century British form in several respects. For one thing, world money came to be regulated by the US Federal Reserve System acting in concert with select central banks of other states, in sharp contrast to the nineteenth-century system of private regulation based on and controlled by the London-centered cosmopolitan networks of *haute finance*. The publicly regulated dollar system endowed the US government with much greater freedom of action than the British government ever enjoyed under the nineteenth-century privately regulated gold standard (Mjoset 1990: 39). Eventually, market constraints drastically reduced this freedom of action. But as long as the US government wielded effective control over world liquidity – as it did throughout the 1950s and most of the 1960s – it could use this control to promote and sustain a generalized expansion of world trade with few precedents in capitalist history (see chapter 4).

Similarly, the chief instrument of world market formation under US hegemony, the General Agreement on Trade and Tariffs (GATT), left in the hands of governments in general, and of the US government in particular, control over the pace and direction of trade liberalization. By unilaterally liberalizing its foreign trade in the nineteenth century, Britain had *ipso facto* forgone the possibility of using the prospect of such a liberalization as a weapon in forcing other governments to liberalize their own trade. By never renouncing the use of this weapon through unilateral free trade, the United States instituted a trade regime that was far less "generous" towards the rest of the world than the British regime. But as Krasner (1979) has pointed out, as long as the United States operated at a higher level in the hierarchy of needs than its allies – as it did throughout the 1950s and 1960s – it could afford to give priority to Cold War objectives and be generous in the negotiation of successive rounds of trade liberalization. A far more extensive degree of *multilateral* free trade was thereby attained under US hegemony compared with British hegemony. Nevertheless, what eventually emerged was not a free trade regime; rather, it was a "patchwork arrangement for world trade that is neither openness nor autarky" (Lipson 1982: 446); or, worse still, a "ramshackle political structure of *ad hoc* diplomatic relations between Japan, EEC and US, and bilateral agreements between these and other minor countries" (Strange 1979: 323).

A third and far more fundamental departure of US from British hegemony has been the tendency for a significant and growing proportion of world trade to be "internalized" within, and administered by, large-scale, vertically integrated, transnational corporations. Data on international "trade," which consists in reality of intra-firm transactions, are not readily available. But various estimates indicate that the proportion of world trade consisting of intra-firm transactions has risen from something in the order of 20–30 per cent in the 1960s to something in the order of 40–50 per cent in the late 1980s and early 1990s. According to Robert Reich, "in 1990 more than half of America's exports and imports, by value, were simply the transfers of such goods and related services *within* global corporations" (Reich 1992: 114; emphasis in the original).

This feature of US hegemony reflects the centrality of direct investment rather than trade in the reconstruction of the capitalist world-economy since the Second World War. As Robert Gilpin (1975: 11) has observed, the essence of direct investment by US transnational corporations "has been the shift of managerial control over substantial sectors of foreign economies to American nationals. In character, therefore, these direct investors in other countries are more similar to the trading companies of the mercantilistic era than to the free traders and finance capitalists that dominated Britain in the nineteenth century." Since the trading companies to which Gilpin refers were the chief instrument in the seventeenth century through which Dutch governmental and business agencies transformed their regional commercial supremacy based primarily on control over Baltic trade into a world commercial supremacy, the transnational expansion of US corporate capital in the twentieth century constitutes another aspect of the "regression" of US hegemony towards strategies and structures typical of Dutch hegemony (see chapters 2 and 4).

There is none the less a fundamental difference between the joint-stock chartered companies of the seventeenth and eighteenth centuries on the one side, and the transnational corporations of the twentieth century on the other. Joint-stock chartered companies were part-governmental, part-business organizations, which specialized *territorially*, to the exclusion of other similar organizations. Twentieth-century transnational corporations, in contrast, are strictly business organizations, which specialize *functionally* in specific lines of production and distribution, across multiple territories and jurisdictions, in cooperation and competition with other similar organizations.

Owing to their territorial specialization and exclusiveness, successful joint-stock chartered companies of all nationalities were very few in number. At no time were there more than a dozen or so, and even fewer were truly successful as governmental or as business enterprises. Nevertheless, individually and collectively, these companies played a key role in consolidating and expanding the territorial scope and exclusiveness of the European system of sovereign states.

Owing to their trans-territoriality and functional specialization, the number of transnational corporations that have prospered under US hegemony has been incomparably larger. An estimate for 1980 put the number of transnational corporations at over 10,000 and the number of their foreign affiliates at 90,000 (Stopford and Dunning 1983: 3). By the early 1990s, according to another estimate, these numbers had risen to 35,000 and 170,000, respectively (*The Economist*, 27 March 1993: 5, as cited in Ikeda 1993).

Far from consolidating the territorial exclusiveness of states as "containers of power," this explosive growth of transnational corporations has become the single most important factor in undermining the substance of that exclusiveness. By about 1970, when the crisis of US hegemony as embodied in the Cold War world order began, transnational corporations had developed into a world-scale system of production, exchange and accumulation, which was subject to no state authority and had the power to subject to its own "laws" each and every member of the inter-state system, the United States included (see chapter 4). The emergence of this free enterprise system – free, that is, from the constraints imposed on world-scale processes of capital accumulation by the territorial exclusiveness of states – has been the most distinctive outcome of US hegemony. It marks a decisive new turning point in the process of expansion and supersession of the Westphalia System, and may well have initiated the withering away of the modern inter-state system as the primary locus of world power.

Robert Reich (1992: 3) speaks of the declining significance of national economies and societies under the impact of "the centrifugal forces of the global economy which tear the ties binding citizens together." Peter Drucker (1993: 141–56) sees a steady deterioration in the power of nation-states under the combined impact of three forces: the "transnationalism" of multilateral treaties and suprastatal organizations; the "regionalism" of economic blocs like the European Union and the North American Free Trade Agreement (NAFTA); and the "tribalism" of increasing emphasis on diversity and identity. Whatever the diagnosis, a general perception has developed that the usefulness and power of nation-states are waning:

> The key autonomous actor in political and international affairs for the past few centuries appears not just to be losing its control and integrity, but to be the *wrong sort* of unit to handle the newer circumstances. For some problems, it is too large to operate effectively; for others, it is too small. In consequence there are pressures for the "relocation of authority" both upward and downward, creating structures that might respond better to today's and tomorrow's forces of change. (Kennedy 1993: 131; emphasis in the original)

Towards a New Research Agenda

Terence Hopkins (1990: 411) has suggested that Dutch, British, and US hegemony should be interpreted as successive "moments" in the formation of the capitalist world system: "Dutch hegemony made possible a capitalist world-economy as an historical social system; British hegemony clarified its underpinnings and moved it to dominion globally; US hegemony furthered its reach, framework, and penetration and at the same time freed the processes that are bringing about its demise." A similar scheme is proposed in this chapter, whereby the inter-state system instituted under Dutch hegemony expanded through two successive reductions in the sovereignty and autonomous capabilities of its constituent units.

British hegemony expanded the system through the inclusion of the settler states which emerged from the decolonization of the Americas and through the elevation of the property rights of subjects above the sovereignty rights of rulers. The system so instituted was still a system of mutually legitimating, exclusive territorial sovereignties, like the original Westphalia System. But it was a system subject to British governance – a governance which Britain was able to exercise by virtue of its control over the European balance of power, over an extensive and dense world market centered on Britain itself, and over a global British empire. Although this governance was widely perceived as being exercised in the general interest of the member states of the system, it involved a lesser exclusiveness of sovereignty rights than was actually enjoyed in the original Westphalia System.

This evolutionary process of simultaneous expansion and supersession of the modern inter-state system was taken one step further by its enlarged reconstitution under US hegemony. As the system came to include the non-Western states that emerged from the decolonization of Asia and Africa, not just the property rights, but also the rights of subjects to a livelihood were elevated *in principle* over the sovereignty rights of rulers. Moreover, constraints and restrictions on state sovereignty came to be embodied in suprastatal organizations – most notably, the UN and the Bretton Woods organizations – which for the first time in the modern era institutionalized the idea of world government (and for the first time in world history, the idea of a world government encompassing the entire globe). With the establishment of the Cold War world order, the United States abandoned Roosevelt's "one worldism" in favor of Truman's "free worldism" and substituted itself for the UN in the governance of the world system. But the scale, scope, and effectiveness of US governance of the world, as well as the concentration of military, financial, and intellectual means deployed for the purpose, far exceeded the ends and means of nineteenth-century British hegemony.

The modern inter-state system has thus acquired its present global dimension through successive hegemonies of increasing comprehensiveness, which have correspondingly reduced the exclusiveness of the sovereignty rights actually enjoyed by its members. Were this process to continue, nothing short of a true world government, as envisaged by Roosevelt, would satisfy the condition that the next world hegemony be more comprehensive territorially and functionally than the preceding one. We are thus back, by a different and more roundabout route, to one of the questions raised in the Introduction. Has the West attained such a degree of world power under US leadership that it is on the verge of putting an end to capitalist history as embedded in the rise and expansion of the modern inter-state system?

There are certainly signs that this is within the realm of historical possibilities as an outcome of the hegemonic crisis of the 1970s and 1980s. Thus, the revitalization in the 1980s and early 1990s of the Bretton Woods and UN organizations shows that the ruling groups of the United States are well aware of the fact that even so powerful a state as the United States lacks the material and ideological resources needed to exercise minimal governmental functions in an increasingly chaotic world. Whether these same groups are willing to renounce the trappings – let alone the substance – of national sovereignty that would be needed for effective action through suprastatal organizations, or whether they are at all capable of devising and articulating a social purpose for such action that would make it legitimate world-wide and thereby increase its chances of success – these are altogether different questions, which for the time being deserve an emphatically negative answer. And yet, there is no reason to suppose that in the present just as in past hegemonic transitions, what at one point appears unlikely or even unthinkable, should not become likely and eminently reasonable at a later point, under the impact of escalating systemic chaos.

The obverse side of this process of world government formation is the crisis of territorial states as effective instruments of rule. Robert Jackson has coined the expression "quasi-states" to refer to states that have been granted juridical statehood and have thereby become members of the inter-state system, but that lack the capabilities needed to carry out the governmental functions associated historically with statehood. In his view, the clearest instances of such a condition are provided by the Third World states that have emerged from the post-Second World War wave of decolonization:

> The ex-colonial states have been internationally enfranchised and possess the same external rights and responsibilities as all other sovereign states: juridical statehood. At the same time, however, many ... disclose limited empirical statehood: their populations do not enjoy many of the advantages traditionally associated with independent statehood.... The concrete benefits which have historically justified the undeniable burdens of sovereign statehood are often limited to fairly narrow elites and not yet extended to the citizenry at large.... These states are primarily juridical. They are still far from complete, so to speak, and empirical statehood in large measure still remains to be built. I therefore refer to them as "quasi-states." (Jackson 1990: 21)

If the condition of quasi-statehood designates a more or less fundamental lack of actual state-making capabilities relative to theoretically or historically informed expectations, then it has been a far more general condition of the modern inter-state system than Jackson supposes. As John Boli (1993: 10–11) has pointed out, the internal and external aspects of national sovereignty are essentially theories about the legitimacy of authority. National polities organized into states are theorized as the pinnacle of legitimate authority, "neither subordinate to the world polity nor defied by local polities or organizations." The theory, however, "is often violated by the facts."

Having examined the facts, Charles Tilly (1975: 39) noted how the history of European state-making itself presents many more instances of failure than of success: "The disproportionate distribution of success and failure puts us in the unpleasant situation of dealing with an experience in which most of the cases are negative, while only the positive cases are well-documented." Even more damning, Ruggie (1993: 156) adds, paraphrasing Hendrik Spruyt, is the fact that "because successor forms to the medieval system of rule other than territorial states have been systematically excluded from consideration, there is no fundamental variation in units on the dependent-variable side in theories of state-building."

Jackson's notion of quasi-states thus rests on a theory of sovereignty based on a handful of "successful" historical experiences of state-making in which "success" itself has come to be assessed exclusively in terms of the capability of creating a viable territorial nation-state rather than in terms of the actual capability of exercising authority in the world system at large. This double bias is well illustrated by the disproportionate role played by France in setting the standards of sovereignty by which the "fullness" of other state-making experiences have been assessed. In the seventeenth and eighteenth centuries France was undoubtedly the most "successful" territorialist organization in Europe as far as nation-state-making was concerned. As such it became a model for other territorialist organizations to imitate and for political historians to study. By the real or imagined standards set by France in nation-state-making, the United Provinces throughout its short life of merely two centuries may be said to have been a quasi-state. Indeed, it never became a nation-state proper. And yet, as far as the making of the modern inter-state *system* is concerned – as opposed to the making of one of the system's most powerful constitutent units – the role played by the transient Dutch state has been incomparably greater than that of the "model" French nation-state. As we shall see, analogous considerations apply to the grossly overvalued city-state-making experience of Venice relative to the world system-making experience of the quasi-city-state, Genoa.

The issue is not one of mere historiographical interest. As noted in the Introduction, in comparison with the real or imagined standards set by the United States over the last century in state-making, let alone in war-making, the states of the rising East and Southeast Asian capitalist archipelago are to varying degrees all quasi-states. Among the "islands" of the archipelago only the largest, Japan, is a nation-state in the full sense of the term, and a highly successful one at that. But even Japan is still a US military protectorate in the world system at large. The two "islands" of intermediate size, South Korea and Taiwan, are also US military protectorates. In addition, neither of them is a nation-state in the full sense – South Korea living in constant hope or fear of being reunited with its northern half, and Taiwan in constant hope or fear of becoming the master or servant of mainland China. Finally, the two smallest but by no means least important "islands," Singapore and Hong Kong, are city-states combining ultramodern technologies and architectures with a political capitalism reminiscent of the Renaissance city-states – the commercial–industrial entrepôt functions exercised by Singapore making it resemble Venice, and the commercial–financial entrepôt functions exercised by Hong Kong making it resemble Genoa.

A different but equally striking combination of ultramodern and early modern traits is present in the quasi-states on which Robert Jackson has focused his attention:

> In Third World regions such as Africa and South Asia, a student of Western history cannot help noticing apparent disjunctions between the existence of Western-looking twentieth-century armies, on the one hand, and the prevalence of military politics reminiscent of the Renaissance, between the apparatus of representative government and the arbitrary use of state power against citizens, between the installation of apparently conventional bureaucracies and the widespread use of governmental organization for individual gain. These disjunctions are more visible in states that have recently escaped from colonial rule than in the rest of the Third World. (Tilly 1990: 204)

The resurgence of early modern forms of military politics in an ultra- or post-modern world is not confined to Third World regions that have recently shaken off colonial rule. Well before the Second World of Communist regimes disintegrated into a host of ethno-nations actually or potentially at war with one another, a RAND report stressed the tendency for warfare to revert to early modern patterns:

> With continuous, sporadic armed conflict, blurred in time and space, waged on several levels by a large array of national and subnational forces, warfare in the last quarter of the twentieth century may well come to resemble warfare in the Italian Renaissance or warfare in the early seventeenth century, before

the emergence of national armies and more organized modern warfare. (Jenkins 1983: 17)

This resurgence of early modern patterns of state- and war-making at the end of a 300-year process of expansion of the modern inter-state system has been accompanied by a wave of challenges to statal authority with few precedents in modern history. In noting this tendency, James Rosenau (1990: 4–5) wondered "whether such developments, coming so fast upon each other, are not the first surfacings of historical departures in which the dynamics of constancy and change are brought into new forms of tension which, in turn, are altering the fundamental structures of world politics." He then suggests that global life may have entered a period of "turbulence" the likes of which it has not experienced since major shifts in all dimensions of world politics culminated in the Treaty of Westphalia in 1648.

Rosenau's "turbulence" broadly corresponds to the systemic chaos which in our interpretative scheme constitutes a recurrent condition of the modern inter-state system. A condition of systemic chaos/turbulence was highly visible at the inception of the system. But it recurred twice, both as a symptom of the breakdown of the system as instituted under one hegemony and as a key ingredient in the reconstitution of the system under a new hegemony.

The increasing systemic chaos/turbulence of the 1970s and 1980s fits this pattern of recurrence well. It can be taken to signal the breakdown of the system as instituted under US hegemony, and it can be projected as a key component of a possible but by no means certain future reconstitution of the system on new foundations. Nevertheless, the resurgence of early modern forms of state- and war-making in the midst of challenges to statal authority of unprecedented scale and scope suggests that there may indeed be something special about the present systemic chaos/turbulence in comparison with earlier manifestations of the phenomenon. It is as if the modern system of rule, having expanded spatially and functionally as far as it could, has nowhere to go but "forward" towards an entirely new system of rule or "backward" towards early modern or even pre-modern forms of state- and war-making.

The system seems to be moving "forward" and "backward" at the same time. This double movement has always been a major feature of the modern world system. In our scheme of things, "old regimes" do not just "persist," as in Arno Mayer's (1981) account of what we have taken to be the era of British hegemony. Rather, they are repeatedly resurrected as soon as the hegemony that has superseded them is in its turn superseded by a new hegemony. Thus, British hegemony reconstituted the modern system of rule on enlarged spatial and social foundations by reviving in new and more complex forms aspects of imperial rule that had been superseded under Dutch hegemony. And so in its turn US hegemony reconstituted the system on enlarged spatial and social foundations by reviving in new and more complex forms aspects of corporate capitalism that had been superseded under British hegemony.

This double movement forward and backward at the same time seems also to characterize the present conjuncture. The difference with previous periods of hegemonic transitions is that the scale and complexity of the modern world system have already become so large as to leave little room for further increases. The double movement and accompanying turbulence may therefore be producing not a new reconstitution of the modern system of rule on enlarged foundations, but its metamorphosis into an altogether different system which revitalizes one aspect or another of early modern or pre-modern modes of rule.

In a similar vein, John Ruggie (1993) has maintained that the chief and most distinctive feature of the modern system of rule has been the differentiation of its subject collectivity into separate, fixed, and mutually exclusive territorial spaces of legitimate dominion. Although the substantive forms and individual trajectories of the states instituted by this differentiation have varied over time, their "species" has been clearly discernible from the seventeenth century to the present day. Today, however, this form of territoriality as the basis for organizing political life seems to be torn apart by a non-territorial, functional space, which has grown within the modern system of rule, but constitutes an institutional negation of that system's exclusive territoriality.

Among the main aspects of this implosion, Ruggie mentions Fredric Jameson's (1984) notion of a "postmodern hyperspace" resulting from the "internalization" of international relations within global capitalism's own institutional forms. Ruggie is unsure about what precisely Jameson means by the term "hyperspace." He none the less finds it useful to designate the tendency whereby "transnationalized microeconomic links ... have created a non-territorial 'region' in the world economy – a decentered yet integrated space-of-flows, operating in real time, which exists alongside the spaces-of-places that we call national economies."

> These conventional spaces-of-places continue to engage in external economic relations with one another, which we continue to call trade, foreign investment, and the like, and which are more or less effectively mediated by the state. In the nonterritorial global economic region, however, the conventional distinctions between internal and external are exceedingly problematic, and any given state is but one constraint in corporate global strategic calculations. (Ruggie 1993: 172)

This corresponds to our earlier contention that the explosive growth in the number of transnational corporations and the transactions within and between them has become the most critical factor in the withering away of the modern system of territorial states as the primary locus of world power. As Ruggie underscores, however, the novelty of the emerging "postmodern hyperspace" can easily be exaggerated, owing to the deficiencies of our perceptual habits. These habits have formed in the conventional spaces-of-places and are wholly inadequate to describe, let alone explain, the development of the singular space-of-flows engendered by the "internalization" of international relations within the organizational structures of world capitalism. Given this inadequacy, nonterritorial spaces-of-flows may have existed unnoticed alongside the national spaces-of-places throughout the history of the modern world system.

Ruggie (1993: 154–5, 173) specifically mentions the resemblance that today's relationship between the transnational economy and national jurisdictions bears to the relationship between medieval juridical authorities and the trade fairs. Local lords could have withdrawn the right to hold a fair located in their domain at any time. But they had no interest in doing so because the fairs were a source of revenue and financial services (money-changing in particular) which other lords would have been only too glad to welcome to their own domains. So the fairs prospered, and although they were no substitute for the institutions of feudal rule, they eventually sapped their vitality.

> They did so because the new wealth they produced, the new instruments of economic transactions they generated, the new ethos of commerce they spread, the new regulatory arrangements they required, the expansion of cognitive horizons they required, and the expansion of cognitive horizons they effected all helped undermine the personalistic ties and the modes of reasoning on which feudal authority rested.

Similarly, today's transnational corporations are no substitute for the governmental institutions of the modern system of rule, as Kenneth Waltz (1979) has insisted. And yet, they may be contributing to their demise through the novel behaviors they generate and the novel space–time constructs they embody. This much was implied by Richard Barnet and Ronald Müller's (1974: 15–16) contention that "[t]he managers of the global corporations are seeking to put into practice a theory of human organization that will profoundly alter the nation-state system around which society has been organized for over 400 years. What they are demanding in essence is the right to transcend the nation-state, and in the process, to transform it." In support of this contention, they quote Carl

A. Gerstacher, chairman of the Dow Chemical company, which was to become a *locus classicus* of the literature on transnational corporations:

> I have long dreamed to buy an island owned by no nation ... and of establishing the World Headquarters of the Dow Company on the truly neutral ground of such an island, beholden to no nation or society. If we were located on such truly neutral ground we could then really operate in the United States as U.S. citizens, in Japan as Japanese citizens, and in Brazil as Brazilians rather than being governed in prime by the laws of the United States.... We could even pay any natives handsomely to move elsewhere. (quoted in Barnet and Müller 1974: 16)

Interestingly enough, this dream of absolute non-territoriality evokes the system of "fairs without place" realized by the Genoese diaspora capitalist class four hundred years earlier. Unlike the medieval fairs, these fairs were tightly controlled by a clique of merchant bankers who held them wherever they liked until they settled on the truly neutral ground of Piacenza. "The Genoese have invented a new exchange," commented the Florentine Bernardo Davanzati sarcastically in 1581, "which they call fairs of Bisenzone [the Italian name for Besançon], where they were held initially. But now they are held in Savoy, in Piedmont, in Lombardy, at Trento, just outside Genoa, and wherever the Genoese choose. Hence, they should be called more appropriately *Utopie*, that is, fairs without place" (quoted in Boyer-Xambeau, Deleplace, and Gillard 1991: 123).

The truth of the matter is that the Genoese fairs were a utopia only if perceived from the vantage point of the space-of-places of the declining city-states and of the rising nation-states. From the vantage point of the space-of-flows of diaspora capitalist classes, in contrast, they were a powerful instrument of control of the entire European system of interstatal payments. Flows of commodities and means of payment that were "external" to the declining and rising states were, in fact, "internal" to the non-territorial network of long-distance trade and high finance controlled and managed by the Genoese merchant elite through the system of the Bisenzone fairs (see chapter 2).

As in the kin-based systems of rule studied by anthropologists, to paraphrase Ruggie (1993: 149), the network of commercial and financial intermediation controlled by the Genoese merchant elite *occupied* places, but was not *defined* by the places it occupied. Marketplaces like Antwerp, Seville, and the mobile Bisenzone fairs were all as critical as Genoa itself to the organization of the space-of-flows through which the Genoese diaspora community of merchant bankers controlled the European system of interstatal payments. But none of these places – Genoa included – in itself defined the Genoese system of accumulation. Rather, the system was defined by the flows of precious metals, bills of exchange, contracts with the Imperial government of Spain, and monetary surpluses which linked these places to one another. If the "pre-modern" analog of the Genoese system of accumulation are kin-based systems of rule, its closest "post-modern" analog is the Eurodollar market, a notable characteristic of which, in Roy Harrod's (1969: 319) words, "is that it has no headquarters or buildings of its own.... Physically it consists merely of a network of telephones and telex machines around the world, telephones which may be used also for purposes other than Euro-dollar deals." The Genoese system had no modern means of communication at its disposal. Physically, however, it consisted as exclusively as today's Eurodollar market of a mere network of communications which could be used for purposes other than the exchange of currencies.

The Genoese were not the only ones to control non-territorial networks of this kind. The Florentine, Lucchese, German, and English "nations" – as diaspora communities of merchant bankers were known in the sixteenth century – also did. In the latter half of the sixteenth century, however, the Genoese "nation" emerged as by far the most powerful among them. In 1617, Suárez de Figueroa went as far as claiming that Spain and Portugal had become "the Indies of the Genoese" (quoted in Elliott 1970b: 96). The hyperbole contained an important element of truth. As we shall detail in the next chapter, in the half-century or so preceding 1617 the "invisible hand" of Genoese capital, operating through the triangle-of-flows that linked Seville, Antwerp, and Bisenzone to one another, had succeeded in turning the power pursuits of Imperial Spain, as well as the industrial pursuits of Genoa's old rival and "model" city-state Venice, into powerful engines of its own self-expansion.

This powerful non-territorial network of capital accumulation was quintessentially capitalist in structure and orientation. According to Braudel (1984: 118), the Genoese approach to capitalism "was far more modern than [that of] Venice," and Genoa as city-state "may have been somewhat vulnerable by virtue of this forward position." If Venice was the prototype of all subsequent capitalist states, as we have argued in this chapter, the Genoese diaspora of merchant bankers was the prototype of all subsequent non-territorial systems of capital accumulation on a world scale:

For three-quarters of a century, "the Genoese experience" enabled the merchant-bankers of Genoa, through their handling of capital and credit, to call the tune of European payments and transactions. This ... must surely have been the most extraordinary example of convergence and concentration the European world-economy had yet witnessed, as it re-oriented itself around an almost invisible focus. For the focal point of the whole system was not even the city of Genoa itself, but a handful of banker-financiers (today we would call them a multinational consortium). And this is only one of the paradoxes surrounding the strange city of Genoa which, though apparently so cursed by fate, tended both before and after its "age of glory" to gravitate towards the summit of world business. To me Genoa seems always to have been, in every age, the capitalist city par excellence. (Braudel 1984: 157)

Here as elsewhere, Braudel's language and hesitations betray the difficulties involved in unveiling a capitalist power that is *not* "contained" by a state in Giddens's sense, but encompasses a system of states. These difficulties are rooted in the bias of our conceptual equipment in favor of the space-of-places that defines the process of state formation and against the space-of-flows of capital that defines the process of capital accumulation. And yet, historically, capitalism as a world system of accumulation and rule has developed simultaneously in both spaces. In the space-of-places – as Braudel puts it in a passage quoted in the Introduction – it triumphed by becoming identified with particular states. In the space-of-flows, in contrast, it triumphed by *not* becoming identified with any particular state but by constructing world-encompassing, non-territorial business organizations.

This simultaneous development in opposite directions has given rise to two closely related but distinct genealogies of modern capitalism. In the genealogy sketched in this chapter, modern capitalism originates in the prototype of the leading capitalist state of every subsequent age: the Venetian city-state. In the genealogy that we shall explore in the rest of the book, modern capitalism originates in the prototype of the leading world-encompassing, non-territorial business organization of every subsequent age: the Genoese diaspora "nation." The first genealogy describes the development of capitalism as a succession of world hegemonies. The second genealogy describes that same development as a succession of systemic cycles of accumulation.

2

The Rise of Capital

The Antecedents of Systemic Cycles of Accumulation

The rise of the contemporary free enterprise system as the dominant structure of the capitalist world-economy constitutes the latest stage of a six-centuries-long process of differentiation of business enterprises from governments. Following Frederic Lane, we can distinguish between these two kinds of organizations on the basis of their objectives, methods employed, and social consequences. Governments are power-oriented organizations which use war, the police force, and judicial procedures, supplemented by appeals to moral sentiments, as characteristic means of attaining their objectives, and which bring into existence systems of law and allegiance. Business enterprises, in contrast, are profit-oriented organizations which use as their customary activities buying and selling, and which bring into existence systems of production and distribution (Lane 1979: 38):

> In examining the organizations actually existing in the Western world about 1900 it is not too difficult to classify them either as governments or as business enterprises. But in examining the oceanic expansion of the fifteenth and sixteenth centuries, we cannot classify in this way the organizations initially involved. Whether we consider their motives, their methods, or their consequences, we find that the key innovating enterprises usually combined characteristics of government with characteristics of business. (Lane 1979: 38–9)

As we shall see, the enterprises that took the lead in the oceanic expansion of the fifteenth and sixteenth centuries already showed considerable specialization in the exercise of either governmental or business functions, and in about 1900 the differentiation between governmental and business organizations was not as complete as Lane's remarks seem to imply. Yet,

Lane's observation captures the essential thrust of the evolutionary pattern of the capitalist world-economy from its beginnings in late medieval Europe to the present day.

Initially, networks of capital accumulation were wholly embedded in and subordinate to networks of power. Under these circumstances, in order to succeed in the pursuit of profit it was necessary for business organizations to be powerful states, as witnessed by the experience of the capitalist oligarchies of northern Italy who were leaders not just in processes of capital accumulation, but in processes of state-making and war-making too. However, as networks of accumulation expanded to encompass the entire globe, they became increasingly autonomous from and dominant over networks of power. As a result, a situation has arisen in which in order to succeed in the pursuit of power governments must be leaders not just in processes of state-making and war-making but in processes of capital accumulation as well.

The transformation of the capitalist world-economy, from a system in which networks of accumulation were wholly embedded in and subordinate to networks of power into a system in which networks of power are wholly embedded in and subordinate to networks of accumulation, has proceeded through a series of systemic cycles of accumulation each consisting of an (MC) phase of material expansion followed by a (CM') phase of financial expansion. As we saw in the Introduction, the notion of successive systemic cycles of accumulation has been derived from Braudel's observation that all major trade expansions of the capitalist world-economy have announced their "maturity" by reaching the stage of financial expansion. Following Braudel, we identify the beginning of financial expansions with the moment when the leading business agencies of the preceding trade expansion switch their energies and resources from the commodity to the money trades. And like Braudel, we take the recurrence of this kind of financial expansion as the main expression of a certain unity of capitalist history from the late Middle Ages to our own days. Unlike Braudel, however, we explicitly conceive of financial expansions as long periods of fundamental transformation of the agency and structure of world-scale processes of capital accumulation.

From this point of view, our systemic cycles of accumulation resemble Henri Pirenne's stages of capitalist development. In surveying the social history of capitalism over a thousand years, from its earliest beginnings in medieval Europe to the early twentieth century, Pirenne observes that for each period into which this history could be divided there was a distinct and separate class of capitalists. That is to say,

the group of capitalists of a given epoch does not spring from the capitalist group of the preceding epoch. At every change in economic organization we find a breach of continuity. It is as if the capitalists who have up to that time been active, recognize that they are incapable of adapting themselves to conditions which are evoked by needs hitherto unknown and which call for methods hitherto unemployed. They withdraw from the struggle and become an aristocracy, which if it again plays a part in the course of affairs, does so in a passive manner only, assuming the role of silent partners. (Pirenne 1953: 501–2)

Their place in promoting further expansion is taken by a new class of capitalists "who . . . permit themselves to be driven by the wind actually blowing and who know how to trim their sails to take advantage of it, until the day comes when . . . they in their turn pause and are distanced by new crafts having fresh forces and new directions."

In short, the permanence throughout the centuries of a capitalist class, the result of a continuous development and changing itself to suit changing circumstances, is not to be affirmed. On the contrary, there are as many classes of capitalists as there are epochs in economic history. That history does not present itself to the eye of the observer under the guise of an inclined plane; it resembles rather a staircase, every step of which rises abrubtly above that which precedes it. We do not find ourselves in the presence of a gentle and regular ascent, but of a series of lifts. (Pirenne 1953: 502)

Our succession of systemic cycles of accumulation does indeed constitute "a series of lifts," each lift being the result of the activities of a particular complex of governmental and business agencies endowed with the capacity to carry the expansion of the capitalist world-economy one step further than the promoters and organizers of the preceding expansion could or would. Every step forward involves a change of guard at the commanding heights of the capitalist world-economy and a concomitant "organizational revolution" in processes of capital accumulation – a change of guard and an organizational revolution which, historically, have always occurred during phases of financial expansions. Financial expansions are thus seen as announcing not just the maturity of a particular stage of development of the capitalist world-economy, but also the beginning of a new stage.

Thus, the starting point of our sequence of systemic cycles of accumulation, which we shall take as the "zero point" in the development of capitalism as world system, is the financial expansion that took off at the *end* of the trade expansion of the thirteenth and early fourteenth centuries. As Janet Abu-Lughod (1989) has shown, this trade expansion encompassed select locations (mostly cities) of the whole of Eurasia and parts of Africa. No single agency or organic complex of agencies can be said to have promoted or organized the expansion. The northern Italian city-states, which were among the main beneficiaries of the trade expansion and became the leaders of the subsequent financial expansion of the European world-economy, did play a critical role in creating regional links in the transcontinental chain of transactions which stretched from England to China. But neither individually nor collectively can these city-states be said to have been the promoters and organizers of the transcontinental trade expansion that made their fortunes. In this respect, their role was important but secondary both absolutely and relative to other organizations, first and foremost the Mongol empire. (See Abu-Lughod 1989: ch. 5; and Barfield 1989 on the impact of the rise and demise of the Mongol empire on the Eurasian trading system.)

Since systemic cycles of accumulation are defined here as consisting of a phase of material expansion followed by a phase of financial expansion promoted and organized by the *same* agency or group of agencies, the trade expansion of the late thirteenth and early fourteenth centuries and the ensuing financial expansion cannot be said to constitute a systemic cycle of accumulation. Nevertheless, it was in the course of this financial expansion that the agencies of the first systemic cycle of accumulation were formed and key features of all subsequent financial expansions were foreshadowed. Neither the origins nor the structure of systemic cycles of accumulation can be fully understood without a preliminary examination of the forces at work in the financial expansion of the late fourteenth and early fifteenth centuries.

The most important feature of this period – as of all closing phases of systemic cycles of accumulation – was a sudden intensification of inter-capitalist competition. Nowhere was this intensification more evident than in the northern Italian capitalist enclave, which became the main seat of the financial expansion. During the preceding trade expansion the relationships between the centers of accumulation of that enclave – that is, its city-states – had been fundamentally cooperative. Cooperation rested primarily on a division of labor among the commercial–industrial activities of the city-states. Even the "big four" occupied fairly distinct market niches in the trading system. Florence and Milan both engaged in manufacturing and in overland trade with northwestern Europe; but while Florence specialized in the textile trades, Milan specialized in the metal trades. Venice and Genoa both specialized in maritime trade with the East; but while Venice specialized in deals with the southern Asian circuit based on the spice trade, Genoa specialized in deals with the Central Asian circuit based on the silk trade.

This structural differentiation among the traffics of the city-states did not only prevent their commercial expansions from getting into one another's way. More importantly, it created strong links of com-plementarity between the businesses of the city-states, thereby making the success of each center conditional on the success of every other center. As John Hicks has underscored in his theoretical account of what he calls "the Mercantile Economy ... in its first form, when it is embodied in a system of city states," in trade, as in industry, there are genuine increasing returns tendencies owing to the fact that a large volume of trade can be organized better than a smaller one so as to reduce the costs of trading. In part, these economies are "internal" to the individual trading center or enterprise in the sense that they can be traced to the larger scale and scope of the operations of that center or enterprise. In part, however, they correspond to what Alfred Marshall has called "external economies" – economies, that is, owing to the fact that the individual trading center or enterprise benefits from being "part of a larger body" (Hicks 1969: 47, 56).

In a system of city-states, "a larger body" means a larger number and variety of politically autonomous trading centers. As the number and variety of such centers increase, the array of commodities that each center can mobilize to expand trade within its specialized market niche becomes more diversified, or the same array can be procured more cheaply to the benefit of profitability. Even more important, Hicks suggests, are lower risks of operation:

> Every trader is operating in an environment of which he has fair knowledge only as concerns those parts that are "nearest" to him; he has much weaker knowledge of parts that may concern him intimately, though they are "farther away". It will always be to his advantage to find ways of diminishing the risks that come from his imperfect knowledge, either directly by increasing knowledge, or indirectly by devising safeguards so that the things which come up out of the darkness may (probably) hurt him less. The evolution of the institutions of the Mercantile Economy is largely a matter of finding ways of diminishing risks. (Hicks 1969: 48)

Hicks goes on to say that "the larger the number of traders who are in contact with one another, the easier it will be to acquire information; even more important, the easier it will be to shift risks – risks that arise for the single trader out of his own ignorance – on to the shoulders of those who in this respect are less ignorant, or who can find it worth their while to become so" (Hicks 1969: 49). Hicks's remarks concerning "traders" apply also – indeed, refer primarily – to trading centers. Thus, there can be little doubt that the specialization of the northern Italian city-states in interrelated but spatially or functionally distinct circuits of trade greatly expanded their collective knowledge of the world-economy in which they operated and thereby reduced the risks involved in trading in a fundamentally insecure or even hostile environment.

In sum, the prosperity of the northern Italian capitalist enclave during the pan-Eurasian trade expansion of the thirteenth and early fourteenth centuries was based on a proliferation in its midst of politically autonomous centers of trade and accumulation and on a division of labor among these centers that reduced the costs and risks of their trade. As long as the trade expansion was in its rising phase, the intensification of competitive pressures inherent in this proliferation of centers remained a mere potentiality. Newcomers could find plenty of market niches which were either "empty" or were eagerly relinquished by established centers. And as they occupied these niches and specialized therein, they created opportunities for established centers to cut costs and risks of operations through a more specialized expansion of their own trade. But even when old and new centers were operating in the same line of business, and therefore seemed to be directly in competition with one another, they were in fact cooperating in creating a volume of trade that was large enough to permit the opening up of new sources of supply – or of new outlets for the disposal of outputs – but would have been too large for a smaller number of units to organize effectively.

To the extent that the centers were actually competing with one another in the procurement of some inputs and in the disposal of some outputs, this competition, to paraphrase Marx (1962: 248), regulated relationships among the members of "an operating fraternity" of capitalist centers so as to make the share of total profits that accrued to each center somewhat proportional to its contribution to the overall expansion of trade. But as soon as a major and lasting disproportion arose between the mass of capital that sought investment in trade on the one side, and what could be so invested without precipitating a drastic reduction in returns to capital on the other, competition between the centers turned into "a fight among hostile brothers." When such a disproportion arose, it was no longer a question of sharing profits but of sharing losses. As a result, the antagonism between the interest of each center and the collective interest of the ensemble formed by all the centers surfaced and transformed competition into "cut-throat competition" – a kind of competition, that is, the primary objective of which is to drive other centers out of business even if it means sacrificing one's own profits for as long as it takes to attain the objective.

We do not know exactly when the change in conjuncture occurred. But we do know that the total value of the transit of merchandise anticipated by tax farmers in the port of Genoa dropped from 4,000,000 Genoese pounds in 1293 to 2,000,000 pounds in 1334 and that in the second half of the century the value in question seldom rose above the latter amount (Martines 1988: 170). Given the importance of Genoa at that time, both as a trading center and as a center of capital accumulation – in 1293 its sea trade being three times the entire revenue of the Kingdom of France (Lopez 1976: 94) – we may safely suppose that at some point in the early fourteenth century, but certainly before 1334, the Eurasian trade expansion had tapered off and the business of the Italian city-states came to be affected by a radical and lasting change in the conjuncture (cf. Abu-Lughod 1989). Be that as it may,

> a cessation of expansion does not mean that the Mercantile Economy settles into an "equilibrium" – the stationary competitive equilibrium beloved of theoretical economists. Each of the centers, at the time when the blockage comes, is still trying to expand its trade; but the competition of the others, which had formerly been tolerated, is now a danger. There had always been squabbles between the centers.... But it is at this point, when the growth of their trade begins to be constricted, that the formidable struggles between them are likely to break out. Such, we may reasonably suppose, was the long war between Venice and Genoa, that lasted for nearly forty years around 1400. (Hicks 1969: 57).

The series of wars that pitted Genoa and Venice against one another in the middle of the fourteenth century actually ended with the Peace of Turin of 1381, by which Venice ousted Genoa from the most profitable markets of the eastern Mediterranean. But these wars between Genoa and Venice were only episodes of a far longer and more general city-state conflict that tore apart and reorganized the northern Italian capitalist enclave. This general city-state conflict lasted for about a century and is what Braudel has called the "Italian" Hundred Years War. After ousting Genoa from the most profitable markets of the eastern Mediterranean, Venice went on to build up a mainland zone (the *Terraferma*). At the same time, Milan took over Lombardy, and Florence became Tuscany. The war eventually ended with the Peace of Lodi of 1454, which institutionalized the northern Italian balance of power (Braudel 1976: I, 339, 388).

It was in this period that, as previously noted, select northern Italian city-states came to function as great powers in European politics. But this was also a period in which the dominant groups of the northern Italian city-states were continually split into opposite factions by violent feuds. These internal feuds were mild and easily recomposed in the city-states that were winning in the competitive struggle, most notably in Venice, but they were severe and uncontainable in the case of those city-states that were losing out (most notably in Genoa). In any event, as vividly portrayed by Jacob Burckhardt (1945: 4–64) in his classic study, Renaissance Italy was one of the clearest historical instances of "war of all against all."

The ruling groups of the city-states were constantly beset by enemies, and the pursuit of profit came to be embedded more firmly than ever in the pursuit of power:

> There were implacable exiles, the leaders of the faction out of power, prowling just beyond reach. There were rival cities, eager to make a profit out of a neighbor's difficulties. And there were usually secret enemies conspiring within the gates. Therefore the state, depending for its survival on power, was compelled constantly to seek more power.... So warfare between city and city became endemic all over northern and central Italy. Only commercial giants like Venice and Genoa could afford to wage their wars on the sea lanes and shake half the peninsula with their quarrels. Mostly the war was with the nearest independent city.... Big cities ate smaller ones.... And these victims had been powerful cities, the conquerors of their smaller neighbors before they were conquered in their turn. Unlikely as it seemed that any one of the rivals could succeed in devouring all the others, no city was strong enough to feel really secure. Under jungle law, the price of survival was incessant alertness. (Mattingly 1988: 49–50)

This is the context in which capitalism as historical social system was born. The intensification of inter-capitalist competition and the increasing interpenetration of this competition with the power struggle within and between city-states did not weaken but strengthened the control of these states by capitalist interests. As the "Italian" Hundred Years War raged on, one city-state after another faced ever more serious fiscal crises due primarily to "truly staggering disbursements ... for military expenditures and accruing interest on the public debt" (Martines 1988: 178). The result was an increasing "alienation" of the city-states to moneyed interest, as Marx called the phenomenon in his discussion of primitive accumulation. The alienation was most thorough in Genoa, where in 1407 the republic's revenues and public administration were put in the hands of the *Casa di San Giorgio*, which incorporated the state's private creditors, and in Florence, where the terrible fiscal crisis that followed the war with Lucca (1429–33) led directly to the takeover of the city's government by the House of Medici. But even in Milan – the least capitalist and most territorialist of the "big four" – the ducal treasury developed close ties with the city's big business and financial families (Martines 1988: 179–80).

This tightening of the control of moneyed interests on the governments of the city-states is a second key feature of the northern Italian financial expansion of the latter fourteenth and early fifteenth centuries. As in all subsequent financial expansions, the alienation of the states to moneyed interests occurred through a transfer of surplus capital – capital, that is, that no longer found profitable investment in trade – to the financing of war-making activities. What capitalist groups could no longer invest profitably in trade, they now invested in the hostile takeover of the markets or of the territories of competitors both as an end in itself and as a means to appropriate the assets and the future revenues of the state within which they operated.

Profitable as it was for the groups that won the struggles, this process of conquest and appropriation was none the less limited in time and space by the decreasing returns to the capital invested in warfare. Once the most profitable markets had been snatched from competitors; once the nearest competitors had been incorporated into one's own domains, so that larger and more difficult to conquer units began to confront one another; and once most of the assets and future revenues of the warring city-states had been mortgaged to moneyed interests – once all these things had happened, the continued investment of surplus capital in war-making activities became increasingly counterproductive for the capitalist groups that had come to control the surviving city-states. As Hicks (1969: 57) notes, inter-mercantile warfare, like cut-throat price competition, is destructive of profits. Why not "behave as modern industrial giants behave when they find themselves similarly placed.... [Why] not seek a way out, by what after all is the normal mercantile method? Why not come to an agreement, tacit or explicit, to divide the market – to keep out of each other's way?"

A new kind of cooperation within and between trading centers thus tended to develop in the course of the struggles that ensued from the cessation of the trade expansion. During the trade expansion, arrangements in restraint of competition were not unknown but the low intensity of competitive pressures made them unnecessary except in special and circumscribed spheres. But once the expansion of the trading system had reached its limits and the most profitable opportunities of war-making had been exploited, the need for such arrangements became more pressing:

> As opportunities in general close in, or seem to close in, the fields in which it becomes tempting to protect oneself by agreements with one's competitors become more extensive. Gradually, in this way, the mercantile economy slips into custom; the merchant is accepting a place in a system of customary rights and duties. The "social gravitation", to which [other kinds of economies are] subject, is expressing itself in this way upon the mercantile economy also. (Hicks 1969: 57–8)

The cooperation between centers of accumulation which tends to develop in the closing phases of trade expansions thus differs radically in origins and consequences from the cooperation that obtains in their opening phases. The latter kind of cooperation is rooted in a structural *weakness* of competitive pressures, owing to the fact that the commercial expansion of each trading center is "naturally" protected by the spatial and/or functional distance that separates its business from the businesses of all the other centers and by the division of labor that makes the profitability and security of the business of each center dependent on the profitability and security of the business of all the other centers. The cooperation that tends to develop in the closing phases of trade expansions, in contrast, is rooted in a structural *intensity* of competitive pressures, owing to the fact that some or all of the more powerful trading centers command more capital than they can invest profitably within their respective market niches and are thus driven to invade the market niches of other centers. As in Marx's "overaccumulation crises" (which we shall discuss in chapter 3) more capital is seeking investment in the purchase and sale of commodities than the structure of the trading system can accommodate without provoking a drastic reduction in the overall profitability and security of trade.

Under these circumstances, cooperation between the centers can succeed in enhancing the overall security and profitability of trade only if it succeeds in restraining the tendency of the centers to plow the profits of trade back in the further expansion of trade. As Hicks put it, "this moment, when expansion is arrested, may from other points of view be a wonderful moment. Profits are still high, but *it is a condition for their maintenance that they should not be invested in further expansion.* Once that condition is accepted, there is wealth, and there is security" (Hicks 1969: 58; emphasis added). In other words, once trade expansions have reached their limits, wealth and security come to depend on a general recognition by the relevant agencies that under existing historical circumstances these limits cannot be overcome and that attempts to do so, instead of preserving, tend to destroy wealth and security. To the extent that this recognition actually materializes in restraining the tendency of trading centers to reinvest surplus capital in the further expansion of their business, competitive struggles can be brought under control and the centers of accumulation can enjoy the best of times:

What can be better? The hurly-burly of the market-place has been brought into order. People have their place in society, places to which they must keep, but which are preserved for them, by protection against the intrusion of others. Through their guilds and suchlike associations, which are the means to this protection, they can explore new forms of human fellowship. . . . It has other blessings also. The vigour which marked the expansion may not immediately be lost; it must turn from trading innovations, but with security and wealth it can be turned to other fields. The expansion of trade had been an intellectual stimulus; but when the point comes that it no longer absorbs the same energy, art can be pursued for art's sake, and learning for the sake of learning.... [It] was after their commercial expansion was completed that Florence and Venice became the homes of the High Renaissance. These are the fruits for which we remember them; but autumn is the season when fruit comes. (Hicks 1969: 58–9)

It is not by chance that Braudel used the same metaphor – "a sign of autumn" – to characterize financial expansions (see the Introduction). For the reaping of the fruits of a bygone phase of material expansion is yet another typical feature of all closing phases of systemic cycles of accumulation that was prefigured in the financial expansion of the latter fourteenth and early fifteenth centuries. Together with the development of high finance (to be discussed presently) the conspicuous consumption of cultural products was the most important way in which these fruits were reaped.

In part, the conspicuous consumption of cultural products was a direct result of the adverse commercial conjuncture which made investments in the patronage of the arts a more useful or even a more profitable form of utilization of surplus capital than its reinvestment in trade (Lopez 1962; 1963). In part, it was a supply-driven phenomenon associated with the invention of mythical collective identities as means of popular mobilization in inter-city-state warfare (cf. Baron 1955). And in part, it was a direct result of the struggle for status among competing factions of merchants whereby "building magnificently became a strategy for distinguishing some families from others" (Burke 1986: 228).

The particular mix of circumstances that produced the Renaissance varied from city-state to city-state, and so did their outcome. But in so far as the *system* of city-states is concerned, the conspicuous consumption of cultural products was integral to a state-making process, that is, to the reorganization of the northern Italian capitalist enclave into a system consisting of fewer, larger, and more powerful political organizations. The anomalous character of the ruling groups of the city-states meant that they could not rely on the automatic, customary allegiance that was available to more traditional kinds of authority. Hence, these groups "had to win and hold that allegiance by intensifying the community's self-consciousness" (Mattingly 1988: 49).

The wars that constantly set the city-states against one another did focus loyalties and win allegiances, particularly for the ruling groups that won the wars. Nevertheless, the expansion of the domains of the city-states that were winning the wars through the incorporation of the territories and populations of the city-states that were losing them, again posed the same problem of loyalty and allegiance in increasingly complex forms. What is more, as the expanding city-states came to play the role of great powers in European politics, problems of domestic legitimation were compounded by problems of external legitimation. Primacy in art and learning was as good a means as any other to win legitimacy on both fronts.

It was also a means that suited well the skills and dispositions of the ruling groups of the city-states.

> It was ... natural for the ruling groups – merchants and professional men – most of them with some legal or notarial training ... and most of them experienced in the haggling of the forum and the market place – to believe that words might be as potent as swords. The faith of the merchants and the politicos in the efficacy of diplomatic and forensic persuasion as an auxiliary to or substitute for military force was probably heightened by the reviving interest in classical literature. In turn, no doubt, this faith strengthened the new humanism and helped give it its prevailing bias towards public rhetoric. The real effectiveness of this form of psychological warfare no one can hope to estimate now. Certainly public opinion among the educated classes was more or less susceptible to propaganda, and certainly, from the time of Petrarch and Cola de Rienzi onward, there was an increasing tendency to try to manipulate this opinion by literary means. (Mattingly 1988: 53–4)

The increasing but never complete substitution of words for swords as means to power was a central aspect of the consolidation of the Italian inter-city-state system in the century of incessant warfare that ended with the Peace of Lodi of 1454. But neither words nor swords would have sufficed to create the prototype of the future inter-state system of the European world-economy had they not been supplemented, or rather, underlain, by the power of money. The feats of words and swords are more easily remembered than those of money. But the most decisive and lasting contribution of the Italian Renaissance to the development of capitalism as world system was in the sphere of high finance. This was the "invisible" sphere in which the agencies and structures of the first systemic cycle of accumulation were formed and to which we must now turn.

The Genesis of High Finance

High finance in its modern, capitalist form is a Florentine invention. Its foundations were laid during the trade expansion of the late thirteenth and early fourteenth centuries. But it came of age only after that expansion had come to an end.

The first extensive financial deals beyond the Alps had been carried on by Sienese businessmen who had travelled to England and the northern kingdoms as papal collectors; and this business with Rome and on Rome's account, which included such "invisible exports" as pilgrimages, indulgences, and dispensations, remained essential to the continental reach and prosperity of Florentine and Sienese banking houses throughout their hey-day in the fourteenth and fifteenth centuries. This huge business required expert management and, as the merchant and chronicler Giovanni Villani observed, the Florentines "quickly recognized the advantage of becoming bankers to the Pope; for thus the largest floating capital in the world would have to pass through their hands" (quoted in Cox 1959: 165; see also de Roover 1963: 1–3, 194–224; Gilbert 1980: ch. 4; Burke 1986: 224).

The leadership of Florentine business enterprises in European high finance was established on the basis of trade in religion on Rome's account in combination with trade in wool on Florence's own account. The rapid expansion of the Florentine wool industry in the late thirteenth century involved a progressive widening of the "catchment area" from which its inputs were purchased and to which its final outputs were sold. As local supplies of raw wool were exhausted, large quantities of roughly woven cloth were imported mainly from the Netherlands and France to be further processed and finished by skilled Florentine artisans. As new competitive supplies of raw wool were found in Spain, Portugal, and England, the production of cloth in Florence expanded, only to be relocated once again on an enlarged scale through the establishment of workshops for the first and coarser stages of the manufacturing process in Brabant, Holland, England, and France, where the best wool was to be found (Cox 1959: 162–3). On the demand side of the equation, outlets in the Italian states were supplemented by rapidly expanding outlets in the Levant where Florentine-finished woolen goods were exchanged for spices, dyes, and other Asian products. And "as quality went on improving," Giovanni Villani noted, "they found their way to France, England and the same markets whence they had originally come, and whence they were sold in exchange for undressed fabrics" (quoted in Cox 1959: 162).

The formation and expansion of Florentine networks of high finance were initially embedded in, and built on, the extensive and dense web of transactions created by the wool trade:

The great bankers were at the same time members of the ... wool guilds so that international banking and commerce in cloth developed co-extensively. As bankers they converted money and debts due in foreign countries into wool; accepted wool as security for loans; allowed the papal dues in foreign countries to be paid in wool; sought trading concessions from feudal lords, especially monopoly of the market for wool, when these rulers requested financial

favors.... [They also] financed the production of cloth at home and abroad ...
[and] provided short-term loans for the marketing of the finished product.
(Cox 1959: 164)

As long as the wool trade continued to grow rapidly and yielded high
returns, it constituted the main dynamic element in the expansion of
Florentine banking networks across Europe. But as its growth rate slowed
and returns fell, Florentine merchant bankers sought, and eventually
found, a new foundation in the rapidly increasing demand for mobile
capital engendered by the power struggle between the emerging territorialist states of Western Europe. For the tapering off of the Eurasian trade
expansion was associated not just with the escalation of competitive
struggles within the Italian system of city-states noted earlier. It was also
associated with the escalation of power struggles in the rest of Europe.
The century of the "Italian" Hundred Years War was also the century of
the better known "Anglo-French" Hundred Years War (1337–1453), of
the Schism that split the papacy (1378–1417), of recurrent bouts of
political anarchy and chaos in the Iberian peninsula, and of the long series
of wars in northern Europe in the course of which the power of the
Hanseatic League waned and Dutch fortunes waxed.

The connections that linked these various strands of the escalation in
the European power struggle to one another and to the tapering off of the
Eurasian trade expansion are too complex to be discussed here. Nevertheless, for what concerns the "Anglo-French" Hundred Years War,
which played a critical role in the development of Florentine high finance,
we should note that during the preceding trade expansion England had
become the largest and most important source of fine wool for Italian and
Flemish manufacturing centers. As Barrington Moore (1966: 5) has
pointed out, this expansion of the wool trade initiated "the strong
commercial impulse that was eventually to rule English society." Its
reverberations "were felt not only in the towns but in the countryside as
well, possibly even more there, and certainly in politics."

The commercial impulse had repercussions not just on state-making
but on war-making activities as well, as witnessed by the fact that on the
eve of the English invasion of France the rulers of England were
apparently superior to their otherwise more powerful French rivals in the
commercialization of war (McNeill 1984: 81–2). We may therefore
suppose that, by invading France, English rulers reckoned that the time
had come to turn into territorial acquisitions their lead over the French
in the commercialization of warfare, or that territorial aggrandizement
was needed to compensate for the negative repercussions of the slowdown or contraction in the wool trade on their state-making and war-
making capabilities. What we do know is that during the quarter of a

century preceding the invasion of France the English balance of payments had experienced a dramatic deterioration, as evinced by the sharp decrease in the 1310s and 1320s of silver coinage in England (see figure 2). Since a very large proportion of English coinage was struck from resmelted foreign coin – 90 per cent or more in the decades in question – changes in the level of English mint production were closely and positively related to changes in the balance of payments (Miskimin 1969: 139).

Having become accustomed to an expanding supply of foreign means of payments in the exercise of their state- and war-making functions, the ruling groups of England reacted to the change in the conjuncture by seeking through war what they could no longer obtain through trade. Direct evidence of the importance of balance of payments considerations in the English invasion can be detected in the fact that the first objective pursued by the English on the continent was to squeeze better terms of trade from their Flemish customers. To this end, they first imposed an embargo on the export of wool to Flanders in collusion with the king of Castile, and then attacked and vanquished the Flemish in the battle of Cansand (1337). At this point, English exports to Flanders resumed, but at prices far more advantageous to the English and on condition that the Flemish made direct loans to Edward III (Miskimin 1969: 92–3).

In and by itself, the extortion of higher prices and forced loans from customers was not a good way of financing a long and costly war because, sooner or later, such a policy would kill the goose that laid the golden egg, as it eventually did by driving the Flemish cloth industry out of business. The extortion, however, was only a tactical move in a wider strategy aimed at "internalizing" the cloth industry within England. Thus, as Flemish clothworkers were subjected to embargoes and to military aggression, they were at the same time encouraged to move to England. And when at the end of the fourteenth century the Flemish industry finally collapsed, many did just that (Miskimin 1969: 93–9). The success of this carrot-and-stick strategy can be gauged from the trends depicted in figure 3, which shows the expansion of the English cloth industry during the Hundred Years War and the parallel "forcible" deindustrialization of one of the three main centers of Flemish cloth production, Ypres.

Commenting on these trends, Harry Miskimin has underscored the "negative-sum game" that underlay them.

Edward III had been triumphantly successful in destroying the Flemish industry and in transferring part of it to England, but the Flemish depression must moderate the claims permitted to the English success. The English accomplishment lay in the transplantation of an industry rather than in the creation of a new area of industrial enterprise.... In the face of a declining world market – the decline at the city of Ypres alone was greater than the entire English export trade – England, through the exercise of national power and the economic control of raw materials, had gained regional economic prosperity at the expense of Flanders. (Miskimin 1969: 95–6)

The conclusion that the expansion of cloth production in England consisted of nothing more than a transplant of an industry, and that the transplant was associated with an overall decline in economic prosperity, becomes even more inescapable once we bring into the picture the "spontaneous" deindustrialization of Florence, which preceded that of Ypres and was even more massive. According to Giovanni Villani, in 1338 there were 200 or more workshops in Florence producing between 70,000 and 80,000 pieces of cloth for a total value of more than 1,200,000 gold florins. Thirty years earlier, there had been about 300 producing over 100,000 pieces of cloth, although these cloths were coarser and about half as valuable (Lopez and Raymond 1955: 71–4; Luzzatto 1961: 106).

Florentine merchants and manufacturers had thus begun to cut cloth production and to concentrate on items of higher quality and greater value well before 1338. But between 1338 and 1378, this tendency became spasmodic. Production was concentrated almost exclusively on higher quality cloth – worth on average twice as much the former product – and fell to 24,000 pieces, never to rise over 30,000 pieces per year during the entire course of the fifteenth century (Cipolla 1952; Luzzatto 1961: 97–8, 106, 141).

The reduction of woolen production in Florence between 1338 and 1378 was larger than either the decline in Ypres from the beginning of the Hundred Years War through the 1380s or the entire growth in English cloth exports over the course of the fourteenth century. However, this drastic curtailment of industrial production in Florence was not the result of any use or threat of violence on the part of English rulers, or anybody else. Rather, it was the expression of the strictly capitalist logic of action that guided Florentine business enterprise.

Then, as now, this logic dictated that capital should be invested in trade and production only as long as returns in these activities were not only positive, but higher than whatever rate justified the exposure of capital to the risks and troubles inseparable from its employment in trade and production and, secondly, compensated its owners for the returns that capital could have earned in financial deals. And then, as now, the intensification of competitive pressures throughout the trading system tended to raise this rate and thereby provoked a major reallocation of capital from the purchase, processing, and sale of commodities to more flexible forms of investment, that is, primarily to the financing of domestic and foreign public debts. This reallocation was not a movement towards some kind of "equilibrium". On the contrary, it was both the expression and the cause of considerable economic, political, and social turbulence.

Economic turbulence climaxed in the "great crash" of the early 1340s triggered in 1339 by Edward III's default on the massive loan of 1,365,000 gold florins – larger, it should be noted, than the entire value of Florentine cloth production in 1338 – with which the Florentine firms of Bardi and Peruzzi had financed the English invasion of France. Ferdinand Schevill (1936: 219) maintains that the Florentine bankers knew that the investment was risky but had become so enmeshed in the finances of the English throne that they could not withdraw. This probably means that Bardi and Peruzzi knew that the golden age of expanding revenues in the wool trade was gone for good and that their best chance of recouping the funds previously advanced to the English crown lay in a big new advance, which would enable Edward III to expand his revenues – and hence his ability to service and repay his debts – through territorial conquests or through the transplant of the Flemish cloth industry within its domains. As it turned out, this was a gross miscalculation since within two years of the beginning of the war Edward III declared himself insolvent and, by so doing, precipitated a major crisis in the European credit system, a run on the banks in Florence and elsewhere, and the collapse of the firms of Bardi and Peruzzi themselves.

The great crash of the 1340s spread havoc in the lives of thousands of ordinary investors and workers in Florence and led to an intensification of the feuds that had traditionally set the different factions of the city's ruling groups against one another. The turmoil in the market, compounded from 1348 by the ravages of the Black Death and subsequent epidemics, destabilized the rule of the merchant classes and created new opportunities for the political emancipation of the laboring classes. In 1338, on the eve of the great crash, more than 30,000 people, about one third of Florence's population, lived by the wages paid out by cloth manufacturers. As cloth production plummeted over the next forty years, the lower strata of the wage labor force – which was only marginally involved in the production of higher quality cloth – rose up in self-protection demanding higher wages, the preservation of existing levels of production, and the right of independent organization. These struggles culminated in the so-called revolt of the *Ciompi* of 1378 when impoverished clothworkers seized state power and put a woolcomber, Michele di Lando, at the head of the republic's government (Cox 1959: 152–3; Dobb 1963: 157–8; Miskimin 1969: 98–9).

This proletarian revolt was swiftly brought under control by the employers through a lock-out which transformed the rebellious workers into a mass of hungry idlers. And when these hungry idlers turned to rioting for food and marched threateningly to the Signoria, di Lando himself at the head of upper-guild workers dealt them a crushing defeat (Cox 1959: 153). As Schevill (1936: 308) observed, the "struggle of the fourteenth century [in Florence] constitutes an early chapter in the very modern conflict between capital and labor, and in the relatively easy victory won by capital reveals the diffficulties which then and ever since have confronted capital's opponents."

Then, as ever since, these difficulties arose from the fact that capital was endowed with a much greater flexibility and mobility than its opponents. As competitive pressures on governmental and business organizations intensified, strictly capitalist organizations were far less constrained by considerations of power or livelihood in the reallocation of their resources than most other organizations – be they the English royal house, or Flemish guilds, or Florence's own guilds. Thus, Florence's leading business enterprises were largely indifferent as to whether the self-expansion of their capital occurred through the purchase, processing, and sale of commodities or through the financing of the struggles that set the various components of the world-economy within which they operated against one another. And as competition drove down returns to capital in trade and production, while the power struggle raised returns in high finance, they began transferring cash surpluses from the first to the second kind of investment – gradually in the early decades of the fourteenth century, precipitously in the middle decades.

There was very little that the strata of the Florentine working class that were hardest hit by this transfer could do to stop, let alone reverse, the tendency that was making their very existence "redundant" as far as the capitalist accumulation of capital was concerned. Ironically, their revolt and momentary seizure of power in 1378, far from weakening, strengthened this tendency and led to its final consolidation. They did so, on the one hand, by bringing to the fore the fundamental conflict of interest that set the upper and the lower strata of the Florentine working class against one another and, on the other hand, by creating a strong political incentive for the various factions into which the Florentine capitalist class was divided to resolve their quarrels and exercise their domination over labor with an iron fist.

It was neither by accident nor by a false perception of their interests that upper-guild workers participated actively in the repression of the rebellious *Ciompi*. For the same tendencies that were impoverishing the lower strata of the Florentine working class in the course of the fourteenth century were creating a bonanza for its upper strata. Returns to capital were not falling in all branches of manufacturing equally, and in some branches they were not falling at all. As surplus capital was transferred ever more massively to the financing of warfare in the Italian inter-city-state system and in the European world-economy at large, demand for means of war boomed to the benefit of Venice's shipyards and even more of Milan's armament industry. But surplus capital was also being transferred to conspicuous consumption, not just of cultural products, but of more mundane goods like high quality textile products. As a result, while the lower strata of the Florentine working class were being made redundant by declining returns in the production of the coarser cloth – the demand for which was at best stagnant and supplied abundantly by increased production in England, Holland, Brabant, and France – the skills and labor of the upper strata found a ready and steady demand in the production of the more luxurious cloth (Miskimin 1969: 99, 153–7).

Florentine big business and wealthy merchant families skilfully exploited the contradictions that these divergent tendencies created within the working class. As they locked out the workers of the lower guilds, they courted the government of Michele di Lando and the workers of the upper guilds. After this policy bore fruit with the final submission of the *Ciompi*, they ejected di Lando and for half a century after 1382 ruled the city with a unity of purpose seldom displayed before the revolt of 1378. Even then, however, they reserved a very different treatment for the lower and the upper strata of the working class. The livelihood of the upper strata was protected more aggressively than before the revolt through prohibitive duties on the import of foreign cloth and other measures aimed at preserving trade secrets and at withholding strategic inputs from competitors. The lower strata, in contrast, were stripped of all protection and rights of independent organization and thereby turned into a floating mass of surplus labor forced by indigence to seek their daily bread in the building boom of the Renaissance (Cox 1959: 154; Miskimin 1969: 99; Martines 1988: 189–90).

The half-century of oligarchical rule by the city's wealthy merchant families ended in 1434 with the takeover of the government and the *de facto* establishment of monarchical rule by the family that had moved ahead of all the others in the accumulation of wealth and capital, the Medici. As previously noted, this takeover was a direct consequence of the crippling fiscal crisis that seized the Florentine republic after its war with Lucca. But if this fiscal crisis can be said to have created the opportunity for the Medici to "buy" the Florentine republic at a bargain price, the ability to do so was the result of a long process of development, which can be traced back to the great crash of the 1340s and in the course of which the House of Medici had become the leading organization in European high finance. Four aspects of this process are germane to our concerns.

First, the fortunes of the Medici were created out of the havoc of the great crash of the 1340s. Having survived the crash, and starting from modest origins, the Medici moved quickly to fill the void left by the collapse of the giant firms of Bardi and Peruzzi and of a host of lesser financiers. Like many other Italian merchant bankers, the Medici relied on a network of correspondents that spanned the entire European world-economy. In addition, however, they established foreign branches controlled directly by the Florentine headquarters in Rome, Venice, Naples, Milan, Pisa, Geneva, Lyons, Basle, Avignon, Bruges, and London (de Roover 1963: 194, 225–346).

Second, the prodigious trans-statal expansion of the House of Medici in the late fourteenth and early fifteenth centuries was based on a strategy of accumulation that gave priority to financial deals with governments but was highly selective in the choice of the governments with which to do business. In the period 1435–50, 90 per cent of the firm's recorded total profits of 289,000 gold florins came from banking and the remainder from two wool shops and one silk shop operated by the firm in Florence. The most profitable of the firm's foreign branches was Rome, which up to 1434 had generated more than half of its revenues. Business with Rome and on Rome's account was indeed the cornerstone of the Medici's financial empire, not just because of the volume of the cash flows involved, but because the chronic indebtedness of the Curia to the House of Medici enabled the latter to mobilize the spiritual and organizational power of the Church to secure the repayment of the lucrative loans it made to subordinate clerics throughout Europe (de Roover 1963: 194–224).

Third, the formation and expansion of the Medici's financial empire was closely associated with the formation and expansion of the state-making capabilities of the House of Medici:

In the early 1470s, when Lorenzo de' Medici sat down to figure out the principal expenditures made by his family between 1434 and 1471, he did not even bother to distinguish the disbursements for architectural and artistic commissions from those for charity and taxes. All were lumped together because all served the one end – the grandeur of his house and its power in the state. Far from regretting the astounding total (663,755 gold florins), he concluded: "I think it casts a brilliant light on our estate and it seems to me that the monies were well spent and I am very pleased with this." (Martines 1988: 243)

This observation shows that Lorenzo de' Medici had a far better sense of the business climate in which the Medici operated than the later historians and social scientists who mistook the Medici's indulgence in pomp and display as the main reason why capital invested in their firm lagged far behind profits. In fact, the Medici profits were high precisely because – to paraphrase Hicks's dictum quoted earlier – they were *not* reinvested in the further expansion of the business that generated them. Had the Medici reinvested in their financial, commercial, and industrial operations the 663,755 gold florins that between 1434 and 1471 they spent in the patronage of the poor, of the arts, and of the state, their firm's operating capital – which according to Raymond de Roover (1963) peaked at about 72,000 florins – would have increased by something like a factor of 10. In all likelihood, an increase of this order would have led the Medici to involve themselves in dubious business ventures, possibly as dubious as the one that ruined Bardi and Peruzzi. In any event, it would have seriously undermined the scarcity of capital that was keeping inter-capitalist competition under control, the Florentine working class in its place, and, more importantly, the Roman Curia and several other European governments in constant need of the Medici's financial assistance.

If the plowing back of the huge profits of the House of Medici in the expansion of its financial, commercial, and industrial operations would have been bad business policy, the seemingly "unproductive" expenditure of a large proportion of these profits in pomp and display was in fact good business policy – quite apart from the aesthetic pleasure and other benefits that it gave the Medici family. For big business in general and high finance in particular were involved in state-making functions to a far greater extent than in later epochs. As Mattingly (1988: 59) notes, the diplomatic function of the foreign branch managers of the House of Medici was always considerable and, after 1434, "it was progressively harder to distinguish between the resident representatives of the Medici bank and the political agents of the Florentine state." Pomp and display were important for public relations in Florence where the expenditures were made, but they were even more important in providing the foreign branch managers with valuable psychological ammunition in their daily struggles to be accepted as equals (or as superiors) when dealing with their aristocratic clientele.

Granted all this, there was none the less a fourth aspect of the long process of development of Florentine high finance which had nothing to do with the business acumen of the Medici and of their managers and without which that business acumen would have gone to waste. This fourth aspect, to paraphrase Weber, was the peculiar political competition and "equilibrium" between Europe's major political structures which began to emerge in the latter half of the fourteenth century. What ruined Bardi and Peruzzi in the 1340s was not so much the fact that they had put all their eggs in one basket. What really ruined them was the fact that they had shifted the bulk of their resources to high finance "too early," that is, *before* the competition for mobile capital among the rising and declining political structures of Europe had assumed the acute character that it did in the late fourteenth and early fifteenth centuries. As a result, neither they nor the English king whose war they financed were aware of the underlying relationship of forces between capitalism and territorialism that was about to emerge in Europe. The two Florentine firms thought that they had no choice but to yield to Edward's pressure and lend him a huge amount of money, when in fact it would have been far better for them to hold out and wait for the financial straits of the English realm to worsen. And Edward, for his part, thought that he could default on the Florentine loan without worrying too much about the future credit standing of the English crown, when in fact in order to win the war he had just launched the English crown needed all the credit it could get.

When the Medici appeared on the scene of European high finance, the situation was quite different. They could, of course, learn from the disastrous experience of Bardi and Peruzzi and be more cautious in making loans, as they no doubt were in choosing Rome as their main client. Nevertheless, the more cautious lending strategy of the Medici would not have yielded the spectacular results it did, were it not for the systemic conditions that they had done nothing to create. As already mentioned, the crash had created a void in the structure of high finance that strengthened the bargaining position of the surviving financiers. In addition, the Black Death multiplied legacies and donations to the Church and thus gave a big boost to Rome's cash flows shortly before the Medici stepped in to manage them, while the Schism of 1378–1417, by splitting the papacy into two competing seats and by complicating its financial transactions, no doubt helped the Medici in establishing their hold over the Curia (cf. Favier 1966; Miskimin 1969: 144–7).

Important as the windfalls and the troubles of the Church were in establishing the leadership of the Medici in European high finance, the more permanent and eventually most important change in systemic circumstances that made the Medici succeed where Bardi and Peruzzi had failed was the competition for mobile capital between France and England engendered by the Hundred Years War. As we can see from figure 2, Edward III's imposition of better terms of trade and forced loans on the Flemish, combined with his default on the Florentine loan, did have a temporary positive effect on his realm's balance of payment and liquidity as measured by the increase in English mint production of the 1340s and early 1350s. By the 1360s, however, this positive effect had vanished, and except for some temporary relief from Calais in the 1420s, for the remaining ninety years of the war England faced a constant shortage of liquidity.

At the roots of this lay the fact that the war itself, being fought on French soil, tended to destroy the English lead over the French in the commercialization of warfare:

As earlier in Italy, an army in the field with its continual appetite for supplies acted like a migratory city. In the short run the effect on the French countryside was often disastrous; in the long run armies and their plundering expanded the role of buying and selling in everyday life.

As a result, by the time the French monarchy began to recover from the squalid demoralization induced by the initial English victories and widespread disaffection among the nobility, an expanded tax base allowed the king to collect enough hard cash to support an increasingly formidable armed force. This was the army which expelled the English from France by 1453 after a series of successful campaigns. (McNeill 1984: 82–3)

Once hostilities ceased, the golden age of Florentine high finance in general, and of the Medici in particular, drew rapidly to a close. As late as 1470, it was still said of the Medici branches in Bruges and London that "[t]hey rule these lands, having in their hands the lease of the trade in wool and alum and all the other State revenues, and from thence they do business in exchange with every market in the world, but chiefly with Rome, whereby they make great gains." But by 1485 the branch in Bruges had been closed and the Medici soon disappeared from the world of European high finance (Ehrenberg 1985: 196–8).

As long as the Hundred Years War lasted, however, the equilibrium between the two contending territorialist organizations, and the constant need for financial assistance imposed on both of them by the commercialization of warfare, created unprecedented opportunities for commercial and financial intermediation which the Medici and other Florentine merchant bankers were well placed to turn to their own advantage, both economically and politically. These opportunities presented the Medici with opportunities for business success that Bardi and Peruzzi never had. By seizing these opportunities, the Medici became one of the wealthiest and most powerful families in Europe. "The Medici," notes Ehrenberg (1985: 52), "hardly ever had more influence over the course of the world's history than that which they exercised at the time of the struggles between Louis XI of France, Edward IV of England, and Charles the Bold of Burgundy." In doing so, however, they became more and more deeply involved in the business of politics, rose to prominence in the ranks of the European aristocracy, and over time let their commercial and financial activities wither away.

Pace Pirenne, this metamorphosis was not primarily the expression of a failure of adaptation to changing business conditions. Rather, it was the expression of an exceptional success in the adaptation to business conditions that were still predominant when the metamorphosis occurred. The career of the Medici was simply the most conspicuous instance of a tendency that, to different degrees and with different modalities, was unfolding in other Italian city-states as well. It was most clearly observable in Venice, which was also the most successful of the city-states in coping with the adverse trade conjuncture of the late fourteenth and early fifteenth centuries:

> The promise and opportunities of Venice's mainland empire, acquired after 1405, worked a profound change in the Venetian patriciate. Providing it with new concerns, with land, governorships, and lucrative offices, the mainland lulled the entrepreneurial initiative of the nobility, gradually rendering it more sedentary. In Pareto's classic formulation, entrepreneurs turned into *rentiers*. (Martines 1988: 171)

In Venice, as in Florence, the conjuncture of the century following the end of the Eurasian trade expansion dictated that surplus capital be transferred from trade to war- and state-making activities. The main difference between the two city-states was that the transfer in Venice occurred more smoothly and yielded higher returns than in Florence, so that a much larger stratum of the Venetian than of the Florentine merchant class could participate in and benefit from political capitalism. That is to say, the same tendency towards the transfer of resources from the business of trade to the business of politics – which in Florence materialized in the highly concentrated form of the irresistible rise of the Medici to monarchs of the city – in Venice materialized in the more diffuse if less spectacular form of the "rentierization" of the entire upper stratum of the city's merchant class.

Although in Venice, as in Florence, the withdrawal from trade of select capitalist elements to become an "aristocracy" was a sign of their successful pursuit of profit rather than of a failure of adaptation to changing business conditions, it is still the case, as Pirenne maintained, that, *once the metamorphosis had occurred*, these elements played a purely passive role in the subsequent expansion of the capitalist world-economy. Thus, when at the end of the fifteenth century the European world-economy entered a new phase of expansion under the impact of the so-called Great Discoveries – the opening up of a direct trade link between Europe and the East Indies, and of the conquest and plunder of the Americas – the capitalist classes of Venice, Florence, and Milan played no active role in the promotion and organization of the expansion. By then, their surplus capital had been fully absorbed by the process of state-making and had thereby lost much of its previous flexibility. Worse still, as we saw in chapter 1, their conspicuous success in the accumulation of wealth and power induced the surrounding territorialist organizations to follow in their path of development but on a much larger scale. As these "modernized" territorialist organizations sought to divert trade from the city-states to their own domains, or to conquer the city-states themselves, the latter were forced to divert an increasing proportion of their resources to protect themselves.

The Great Discoveries and the trade expansion which they engendered were integral aspects of the attempt of territorialist rulers to divert trade from the Italian city-states to their own domains. As such, they ran counter to the interests of the ruling groups and capitalist classes of these city-states, and occurred behind their back or against their will. There was none the less an important exception to this general rule. This exception was the Genoese capitalist class, which actively promoted, monitored, and benefited from the trade expansion from beginning to end and thereby gave rise to the first of our systemic cycles of accumulation.

The First (Genoese) Systemic Cycle of Accumulation

As anticipated in the Introduction, our notion of systemic cycles of accumulation is derived from Braudel's observation that the maturity of every major development of the capitalist world-economy is heralded by a particular switch from trade in commodities to trade in money. Braudel makes this observation in connection with the Dutch switch that took place in about 1740, which he likens to the British switch of the late nineteenth century and to two earlier Genoese switches, one in the fifteenth and one in the sixteenth century. It may seem curious at first sight that Genoese merchant bankers, rather than the more famous Florentine or Augsburg financiers, should be singled out as the true predecessors of Dutch and British finance capitalism. Braudel does not make the reasons of this choice explicit, but the choice is none the less justified on various grounds, some of which bear directly on our definition of systemic cycles of accumulation.

Let us begin by noting that Genoese finance capitalism developed in the latter half of the fourteenth century under the impact of the same systemic circumstances as the finance capitalism of other Italian city-states. As competitive pressures intensified and the power struggle escalated, surplus capital that no longer found profitable investment in trade was held liquid and used to finance the growing public debts of the city-states, whose assets and future revenues were thereby alienated more thoroughly than ever to their respective capitalist classes. Genoa was in the forefront of this movement, and with the formation of the *Casa di San Giorgio* in

1407, it created an institution for the control of public finances by private creditors which in this respect was not to be paralleled in effectiveness or sophistication until the Bank of England was established almost three centuries later.

From the start, however, the development of Genoese finance capitalism showed peculiarities of its own. Thus, the takeover of Genoese public finances by the private creditors incorporated in the *Casa di San Giorgio* did not mark the beginning of the takeover of the Republic's government by moneyed interests and of an ever-increasing diversion of surplus capital to state-making activities, as in different ways was happening in Venice and Florence. On the contrary, the establishment of the *Casa di San Giorgio* simply institutionalized a dualism of power and an inherent political instability that had long characterized the Genoese state and would continue to do so until Andrea Doria's constitutional reforms of 1528. "The whole history of the Genoese *quattrocento*," according to Jacques Heers, "is the history of a true social and political crisis." But it was in this same century of permanent social and political crisis that Genoa became the city where capitalism developed

> in all its forms, with its precise and modern techniques; where capital [came] to control every economic activity; where banks [came] to occupy a position of great importance. Hence, a city that saw the rapid formation of a class of rich and powerful businessmen involved simultaneously or successively in banking, in commerce, and in industry; in short, a class of big capitalists in the most modern sense of the word. (Heers 1961: 610)

From this point of view, Genoese capitalism in the fifteenth century was developing along a path that diverged radically from that of all the other big Italian city-states. To different degrees and in different ways, Milanese, Venetian, and Florentine capitalism were all developing in the direction of state-making and of increasingly "rigid" strategies and structures of capital accumulation. Genoese capitalism, in contrast, was moving in the direction of market-making and of increasingly "flexible" strategies and structures of accumulation. This exceptionalism had deep roots in a unique combination of local and systemic circumstances.

Locally, the deepest roots of Genoese exceptionalism lay in the aristocratic origins of Genoese capitalism and in the precociousness with which the Genoese city-state had annexed the surrounding countryside. By the time Venice began to annex the *Terraferma*, Milan Lombardy, and Florence Tuscany, Genoa had long extended its jurisdiction over most of Liguria – from Porto Venere to Monaco, and from the sea to the ridge of the Apennines, as the Genoese government liked to claim. The claim was none the less largely nominal because much of the long, narrow, and mountainous territory enclosed by these boundaries was divided into fiefs of the small and highly exclusive Genoese landed aristocracy. This landed aristocracy had provided the mercantile expansion of Genoa with its initial entrepreneurial impulse, and had remained at the head of the most important Genoese commercial undertakings through the peak of that expansion in the late thirteenth century. But as returns to resources invested in trade fell, the Genoese landed aristocracy moved fast to "refeudalize" itself by transferring resources back to the appropriation of rural space and to the formation of powerful private armies – space and armies which the Genoese government had no means of controlling, let alone commanding (Heers 1961: 538, 590–1).

In Genoa, the reallocation of surplus capital from long-distance trade to investment in landownership and state-making thus occurred differently, and with opposite social consequences, compared with Venice or Florence. In Venice, and to a lesser extent in Florence, the reallocation was promoted and organized by the urban merchant classes themselves as a means to the twofold end of finding a secure store of value for the surplus capital which they controlled and of buttressing their power both domestically and internationally. In Genoa, in contrast, the reallocation was promoted and organized by a landed aristocracy reinvigorated by the preceding commercial expansion, as a means to the end of reaffirming on a larger scale its monopolistic control over the use of violence and over territorial and demographic resources. Far from benefiting the urban merchant classes, this kind of reallocation created an insurmountable social barrier to the domestic expansion of their wealth and power. To be sure, the Genoese urban merchant classes had benefited greatly from their association with a commercially minded landed aristocracy. But as the trade expansion drew to a close and the landed aristocracy turned the rural domains of the Genoese state into "fiefs" of its own, this very association blocked the transformation of the Genoese urban merchant classes into an aristocracy along the Venetian or the Florentine paths, and condemned them instead to hold the bulk of their surplus capital in liquid form:

S'il est relativement facile d'accéder à la classe des marchands ou des banquiers, si l'on peut ... prendre assez vite le titre de "nobilus", la classe des seigneurs, la noblesse foncière, est sévèrement fermée. Quelques très rares exceptions mises à part, on ne voit pas de seigneurs vendre leurs châteaux ou leur droit à des marchands. Le régime de l'indivision et de l'administration en commun maintient plus solide la tutelle des lignages. ... Le divorce entre les deux [classes] est très net: propriétés, genre de vie, idéal. Leurs intérêts sont souvent complètement opposés. Leurs conceptions politiques aussi. Les uns veulent une Commune bourgeois et ont réalisé déjà leur idéal de bon gouvernement à San Giorgio; les autres désirent le maintien de leurs privilèges et visent si possible une seigneurie à la façon du duché de Milan. L'opposition entre ces deux classes dirigeantes qui disposent de moyens très différents, mais puissants, explique les troubles politiques dont souffre la cité.

While it may be relatively easy to rise to the merchant or banking class ... and acquire the title of "nobilus" quite quickly, entry into the nobility or landed aristocracy is firmly closed. A few rare exceptions apart, one does not find aristocrats selling their castles or their commercial rights. The system of joint ownership and of shared administration preserves the lineage. . . . The separation of the two [classes] is clear-cut: property, lifestyle, aspirations. Their interests are often completely opposed. Likewise their political ideas. One class wants a bourgeois polity and has already realized its ideal in San Giorgio; the other wishes to retain its privileges, and envisages, if possible, a seignory like that of the Duchy of Milan. This opposition between the two ruling classes, who have such different, yet powerful means at their disposal, explains the political turmoil from which the city suffers. (Heers 1961: 561–2)

The establishment of the *Casa di San Giorgio* in 1407 can thus be interpreted as a critical moment in the process of self-organization of the Genoese capitalist class in a situation of fundamental political impasse between the power of money and the power of the sword. The escalation of the competitive struggle between the city-states, by inflating Genoa's public debt, strengthened the hand of the city's moneyed interests, but not sufficiently to overcome the power of the landed aristocracy. The latter controlled the means of violence and the sources of ground rent in the surrounding countryside and continued to participate in the city's governmental and business processes if and when it was in its own interests. Nevertheless, the fact that the power of money could not overcome the power of the sword did not mean that the moneyed interests could not organize themselves more effectively to match the solidarity of the landed aristocracy. This indeed is what was achieved by the incorporation of the private creditors of the Genoese government in the *Casa di San Giorgio*.

The self-organization of moneyed interests did nothing to stabilize political life in Genoa. Ever since 1339 – when a popular revolt against the government of the aristocracy had installed a commoner as Doge – the head of the Genoese government had always been chosen from the ranks of the so-called *popolo*, that is, commoners. Nominally, the Doge was the military leader of the Genoese state, but real military power had remained firmly in the hands of the landed aristocracy. With the formation of the *Casa di San Giorgio*, the administration of the government's revenues was progressively taken over by this organization, so that the military impotence of the Genoese government was compounded by its financial disempowerment.

If the financial disempowerment of the Genoese government did not help in bringing stability to Genoa's political life – which remained as turbulent as ever – it did none the less contribute to solving the city's financial troubles and to fostering the technical virtuosity of the Genoese capitalist class in the money trades. The ideology of "sound money" reached its apogee in nineteenth-century Britain and has found its most dogmatic supporters in late twentieth-century US academic circles. But its practice first flourished in fifteenth-century Genoa.

The central tenet of this practice was the notion that the availability of "good money" was essential to the processes of capital accumulation. Then, as now, capitalist organizations – be they business enterprises, governments, or combinations of the two – needed a sound and reliable unit of account with which to measure the profit and losses of their commercial and financial operations. If no such standard was available, then as now, these organizations were bound to mistake losses for profits, and vice versa, simply because of variations in the value of the means of payments with which their business was carried out. They were bound, that is, to fall victim to so-called monetary illusions. But were they to command a unit of account that effectively discounted these variations, far from falling victims to monetary illusions, they could profit hand-somely from the monetary illusions of those from whom they bought and borrowed, and to whom they sold and lent.

The merchant bankers of fifteenth-century Genoa understood very well that it was neither in their power nor in their interest to eliminate variations in the value of actually circulating money, including the money that circulated in Genoa – what they called "current money." But by the middle of the century they had come to realize that it was both in their interest and in their power to introduce an invariant unit of account with which to settle their mutual business, assess accurately the profitability of their far-flung commercial and financial deals, and be in a position to profit rather than lose from variations in time and space in the value of actually circulating money. Thus, in 1447 a law was passed requiring all business accounts relating to currency exchanges to be held in gold coin of fixed weight – a unit of account which soon became the *lira di buona moneta*, sometimes also called *moneta di cambio*. From the early 1450s onwards, this "good money" became the standard unit of Genoese business accounts not just for currency exchanges but for all transactions, whereas "current money" of variable value remained the standard means of exchange (Heers 1961: 52–5, 95–6).

This monetary reform gave new impulse to the ongoing flourishing of monetary instruments and techniques. If modern high finance was a Florentine invention, the real birthplace of modern finance capitalism in all its forms was mid-fifteenth-century Genoa:

[L]es techniques génoises sont, dès le milieu du Quattrocento, celles qui caractérisent le capitalisme de l'ère moderne. Chèques et lettres de change sont d'un emploi courant et le principe de l'endossement y est admis; l'essentiel des paiements s'effectue par virements des comptes et la ville dispose d'une monnaie de banque stable et facile. C'est pourquoi on trouve, sans doute, moins nécessaire de recourir à l'affaiblissement de la monnaie pour augmenter les moyens de paiement.... C'est une période de monnaie beaucoup plus stable. Car Gênes, contrairement aux régions voisines moins évoluées (à la France surtout), *dispose d'une abondance relative des moyens de paiements*. Elle connaît le secret du régime capitaliste moderne qui consiste à "retarder les paiements ou les remboursements et faire perpétuellement chevaucher ces retards les uns sur les autres"; d'un régime "qui mourrait d'un apurement simultané de tous les comptes."

Genoese [monetary] techniques, from the middle of the Quattrocento, are those characteristic of present-day capitalism. Cheques and bills of exchange are in current usage and the principle of endorsement is accepted; most payments are made through bank transfer and the city has at its disposal a stable and ready money of account. This is why it was undoubtedly less necessary to resort to monetary devaluation to increase the means of payment.... It is a period of much more stable money. Because Genoa, unlike its neighbouring, but less advanced regions (France especially), *has at its disposal a relative abundance of means of payment*. It knows the secret of the modern capitalist system which consists of "delaying payments and settlements and continuously making these deferrals overlap one another"; a system "which would collapse if all the accounts were cleared simultaneously." (Heers 1961: 96; emphasis added; quotations from Bloch 1955)

Neither the political troubles, nor the relative abundance of means of payments, nor indeed the technical virtuosity of Genoese capitalism in the fifteenth century were the outcome of local circumstances alone. On the contrary, developments in Genoa were radically shaped by the wider Italian, European, and Eurasian systemic contexts, which were only in small part the making of Genoa. The most important of these systemic circumstances was no doubt the disintegration of the Eurasian trading system within which Genoa's commercial fortunes of the late thirteenth and early fourteenth centuries had been made.

These fortunes were built primarily on the competitiveness of the Central Asian trade route to China and on the success with which Genoese enterprise managed to establish a quasi-monopolistic control over the Black Sea "terminal" of this route. As long as the Mongol empire ensured access to and security of the Central Asian route, and Genoa retained its military superiority in the Black Sea region, Genoese trade prospered and Genoese enterprises grew in scale, scope, and number. But as soon as the decline of Mongol power made the Central Asian trade route less competitive and secure, and the rise of Ottoman power in Asia Minor undermined and then destroyed Genoese supremacy in the Black Sea region, the wheel of fortune turned. The prosperity of Genoese trade waned and the inflated Genoese military–commercial apparatus suddenly faced the imperative of fundamental restructuring (cf. Heers 1961: 366–72; Abu-Lughod 1989: 128–9).

Genoa's response to the squeeze on profitable trade opportunities along the Central Asian route was to seek even tighter control over the other trades that were developing in the Black Sea region – grain, timber, furs, and slaves. As Heers (1961: 367) notes, the War of Chioggia against Venice (1376–81) was essentially a war fought in an attempt to impose a commercial monopoly in the Black Sea. But as we know, the attempt backfired: Genoa lost the war, and the Peace of Turin imposed even tighter Venetian control over Asian trade via the southern route. From then on, Genoa's power in the Black Sea and in the eastern Mediterranean declined rapidly under the impact of rapid Turkish advances, while opportunities to redirect expansion closer to home were held in check by Catalan–Aragonese power in the northwestern Mediterranean.

Genoese trade was thus hit particularly hard by the tapering off of the expansion in Eurasian trade. It was also hit far harder than the trade of any of the other big Italian city-states. Milan's metal trades benefited greatly from the escalation of warfare across Europe; after the traumatic restructuring of the 1340s, Florentine business found new, fairly well protected, and highly profitable market niches in high-quality textile production and in high finance; and Venice profited far more than it lost from the same trends and events that were causing Genoa's troubles. As Abu-Lughod (1989: 129) puts it, "Venice's 'bet' on the southern sea route proved a fortunate one." The Central Asian route controlled by Genoa and the southern Asian route controlled by Venice were somewhat complementary but for the most part competed with one another. Hence, the disruption and eventual closure of the northern route eased competitive pressures on Venetian trade, and of course that became even greater once Genoa's presence in the eastern Mediterranean had been curtailed by its defeat in the War of Chioggia.

Trends and events in Genoa in the latter half of the fourteenth century and in the fifteenth century were profoundly influenced by this squeeze on Genoese networks of long-distance trade and by the concomitant deterioration in the city's power position in the Mediterranean world-economy and in the Italian city-state system. The rapid closing down of Genoa's Central Asian route to China, the closing in of Ottoman, Venetian, and Catalan–Aragonese power on Genoese trade in the Mediterranean, the rise of powerful city-states all around Genoa's metropolitan domains – this configuration of circumstances must have looked quite hopeless to the Genoese. And it certainly makes sensible the decision of the Genoese landed aristocracy to withdraw from commerce and to invest the profits of trade in land, castles, and armies in the Ligurian region.

Sensible as it was, this retrenchment deepened the crisis of over-accumulation which "afflicted" the bourgeois element of the Genoese merchant classes. As already noted, it considerably narrowed the oppor-tunities open to the bourgeoisie in finding rewarding outlets for its surplus capital in landownership and state-making. Worse still, it deprived the Genoese bourgeoisie of much needed protection in the world-economy at large.

For the Genoese bourgeoisie, unlike the Venetian, had never been self-sufficient in organizing the protection needed by its long-distance traffics – a task which had always been undertaken by the Genoese landed aristocracy-turned-merchant. As long as the interest of this aristocratic element in commercial enterprise remained strong, the arrangement had its advantages because it enabled the bourgeoisie to concentrate on, and specialize in, strictly commercial pursuits. But as that interest waned and the landed aristocracy withdrew from commerce, the bourgeoisie was left unprotected in an increasingly hostile world.

Under these circumstances it was only natural for a large fraction of Genoese capital and commercial personnel to fall back on the Genoese domestic economy in spite of the lack of attractive investment opportun-ities in landownership and state-making activities. This domestic implo-sion of the Genoese regime of accumulation was the single most important factor underlying the tendencies which we have seen charac-terized Genoa in the fifteenth century – political turbulence, over-abundance of means of payments, and the creation of new monetary instruments and techniques. In and by themselves, however, these tendencies could not and did not resolve the crisis of overaccumulation of which they were an expression. Even virtuosity in the money trades, which would later become a key ingredient of Genoese capitalist expansion, did very little to resolve the crisis of Genoese capitalism for most of the fifteenth century.

Deep down, however, and in response to the crisis, Genoese networks of trade and accumulation were being restructured radically and in a way that, over time, turned Genoese merchant bankers into the most powerful capitalist class of sixteenth-century Europe. Genoese military–commercial power was being squeezed out of the Black Sea and eastern Mediterranean regions by Turkish and Venetian power and was simulta-neously held in check in the northwestern Mediterranean by Catalan and Aragonese power. Nevertheless, as John Elliott (1970a: 38) observes, while the war between the Genoese state and the Catalan–Aragonese federation was waged indecisively for most of the fifteenth century, Genoese capital outmaneuvered Catalan capital throughout the Iberian peninsula. The earliest victory was won in the sphere of high finance. Genoese merchant bankers promptly seized the opportunities created by the collapse of Barcelona's leading private banks in the crash of the early 1380s to become the most important financiers in the Iberian region – very much as the Medici on a grander scale had taken advantage of the collapse of Bardi and Peruzzi in the crash of the 1340s. However, the victory that proved most decisive in the making of subsequent Genoese fortunes was the takeover of Castilian trade:

> The growth of Castile's wool trade had created new commercial opportunities, which the Catalans, embattled on so many fronts, were in no position to seize. It was, instead, the Genoese who settled in Córdoba, Cadiz, and Seville, built up a solid alliance with Castile, and secured control of the wool exports from Spain's southern ports. Once they had obtained this foothold, the Genoese were well placed to entrench themselves at one strategic point after another in the Castilian economy, and so prepare the way for their future participation in the lucrative trade between Seville and Castile's colonial empire. This Genoese predominance decisively influenced the course of sixteenth-century Spanish development. If the Catalans rather than the Genoese had won the struggle for entry into the Castilian commercial system, the history of a united Spain would have taken a profoundly different turn. (Elliott 1970a: 39)

And so would have the history of the capitalist world-economy. For all we know, we would be speaking here of a "Catalan" or "Spanish" systemic cycle of accumulation – or, perhaps, we would not be speaking of systemic cycles of accumulation at all. The reason why we are speaking of a Genoese cycle, however, is not that at a critical juncture the Catalans were "embattled on so many fronts," since the Genoese were embattled on even more fronts. In part, to paraphrase Abu-Lughod's dictum concerning Venice, the reason is that the Genoese "gamble" on Castilian trade proved a fortunate one. Even more than in the case of the Venetian "gamble" on the southern Asian trade route, chance was none the less only a minor part of the Genoese story.

The most important part was that the Genoese placed their "bets" very carefully and, more important, backed them up with a repertoire of monetary and organizational means that few, if any, of their actual or potential competitors could match. In a sense, the matrix of the sixteenth-century fortunes of the Genoese capitalist class were its "misfortunes" of the late fourteenth and early fifteenth centuries. As the military–commercial empire that the Genoese had built in earlier centuries began to disintegrate, and the Genoese landed aristocracy withdrew from commerce to "refeudalize," the bourgeois element of the Genoese merchant classes came to be "afflicted" by a serious and chronic disproportion between, on the one side, its huge reserves of money, information, business know-how, and connections, and, on the other side, its meager capabilities to protect itself and its traffics in an increasingly competitive and hostile world. The Iberian peninsula was the place that offered the best prospects of a prompt and favorable resolution of this fundamental disproportion for three main reasons.

As we can see from figure 4, the southern part of the Iberian peninsula and the nearby Maghreb were the regions of the Mediterranean that had been more thoroughly "monopolized" by Genoese enterprise. It was only natural that Genoese business would respond to increasing pressure elsewhere by retreating to this stronghold. And so it did and, among other things, in the first half of the fifteenth century it transformed the still independent kingdom of Granada – by far the most prosperous agro-industrial center of the region – into "a true Genoese economic colony" (Heers 1961: 477; 1979: ch. 7).

Second, the Iberian peninsula, for Genoese business, was not just the natural stronghold to which to retreat, but also the natural outpost from which to advance in search of the supplies of which it was being deprived. As the Venetians tightened their control over German silver and Asian spices, it became imperative for Genoese business, minimally, to tighten its control over the African gold that was being brought to Maghreb ports by the Saharan caravan trade and, optimally, to find an Atlantic trade route to the East to replace the lost Central Asian route. From both points of view, a strong presence in the Iberian peninsula was of great strategic importance (Heers 1961: 68–9, 473; 1979: chs 4 and 8; Pannikar 1953: 23).

Third, and most important, the Iberian peninsula, for the Genoese capitalist class, was the most promising place to find what it needed most: effective and enterprising "protection-producing" partners who could be enticed to assume the role formerly played by the Genoese landed aristocracy. The territorialist rulers of emerging Portugal and Spain appeared very early to be eminently suitable for the purpose thanks to the combination of religious fanaticism and political entrepreneurship which made them resemble closely the Genoese aristocrats-turned-merchants of earlier times. The most famous of the precursors and inspirers of the European Discoveries, the Portuguese prince, Henry the Navigator, was a "staunchly medieval figure . . . [obsessed] with the idea of the Crusade" (Parry 1981: 35–6). And the most successful of the entrepreneurs of the Discoveries, Queen Isabella of Castile, was the leader of a new crusade aimed at expanding the territorial domain of Christian and Castilian power:

The expulsion of the Jews, the violent baptism of the Moors of Granada, the extraordinary powers entrusted to the new Inquisition . . . represented both a reaction against the intensified Muslim pressure on Christendom since the fall of Constantinople, and an intensification of religious fervor, and so of religious intolerance, in Spain. This intensification of zeal, this new enthusiasm for conversion, quickly traveled to the New World, where it was to find new and more effective forms of expression. (Parry 1981: 29)

The spirit of the crusade went hand in hand with a prompt adherence to the spirit of the Renaissance, the encouragement of learning, the cult of the individual and, above all, the new art of politics:

> Like many Italian rulers, Isabella of Castile owed her throne to a mixture of war and diplomacy. A masterful restoration of public order and discipline was one of her major achievements.... Machiavelli's principles of statecraft had no more successful exemplars than Ferdinand of Aragon and John II of Portugal.... [This] cult of governmental expediency ... helped to prepare men's minds for the immense task of political and administrative improvisation which was to confront Spanish government in the New World. (Parry 1981: 32–3)

Henri Pirenne once remarked that the Genoese, unlike the Venetians, were not "merchants from the very beginning" and "reminded one rather of the Christians of Spain. Like them they made war upon the infidel with a passionate religious enthusiasm; a Holy War, but a very profitable one.... In them religious passion and the appetite for lucre were merged in a spirit of enterprise" (quoted in Cox 1959: 181). The analogy can be taken further by noting that the trans-oceanic expansion of Iberian commerce in the late fifteenth and early sixteenth centuries – like the expansion of Genoese commerce in earlier epochs, but unlike the expansion of Venetian commerce at any time – was promoted and organized by a dichotomous entrepreneurial agency held together by an organic relationship of "political exchange."

The substantive meaning of the expression "political exchange" as used here is a variant of Schumpeter's (1954: 138) contention that "without protection by some non-bourgeois group, the bourgeoisie is politically helpless and unable not only to lead its nation but even to take care of its particular class interest." In Schumpeter's view, the main historical exception to this rule was the management of the affairs of city-states like the Venetian and Genoese republics – an exception which he attributes to the fact that "[b]efore the advent of the modern metropolis, which is no longer a bourgeois affair, city management was akin to business management." Even the Dutch republic was only a partial exception to this rule, as witnessed by the fact that "in practically every emergency [the merchant's republic] had to hand over the reins to a warlord of feudal complexion."

The rise of national states proper put the business of state- and war-making further beyond the reach of the bourgeoisie and produced an "amphibial" structure of rule consisting of a bourgeois and an aristocratic element: "All this was more than atavism. It was an active symbiosis of two social strata, one of which no doubt supported the other economically but was in turn supported by the other politically." That this was no mere atavism but an active symbiosis is best demonstrated by the English experience:

> The aristocratic element [in England] continued to rule the roost *right to the end of intact and vital capitalism.* No doubt that element ... currently absorbed the brains from other strata that drifted into politics; it made itself the representative of bourgeois interests and fought the battles of the bourgeoisie; it had to surrender its last legal privileges; but with these qualifications, and for ends no longer its own, it continued to man the political engine, to manage the state, to govern. (Schumpeter 1954: 135–7; emphasis in the original)

Schumpeter's contention broadly corresponds to our earlier claim that, by the *Communist Manifesto*'s definition of the capitalist state ("but a committee for managing the common affairs of the whole bourgeoisie"), the hegemonic capitalist states of increasing size and complexity that created and expanded the modern interstate system appear to have been increasingly diluted versions of the ideotypical standards of the capitalist state realized by Venice in early modern times. In both contentions, the relationship of political exchange which links the capitalist to the non-capitalist component of hegemonic ruling groups concerns exclusively state-making processes. The thesis advanced here, in contrast, is that even in world-scale processes of capital accumulation the agency of expansion has been dichotomous in structure.

More specifically, it is maintained that the material expansion of the first (Genoese) systemic cycle of accumulation was promoted and organized by a dichotomous agency consisting of an (Iberian) aristocratic territorialist component – which specialized in the provision of protection and in the pursuit of power – and of a (Genoese) bourgeois capitalist component – which specialized in the buying and selling of commodities and in the pursuit of profit. These specializations complemented one another, and their mutual benefits brought together – and as long as they lasted, held together – the two heterogeneous components of the agency of expansion in a relationship of political exchange in which, on the one side, the pursuit of power of the territorialist component created profitable trade opportunities for the capitalist component and, on the other side, the pursuit of profit of the latter strengthened the effectiveness and efficiency of the protection-producing apparatus of the territorialist component.

In the fifteenth century, Iberian territorialist rulers and Genoese capitalist merchant bankers were brought together in a relationship of this kind for the simple reason that each side could provide the other with what it most needed; and the relationship endured because this relationship of complementarity was continually reproduced by the successful specialization of both sides in their respective pursuits. What the Genoese capitalist class most needed in the fifteenth century was an enlargement of its commercial space sufficient to accommodate its huge surplus of capital and personnel and to keep alive its far-flung business networks. The more intensive exploitation of its market niche in the southwestern Mediterranean was just a palliative which at best slowed down implosion and decline. What it really needed to resolve its long crisis was a major breakthrough which, however, the Genoese state, embattled on many fronts and internally divided, was in no position to undertake.

Nor was such an undertaking within the narrowly calculating horizon of the Genoese capitalist class acting on its own. To be sure, the pursuit of profit had long spurred Genoese business to explore the west African coast:

> It was when gold was particularly high in value ... that the Vivaldi brothers of Genoa tried to circumnavigate Africa in the late 13th century, two centuries before Vasco da Gama. They lost their way, but the sailors sent to look for them by the capitalist who had financed them, Teodisio d'Oria, re-discovered the "Happy Isles" of antiquity, the Canaries.... After 1350 these attempts ceased because the ratio of gold to silver returned to a more normal level, and economic activity in Europe decreased; when around 1450 it picked up again and gold increased in value, the Oceanic and African expeditions began again. (Vilar 1976: 47–8)

Thus, Genoese capitalists sponsored an ambitious expedition across the Sahara in 1447 and two voyages along the west African coast in the 1450s – all in search of direct access to African gold. But the slow returns of this kind of undertaking and, above all, the very *incalculability* of the prospective financial costs and benefits of expansion in uncharted waters made Genoese capital reluctant to proceed in this direction with the determination and resources needed to make a breakthrough. As Heers observes with specific reference to Genoese merchant bankers,

> [l]'homme d'affaires italien est trop volontiers présenté comme avide de tenter quelque grosse opération risquée et très lucrative. Ce n'est plus tellement le cas au XVe siècle. Ni le commerce, ni la finance ne sont des "aventures", mais des industries exercées sur une échelle de plus en plus grande et dont les techniques

bien rodées laissent peu de place au hasard.

The Italian businessman is too readily portrayed as overeager to risk a hazardous but lucrative venture. That was no longer the case in the fifteenth century. Neither commerce nor finance are "adventures" but are industries run on a bigger and bigger scale and whose tried and tested techniques leave little to chance. (Heers 1961: 53)

In short, the Genoese capitalist class in the fifteenth century can be described as being caught in a fundamental impasse. On the one hand, the loss of the long-distance trade opportunities of earlier times led to domestic competitive struggles and endless feuds which were destructive of profits and to the withering away of unused or unusable business networks and resources scattered all over the world-economy. On the other hand, the opening up of new long-distance trade opportunities on a scale sufficient to reverse these tendencies involved risks that were not just high but incalculable and, as such, beyond the horizon of rational capitalist enterprise. In other words, the very logic of profit-making restrained the self-expansion of Genoese capital and thereby threatened it with self-destruction.

The obvious way out of this impasse was to enter into a relationship of political exchange with territorialist rulers like the Iberians who were driven to open up new commercial spaces by motives other than calculable profit and furthermore were so badly in need of the kind of services that the Genoese capitalist class was best equipped to provide as to let it free to organize its traffic in currencies and commodities as it saw fit. The spirit of the crusade was an excellent guarantee that Iberian expansion in uncharted waters would proceed unencumbered by constant rational calculations of pecuniary costs and benefits. And adherence to the spirit of the Renaissance was as good a guarantee as any that the promoters and organizers of the expansion would continue to appreciate the advantages of association with one of the largest, most solvent, and best connected merchant classes of the time – a class, moreover, that was already well entrenched in the southern part of the Iberian peninsula. As the association formed and the so-called Great Discoveries consolidated it, Genoese capitalism was finally delivered from its long crisis and propelled towards its moment of greatest expansion.

By 1519 the power of Genoese capital was already such as to enable it to play a critical role in the election of Charles V, then king of Spain, to the title of emperor at the expense of the French king, Francis I. On this occasion, Ehrenberg (1985: 74) maintains, the German Electoral princes "would never have chosen Charles had not the Fugger helped his cause with their cash, and still more with their powerful credit." But the operation would never have succeeded had not Genoese merchant bankers mobilized their bills of exchange to enable the Fuggers and the Welsers to have at their disposal the money that was needed at short notice in many different places to buy the votes of the German princes (Boyer-Xambeau, Deleplace, and Gillard 1991: 26).

Over the next forty years the fortunes of the Fuggers grew spectacularly, only to decline rapidly in a morass of bad credits, depreciating assets, and increasing indebtedness. In this period the Fuggers' centrality in European high finance resembled that of the Medici a century earlier, although the papal foundations of the Medici's business were far more solid than the imperial foundations of the Fuggers' business. This centrality has led some historians to speak of the age of Charles V as the "age of the Fuggers." If centrality in high finance is all that this phrase is meant to imply, the designation is accurate. But the most important tendencies of the capitalist world-economy at this time were not unfolding in the sphere of high finance. Behind the scenes, the less visible power of Genoese business continued to grow through the consolidation and further expansion of its system-wide trade networks until, in the fullness of time, it felt strong enough to make its own bid for control over the finances of Imperial Spain at the expense of the exhausted Fuggers and other Augsburg financiers operating out of Antwerp.

What eventually exhausted the Fuggers and cleared the way for the Genoese bid was above all the narrow spatial and functional base of their business fortunes – a narrowness that made them the servants rather than the masters of Charles V's continual financial straits. From the very start, their business combined trade in silver and copper with loans to German princes. Their strategy of accumulation was simple enough: the profits of trade in metals were invested in loans to princes in exchange for rights or properties in mines, which in turn enabled them to expand their trade in metals and the mass of profits that could be turned into new loans, mineral rights, and properties, and so on in an "endless" expansionary chain. At the beginning of the sixteenth century, the self-expansion of capital according to this simple formula suddenly accelerated and became truly explosive by virtue of an exceptionally favorable conjuncture for German silver created by the arrival in Europe of the Portuguese supply of Asian spices. In Antwerp this created an alternative market for German silver, the supply of which had thus far been under the monopsonistic domination of the Venetian market. As a result, the capital of Augsburg merchant bankers suddenly multiplied in value and provided them with the means needed to select the emperor of their choice in the election of 1519 (Ehrenberg 1985: 64–74; Braudel 1984: 148–50).

Soon after 1519, however, the favorable conjuncture that had made the fortunes of the Augsburg merchants began drawing to a rapid close. Over the next decade or so, the arrival of the Spanish supply of American silver in Europe diverted a good part of the Portuguese traffic in Asian spices to Seville and, worse still, began outcompeting German silver in all European markets, leading to a virtual stoppage of production in German mines after 1535 (Braudel 1984: 150). The adverse conjuncture induced the Fuggers to become ever more heavily enmeshed in financing the endless wars of their imperial partner-master. According to an agent of the Welsers, by the mid-1540s "the Fugger were tired of Imperial loans; they had already let themselves in so deep that they had to wait a long time before they could get their money again." In the early 1550s, Anton Fugger complained repeatedly to his agent, Matthew Oertel, that "no Resolution as to our debts will come from the Court. Verily in these heavy times they have much else to do, but it is yet hazardous and these affairs are tedious." These complaints notwithstanding, the Fuggers were drawn into new and bigger loans in a vain attempt to entice Charles V to repay or at least service his existing debts. And this they did by themselves borrowing more and more heavily in Antwerp's financial market (Ehrenberg 1985: 101, 109–14):

> So the thing went on. Instead of the Fugger having their old advances repaid, [in 1556–57] they had to lend the House of [Habsburg] in a space of one and a half years, more money than they had ever lent before in so short a time. [The Emperor's secretary] Erasso fairly pumped them dry; and they got no thanks for this either from him or his master. (Ehrenberg 1985: 114)

Having squeezed all there was to be squeezed out of the Fuggers, the Habsburg stopped borrowing from them after 1557 and relied more and more exclusively for this purpose on the Genoese, who "had known how to render themselves indispensable to the Spanish court, while the Fuggers, tied by their past and their lack of enterprise, were kept to the Spanish business and the old markets, and were prevented from making use of the fresh centres of trade and finance which were then developing" (Ehrenberg 1985: 119). Although superficially the power of the Fuggers at its height resembled that of the Medici a century earlier, their story was thus a replica of the vicissitudes of the Bardi and Peruzzi two centuries earlier. They did not go bankrupt like the Bardi and Peruzzi but, like them, they overextended themselves at the wrong time, with the result that their business was ruined by the Habsburg default of 1557 and by the crisis that over the next five years shook the European financial and trading system to its foundations.

The true Medici of the sixteenth century were a clique of Genoese merchant bankers, the so-called *nobili vecchi*, who in the midst of the crisis abandoned trade to become the bankers of the government of Imperial Spain in the nearly absolute certainty that in this role they would make rather than lose money. This switch from trade to high finance of the *nobili vecchi* is taken by Braudel as the beginning of what, following Ehrenberg and Felipe Ruíz Martin, he calls the "age of the Genoese" (1557–1627). During these seventy years, Genoese merchant bankers exercised a rule over European finances comparable to that exercised in the twentieth century by the Bank for International Settlements at Basle – "a rule that was so discreet and sophisticated that historians for a long time failed to notice it" (Braudel 1984: 157, 164).

This rule was exercised through the organization, control, and management of an invisible link between the more than ever overabundant supply of money capital of northern Italy and the permanent financial straits of Imperial Spain:

> By means of the dominant system of the Piacenza fairs, the capital of the Italian cities was all drained towards Genoa. And a multitude of small investors, Genoese and others, entrusted their savings to the bankers for modest returns. There was thus a permanent link between the finances of Spain and the economy of the Italian Peninsula – hence the upsets which regularly followed the bankruptcies in Madrid; the 1595 bankruptcy was passed on and did much damage to the savers and investors of Venice. At the same time in Venice itself, the Genoese, since they controlled the supply of silver which they delivered in vast quantities to the *Zecca*, had acquired control of currency exchange and maritime insurance. (Braudel 1984: 168)

The Genoese financiers who created, managed, and profited from this systemic link between Iberian power and Italian money were themselves affected by a whole series of crises – in 1575, 1596, 1607, 1627, and 1647 – all of which had Spanish origins. Unlike the Fuggers, however, they were not ruined by these crises since they always managed to shift losses and disruptions onto clients or competitors. To be sure, Genoese rule over European high finance eventually withered away and then ceased altogether. But the fruits of that rule remained intact, and more than two centuries later found a new field of investment in the political and economic unification of Italy, of which Genoese finance capital was one of the main sponsors and beneficiaries (Braudel 1984: 162, 169–73).

Genoese rule over European high finance continued by other means the organic relationship of political exchange that since the fifteenth century had intertwined the fortunes of the Genoese capitalist class with those of Iberian territorialist rulers. Finance rather than trade had now become the primary locus of the relationship, but the relationship remained beneficial to both partners. The shift in locus propped up not just the profitability of Genoese business but the power pursuits of Imperial Spain as well. "What made the Genoese merchants so indispensable to the king of Spain was their ability to convert the intermittent flow of silver from America to Seville into a steady stream." After 1567, the Spanish troops fighting in the Netherlands demanded and obtained regular monthly payments in gold coin. "So the Genoese had to convert American silver into gold" (Braudel 1982: 524–5). As Ehrenberg pointed out, "it was not the Potosi silver mines, but the Genoese fairs of exchange which made it possible for Philip II to conduct his world power policy decade after decade" (quoted in Kriedte 1983: 47).

Over time, no amount of technical virtuosity on the part of Genoese financiers could keep at bay the effects of increasingly unfavorable systemic circumstances which, as we shall see, Genoese strategies of accumulation tended to worsen rather than improve. The withering away of Genoese dominance in European high finance, the progressive erosion of the power of Imperial Spain, and the break-up of the Genoese–Iberian alliance cannot be understood except in the context of the escalating competitive power struggles that made the fortunes of Dutch capitalism. But before we proceed to examine the rise of Dutch capitalism to the dominant structure of the European world-economy, let us underscore what was most original about the Genoese-led financial expansion of the late sixteenth century.

Unlike the Florentine-led financial expansion of the late fourteenth century, it constituted the high-point of a pattern of capital accumulation that was both systemic in scope and homogeneous in agency and structure. In this pattern, a major material expansion of the European world-economy, through the establishment of new trade routes and the incorporation of new areas of commercial exploitation, was followed by a financial expansion that tightened the dominance of capital over the enlarged world-economy. Moreover, a clearly identifiable capitalist class (the Genoese) encouraged, monitored, and benefited from both expansions in virtue of a structure of capital accumulation which for the most part had already come into existence when the material expansion began.

This pattern is what we shall understand by a "systemic cycle of accumulation." First established by the Genoese capitalist class in the sixteenth century, it was repeated three more times under the successive leadership and dominance of the Dutch, British, and US capitalist classes. In this succession, financial expansions have always been the initial and concluding moments of systemic cycles. Thus, just as the financial expansion of the late fourteenth and early fifteenth centuries had been the cradle of the Genoese cycle, so the financial expansion of the late sixteenth and early seventeenth centuries was the cradle of the Dutch cycle, to which we shall now turn.

The Second (Dutch) Systemic Cycle of Accumulation

As argued in earlier sections of this chapter, the financial expansion of the late fourteenth and early fifteenth centuries was associated with an intensification of inter-capitalist competition in the form of inter-city-state warfare and violent intra-city-state conflicts on the one side, and with a parallel intensification of the power struggle among and within territorialist organizations on the other side. The "Italian" Hundred Years War was taken as the clearest and most important expression of the first tendency, and the simultaneous "Anglo-French" Hundred Years War as the clearest and most important expression of the second tendency. The financial expansion of the late sixteenth and early seventeenth centuries was also associated with an escalation of inter-capitalist and inter-territorialist struggles, but in forms which were far more complex and hence more difficult for the observer to identify.

A first difficulty arises from the fact that inter-territorialist struggles never really de-escalated after the end of the "Anglo-French" Hundred Years war and the pacification of the territories that became Spain. As soon as the unification of Spain was completed, the Anglo-French struggle was replaced by a Franco-Spanish struggle for control over the Italian political space, where most of the power of money and religion was still concentrated. This struggle engendered a continual state of warfare in Italy and elsewhere throughout the first half of the sixteenth century, and blurs the escalation of conflicts of the second half of the century, which began with the outbreak of wars of religion in Germany in the late 1540s and 1550s and of the war of Dutch independence in the late 1560s.

This difficulty is compounded by the fact that the main agencies of inter-capitalist cooperation and competition were no longer easily identifiable organizations like the Italian city-states of earlier times. For in the century following the Peace of Lodi (1454), the city-states had ceased, individually and collectively, to be the primary agencies of processes of capital accumulation. The increasing involvement of their resident bourgeoisies – as opposed to their diaspora bourgeoisies – in state-making activities (except in Genoa) made them unwilling or incapable of keeping abreast of ongoing changes in the capitalist world-economy. What is more, as Mattingly (1988: 52, 86) has pointed out, their very success in these activities made them "blind to the fact that the tallest giants among the Italian states were pigmies beside the monarchies beyond the Alps." Having grown "rashly confident of their ability to summon the barbarians when they might be useful and send them home if they became embarrassing ... they failed to understand the catastrophe that overwhelmed them" once France and Spain felt ready to face each other in the Italian arena.

Of the big four Italian city-states, Venice was the only one that managed to retain considerable power *qua* state throughout the sixteenth century in the emerging political landscape of Europe. But it did so at the cost of falling behind old and new competitors in the accumulation of capital. To be sure, it was precisely in the century following the Peace of Lodi that Venice industrialized rapidly to become the leading manufacturing center of Europe. This late industrialization, however, only counterbalanced the negative effects of the contraction and obsolescence of Venice's long-distance trade networks, but did not reverse its decline relative to more dynamic centers of capital accumulation (Braudel 1984: 136).

These more dynamic centers were no longer city-states – the Genoese city-state itself having long ceased to be the primary locus of the self-expansion of Genoese capital. Nor were they cities such as Antwerp, Seville, and Lyons, as it is often maintained, confusing cities *qua* places with cities *qua* agencies. Unlike fourteenth-century Venice, Genoa, Florence, and Milan, sixteenth-century Antwerp, Seville, and Lyons were not agencies or even centers of processes of capital accumulation. They were neither autonomous governmental organizations nor autonomous business organizations. They were simple market*places* – central markets of the European world-economy to be sure, but none the less places subjected politically to the authority of Imperial Spain (Antwerp and Seville) or France (Lyons), and economically to the trans-statal activities of foreign business organizations, which neither represented nor had any allegiance to the cities in question except as convenient places in which to meet and deal with one another.

The most important among these foreign business organizations consisted of expatriate capitalist groups which identified themselves and were recognized as "nations" in relation to one another and to the governments of the various market cities in which they resided, whether permanently or temporarily. As Boyer-Xambeau, Deleplace, and Gillard (1991) have shown in great detail, these trans-statal "nations" exercised a truly dominant influence over the commercial and monetary system of sixteenth-century Europe. This dominance was based on mastery of a monetary instrument – the bill of exchange – in a politically heterogeneous economic space criss-crossed by a great variety of circulating currencies, which the "nations" of merchant bankers managed to organize for their own benefit into a homogeneous commercial and financial space through the use of stable units of account – the *monete di cambio*.

Although most "nations" were involved in trade in commodities of one kind or another, the largest profits were made not in the buying and selling of commodities but in exchanging currencies for one another through bills of exchange. For bills of exchange enabled merchant bankers organized in "nations" to appropriate as profits differences in the values of currencies from place to place at any given time and from one time to another in the same place. Since these differences in the sixteenth century were huge, so were the profits of the "nations" that were best positioned to appropriate them.

Contrary to quite widespread beliefs at the time, this highly profitable activity did render a useful service to ordinary merchants and to the various sovereigns under whose jurisdictions the "nations" of merchant bankers operated. The service consisted of relieving their clients of the risks and trouble of carrying valuable means of payments to and from the distant places where their purchases were made and their goods were sold and also of having to exchange these means of payments in unfamiliar and unpredictable environments. One of the reasons why the money-changing activities of the "nations" were highly profitable is precisely that this service was extremely useful to a vast clientele, and yet its provision involved little risk and trouble for the merchant bankers who were organized in extensive and cohesive "nations." For one thing, this organization enabled its members to undertake the transport, not of all the means of payments whose movement through space and time they managed, but only of a very small fraction corresponding to movements that were not balanced by more or less roundabout movements in the opposite direction. Moreover, the simultaneous presence of a "nation" in the most important marketplaces of the European world-economy made these places familiar and predictable environments for all its members regardless of where they resided or operated. In short, what would have been a costly and risky venture for the "nation's" clients was a costless and risk-free venture for the "nation's" members, and this difference translated into large and steady profits.

The size and steadiness of these profits did not depend on the extent and degree of cooperation realized within each "nation" alone. It depended also on the extent and degree to which the most important "nations" cooperated with one another in coordinating their operations and in complementing each other's spatial or functional specialization. It is above all in this sphere that an escalation of inter-capitalist struggles is most clearly observable from the crisis of 1557–62 onwards.

According to Boyer-Xambeau, Deleplace, and Gillard (1991: 26–32 and *passim*), up to that crisis the most important group in the organization and management of the European commercial and monetary system was the Florentine "nation," which was centered in Lyons and exercised a predominant influence on that city's fairs. Born a century earlier under the hegemony of the Medici, the Florentine "nation" came of age only in the sixteenth century when the renewed political troubles of Florence produced a constant stream of exiles who settled in France – particularly in Lyons, which they turned into a "French Tuscany." Of lesser but rapidly increasing importance was the Genoese "nation" whose fortunes grew in step with the expansion of Iberian trade with Asia and the Americas. Four other nations played a more peripheral but none the less significant role in the regulation of the European commercial and monetary system – the German and the English in Antwerp, the Milanese in Lyons, and the Lucchese first in Antwerp and then in Lyons. It should be noted for future reference that neither Venice nor Holland – the greatest capitalist powers of the fifteenth and seventeenth centuries, respectively – were represented in this cosmopolitan ensemble of capitalist "nations."

For most of the first half of the sixteenth century relationships between the various components of this cosmopolitan ensemble were basically cooperative. Each "nation" specialized in a particular market niche defined by a merchandise (textiles for the English; alum, silver, and copper for the German; metal products for the Milanese; staples of various kind for the Lucchese) or by a predominant relationship of political exchange with one of the two most powerful territorialist organizations of the European world-economy (with France for the Florentine; and Spain for the Genoese). By pooling at fairs, as in Lyons, or in more continuous commodity and money exchanges, as in Antwerp, the promises of payment, the information, and the connections acquired in dealing with overlapping but distinct clienteles, the various "nations" cooperated with one another in attaining three main results.

First, they ensured that the largest possible number of promises of payment would offset one another directly or indirectly, thereby minimizing the actual transport of currencies that the "nations" had to undertake. Second, they pooled a better knowledge of conditions affecting trends and fluctuations in exchange rates than they would have been able to acquire on their own. And third, they involved one another in profitable commercial or financial deals, such as the election of the emperor in 1519, which would have been too big or risky for the members of a single "nation" to undertake but not for a "multinational" joint venture. These outcomes of cooperation were the main reason for the various "nations" to converge in specific places at specific times and thus create and keep alive central marketplaces like Antwerp and Lyons. But as soon as these outcomes declined in importance for one or more of the core "nations," cooperation was displaced by competition and the centrality of cosmopolitan marketplaces like Antwerp and Lyons was progressively undermined and eventually destroyed.

A displacement of this kind began in the 1530s when the crowding out of German by American silver supplies destroyed the commercial foundations of the German "nation" and strengthened those of the Genoese "nation." It was also in the 1530s that the Genoese began to hold their own fairs in competition with the Lyons fairs, which were controlled by the Florentine "nation." In spite of these early signs of an escalation in inter-capitalist competition, relationships between the main "nations" remained basically cooperative through the 1540s and early 1550s.

The real escalation only began with the crisis of 1557–62. As previously noted, it was in the course of this crisis that German capital was crowded out of high finance by Genoese capital. More important, the Genoese introduced the system of the *asientos* – contracts with the Spanish government that gave the Genoese almost complete control over the supply of American silver in Seville in exchange for gold and other "good money" delivered in Antwerp, which was quickly becoming the main center of operation of the Spanish Imperial army. At this point, the Genoese "nation" lost all interest in cooperating with the Florentine "nation" and began making aggressive use of the supply of American silver to divert Italian liquidity (gold and bills of exchange) from the Lyons fairs to its own "Bisenzone" fairs. Although these fairs still bore the Italian name of Besançon – from where they had been held initially – they were in fact mobile (held at Chambéry, Poligny, Trento, Coira, Rivoli, Ivrea, and Asti) to suit the Genoese (Boyer-Xambeau, Deleplace, and Gillard 1991: 319–28, 123).

By 1579, when the Bisenzone fairs settled at Piacenza in the Duchy of Parma, a tightly controlled and highly profitable triangle had been established through which the Genoese pumped American silver from Seville to northern Italy, where they exchanged it for gold and bills of exchange, which they delivered to the Spanish government in Antwerp in exchange for the *asientos* which gave them control over American silver in Seville (see figure 5). By the end of the 1580s, the progressive centralization of the supply of American silver and northern Italian gold and bills of exchange within the Genoese triangle made the decline of Lyons as the central money market irreversible. Although Antwerp was one of the three corners of the Genoese triangle, its vitality as a central commodity and money market had been sapped much earlier. The crowding out of the Germans and the increasing exclusiveness of the Genoese–Iberian connection alienated the English who, in the late 1560s, returned home under Thomas Gresham's leadership to convince Elizabeth I of the importance of making England independent of foreigners not just in trade but in finance as well (see chapter 3).

The consolidation of the system of the Piacenza fairs thus marked the end of the system of cooperating "nations" which had governed the capitalist engine of the European world-economy in the first half of the sixteenth century. The Genoese had won the day, but this early victory in the battle for supremacy in high finance was only the prelude to a much longer struggle. This was the war of Dutch independence, in which the Genoese let their Spanish partners do the actual fighting, while they profited behind the scenes by transforming silver delivered in Seville into gold and other "good money" delivered in Antwerp near the theater of operations. Without this war there probably would have been no "age of the Genoese." But it was this same war that eventually dislodged the Genoese from the commanding heights of the capitalist world-economy.

When in 1566 Spanish troops were sent to occupy the Netherlands – basically to enforce taxation – the move backfired. The Dutch rebels took to the seas and developed outstanding abilities not just in tax evasion, but in imposing on the finances of Imperial Spain a kind of "inverted" fiscal squeeze through piracy and privateering. For eighty years – that is, up to the end of the Thirty Years War – the finances of Imperial Spain were thus subjected to a major and growing drain, which strengthened the Dutch rebels and weakened Spain absolutely and relative to subordinate and competing territorialist organizations, France and England in particular. And as the imperial center weakened, wars and rebellions proliferated until the Peace of Westphalia institutionalized the emerging European balance of power.

Throughout these struggles the primary source of Dutch wealth and power was control over supplies of grain and naval stores from the Baltic. These supplies had been made absolutely essential to the conduct of war by land and sea in Europe by the exhaustion of competing Mediterranean supplies in the first half of the sixteenth century. The more the Dutch succeeded in holding in check Iberian power and in drawing other states into the conflict, the more they profited from control over trade with the Baltic. Supplemented by the inverted fiscal squeeze imposed on Spain, these profits were the primary and original source of the "embarrassment of riches" (Schama 1988) which characterized Dutch capitalism from the very start. In this sense, Baltic trade was indeed Amsterdam's *moeder commercie* – the underlying foundation of the city's fortunes (cf. Boxer 1965: 43; Kriedte 1983: 78).

Baltic trade was highly profitable but stagnant. In the course of the two centuries during which the commercial fortunes of Amsterdam rose and declined – that is, from the middle of the sixteenth to the middle of the eighteenth century – the *volume* of grain shipments from the Baltic to Western Europe shows a great deal of fluctuation but a stagnant and eventually a declining secular trend. In the first century or so, this stagnation was partly counteracted by an increase in the shipment of other commodities (such as Swedish iron) and by an increase in the share of Baltic grain carried on Dutch ships. But even if we take these increases into account, the overall tendency throughout the golden age of Dutch commerce was one of sluggish growth in the volume of commodities exchanged with the Baltic region (see figure 6).

There is no contradiction between the fact that the volume of Baltic trade was stagnant and its characterization as the "mother trade" of the commercial fortunes of the Dutch. This characterization simply conveys the notion that the profits of Baltic trade were largely gifts of geography and history – a surplus that was more the source than the result of the development of Dutch capitalism. As in the development of capitalism in northern Italy three centuries earlier, all the Dutch merchants had to do to become leaders in processes of capital accumulation was to "permit themselves to be driven by the wind actually blowing and [to learn] how to trim their sails to take advantage of it," as Pirenne put it in his previously quoted, metaphorical description of the rise of new leading capitalist "classes" in general. As Pirenne suggests, to do so successfully required courage, entrepreneurship, and boldness. But as in the case of the Italian mercantile communities that preceded the Dutch – or, for that matter, of the English and North American communities that followed them – no amount of courage, entrepreneurship, and boldness would have helped the Dutch to become the new leading capitalist "class" of the European world-economy so quickly and so successfully had they not happened to dwell in the place and at the time that were both just right to catch "the wind actually blowing."

This "wind" has always been the outcome of systemic circumstances which were the unintentional effect of the actions of a multiplicity of agencies, first and foremost of the agency that was in the process of being displaced from the commanding heights of the world-economy. In the case of the Dutch, these systemic circumstances consisted of a fundamental temporal and spatial disequilibrium between the demand for, and the supply of, grain and naval stores in the European world-economy at large. For most of the sixteenth century and in the first half of the seventeenth, demand was large and growing rapidly, mostly in the West, owing to the inflow of American silver and to the escalation in the power struggle by land and sea between the states of the Atlantic seaboard. But supply could not and was not growing as fast as demand and, furthermore, with the exhaustion of Mediterranean supplies it came to be concentrated in the Baltic region.

Thanks to the earlier decline of the power of the Hanseatic League and to its own seafaring traditions rooted in fishing and in the carrying of bulk goods along the coasts of the northern seas, the Dutch mercantile community had been uniquely positioned to exploit this chronic temporal and spatial disequilibrium between demand and supply. By stepping in and establishing tight control over the transfer of Baltic supplies through the Sound, the Dutch had come to occupy what in the course of the sixteenth century turned into the most strategic market niche of the European world-economy, and thus became the beneficiaries of a large and steady stream of money surpluses which they further augmented by imposing an inverted fiscal squeeze on Imperial Spain.

A good part, probably the largest part, of these surpluses was "surplus capital" – capital that could not be invested profitably in the activities out of which it stemmed. Had the surpluses been plowed back into Baltic trade, the most likely outcome would have been an upward pressure on purchase prices, and/or a downward pressure on sale prices, which would have destroyed its profitability. Like the Medici in the fifteenth century, however, the merchant elite who had been bred and fed by the accumulation of these surpluses, and who had come to control their utilization, knew better than to plow profits back into the expansion of Baltic trade, and carefully abstained from doing so.

Dutch surplus capital instead was utilized in ways analogous to those pioneered by the northern Italian capitalist classes when similarly placed in the late fourteenth and early fifteenth centuries. Some went in rent-bearing assets, particularly land, and in the development of commercial agriculture. In this respect, the main difference between the Dutch and their Italian predecessors was the precociousness with which Dutch merchants turned into a rentier class.

The capitalist classes of the Italian city-states acquired a rural space large enough to allow sizeable investments in land and commercial agriculture only *after the end* of their mercantile expansion. The Dutch, by contrast, acquired such a space in the very process of constituting themselves into a sovereign state. Investment in land and other rent-bearing assets thus became an early feature of Dutch capitalism as witnessed by the fact that already in 1652 – that is, *long before the end* of the Dutch mercantile expansion – it was complained widely and authoritatively that the interests of trade were neglected because "the *Heeren* [regents] were not merchants, but drew their income from houses, lands and investments" (statement by the historian Lieuwe Aitzema, quoted in Wilson 1968: 44; see also Boxer 1965: ch. 2).

A second analogy between the Dutch and earlier Italian strategies of surplus capital utilization was investment in war-making and state-making activities. Very early in their struggle against Spain, Dutch merchants entered into an informal relationship of political exchange with the English monarchy, who provided them with protection in exchange for special consideration in trade and finance. This even led to proposals of union between the English and Dutch polities. "Union had been proposed under Elizabeth, by the Dutch, and offered again on terms very favorable to Dutch merchants in 1614–19." But nothing came of these proposals (Hill 1967: 123).

In all likelihood, the main reason why Dutch merchants turned down the favorable English offer was that in the meantime they had entered into an organic and formal relationship of political exchange with a local territorialist organization, the House of Orange. The essential feature of this relationship was the provision by the Dutch merchant class of liquidity, business knowledge, and connections, in exchange for the provision by the House of Orange of war-making and state-making capabilities, particularly in the organization of protection on land. The result was a governmental organization, the United Provinces, that fused the advantages of capitalism and territorialism far more effectively than any of the northern Italian city-states, including Venice, had ever managed to do. English protection was simply no longer needed, no matter on how favorable terms it was offered.

A third analogy between Dutch and earlier Italian patterns of surplus capital utilization was investment in the conspicuous consumption of cultural products through the patronage of the arts and other intellectual pursuits. Notwithstanding its supremacy in high finance, the Genoese capitalist class never distinguished itself in this kind of conspicuous consumption – presumably because of its lack of involvement in state-making activities. Not so the Dutch, who in this sphere too showed their precociousness by leading the way in the consumption of cultural products throughout the Age of the Genoese. Just as fifteenth-century Venice and Florence had been the centers of the High Renaissance, so early seventeenth-century Amsterdam became the center of the transition from the "climate of the Renaissance," which had pervaded Europe in the previous two centuries, to the "climate of the Enlightenment," which was to pervade Europe in the next century and a half (Trevor-Roper 1967: 66–7, 93–4; see also Wilson 1968: chs 7–9).

From all these points of view, the Dutch strategy of surplus capital utilization bore a closer resemblance to the strategy previously pursued by the Venetians than to the strategies of any other northern Italian capitalist class. Unlike the Venetians, however, the Dutch went on to become the leaders of a commercial expansion of the entire European world-economy, thereby turning Amsterdam not just into the "Venice of the North," as is generally acknowledged, but into the "Genoa of the North" as well. For in the fifteenth century the Venetians did nothing to lead surplus capital towards the creation of a new and larger commercial space. Having succeeded in excluding the Genoese from the Levant trade (Venice's own "mother trade"), they fell back on a strategy of regional, that is, eastern Mediterranean, specialization aimed at tightening their hold on this trade; and once this policy began to yield decreasing returns, they went ever more deeply into manufacturing. This strategy enabled

Venice to remain a model of state-making for centuries to a much greater extent than the United Provinces, let alone the Genoese Republic, ever was. Nevertheless, in and by itself this strategy did not open up new profitable investment opportunities for the surplus capital that was "embarrassing" the whole of northern Italy. It was thus left to the politically and militarily weaker Genoese to turn the northern Italian financial expansion of the fifteenth century into a new commercial expansion of systemic significance, which they did by specializing in strictly business pursuits and letting their Iberian partners take care of the required state- and war-making activities.

In contrast to both strategies of accumulation – the Venetian strategy of regional consolidation based on self-sufficiency in state- and war-making, and the Genoese strategy of world-wide expansion based on a relationship of political exchange with foreign governments – the Dutch in the early seventeenth century moved in both directions simultaneously and fused the two strategies into a harmonious synthesis. This was based on a domestic relationship of political exchange which made Dutch capitalism self-sufficient in war-making and state-making, and combined regional con-solidation with world-wide expansion of Dutch trade and finance. In an often quoted passage, written in 1728 when the Dutch-led phase of commercial expansion of the European world-economy was drawing to a close, Daniel Defoe pinpointed the central aspect of this strategy:

> The Dutch must be understood as they really are, the Middle Persons in Trade, the Factors and Brokers of Europe ... they *buy* to *sell* again, *take* in to *send* out, and the greatest Part of their vast Commerce consists in being supply'd from All Parts of the World, that they may supply All the World again. (quoted in Wilson 1968: 22; emphasis in the original)

This statement can be read as consisting of two parts which provide a description, not just of the most typical feature of the Dutch commercial system from its rise to systemic significance in the sixteenth century to its demise in the eighteenth century, but also of the *expansion* in the scale and scope of that system. For the first part of the statement, which refers to Europe, can be taken to describe the *original* function of the Dutch as the Venetians of the North, as the "middle persons" of Baltic trade, as the intermediaries between northeastern European supplies of grain and naval stores on the one side, and western European demand for such supplies on the other side. The second part of the statement, in contrast, refers to the entire world and can be taken to describe the *mature* function of the Dutch as the Genoese of the North, as the "middle persons" of global commerce, as the intermediaries between world supply in general and world demand in general.

This reading of Defoe's statement is implicit in Braudel's contention that the first condition of Dutch commercial supremacy was Europe, and the second was the world: "Once Holland had conquered the trade of Europe, the rest of the world was a logical bonus, thrown in as it were. But in both cases, Holland used very similar methods to impose her commercial supremacy or rather monopoly, whether close at home or far away" (Braudel 1984: 207).

This expansion of the scope of the Dutch commercial system from regional to global was propelled and sustained by the *combination* of three related policies. A first policy aimed at transforming Amsterdam into the central entrepôt of European and world commerce. By central-izing in Amsterdam the storage and exchange of what happened to be the most strategic supplies of European and world commerce at any given time, the Dutch capitalist class developed unprecedented and unparal-leled capabilities to regulate and profit from the disequilibria of the European world-economy:

> The rule was always the same: buy goods directly from the producer for a low price, in return for cash or, better still, advance payments; then put them in store and wait for prices to rise (or give them a push). When war was in the air, which always meant that foreign goods became scarce and went up in price, the Amsterdam merchants crammed their five- or six-storey warehouses to bursting-point; on the eve of the war of Spanish Succession, ships could not unload their cargoes for lack of storage space. (Braudel 1982: 419)

The visible weapons of this policy were

> the great warehouses – bigger and more expensive than a large ship – which could hold enough grain to feed the United Provinces for ten or twelve years (1670), as well as herrings and spices, English cloth and French wines, salpetre from Poland or the East Indies, Swedish copper, tobacco from Maryland, cocoa from Venezuela, Russian furs and Spanish wool, hemp from the Baltic and silk from the Levant. (Braudel 1982: 418–19; see also Barbour 1950: 75)

But a far more important though less visible weapon wielded by the Dutch in their attempts to divert commodity trade to Amsterdam from other entrepôts, or from direct exchanges between producers and consumers, was their superior command over liquidity. Thanks to this they succeeded decade after decade in pre-empting the bids of actual or potential competitors. They were thus able to exploit alone the ever-growing demand for money of the producers, and so obtain supplies at low prices in return for ready cash or advance payments (cf. Braudel 1982: 419–20).

This brings us to the second component of the strategy of accumulation which propelled and sustained the ascent of the Dutch capitalist class from regional to global commercial supremacy. This component was the policy of transforming Amsterdam not just into the central warehouse of world commerce but also into the central money and capital market of the European world-economy. The key tactical move in this respect was the creation in Amsterdam of the first stock exchange in *permanent* session.

The Amsterdam Bourse was not the first stock market. Stock markets of various kinds had sprung up and flourished in Genoa, at the Leipzig fairs, and in many Hanseatic towns in the fifteenth century, and state loan stocks had been negotiable much earlier in the Italian city-states. "All [the] evidence points to the Mediterranean as the cradle of the stock market.... But what was new in Amsterdam was the volume, the fluidity of the market and the publicity it received, and the speculative freedom of transactions" (Braudel 1982: 100–1).

The power of the Amsterdam Bourse to attract the supply of and the demand for idle money and credit from all over Europe at the expense of the Genoese fairs grew rapidly at the turn of the sixteenth and seventeenth centuries, and became overwhelming after the crisis of 1619–22 (Braudel 1982: 92). The already overabundant liquidity commanded by the Dutch capitalist class by virtue of its control over Baltic supplies and of the inverted fiscal squeeze imposed on Spain thus came to be supplemented by mobilization and rerouting of surplus capital from all over Europe to the Amsterdam Bourse and to the banking institutions that the Dutch established to service the Bourse – first and foremost, the *Wisselbank* founded in 1609 to carry out functions typical of future central banks. The superior command over liquidity on which the commercial supremacy of Dutch entrepôt capitalism rested was thus consolidated and raised well above what would be in the power of any rival group to challenge for a long time to come. The centralization in Amsterdam of transactions and speculation in commodities, in turn, expanded the city's effective demand for money and, therefore, the power of its Bourse and of its banking institutions to attract money capital, whether idle or not, from all over Europe. A virtuous circle of expansion was thus established whereby the increasing commercial and financial centrality of Amsterdam made it imperative for all European business and governmental organizations of any importance to be represented at Amsterdam's Bourse; and "[since] the important businessman and a host of intermediaries met here, business of every sort could be transacted: operations in commodities, currency exchange, shareholding, maritime insurance" (Braudel 1982: 100).

This virtuous circle of expansion would never have got off the ground, let alone produce the spectacular results it did, were it not for a third policy which complemented and sustained the policies that promoted the transformation of Amsterdam into the central entrepôt of world commerce and world finance. This consisted in launching large-scale joint-stock companies chartered by the Dutch government to exercise exclusive trading and sovereignty rights over huge overseas commercial spaces. These companies were business enterprises which were supposed to yield profits and dividends but also to carry out war-making and state-making activities on behalf of the Dutch government.

In this capacity, as Maurice Dobb (1963: 208–9, quoting Sombart) remarked, the chartered companies of the seventeenth century were not unlike the Genoese *maone*, associations of individuals established in view of a profit to undertake war-making and state-making functions, such as the conquest of Caffa and the colonization of Chios. These associations had played a crucial role in the original formation of the Genoese capitalist class during the commercial expansion of the thirteenth and early fourteenth centuries but were subsequently displaced by more flexible organizational structures, of which the trans-statal Genoese "nation" discussed above was the most important. In the seventeenth century, the Dutch were not alone, nor indeed the first, to revive the tradition of the Genoese *maone*, the English East India Company having received its charter in 1600 and other English companies even earlier. Yet, throughout the seventeenth century the Dutch VOC (*Verenigde Oost-Indische Compagnie*), chartered in 1602, was by far the greatest success of this revival – a success which took the English a century to imitate and even longer to supersede (Braudel 1982: 449–50).

For the Dutch chartered companies were both beneficiaries and instruments of the ongoing centralization in Amsterdam of world-embracing commerce and high finance – beneficiaries because this centralization granted them privileged access to remunerative outlets for their outputs and to economical sources from which to procure their inputs, including outlets or sources for the disposal or procurement of surplus capital, depending on their stage of development and on fluctuations in their fortunes. But chartered companies were also powerful instruments of global expansion of Dutch commercial and financial networks, and from this point of view their role in the overall strategy of accumulation of the Dutch cannot be emphasized strongly enough.

For one thing, chartered companies were the medium through which the Dutch capitalist class established *direct* links between the Amsterdam entrepôt on the one side, and producers from all over the world on the other side. Thanks to these direct links, the ability of the Dutch capitalist class to centralize the commercial transactions that mattered in Amsterdam, as well as its ability to monitor, regulate, and profit from the disequilibria of world trade, were greatly enhanced. At the same time, chartered companies played a decisive role in the rise of Amsterdam to the status of world financial center. For investment and speculation in the shares of chartered companies – first and foremost of the VOC – were the single most important factor in the successful development of the Amsterdam Bourse into the first stock market in permanent session (Braudel 1982: 100–6; 1984: 224–7; Israel 1989: 75–6, 256–8).

Without a large, profitable, and fast-growing joint-stock company like the VOC, such a development may never have taken place, or at least not in time to beat the old (Genoese) or the new (English) competition in high finance. But the VOC was an epochal success, and so was the strategy of accumulation to which it belonged. For more than a century, from circa 1610–20 to circa 1730–40, the upper strata of the Dutch merchant class remained the leaders and governors of the European capitalist engine. Throughout this period, the Amsterdam Bourse remained the central regulatory mechanism through which idle capital was rerouted towards new trade ventures, some of which were directly controlled by the inner circle of the Dutch capitalist class but most of which could be safely and profitably left in the hands of lesser Dutch and foreign (primarily English) enterprises.

Through the Bourse, capital was recycled from profitable but stagnant or contracting lines of business like Baltic trade to new but promising lines of business, and continually reshuffled among governments and business enterprises depending on prospective returns and risks. By promoting and organizing this recycling and reshuffling, the Dutch merchants, and their upper capitalist stratum in particular, could profit not just from the activities initiated or controlled by them but also from the military, commercial, and industrial ventures promoted and organized by others. But the capabilities of the Dutch to turn the undertakings and activities of others into so many means of expansion of their commercial supremacy were not unlimited. The very success of the Dutch strategy of accumulation soon brought into being forces that constrained, undermined, and eventually destroyed the capabilities of the Dutch world trading system to go on expanding indefinitely.

These forces were variants of what later came to be known as "mercantilism." These variants were many and their success very uneven. But whatever their *individual* successes and failures, the *spread* of multiple mercantilisms in the late seventeenth and early eighteenth centuries created an environment in Europe and in the world at large in which the Dutch commercial system could not survive, no matter what the Dutch did or did not do.

All variants of mercantilism had one thing in common: they were more or less conscious attempts on the part of territorialist rulers to *imitate* the Dutch, to become themselves capitalist in orientation as the most effective way of attaining their own power objectives. The Dutch had demonstrated on a world scale what the Venetians had already demonstrated on a regional scale, namely, that under favorable circumstances the systematic accumulation of pecuniary surpluses could be a far more effective technique of political aggrandizement than the acquisition of territories and subjects. The more the Dutch succeeded in their endless accumulation of capital, and the more this accumulation was turned into ever-growing capabilities to shape and manipulate the European political system, the more European territorialist rulers were drawn into the Dutch path of development, that is, into imitating as much as they could (or thought desirable) of Dutch trade, war-making and state-making techniques. The creation of world-embracing commercial empires, the rerouting of commodity and money flows to entrepôts within one's own control and jurisdiction, the systematic accumulation of pecuniary surpluses in the balance of payments with other domains, were all expressions of this imitative predisposition of territorialist organizations.

But mercantilism was not just the imitative response of territorialist rulers to the challenges posed by world-embracing Dutch capitalism. Equally important was the tendency to reaffirm or re-establish the territorialist principle of autarky in the new form of "national economy-making," and to counterpose that principle to the Dutch principle of universal intermediation. The central aspect of this tendency was the strengthening of "forward and backward linkages," in Albert Hirschman's (1958) sense, between the consumers and the producers of a given territorial domain – a strengthening which involved not just the establishment of intermediate (mainly "manufacturing") activities linking domestic primary production to domestic final consumption, but also the forcible "delinking" of producers and consumers from relationships of dependence on foreign (primarily Dutch) purchases and sales.

These two tendencies were typical of all the variants of mercantilism, although some variants – most notably the English – were more inclined to build a commercial empire overseas than a national economy at home, while others – most notably the French – showed the opposite tendency. Either way, by the late seventeenth century, the success of English and French mercantilism was already imposing serious constraints on the capabilities of the Dutch world trading system to go on expanding in scale and scope. As expansion tapered off, the system began to crack. But the straw that broke the camel's back was the spread of mercantilism to the region that had been feeding the "mother trade" of the Dutch commercial system:

The basic reason for the decisive decline of the Dutch world-trading system in the 1720s and 1730s was the wave of new-style industrial mercantilism which swept practically the entire continent from around 1720.... Down to 1720 countries such as Prussia, Russia, Sweden, and Denmark–Norway had lacked the means and, with the Great Northern War in progress, the opportunity, to emulate the aggressive mercantilism of England and France. But in the years around 1720 a heightened sense of competition among the northern powers, combined with the diffusion of new technology and skills, often Dutch or Huguenot in origin, led to a dramatic change. Within the next two decades most of northern Europe was incorporated into a framework of systematic industrial mercantilist policy. (Israel 1989: 383–4)

There was nothing that Dutch merchants could do to contain, let alone reverse, this tidal wave of mercantilism. Such a containment was well beyond their organizational capabilities. But what was not beyond their organizational capabilities, and indeed was the most sensible course of action for them to undertake under the circumstances, was to withdraw from trade and concentrate on high finance in order to benefit from, instead of succumbing to, the spread of mercantilism. For the heightened competition among the territorialist organizations of Europe, which was undermining the viability of the Dutch world system of trade, was also widening and deepening the need for money and credit of governments in general – a need which Dutch business networks were well placed to service and profit from. The Dutch capitalist class promptly seized this opportunity and, from about 1740, its leading elements began switching from trade to an ever more exclusive specialization in high finance.

As in the case of the previous financial expansions of Florentine and Genoese capital, the switch of the Dutch from trade to finance occurred in the context of a major escalation of inter-capitalist and inter-territorialist struggles. This time, however, the two kinds of struggle had become completely fused into conflicts between nation-states that were capitalist and territorialist at the same time. At first, the escalation of these conflicts took the form of commercial warfare between England and France, which in the course of the commercial expansion of the early seventeenth century had emerged as the two most powerful competitors. Participation in the War of the Austrian Succession (1740–48), according to H.W.V. Temperley, "the first of English wars in which trade interests absolutely predominated, in which war was waged solely for the balance of trade rather than the balance of power" (quoted in Wallerstein 1980: 256), was soon followed by the decisive confrontation of the Seven Years War (1756–63). Just as the Venetians had ousted the Genoese from the eastern Mediterranean with the Peace of Turin of 1381, so now the English ousted the French from North America and India with the Treaty of Paris of 1763.

This time, however, the victor in the inter-statal struggle was itself torn apart by an internal feud. A dispute between the British government and its North American subjects over the distribution of the costs and benefits of their joint victory over the French quickly escalated into the American War of Independence, which the French government readily exploited in an attempt to recover its previous loss of power and prestige. But victory in the American War of Independence backfired. A fiscal dispute over the distribution of the costs of war broke out in metropolitan France itself and the ensuing Revolution reverberated in generalized warfare throughout the European world-economy (see chapter 1).

Initially at least, this escalation of struggles between and within territorialist organizations created extremely favorable demand conditions for the financial deals in which the Dutch capitalist class had come to specialize:

> By the 1760s, all the states of Europe were queuing up in the offices of the Dutch money-lenders: the emperor, the elector of Saxony, the elector of Bavaria, the insistent king of Denmark, the king of Sweden, Catherine II of Russia, the king of France and even the city of Hamburg (although it was Amsterdam's successful rival) and lastly, the American rebels. (Braudel 1984: 246–7)

Under these circumstances, it was only natural that the Dutch capitalist class would choose to distance itself from the struggles that raged between and within territorialist organizations, and concentrate instead on exploiting the competition for mobile capital these struggles generated. The capabilities of the Dutch to continue profiting from this competition long after the golden age of their commercial supremacy had passed were of course not unlimited. The territorialist revival in mercantilist clothes which was sweeping Europe eventually caught up with the Dutch who, under the pressure of territorialist interests in their midst, which the House of Orange was only too keen to lead and organize, were drawn into the struggles with disastrous consequences. Thus, in the war that followed from the American rebellion, the Dutch sided with France against Britain. As in the case of France, however, the United Provinces gained nothing from Britain's defeat. On the contrary, the British retaliated viciously, and in the course of the fourth Anglo-Dutch War (1781–84) they annihilated what was left of Dutch seaborne power, occupied Dutch-held Ceylon, and gained access to the Moluccas.

This defeat and the ensuing "Batavian" Revolution and Orangist counter-revolution hastened the displacement of Amsterdam by London as the financial entrepôt of the European world-economy. This was completed in the course of the Napoleonic Wars, which wiped the United Provinces off the map of Europe. By then, however, it was more than half a century since the Dutch had pulled out of trade to specialize in high finance, and in the course of that half-century the Dutch financiers had their own "wonderful moment" during which they could enjoy the unprecented spectacle (a profitable spectacle, to boot) of the great territorialist rulers of Europe queuing up in their offices begging for a loan.

Once again, *and on a grander scale*, one capitalist class had successively promoted and financed, monitored and profited from, and, in the fullness of time, withdrawn from, a commercial expansion that encompassed a multiplicity of power and trade networks. Capitalism as a world system was here to stay. From now on, territorialism could succeed in its objectives only by "internalizing" capitalist techniques of power. This, as we shall see, was to be the central feature of the third (British) systemic cycle of accumulation.

The Dialectic of State and Capital

Before we proceed to examine the third (British) systemic cycle of accumulation, our description of the Genoese and Dutch cycles must be completed by a brief examination of the "organizational revolution," which in spite of all the similarities between the two cycles, sets them apart as distinct stages of capitalist development. For the strategies that structured the Dutch cycle were in key respects not just different from but antithetical to the strategies that had structured the previous Genoese cycle. The differences between the two cycles are many and complex but they can all be traced to the fact that the Dutch regime of accumulation, in comparison with and in relation to the Genoese, "internalized protection costs."

The notion of an "internalization of protection costs" has been introduced by Niels Steensgaard (1974) to explain the striking success in the seventeenth century of European chartered companies operating in the East Indies. By being self-sufficient and competitive in the use and control of violence, these companies "produced" their own protection, to use Lane's (1979: 22–8) terminology, at costs that were lower and more calculable than the costs charged to caravans and ships by local powers in the form of tribute, fees, and outright extortions. What local traders had to pay in tribute, fees, and extortions, the companies could either pocket as profit or pass on in the form of lower prices to their customers and/or in the form of higher purchase prices to their suppliers. If the saving was passed on in one of these two forms, the chartered companies expanded their selling and buying activities at the expense of local competitors; if they were not, the companies expanded their reserves of liquidity or their assets, thereby enhancing their subsequent capabilities to eliminate or subordinate local competitors as well as to cope with rivals in the world-economy at large.

More specifically, as Steensgaard himself put it in a summary statement of his argument,

[like] the trading empire of the Portuguese king, the companies were integrated, nonspecialized enterprises, but with one remarkable difference. They were run as a business, not as an empire. By producing their own protection, the companies not only expropriated the tribute but also became able to determine the quality and cost of protection themselves. This meant that protection costs were brought within the range of rational calculation instead of being in the unpredictable region of 'the acts of God or of the King's enemies.' (Steensgaard 1981: 259–60)

Our main concern here is not so much with this special aspect of the internalization of protection costs pioneered by the Dutch through the VOC but with the far more general aspect of such an internalization which can be inferred by comparing the Dutch and the Genoese systems or regimes of accumulation on a world scale. In this comparison, the internalization of protection costs appears as the development that enabled the Dutch capitalist class to carry systemic processes of capital accumulation one step further than the Genoese capitalist class could. But it appears also as a step backward in the process of differentiation between business and governmental organizations.

In order to identify this double movement – forward and backward at the same time – it is necessary to begin by defining the main features of the Genoese regime of accumulation in relation to the Venetian regime. As Braudel has put it, "[in] Venice the state was all; in Genoa capital was all" (1982: 444; see also Abu-Lughod 1989: 114 and *passim*). What we shall understand by this dichotomy is that, while in Venice the strength of capital rested squarely on the self-reliance and competitiveness of the coercive apparatus of the state, in Genoa capital stood on its own feet and the power of the Genoese state, such as it was, was dependent on the dispositions and capabilities of Genoese capital. The difference could be observed at various levels.

In the struggle over markets, or even in the defense of the city itself, the war-making and state-making capabilities of the Genoese republic were not competitive. Not only had Genoa lost the war with Venice for control over Levant trade; in addition, "Genoa was constantly surrendering to other powers, either forcibly, voluntarily or out of prudence ... whereas Venice ... remained impregnable, yielding for the first time only in 1797 – and then to Bonaparte" (Braudel 1984: 158).

Closely related to this inherent weakness of the Genoese state was its reliance on private capital for its finances and even for the undertaking of war-making and state-making functions. We have already mentioned the *maone*. Equally important in this connection were the *compere*, state loans secured against the revenues of the government. In 1407, "*compere* and *maone* were brought together in the *Casa di San Giorgio*, which was in effect a state within the state, one of the keys to the secret and paradoxical history of the republic" (Braudel 1982: 440).

No such institution existed in Venice. Here the state was firmly in control of its own finances and, far from relying on private associations to carry out war-making and state-making functions, it intervened actively in providing individual merchants and private associations with the basic infrastructure which they required to carry out their business. "The system of the *galere di mercato* was one of these interventionist measures by the Venetian state, inspired by hard times." The system was based on vessels built, owned, and organized in defensive convoys by the government but leased to merchants at an annual auction, so that "the 'private sector' was able to make use of facilities built by the 'public sector.'" Through this system, Venice steadily expanded

> the tentacular network which [she] maintained in the Mediterranean, with one extra long arm snaking to Bruges ... after 1314, when the *galere di Fiandra* were introduced.... [The system] was probably operating at full capacity in about 1460, when the Venetian government introduced the *galere di trafego*, the curious shipping line which greatly stepped up Venice's trade with North Africa, giving access to the gold of the Sudan. (Braudel 1984: 126–7)

But this was not all. In addition, the Venetian state was extremely active and effective in forcing commodity flows through Venice:

> Every German merchant had to deposit his merchandise in [a compulsory segregated residence, the *Fondaco dei Tedeschi*] and lodge in one of the rooms provided, sell his goods under the watchful eye of the Signoria's agents and use the proceeds to buy Venetian goods.... On the other hand, Venice forbade her own merchants to buy and sell directly in Germany. As a result, the Germans were obliged to come to Venice in person to buy cloth, cotton, wool, silk, spices, pepper and gold ... delivering to the merchants of Venice iron, hardware, fuştians ... and, from the mid-fifteenth century onwards, ever-larger quantities of silver currency. (Braudel 1984: 125)

The Genoese government had neither the will nor the power to impose these kinds of restriction on the activities of its own and of foreign merchants. The greater freedom of transactions which it allowed did attract some German buyers, but "the Germans could find nothing there they could not also find in Venice, which had become a sort of universal warehouse of the world as Amsterdam was to be, on a larger scale, in a later century. How could they resist the convenience and temptation of a city lying at the heart of the world-economy?" (Braudel 1984: 125).

From all these points of view, Venice's state-centered regime of accumulation appears to have been far more successful than Genoa's capital-centered regime. This was certainly true in the short run, bearing in mind that, in these things, a century is even more of a "short run" than Joseph Schumpeter thought. But in the longer run, it was not the Venetians but the Genoese that went on to promote, monitor, and benefit from the first world-embracing cycle of capital accumulation. This brings us to another major difference between the two regimes of accumulation.

The very success of the Venetian regime of accumulation, combined with the fact that this success rested on the power of the state, enhanced the introversion of Venetian capitalism and its lack of innovative thrust. In Venice, the main personifications of capital tended to be or become parochial and inward-looking. Bankers and financiers were "entirely taken up with the activity of the Venetian market and were not at all tempted by the possible transfer of their business to the outside world and the search for foreign custom" (Gino Luzzatto, quoted in Braudel 1984: 131).

Except in state- and war-making, the main innovative thrust of northern Italian capitalism did not come from Venice. In manufacturing, banking, and the formation of large firms, the initiative had come traditionally from Florence and other Tuscan city-states. In the opening up of new trade routes, including the new routes added by the Venetian government to the system of the *galere*, the initiative had come from the Genoese. Untroubled by long class wars as Florence was, or by endless feuding as Genoa was, or by a deep-seated insecurity in its trade and power relations with the wider world within which it operated as both Florence and Genoa were, Venice

> was content to settle for tried and trusted methods.... [She] was from the start trapped by the logic of her own success. The true doge of Venice, standing opposed to all forces of change, was the city's own past, the precedents to which reference was made as if they were the tablets of the law. And the shadow looming over Venice's greatness was that of her greatness itself. (Braudel 1984: 132)

In sharp contrast to this pattern, Genoese capitalism was subject to a strong centrifugal and innovative thrust, which intensified with the disintegration of the Genoese military–commercial empire in the Mediterranean and Black Sea regions:

[Genoa] manufactured goods, for other people; sent out her shipping, for other people; invested, but in other places.... But how was [the] security and profitability [of Genoese capital] to be protected in the outside world? This was Genoa's constant worry: she had to live forever on the *qui-vive*, obliged to take risks and at the same time to exercise great prudence.... Time after time, Genoa changed course, accepting on each occasion the need for another metamorphosis. Building up one foreign empire after another for her own use, then abandoning it once it became unworkable or uninhabitable, devising and creating another ... – such was the destiny of Genoa, a fragile creation and an ultra-sensitive seismograph, whose needle quivered whenever there were stirrings in the rest of the world. A monster of intelligence – and of hard-heartedness if necessary – was Genoa not doomed to eat or be eaten? (Braudel 1984: 162–3). ˙

Just as Venice's inherent strength in state- and war-making was its weakness, so Genoa's weakness in these same activities was its strength. In an attempt to beat Venetian competition, or because they had been beaten by it, Genoese merchants forced their way into every corner of the European world-economy and opened up new trade routes within and beyond its geographical boundaries. By the beginning of the fifteenth century, they had settlements in the Crimea, Chios, North Africa, Seville, Lisbon, and Bruges. Even though they lost their trading posts in the Crimea to Ottoman occupation in 1479, before long they had set up business in Antwerp – the central warehouse of Iberian world commerce – and in Lyons (Braudel 1982: 164; 1984: 164).

As a result, the Genoese capitalist class came to control a cosmopolitan commercial and financial network of unprecedented and unparalleled scale and scope. Wherever they set up business, the Genoese were a "minority" but, as Braudel observes, a minority constituted a solid and ready-made network:

The Italian merchant who arrived empty-handed in Lyons needed only a table and a sheet of paper to start work, which astonished the French. But this was because he could find on the spot his natural associates and informants, fellow-countrymen who would vouch for him and who were in touch with all the other commercial centers in Europe – in short everything that goes to make up a merchant's credit and which might otherwise take years and years to acquire. (Braudel 1982: 167)

Genoese merchants were not the only ones to control and operate far-flung networks of this kind. As previously noted, they were only one of several expatriate business groups organized in "nations" that were recognized as such by other business groups and by the governments of the places in which they resided. In addition, there were Jewish,

Armenian, and other diaspora merchant networks that were not recognized as "nations." But owing to the long history of the Genoese in building one trade empire after another, in the sixteenth century their trans-statal commercial and financial networks endowed them with a distinct competitive advantage, not just over other trans-statal "nations," but also over their Venetian rivals who were conspicuous by their absence in this kind of trans-statal networking.

In sum, in the course of the secular competitive struggle that set the one against the other, the Venetian and the Genoese regimes of accumulation developed along divergent trajectories, which in the fifteenth century crystallized into two opposite elementary forms of capitalist organization. Venice came to constitute the prototype of all future forms of "state (monopoly) capitalism," whereas Genoa came to constitute the prototype of all future forms of "cosmopolitan (finance) capitalism." The ever-changing combination and opposition of these two organizational forms and, above all, their ever-increasing scale and complexity associated with the "internalization" of one social function after another, constitute the central aspect of the evolution of historical capitalism as a world system.

A comparison of the two systemic cycles of accumulation sketched thus far reveals that, right from the start, the evolution of historical capitalism as a world system did not proceed in linear fashion, that is, through a series of simple forward movements in the course of which old organizational forms were superseded once and for all by new ones. Rather, each forward movement has been based on a revival of previously superseded organizational forms. Thus, whereas the Genoese cycle of accumulation was based on the supersession of Venetian state (monopoly) capitalism by an alliance of Genoese cosmopolitan (finance) capitalism with Iberian territorialism, this alliance was itself superseded at a later time by the Dutch revival of state (monopoly) capitalism in a new, enlarged, and more complex form.

This double movement – forward and backward at the same time – reflects the self-limiting and dialectical nature of all the organizational innovations that, historically, have propelled processes of capital accumulation on a world scale outward and onward in space and time. Thus, in the fifteenth century the Genoese entered into an organic relationship of political exchange with Iberian territorialist organizations as the most reasonable way – if not the only way – in which to bypass the limits imposed on the expansion of their capital by the closing in on their trade networks of Ottoman, Venetian, and Aragonese-Catalan power; and our argument has been that this course of action was highly successful. To this we should now add that the price of this success was a further weakening of the state- and war-making capabilities of the Genoese government. This weakening, in turn, left Genoese cosmopolitan (finance) capitalism hostage to the territorialist tendencies and capabilities of its Iberian allies and vulnerable to the resurgence of state (monopoly) capitalism in more complex and powerful forms.

The absolute and relative weakening of Genoese cosmopolitan capitalism was the inevitable long-term result of the "division of labor" inherent in the political exchange between Genoese capital and Iberian states. The advantage of this exchange was that each of the two partners could *specialize* in the performance of those functions for which it was best equipped, while relying on the other partner for the performance of those functions for which it was worst equipped. Through this exchange and division of labor, Iberian rulers could mobilize the most competitive and powerful cosmopolitan network of trade and finance in existence in support of their territorialist pursuits, while Genoese merchant bankers could mobilize the most competitive and powerful war- and state-making apparatus in existence in support of their capitalist pursuits.

Whatever the effects of this division of labor on the predispositions and capabilities of Iberian rulers – though these need not concern us here – its effect on the Genoese capitalist class was to induce it to "externalize" protection costs further. That is to say, instead of becoming self-reliant and competitive in those state- and war-making activities that were necessary to protect their commerce effectively, the Genoese became over-reliant on whatever "free ride" they could squeeze out of the defensive apparatus of their Iberian partners. This seemed a good way of economizing on costs; and indeed it was. In fact, this externalization of protection costs might well have been the single most important factor in the success of the Genoese in promoting, monitoring, and profiting from the systemic cycle of accumulation which we have named after them.

Nevertheless, the externalization of protection costs was also the main limit of this success, because the Genoese had little or no control over the *direction* in which the "free ride" the Iberian states were providing was taking them. To be sure, the Genoese could jump off the "boat" of the Iberian rulers as soon as it was no longer profitable to stay aboard – as they did when they pulled out of trade in 1557 or when they discontinued the system of the Piacenza fairs in the late 1620s. But this was precisely the limit of Genoese cosmopolitan capitalism. Their traditional versatility in jumping on and off particular enterprises enabled them to profit from enterprises organized by others, but at the same time it limited their ability to influence, let alone determine, the strategy and structure of each and every enterprise from which they profited.

The increasing and ultimately complete externalization of protection costs was the main limit of the Genoese regime of accumulation. This became evident as soon as the Dutch regime of accumulation began to outgrow its regional dimensions to become a true world system. For the strength of this regime in comparison with, and in relation to, the Genoese regime was a total internalization of protection costs within the agency of capital accumulation.

The Dutch regime, like the Venetian, was rooted from the start in a fundamental self-reliance and competitiveness in the use and control of force. It was this that enabled the Dutch capitalist class to establish and reproduce its exclusive hold on Baltic trade and to supplement the profits of this trade with an inverted fiscal squeeze on Imperial Spain through plunder – the "original" sources of capital accumulation, Dutch style. Our argument has been that the enlarged reproduction of this mode of accumulation was based on a three-pronged strategy which successfully transformed Amsterdam into the central entrepôt of world commerce and high finance and brought into existence large-scale joint-stock chartered companies. In sketching this strategy of accumulation, we have underscored the process of circular and cumulative causation through which success in any one sphere bred success in the other two. To this we must now add that success in each and every one of the three spheres rested on a prior and continuing internalization of protection costs by the Dutch capitalist class organized in the Dutch state.

Whether in diverting traffic from Antwerp to Amsterdam or in fostering Dutch commercial supremacy, the self-reliance and competitiveness of the coercive apparatus of the Dutch state was as key an ingredient in the Dutch regime of accumulation as it had been in the Venetian:

> It was the Dutch state ... which blocked the Scheldt estuary after 1585, paralyzing Antwerp, and which, in 1648, compelled Spain to accept permanent trade restrictions on both the Scheldt and the Flemish coast, as well as to grant the Dutch favorable trade terms in Spain itself. It was the federal Dutch state which forced Denmark to keep the Sound open and the Sound tolls low.... By 1651 England was resorting to the deliberate use of force to disrupt Dutch commerce; only the efforts of the Dutch state prevented Dutch shipping from being swept from the seas.... Furthermore, the Dutch could not have imposed their trade supremacy in Asia, West Africa, and, more sporadically, in the Caribbean and Brazil had the States General not set up and armed politico-commercial organizations of unprecedented scope and resources not just with regard to the scale of their business operations but also in respect of their military and naval power. (Israel 1989: 411)

Dutch success in these spheres was in itself a sufficient condition for the decline of Genoese supremacy in high finance. Even here, however, the self-reliance and competitiveness of the Dutch in the use and control of force played a direct role in ensuring that the Dutch, and no one else, would be the heir to the Genoese:

Spain needed a *reliable* system for the transport of her funds. The Genoese solution, consisting of transferring funds by means of bills of exchange, an elegant arrangement but one that depended on control of an international network of payments, was succeeded by the easy solution of appointing as transporters the very people whose piracy, acts of war and attacks by sea Spain feared. After 1647 or 1648, the ultimate irony, the Spanish silver so essential for the administration and defence of the southern provinces of the Low Countries was transported not in English but in Dutch ships – possibly even before the separate peace of Munster ... had been signed. (Braudel 1984: 170)

At about the same time, we find another and even more direct piece of evidence of the greater advantages of self-reliance and competitiveness in the use and control of violence relative to the advantages of commercial virtuosity and sophistication. Having been ousted from the center of high finance, in 1647 the Genoese set up their own *Compagnia delle Indie Orientali* and, in an elegant move presumably aimed at minimizing operating costs as well as the risks of aggressive Dutch counter-measures, hired Dutch ships and sailors, and sent them out to the East Indies. Not at all impressed by this move, however, "the VOC replied by seizing the ships, arresting the Dutchmen, and sending the Genoese back home" (Israel 1989: 414, citing E.O.G. Haitsma Mulier).

The internalization of protection costs enabled the Dutch to carry systemic processes of capital accumulation much further than the Genoese strategy of externalizing protection costs had or could have done. To be sure, just as the Genoese had jumped on other people's "boats," so "[the] Dutch were by and large stepping into other men's shoes" (Braudel 1984: 216). In particular, if the Dutch, unlike the Venetians two centuries earlier, could turn their regional trade supremacy so swiftly and successfully into a world commercial and financial supremacy, it was because others had already established a direct sea route to the East Indies. What is more, these "others" had become foes, and from the start expansion in the Indian Ocean and the Atlantic was conceived of and carried out by the Dutch as an extension in space and time of their struggle against Imperial Spain, as witnessed by the fact that the charters of the VOC and of the Dutch West India Company (the WIC) stressed among their main purposes the objective of attacking the power, prestige, and revenues of Spain and Portugal.

But this antagonism towards Iberian power is precisely what differentiated the Dutch from the Genoese commercial expansion, and enabled the former to carry systemic processes of accumulation much further than the latter could. For, by taking the political organization of commercial space into their own hands, the Dutch could bring the capitalist logic of action to bear on protection costs in the extra-European world.

This tendency was most evident in the Indian Ocean, where the Portuguese had carried the day both before and after their incorporation into the Spanish empire in the 1560s. Here, as elsewhere, Portuguese enterprise bore the marks of the religious fervor and intolerance that had driven Iberian rulers to undertake overseas expansion in the first place:

> The crusading tradition of the Portuguese, and the uncompromising ortho-
> doxy and vigour of their missionaries, severely hampered their commercial and
> diplomatic endeavours. In an area where Islam was the dominant religion and
> was spreading rapidly among both Hindu and pagan peoples, the Portuguese
> often found themselves committed beforehand to religious hostility, in places
> where their interests would have been better served by commercial treaties.
> (Parry 1981: 244)

More importantly, the territorialist tendencies that characterized Iberian rulers had led the Portuguese in South Asia to spread themselves thinly, to increase rather than decrease protection costs in the region, and to make themselves vulnerable to the arrival of more "economizing" competitors from Europe. By seizing sources of supply, by destroying Arab ships, and by increasing the risks of capture for local traders in general, the Portuguese had greatly raised the protection costs of the Red Sea route, thereby succeeding for some decades in creating profound difficulties for their Arab and Venetian competitors:

> But at the same time the Portuguese king had created for his own spice-trading
> enterprise some high protection costs also, the costs of overawing Indian
> princes, seizing trading posts, and maintaining naval control of the Indian
> Ocean.... In trying to cut off the Red Sea Route [he] had assumed high
> protection costs for his own enterprise. He could not later lower spice prices
> substantially and still cover his own costs. (Lane 1979: 17–18)

As a consequence, the Red Sea route was never closed completely. In fact, after some reorganization to meet the new competition, the Arabs and Venetians managed to recover quite a lot of the ground lost to the Portuguese. In this they might have been helped by the consolidation of the Ottoman empire, which did not simply impose taxation, but also encouraged trade through its domains by providing security in its ports and overland routes, by building and maintaining roads and hostels, by allowing considerable freedom of trade to local merchants, and by cooperating with foreign merchants (Kasaba 1992: 8). Whether or not the consolidation of the Ottoman empire helped, eastern products continued to be transported in large quantities by the old routes, "and though the Portuguese preyed intermittently upon this trade, they could not prevent it" (Parry 1981: 249).

The Portuguese were thus forced to "[find] their place, not as a conquering empire, but as one of many competing and warring maritime powers in the shallow seas of the [Indonesian] archipelago" (Parry 1981: 242). Their shipping in the Indian Ocean remained "one more thread in the existing warp and woof of the Malay–Indonesian interport trade" (Boxer 1973: 49). Their regime, "built upon war, coercion and violence, did not at any point signify a stage of 'higher development' economically for Asian trade" (van Leur 1955: 118). Within the Indian Ocean constellation of powers, the position of the Portuguese as a *primus inter pares*, as well as the profitability of their trade, depended exclusively on their superior seaborne strength. "The appearance in eastern waters of an enemy who could defeat them at sea would damage their power and their trade severely. The Turks had several times tried and failed. In the end it was a European enemy [the VOC] who succeeded" (Parry 1981: 249).

The capability of the VOC to defeat the Portuguese at sea was a necessary but by no means a sufficient condition of the profitable incorporation of the East Indies, or parts of it, into the Dutch commercial empire. The Dutch soon realized that the profitable expansion of their trade in the Indian Ocean required a major restructuring of local networks of trade and power:

[Spices] were cheap and plentiful throughout the islands. There were many alternative sources of supply and many routes of shipment to India, the Near East and Europe. If the Dutch company were to become one more among many competing carriers, the result would be to raise prices in Indonesia and probably to glut the European market. To ensure a cheap and regulated supply in the East and a steady high price in Europe, a monopoly was necessary. This could be achieved only by doing what the Portuguese had failed to do; by controlling all the main sources of supply. (Parry 1981: 249– 50)

The creation of supply and demand conditions favorable to the profitable expansion of the VOC in the East Indies involved a wide range of military actions and territorial conquests. Some were aimed at eradicating alternative sources of supply, as in the case of those Molucca islands, where clove trees were deliberately uprooted, or of Cochin in India, which was occupied to prevent competition from the production of inferior but cheaper cinnamon. Some were aimed at promoting and enforcing specialization among different islands, as in the case of Amboyna, which became the clove island, of the Bandas, which became the mace and nutmeg islands, and of Ceylon, which became the cinnamon island. Some were aimed at excluding competitors from sources of supply that could not be controlled directly, as in the case of the Bantan sultanate of Java, whose pepper became a Dutch monopoly and whose ports were closed to other foreigners, while some were aimed at eliminating actual or potential competing centers of commodity exchange, as in the case of Macassar in the Celebes, taken by force to prevent it from becoming a base of free trade in spices (Parry 1981: 250–2; Braudel 1984: 218).

In these and other instances, the record of Dutch brutality in enslaving the indigenous peoples (literally and metaphorically) or in depriving them of their means of livelihood, and in using violence to break their resistance to the policies of the Company, matched or even surpassed the already abysmal standards established by the crusading Iberians throughout the extra-European world. But this brutality was wholly internal to a business logic of action and buttressed, instead of undermining, profitability:

> The historian, while horrified by such a record of brutality, cannot but be entertained by the calculated, extraordinary and sometimes grotesque web of interlocking purchases, cargoes, sales and exchanges. Fine spices did not find a ready market only in Holland: India consumed twice as much as Europe, and in the Far East they were a sought-after exchange currency, the key that opened many markets, just as the grain and ships' masts of the Baltic were in Europe. (Braudel 1984: 218–9)

The VOC thus combined what the Portuguese had already brought to the Indian Ocean (superior seaborne power and a direct organizational link with European markets for eastern products) with what was missing from Iberian enterprise: namely, an obsession with profit and "economizing," rather than with the crusade; a systematic avoidance of military involvements and territorial acquisitions that had no direct or indirect justification in the "maximization" of profit; and an equally systematic involvement in whatever activity (diplomatic, military, administrative, etc.) seemed best suited to seize and retain control over the most strategic supplies of Indian Ocean trade. In this comparison with Portuguese enterprise, the VOC did not so much internalize as it *economized on* protection costs. It cut down on involvements that did not yield satisfactory financial returns and supplemented the visible and expensive power of its violence-employing, violence-controlling apparatus with the invisible and, once acquired, self-financing power yielded by exclusive control over supplies of fine spices from the Indian Ocean area.

In this way the VOC "duplicated" in the Indian Ocean the state (monopoly) capitalism which the Dutch merchant elite had already practiced successfully in Europe. In the Indian Ocean, as in Europe, the decisive weapon wielded by the Dutch in the struggle for wealth and power was exclusive control over a regionally strategic supply – grain and naval stores in Baltic trade, fine spices in Indian Ocean trade. And in both instances, the acquisition and retention of this exclusive control rested on the deployment of a self-reliant and competitive war- and state-making apparatus.

It was this duplication of state (monopoly) capitalism that enabled the Dutch merchant elite, poised at the commanding heights of the Dutch state and of the "parastatal" VOC, to carry systemic processes of capital accumulation further than the cosmopolitan (finance) capitalism of the Genoese merchant elite had been able to do. Like the Genoese and unlike the Venetians, the Dutch broke out of the straitjacket of regional commerce to "maximize" profits on a world scale. But like the Venetians and unlike the Genoese, they never externalized protection costs and thus could bring an economizing logic of action to bear on commercial expansion in the extra-European world.

Once again, however, the main strength of a regime of accumulation (the Dutch, in this case) in relation to the regime which it superseded (the Genoese) was also its main weakness in relation to the forces that it brought into being (mercantilism). This contradiction found its clearest and most significant expression in the unintended and paradoxical result of Dutch success in the East Indies. The Dutch had gone into the Indian Ocean vowing to themselves and to others that they would stick to trade and avoid dissipating their energies in territorial conquest – a dissipation to which they attributed the decline of Portuguese wealth and power. But eventually they "found themselves . . . acquiring far more actual territory than the Portuguese ever possessed" (Parry 1981: 249–50). In part, these territorial acquisitions were a direct result of the restructuring of trade and power networks through which the VOC established its exclusive control over fine spices and, as such, they were integral to profitable trade pursuits. In part, however, they were the result of unplanned developments, which gradually transformed the VOC into a territorial, and in some ways territorialist, mini-empire.

The more the VOC succeeded in the pursuit of profit, the more powerful it became in what Ravi Palat (1988) has called the Indian Ocean "inter-state system." This growing power enhanced its freedom of action not just in regulating the demand and supply conditions of its trade, but in the imposition of tribute in the undisguised form of "contingencies" (tributes in kind) or in the covert form of "forced deliveries" (trading contracts exceptionally favorable to the VOC). Gradually, these two sources of revenue came to supply the bulk of its income and were increasingly confused both with one another and with the proceeds of ordinary trade (Parry 1981: 254).

The protection and enlarged reproduction of these revenues involved continuous struggles against the peoples subjected to the rule of the Company, against the many maritime princes and their subjects who had been driven to piracy by the policies of the Company (just like the Dutch themselves had been driven to piracy by the policies of Imperial Spain), and against European governments and business enterprises whose power was being undermined by the successes of the VOC or who were attempting to replicate these successes. Slowly but inevitably, the combination of these struggles led the VOC into widespread territorial annexations, far beyond anything that originally had been planned or deemed desirable (Boxer 1965: 104–5).

This development had an adverse effect on the Dutch regime of accumulation. For one thing it added a new twist to the "demonstration effect" which was drawing an increasing number of European states into the Dutch path of development. The Dutch, like the Venetians before them, had shown that capitalist techniques of power could yield considerable results in the European context. The prodigious success of the VOC in the second half of the seventeenth century in building a far more powerful Indian Ocean empire than the Portuguese had managed to do in the previous 150 years showed that, under favorable circumstances, capitalist techniques of power could beat territorialist techniques on the very terrain of territorial expansion. If a one-sided concentration on the pursuit of profit had enabled the Dutch to create a powerful mini-empire out of "thin air" – a charter by a government that was still struggling for its own sovereignty, and an open "credit line" on the Amsterdam financial market – what prevented territorialist organizations from building even more powerful empires by themselves becoming capitalist in orientation?

The successes of the VOC in empire-building thus added a new stimulus to the mercantilist wave that was undermining Dutch commercial supremacy from within and without. In addition, it had a second and more adverse effect on the Dutch regime of accumulation. As in many twentieth-century corporations, the very success and self-sufficiency of the VOC increased the power of the managerial bureaucracy that was responsible for its day-to-day operations. And this greater power came to be exercised at the expense not so much of the board of directors of the company (the *Heeren XVII*), as of the VOC's shareholders. As a consequence, a growing percentage of the actual and potential surpluses of the VOC was diverted from the payment of dividends to the bureaucratic expansion of the VOC and, above all, to licit and illicit rewards for the entourage of the *Heeren XVII* and the top management of the company (cf. Braudel 1984: 223–32).

The main effect of this tendency – at least from the point of view that concerns us here – was to strengthen the comparative attractiveness of investment and speculation in foreign, particularly English, stocks and shares on the Amsterdam stock exchange. "It was to England ... that the surplus capital of Dutch businessmen now began to flow" (Braudel 1984: 225–6, 261–2). The Amsterdam stock exchange, which in the early seventeenth century had functioned as a powerful "suction pump" siphoning surplus capital from all over Europe into Dutch enterprise, a century later thus turned into an equally powerful machine that pumped Dutch surplus capital into English enterprise. The prodigious success of the VOC in South Asia thus backfired on the Dutch regime of accumulation. It created a new enticement for territorialist organizations to imitate and compete with the Dutch, and then pushed Dutch surplus capital towards financing the most successful among the new competitors.

3

Industry, Empire, and the "Endless" Accumulation of Capital

The Third (British) Systemic Cycle of Accumulation

Throughout the eighteenth century, London gained ground on Amsterdam as a rival center of high finance. This was a result both of British successes in the struggle with France and lesser competitors for exclusive control over trade with the extra-European world and of the transfer of Dutch surplus capital to British enterprises. Ironically, however, it was the defeat of Britain by its North American subjects backed by the French in alliance with the Dutch that initiated the terminal crisis of Dutch rule in high finance.

As previously noted, Britain's retaliation against the Dutch after the War of American Independence annihilated the latter's seaborne power and inflicted significant losses on their commercial empire in the East Indies. As a consequence, one of the recurrent crises that had been undermining the Amsterdam financial market since the early 1760s swept away its central position in the European world-economy. In the previous crises, as a contemporary observer, M. Torcia, wrote in 1782, "[Amsterdam's] merchant bankers were to rise again like the phoenix, or rather to emerge from their own ashes and identify themselves in the end as the creditors of the ruined stock market" (quoted in Braudel 1984: 271). But the phoenix that rose from the ashes of the Dutch crisis of 1780–83 was London as the new governing center of world finance.

As with the end of Genoese financial supremacy 160 years earlier, and of British financial surpemacy 140 years later, the end of Dutch rule in high finance did not spell the ruin of Dutch capital. As Braudel (1984: 266) remarks, Amsterdam "continued to lead a profitable existence – and it is still today one of the high altars of world capitalism." But Dutch financial supremacy did wither away. Through the 1780s, and to a lesser extent the 1790s, Dutch rule in high finance coexisted uneasily with the emerging British rule, just as Genoese rule had done with the emerging Dutch rule in the 1610s and early 1620s. These were periods of transition, *interregna*, characterized by a dualism of power in high finance analogous to the one described by Charles Kindleberger (1973: 28 and *passim*) with reference to the Anglo-American dualism of the 1920s and early 1930s.

During all these periods of transition the ability of the previous center of high finance to regulate and lead the existing world system of accumulation in a particular direction was weakened by the rise of a rival center which, in its turn, had not yet acquired the dispositions or the capabilities necessary to become the new "governor" of the capitalist engine. In all these cases the dualism of power in high finance was eventually resolved by the escalation into a final climax (successively, the Thirty Years War, the Napoleonic Wars, the Second World War) of the competitive struggles that, as a rule, mark the closing (CM') phases of systemic cycles of accumulation. In the course of these "final" confrontations, the old regime of accumulation ceased to function. Historically, however, it was not until *after* the confrontations had ceased that a new regime was established and surplus capital found its way back into a new (MC) phase of material expansion.

During the French Wars, Britain's newly acquired commanding position in European high finance translated into virtually unlimited credit for its power pursuits. Suffice to mention that by 1783, the £9 million paid annually by the British government to service debts absorbed no less than 75 per cent of the budget and was the equivalent of more than a quarter of the total annual value of British trade. And yet, between 1792 and 1815 public expenditure in Britain could be increased almost six times, from £22 million to £123 million, partly through indirectly induced domestic inflation but mostly through new loans which, by 1815, raised the sum needed annually to service the debt to £30 million (Jenks 1938: 17; Ingham 1984: 106).

As a result of this explosive growth in public indebtedness and expenditures, the British capital goods industry experienced a phenomenal expansion. The iron industry in particular acquired a capacity well in excess of peacetime needs, as the post-war depression of 1816–20 demonstrated. However, overexpansion created the conditions for renewed future growth by giving British iron masters unparalleled incentives to seek new uses for the cheap products that their new, large-scale furnaces could turn out (McNeill 1984: 211–12). These opportunities were found in the iron railway and in iron ships. Railways in particular,

came to be built because contracting organizations needed work, iron masters orders, bankers and business organizers a project to work upon. And railway building became a service which Great Britain could dump abroad when her financial and constructing plant could not be kept employed at home. (Jenks 1938: 133–4)

Combined with the contemporaneous spread of mechanization within the textile industry, these innovations transformed the British capital goods industry into an autonomous and powerful engine of capitalist expansion. Up to the 1820s, enterprises specializing in the production of fixed capital goods had very little autonomy from their customers, whether governmental or business organizations, which, as a rule, subcontracted or closely supervised the manufacture of whatever fixed capital goods they required and did not themselves produce. But as mechanization increased the number, range, and variety of fixed capital goods in use, the enterprises that specialized in their production actively sought new outlets for their merchandise among the actual or potential competitors of their established clientele (Saul 1968: 186–7).

By the early 1840s, production of the new capital goods for the domestic market began yielding rapidly diminishing returns. But the continued unilateral liberalization of British trade created the conditions for a major boom in world trade and production. British capital goods found a ready demand among governmental and business organizations from all over the world. And these organizations in turn stepped up their production of primary inputs for sale in Britain in order to procure the means necessary to pay for the capital goods or to service the debts incurred in their purchase (Mathias 1969: 298, 315, 326–8).

The combined effect of these tendencies was a system-wide speed-up in the rate at which money capital was converted into commodities – particularly but not exclusively in the new means of transport by land and sea. Between 1845–49 and 1870–75, British exports of railroad iron and steel more than tripled and those of machinery increased nine-fold. During the same period, British exports to Central and South America, the Middle East, Asia, and Australasia increased some six-fold. The net that linked the various regions of the world-economy to its British center was visibly widening and tightening (Hobsbawm 1979: 38, 50–1).

The result of this acceleration in the material expansion of capital was the globalization of the capitalist world-economy:

[The] geographical size of the capitalist economy could suddenly multiply as the intensity of its business transactions increased. The entire globe became part of this economy.... Looking back from almost half a century later H.M. Hyndman ... quite rightly compared the ten years from 1847 to 1857 with the era of the great geographical discoveries and conquests of Columbus, Vasco da

Gama, Cortez and Pizarro. Though no dramatic new discoveries were made and ... few formal conquests by new military conquistadors, for practical purposes an entirely new economic world was added to the old and integrated into it. (Hobsbawm 1979: 32)

This analogy with the era of the great discoveries and conquests can be taken a step further. Just as the material expansion of capital of that era came to a close with the financial expansion of the Age of the Genoese, so from about 1870 onwards the nineteenth-century (MC) phase of material expansion ended in a (CM') phase of financial expansion. This is, of course, the period that Marxists, following Rudolf Hilferding, have identified as the stage of "finance capital." As we would expect, Braudel takes issue with Hilferding's characterization of "finance capital" as a *new* stage of capitalist development:

Hilferding ... sees the world of capital as a range of possibilities, within which the financial variety – a very recent arrival as he sees it – has tended to win out over the others, penetrating them from within. It is a view with which I am willing to concur, with the proviso that I see the plurality of capitalism as going back a long way. Finance capitalism was no newborn child of the 1900s; I would even argue that in the past – in say Genoa or Amsterdam – following a wave of growth in commercial capitalism and the accumulation of capital on a scale beyond the normal channels for investment, finance capitalism was already in a position to take over and dominate, for a while at least, all the activities of the business world. (Braudel 1984: 604)

The main thrust of this study, being itself derived from Braudel's notion of financial expansions as the "sign of autumn" of major capitalist developments, naturally lends support to the view that "finance capitalism was no newborn child of the 1900s," but had important precedents in Genoa and Amsterdam. But our analysis also enables us to draw a distinction between two opposite notions of finance capital which reduces considerably the historical significance of Hilferding's notion. As argued elsewhere (Arrighi 1979: 161–74), Hilferding's notion of finance capital not only differs from but in key respects is the antithesis of the notion of finance capital put forward at about the same time by John Hobson in his study of imperialism. Following Lenin (1952), Marxists (as well as most of their critics) have generally collapsed Hobson's notion into Hilferding's and thus missed the opportunity of distinguishing between the opposite forms of finance capitalism which these two notions convey and of uncovering the dialectical relationship that links the two.

As it turns out, these two forms of finance capitalism are nothing but expanded and more complex variants of the two elementary forms of capitalist organization that we have identified as state (monopoly) capitalism and cosmopolitan (finance) capitalism. Hilferding's notion corresponds to the first, and provides a fairly accurate picture of the strategies and structures of German capital in the late nineteenth and early twentieth centuries, as we shall see in chapter 4. Hobson's notion, in contrast, corresponds to the second and captures the essential traits of the strategy and structure of British capital during the same period. As such, it is far more useful than Hilferding's in the analysis of the late nineteenth-century financial expansion as the closing phase of the third (British) systemic cycle of accumulation.

Hobson sees this financial expansion as being promoted by two distinct agencies. One is what he calls "investors," that is, the holders of Braudel's "surplus capital" – money capital that accumulates beyond the normal channels for investment in commodities and creates the "supply" conditions of the financial expansion. In Hobson's view, the main source of this surplus capital was "tribute from abroad" in the form of interest, dividends, and other remittances. As subsequently documented by Leland Jenks (1938), this was indeed the "original" source of the nineteenth-century migration of capital from Britain (see also Knapp 1957). Moreover, ever since London had taken over the role of central money market of the European world-economy from Amsterdam, the flow of income from abroad had been supplemented by a significant inflow of foreign surplus capital seeking investment through the City (Platt 1980; Pollard 1985). Nevertheless, these flows alone cannot account for the waves of increasing height and/or length that came to characterize the export of capital from Britain in the late nineteenth and early twentieth centuries (see figure 7).

This behavior on the part of British foreign investment can only be understood in conjunction with the coming of the so-called Great Depression of 1873–96, which was nothing but a protracted period of cut-throat price competition:

The years from 1873 to 1896 seemed to many contemporaries a startling departure from historical experience. Prices fell unevenly, sporadically, but inexorably through crisis and boom – an average of about one-third on all commodities. It was the most drastic deflation in the memory of man. The rate of interest fell too, to the point where economic theorists began to conjure with the possibility of capital so abundant as to be a free good. And profits shrank, while what was now recognized as periodic depressions seemed to drag on interminably. The economic system appeared to be running down. (Landes 1969: 231)

In reality, the economic system was not "running down," nor was the Great Depression so startling a departure from historical experience as it seemed to its contemporaries. Production and investment continued to grow not just in the newly industrializing countries of the time (most notably, in Germany and the United States) but in Britain as well – so much so that a later historian was to declare that the Great Depression of 1873–96 was nothing but a "myth" (Saul 1969). Nevertheless, there is no contradiction in saying that there was a Great Depression at a time of continuing expansion in production and investment. On the contrary, the Great Depression was *not* a myth, precisely because production and trade in Britain and in the world-economy at large had expanded and were still expanding *too* rapidly for profits to be maintained.

More specifically, the great expansion of world trade of the middle of the nineteenth century, like all the phases of material expansion of previous systemic cycles of accumulation, had led to a system-wide intensification of competitive pressures on the agencies of capital accumulation. An increasing number of business enterprises from an increasing number of locations across the UK-centered world-economy were getting in one another's way in the procurement of inputs and in the disposal of outputs, thereby destroying one another's previous 'monopolies' – that is, their more or less exclusive control over particular market niches:

This shift from monopoly to competition was probably the most important single factor in setting the mood for European industrial and commercial enterprise. Economic growth was now also economic struggle – struggle that served to separate the strong from the weak, to discourage some and toughen others, to favour the new ... nations at the expense of the old. Optimism about the future of indefinite progress gave way to uncertainty and a sense of agony. (Landes 1969: 240)

From this point of view, the Great Depression of 1873–96 was not at all a departure from historical experience. As we have seen in chapter 2, all previous material expansions of the capitalist world-economy ended in an escalation of competitive struggles. To be sure, for about thirty years the escalation of competitive struggles which marked the end of the mid-nineteenth-century world trade expansion did not assume the form of open inter-state warfare, as it had done from the start on previous occasions. This lag can be traced to two main circumstances which distinguished the third (British) systemic cycle of accumulation from the first two. One relates to the "imperialism", the other to the "free tradism" of the British regime of rule and accumulation.

In the first circumstance, suffice it to say that at the time of the tapering off of the mid-nineteenth-century world trade expansion, British power in the world system at large was at its height. In the Crimea Czarist Russia had just been put in its place, and France, which had participated in the

Crimean war, was in turn put in its place soon after by Prussia. British mastery of the European balance of power was supplemented and complemented by the consolidation of Britain's territorial empire in India after the so-called Great Mutiny of 1857. Control over India meant a command over financial and material resources – including military manpower – which no state, or likely combination of states, could match, and that no ruling group could for the time being challenge militarily.

At the same time, Britain's unilateral free trade regime connected the entire world to Britain. Britain became the most convenient and efficient "marketplace" to procure the means of payment and means of production and to dispose of primary products. To borrow an expression from Michael Mann (1986), states were "caged" in a UK-centered global division of labor which for the time being further restrained their dispositions and capabilities to wage war on the leading capitalist state and on one another. Nevertheless, business enterprises were not equally restrained. The protracted and generalized cut-throat price competition of the late nineteenth century did in itself constitute a major escalation of inter-capitalist struggles – an escalation which eventually assumed the customary form of generalized inter-state warfare.

Moreover, as in all previous systemic cycles of accumulation, the intensification of competitive pressures brought on by the phase of material expansion was associated from the start with a major switch from trade and production to finance on the part of the British capitalist class. The second half of the nineteenth century was characterized not just by great waves of capital exports out of Britain, as previously noted, but also by an expansion of British provincial banking networks combined with an increasing integration of these networks with the networks of the City (Kindleberger 1978: 78–81; Ingham 1984: 143). This combination of circumstances suggests a close connection between the intensification of competitive pressures on British business and the late nineteenth-century financial expansion. As long as the mercantile expansion was in its phase of increasing returns, the main function of British provincial banking networks had been to transfer monetary resources – mostly in the form of revolving and open credits – from local, mostly agrarian, enterprises with a surplus of liquidity to other local enterprises with a chronic shortage on account of their high rate of growth or high ratio of fixed to working capital, or both (cf. Pollard 1964; Cameron 1967; Landes 1969: 75–7). But as soon as the mid-century great leap forward pushed the mercantile expansion into a phase of decreasing returns and intensifying competitive pressures, British provincial banking networks came to perform an entirely different function.

Increasingly, it was no longer just agrarian enterprises that were accumulating large cash surpluses (partly from rents, partly from profits) far in excess of what could be reinvested safely and profitably in their established lines of business. Also commercial and industrial enterprises, which hitherto had been expanding so fast as to absorb their own as well as other enterprises' cash surpluses, began to find that the large mass of profits which, in the aggregate, were accumulating in their books and bank deposits could no longer be reinvested safely and profitably in the lines of business in which they were being made. Rather than invest this surplus in new lines of business, in which they had no particular comparative advantage at a time of intensifying competitive pressures, or invest it in stepping up the competitive struggle within their own line of business, which was often problematic in view of the cohesive social organization of British business in "industrial districts" (see chapter 4) many of these enterprises must have chosen a far more sensible course of action: that is, keep at least part of their capital liquid and let the City, via the provincial banks or directly through brokers, take care of its investment in whatever form and in whatever location of the world-economy promised the safest and the highest returns: "A main attraction for joining Lombard Street was the prospect for fuller and more remunerative employment of surplus cash" (Sayers 1957: 269).

This brings us to Hobson's second agency of the late nineteenth-century financial expansion. In his view, the holders of the money capital that sought investment through the City were only "the cat's paws of the great financial houses" – financial houses to which he attributed the collective role of "governor of the imperial engine":

> These great businesses – banking, broking, bill discounting, loan floating, company promoting – form the central ganglion of international capitalism. United by the strongest bonds of organization, always in closest and quickest touch with one another, situated in the very heart of the business capital of every State ... they are in a unique position to manipulate the policy of nations. No great quick direction of capital is possible save by their consent and through their agency. Does any one seriously suppose that a great war could be undertaken by any European State, or a great State loan subscribed, if the house of Rothschild and its connexions set their face against it? (Hobson 1938: 56–7)

Eventually, as Hobson himself foresaw, cosmopolitan finance capital would lose control of the "imperial engine" as a direct consequence of its encouragement of the territorialist predispositions of the ruling groups of Imperial Britain (Arrighi 1983: ch. 4 and *passim*). But for almost half a century so-called *haute finance* functioned, in Karl Polanyi's words, "as the main link between the political and the economic organization of the world":

The Rothschilds were subject to no *one* government; as a family they embodied the abstract principle of internationalism; their loyalty was to a firm, the credit of which had become the only supranational link between political government and industrial effort in a swiftly growing world economy. In the last resort their independence sprang from the needs of the time which demanded a sovereign agent commanding the confidence of national statesmen and of international investors alike; it was to this vital need that the metaphysical extraterritoriality of a Jewish bankers' dynasty domiciled in the capitals of Europe provided an almost perfect solution. (Polanyi 1957: 10)

To be subject to no *one* government did not mean, of course, complete freedom of action. The most important limit on the autonomy of the Rothschilds was the limit implicit in the political exchange that linked them to Imperial Britain via the Bank of England and the Treasury. In this political exchange, as noted in chapter 1, the protection and preferential treatment which the financial network controlled by the Rothschilds received from the British government had its counterpart in the incorporation of that network in the power apparatus through which Britain ruled the world.

This cosmopolitan network of high finance was not as peculiar to the last third of the nineteenth century and the first third of the twentieth century as Polanyi thought. Its similarities with the cosmopolitan network that had regulated the European monetary system three centuries earlier during the Age of the Genoese are quite striking. We may well say that the Rothschilds were to the late nineteenth-century German-Jewish financial network centered on London what the *nobili vecchi* had been to the late sixteenth-century Genoese network. Both groups were the "governors," not of the "imperial engine," but of the finances of the imperial engine. They were business cliques who, in view of a profit and by means of the cosmopolitan business network which they controlled, acted as the "invisible hand" of an imperial organization – Imperial Britain and Imperial Spain, respectively. Thanks to this "invisible hand," both imperial organizations could reach and control a greater number and variety of power and credit networks than they would have ever been able to do just by deploying the "visible hand" of their state- and war-making apparatuses.

Instrumentality ran both ways. Neither the Rothschilds nor the *nobili vecchi* were mere instruments of the imperial organizations which they "serviced." Both cliques belonged to a wider circle of merchant bankers who had jumped on the boat of a territorialist organization and had skilfully turned the expansion of the latter into a powerful engine of the self-expansion of the commercial and financial networks which they themselves controlled. Just as the *nobili vecchi* were part of a wider circle of Genoese merchant bankers who had jumped on the boat of Iberian oceanic expansion only to emerge a century later as the "central bankers" of Imperial Spain, so the Rothschilds were part of a larger circle of German-Jewish merchant bankers who had jumped on the boat of Britain's industrial expansion only to emerge half a century later as the "central bankers" of Imperial Britain.

Both groups had started from positions of comparative powerlessness. The *nobili vecchi* were *fuoriusciti* – one of the many groups of exiles produced by the endless feuding of late medieval and early modern Genoa and northern Italy. The Rothschilds were one of the many business families that had fled war-torn and increasingly "regulated" Napoleonic Europe to seek refuge in comparatively peaceful and "unregulated" Britain. Whatever power either clique had, it lay in the cosmopolitan commercial networks to which they belonged – that is, primarily in the knowledge and connections that membership of those networks entailed. Just as the "Italian merchant who arrived empty-handed in Lyons needed only a table and a sheet of paper to start work," as Braudel put it in a passage quoted earlier, so a table and a sheet of paper was all that the German-Jewish merchants who arrived empty-handed in Manchester needed to start anew a successful business career:

> Young Rothschild and his countrymen brought a tradition of cash buying when the market was low, small profit margins, volume trade and rapid turnover of stock that set a cracking pace in Manchester and by degrees brought most of the continental trade into their warehouses. Backed by Frankfurt and Hamburg capital, their resources were often superior to local merchants served by Manchester's underdeveloped banking system. (Chapman 1984: 11; see also Jenks 1938)

Finally, when in the fullness of time the Rothschilds jumped off the boat of trade to concentrate on banking and finance – just as the *nobili vecchi* had done after the crash of 1557–62 – they could come to occupy and hold the center of high finance for more than half a century only because they had been able to take advantage of the mid-nineteenth-century commercial boom so as to expand and seize control of the cosmopolitan business network to which they belonged. As the boom intensified competition and curtailed profits in the commodity trades, this expanded and centrally controlled network could be turned into a powerful conveyor belt that pulled "idle" capital into the City of London only to send it out again. This idle capital was pulled in not only from Britain, where it was accumulating very fast, but from all over Europe. As Rozenraad, President of the Foreign Chambers of Commerce in London, once remarked,

Great Britain acts only as an intermediary, as honest broker working in all parts of the world, taking over – to a great extent with the money of her customers – the loans of other nations. . . . In a word, although the investment power of Britain is very great, London is the principal intermediary between Europe and other parts of the world for the placing of foreign securities here. (Quoted in Ingham 1988: 62)

Just as the central feature of the system of the Piacenza fairs in the Age of the Genoese had been direct access to the "idle capital" of northern Italy, so, in the words of Stanley Chapman (1984: 50), "the significant feature of the 'Rothschildesque' structure after 1866 was direct access to [continental] European capital."

There were, of course, important differences between the Age of the Genoese (1557–1627) and what, by analogy, we may call the Age of the Rothschilds (1866–1931). In part, these differences reflected the much greater scale and scope of the operations of cosmopolitan finance capital in the second period. Thus, the catchment area of the City of London under the Rothschilds was incomparably greater in scale and scope than the catchment area of the Piacenza fairs under the *nobili vecchi* three hundred years earlier, regardless of whether we "measure" it in terms of the networks from which surplus capital was procured or in terms of the networks to which surplus capital was reallocated.

In part, however, differences between the Age of the Genoese and the Age of the Rothschilds reflected the opposite outcomes of the power pursuits of their respective territorialist partners, sixteenth-century Imperial Spain and nineteenth-century Imperial Britain. Thus, whereas the consolidation of the "Rothschildesque" structure of high finance was associated with Landes's "most drastic *deflation* in the memory of man," the consolidation of the "Bisenzone" fairs, once they had settled at Piacenza, was associated with so drastic an *inflation* that historians refer to it as the price revolution of the sixteenth century. This divergent behavior of prices during the financial expansions of the first (Genoese) and of the third (British) systemic cycles of accumulation can be traced for the most part to the fact that in the nineteenth century Britain *succeeded* in building by other means the kind of world empire that Spain *fought in vain* to build on a smaller scale in the sixteenth century. What these "other means" were – coercive rule in the East and rule through the world market and the balance of power in the West – has been anticipated in chapter 1, and will be further elaborated at various points in this and the next chapter. Our concern here is with the relationship between war/peace and inflation/deflation on the one side, and between long-term fluctuations in prices and systemic cycles of accumulation on the other.

Historically, major wars have been the single most important factor in feeding inflationary tendencies in the European world-economy (Goldstein 1988). We may therefore suppose that the succession of wars fought by Spain in a vain attempt to establish and enforce imperial rule in Europe provide a good part of the explanation of why the sixteenth century was a time of drastic inflation, both absolutely and in comparison with the nineteenth century. Conversely, we may suppose that Britain's Hundred Years' Peace (1815–1914) provides a good part of the explanation of why the nineteenth century was a time of drastic deflation, both absolutely and in comparison with the sixteenth century.

More important for our present purposes, the opposite behavior of prices during the Genoese and the British financial expansions – whatever its actual reasons – provides strong evidence in support of the contention advanced in the Introduction that price logistics or "secular (price) cycles" are not valid indicators of what is specifically capitalist in systemic processes of capital accumulation. Thus, if we take indicators that reflect more accurately than movements in prices the changing circumstances of the commodity trades in which the capitalist agencies positioned at the commanding heights of the world-economy were more directly involved, the Age of the Genoese and that of the Rothschilds begin to look very similar.

These indicators are shown in figures 8 and 9. Charts A depict indicators of the overall expansion of sixteenth-century Spanish trade (figure 8) and of nineteenth-century British trade (figure 9). Charts B depict indicators of the expansion of the particular commodity trades that made the fortunes of the Genoese in the sixteenth century and of the Rothschilds in the nineteenth century: silver (figure 8) and raw cotton (figure 9), respectively.

All the charts show variants of a common pattern consisting of a phase of rapid/accelerating growth, which corresponds to our (MC) phase of material expansion, followed by a phase of slower/decelerating growth – our (CM') phase of financial expansion. In chart 9A, the pattern is somewhat disturbed by the sharp increase in the value of British imports during the First World War and the immediate post-war years. Nevertheless, even if we take the still "abnormally" high level of British imports in 1921–25 as the basis of calculation, the rate of growth of the series in the fifty years following 1871–75 was on average less than half what it had been in the preceding fifty years.

The logic that underlies the common pattern revealed by the four charts in figures 8 and 9 will be discussed in the closing section of this chapter. For now let us simply note that the financial expansions of the Genoese and of the British cycles of accumulation were both the culminating moments of world trade expansions, one centered on Spain, the other on Britain. The opposite trends in prices typical of the two financial expansions conceal this common pattern. In both cycles, a phase of accelerating investment of money capital in the expansion of world trade resulted in intensifying inter-capitalist competition in the purchase and sale of commodities. In one instance, the bidding up of purchase prices prevailed; in the other, the bidding down of sale prices prevailed. But whatever the impact on the general price level, intensifying competition resulted in a "precautionary" or "speculative" withdrawal of cash flows from trade. This in turn was both the cause and the consequence of the emergence of profitable opportunities in world financial intermediation – opportunities which select cliques of merchant bankers and financiers (the Genoese *nobili vecchi* in the late sixteenth century, the Rothschilds in the late nineteenth and early twentieth centuries) were particularly well placed to seize and turn to their own advantage.

In doing so, the leaders and governors of financial expansions tended to give temporary relief to the competitive pressures that depressed returns to capital, and thereby contributed to the transformation of the end of the material expansion into a "wonderful moment" for a wider circle of capitalist accumulators. "Depression", wrote Thorstein Veblen (1978: 241) shortly after the end of the Great Depression of 1873–96, "is primarily a malady of the affections of the business men. That is the seat of the difficulty. The stagnation of industry and the hardship suffered by the workmen and other classes are of the nature of symptoms and secondary effects." To be efficacious, therefore, remedies must be such "as to reach this emotional seat of the trouble and . . . restore profits to a 'reasonable' rate."

In the last quarter of the nineteenth century cut-throat price competition had indeed reduced profits to "unreasonably" low levels, and optimism had given way to uncertainty and a sense of agony. It is in this sense that the Great Depression of 1873–96 is not a myth. As Eric Hobsbawm (1968: 104) put it, "if 'depression' indicates a pervasive – and for the generations since 1850 a new – state of mind of uneasiness and gloom about the prospects of the British economy, the word is accurate." But then, suddenly, and as if by magic,

the wheel turned. In the last years of the century, prices began to rise and profits with them. As business improved, confidence returned – not the spotty, evanescent confidence of the brief booms that had punctuated the gloom of the preceding decades, but a general euphoria such as had not prevailed since . . . the early 1870s. Everything seemed right again – in spite of rattlings of arms and monitory Marxist references to the "last stage" of capitalism. In all of western Europe, these years live on in memory as the good old days – the Edwardian era, *la belle époque*. (Landes 1969: 231)

Needless to say, there was nothing magic in the sudden restoration of profits to a more than "reasonable" level, and even less in the consequent rapid recovery of the European bourgeoisie from its late nineteenth-century malady. As in the closing phases of all previous systemic cycles of accumulation, states began to compete keenly for the mobile capital that had been withdrawn from trade and was being made available as credit. Starting in the 1880s, military expenditures by European powers began to increase exponentially – the total for Great Britain, France, Germany, Russia, Austria-Hungary, and Italy rising from £132 million in 1880, to £205 million in 1900 and to £397 million in 1914 (Hobsbawm 1987: 350). And as inter-state competition for mobile capital intensified, profits recovered.

On the one hand, surplus capital found a new outlet in an increasing range of speculative activities which promised an easy and privileged access to the assets and future revenues of the governments engaged in the competitive struggle. The more widespread and intense inter-state competition for mobile capital became, the greater the opportunities for those who controlled surplus capital to reap speculative gains and the stronger, therefore, the tendency for capital to shed its commodity form. As can be seen from figure 7, the wave of capital exports from Britain during the Edwardian era far surpassed in height and length the previous two waves. The expansion of capital invested in speculative activities was in fact greater than it appears from figure 7, since the actual flow of capital out of Britain was often only a fraction of the capital floated and subscribed in London. In any event, while initially most of this expansion was no doubt financed by the steadily expanding inflow from abroad of interest and dividends on previous investments, an increasingly significant portion of the expansion must have been financed by a speed-up in the domestic conversion of commodity capital into money capital.

On the other hand, as surplus capital moved ever more massively out of trade and production, the enterprises that either could not or chose not to move out of trade and production found themselves relieved of the competitive pressures that had been curtailing their profit margins. This relief materialized from the 1880s onward in a steady improvement in Britain's terms of trade. But its most important manifestation was the overall decline of British real wages after the mid-1890s, which reversed the rapidly rising trend of the previous half-century (Saul 1969: 28–34; Barrat Brown 1974: table 14):

Arguing ... in terms of the power of organized labor, it might be suggested that during the highly competitive environment of falling prices, unions were able to squeeze profits between stable wages and market-controlled prices. ... But when the trend of prices was reversed in the less competitive environment after 1900 even strong unions could only push up the whole cost and price structure, and prices and profits kept pace with wages. Discounting the rise over the Boer War years, from 1896 to 1914 real wages fell slightly, in very marked contrast to the previous three decades. (Saul 1969: 33)

In short, just as the Great Depression of 1873–96 had been primarily a malady of businessmen depressed by "excessive" competition and "unreasonably" low profits, so the "beautiful times" of 1896–1914 were first and foremost a recovery from this malady following the dampening of inter-enterprise competition and a consequent upturn in profitability. But in so far as the expansion of trade, production, and working-class incomes were concerned, we can hardly speak of an upturn. Like all the wonderful moments that had characterized the closing phases of previous cycles of accumulation, the moment was wonderful only for a minority, and even for that minority it was short-lived. Within a few years, the "rattling of arms" – which was music to the ears of the European bourgeoisie as long as it inflated profitability by intensifying inter-state competition for mobile capital – turned into a catastrophe from which nineteenth-century capitalism would never recover.

In this respect, Edwardian Britain reproduced in highly compressed form and under radically different world-historical circumstances some of the tendencies that had already been at work in Florence during the very first financial expansion of the European world-economy. In both situations, the massive relocation of surplus capital from industry to finance resulted in unprecedented prosperity for the bourgeoisie, partly at the expense of the working class. In early modern Florence, the tendency eventually resulted in the takeover of the government by finance capital; in twentieth-century Britain, it eventually resulted in the takeover of the government by labor. But in both situations the beautiful times of the bourgeoisie were a sign of the supersession of existing capitalism.

Even closer is the resemblance between the Edwardian era and what is known as the "periwig period" of Dutch history – a period that broadly corresponds to the phase of financial expansion of the Dutch cycle of accumulation, particularly to the closing two or three decades of the expansion. As in Florence 400 years earlier and in Britain 125 years later, the financial expansion of the latter half of the eighteenth century was associated in Holland with widespread processes of "deindustrialization" (most clearly reflected in shipbuilding) and with a contraction in working-class incomes. "The merchant-bankers and the wealthy rentiers might never have 'had it so good,'" notes Charles Boxer (1965: 293–4), but as an eyewitness reported at the end of the period, "'the well-being of that class of people who lead a working life [was] steadily declining.'" And as in Renaissance Florence or in Edwardian Britain, or for that matter in Reaganite America, the capitalists-turned-rentiers of periwig Holland were only concerned with the very short run. "Each one says," wrote the periodical *De Borger* in 1778, "'it will last my time and after me the deluge!' as our [French] neighbors' proverb has it, which we have taken over in deeds if not in words" (quoted in Boxer 1965: 291).

The "deluge" for the Dutch republic came soon afterwards with the Patriots' Revolution of the early to mid-1780s – "insufficiently recognized for what it was, the first revolution on the European mainland, the forerunner of the French Revolution" (Braudel 1984: 275) – with the subsequent Orangist Counter-revolution, and with the final demise of the republic under Napoleon. Nothing of the sort happened, of course, in Britain after the Edwardian *belle époque*. On the contrary, victory in the First World War translated into a further expansion of Britain's territorial empire. Nevertheless, the costs of empire had begun exceeding its benefits by a good margin, thereby preparing the ground for its dismantling by the Labour government after the Second World War. But even before the empire was dismantled, the collapse of the British pound's gold standard in 1931 marked the terminal crisis of British rule over the world's money. As Polanyi (1957: 27) put it, "the snapping of the golden thread was the signal for a world revolution."

The Dialectic of Capitalism and Territorialism

As Geoffrey Ingham has pointed out, if the promoters of the reforms that led after the end of the Napoleonic Wars to the establishment of the free trade/gold standard regime had any specific economic interests in mind, it was the interests of British entrepôt trade, which had grown and prospered through the capture of Dutch and French commerce:

> Huskisson [President of the Board of Trade] believed that such policies would make Britain the Venice of the nineteenth century. Ironically, critics of Britain's entrepôt roles invoked the same comparison at a later date. At the end of the nineteenth century, many observers pointed out that the Venetian decline was the result of having based wealth and power on such insecure and uncontrollable mercantile activities. It was far better, they argued, to build a strong domestic productive base. (Ingham 1984: 9)

Both before and after the great mid-nineteenth-century trade expansion, British capitalism thus appeared to its contemporaries as a new variant of older forms of entrepôt capitalism. This indeed was the main similarity between the British and the earlier Dutch regime of accumulation. Like the Dutch, the British regime was still based on the principle of commercial and financial intermediation – the principle, that is, of buying in order to resell, of taking in in order to send out, of being supplied by the whole world in order to be able to supply the whole world again.

England's role as the clearing-house of the world-economy preceded and outlasted its role as the "workshop of the world" (Rubinstein 1977: 112–13). The industrial revolution and the defeat of Napoleon's imperial bid simply consolidated and expanded the scope of British entrepôt capitalism:

> [The] combination of the Industrial Revolution at home and the destruction after Waterloo of any barrier or competition to English global hegemony overseas brought into being a quite new form of world economy, in which British manufacturers possessed overwhelming preponderance amid generalized international free trade. As the density of commercial exchanges multiplied between ever more states and regions drawn into a common network, the functional necessity for a central switchboard to direct its flows grew steadily. The regular reproduction of multilateral transactions, in a world economic space segmented into independent political units, depended on the existence of at least one major clearing-house of universal scope. English industry and the English navy ensured that there would be *only* one. Amsterdam, isolated and sidelined by the Continental System, never recovered from the war-time blockade. With the submergence of Holland and the defeat of France, London had no possible rivals after 1815. (Anderson 1987: 33; emphasis in the original)

Taking issue with Ingham's and Anderson's characterization of nineteenth-century British capitalism as primarily commercial and financial in structure and orientation, Michael Barrat Brown has underscored its imperial and agro-industrial foundations. By the time the great mid-century expansion of British and world trade took off, Britain had already conquered a territorial empire of unprecedented and unparalleled scale and scope:

> [Contrary] to the views equally of Lenin and of Gallagher, Robinson and Fieldhouse, now repeated by Ingham and Anderson, most of the British Empire had already been established by 1850 – not only in Canada, and the Caribbean, Madras, Bombay and the Cape Coast from the seventeenth century, but in Gibraltar, Bengal, Ceylon, the Cape, Botany Bay, Penang, Guiana and Trinidad by the end of the eighteenth; and to these were added by 1850 virtually the whole of India, plus Hong Kong, Australia, New Zealand, Natal. Further increments, then, were almost entirely on the African continent. (Barrat Brown 1988: 32; see also Barrat Brown 1974: 109–10, 187)

Moreover, this far-flung territorial empire was primarily an agro-industrial rather than a commercial–financial complex:

To believe that British capital had basically a banking and merchanting role in the Empire would require us to suppose that there had been in the Empire no sugar and cotton plantations, no tea and rubber estates, no gold, silver, copper and tin mines, no Lever Brothers, no oil companies, no Chartered Company, no Dalgety, no British-owned railways and other utilities or mills and factories overseas. (Barrat Brown 1988: 31)

From the perspective adopted in this study, there is no real contradiction between the views of Ingham and Anderson on the one side, and Barrat Brown on the other. As we have underscored in chapter 1, and again in sketching the third (British) systemic cycle of accumulation, Britain in the nineteenth century did follow the developmental path of Venice and of the United Provinces; but it also followed the developmental path of Imperial Spain or, more precisely, of the Genoese–Iberian capitalist–territorialist complex. Once we acknowledge this hybrid structure of the developmental path of nineteenth-century British capitalism, the thesis of the "nightwatchman state" as applied to Victorian England does indeed become untenable. "What sort of nightwatchman was this who prepared the ground for every single activity of the building's occupants and not only watched against unfriendly acts from outside but effectively ruled the seven seas and established colonial outposts in every continent?" (Barrat Brown 1988: 35). Nevertheless, the "industrialism" and "imperialism" of nineteenth-century Britain were integral aspects of its *enlarged* reproduction of the strategies and structures of Venetian and Dutch entrepôt capitalism. It was precisely by being industrial and imperial in ways that neither Venice nor the United Provinces had ever been that Britain could exercise the functions of world commercial and financial entrepôt on a much grander scale than its predecessor ever dreamt of doing.

For the "industrialism" and "imperialism" of the British regime of accumulation in comparison with the preceding Dutch regime were expressions of a double movement – forward and backward at the same time – analogous to the one that had characterized the transition from the first (Genoese) to the second (Dutch) systemic cycle of accumulation. Just as in the late sixteenth and early seventeenth centuries the Dutch regime of capital accumulation on a world scale superseded the Genoese regime through a forward movement consisting of an internalization of protection costs, so in the late eighteenth and early nineteenth centuries the British regime superseded the Dutch through an internalization of production costs, of which industrialism was the main expression. And just as the Dutch regime had internalized protection costs through a backward movement consisting of a revival of the organizational structures of Venetian state monopoly capitalism, which the Genoese regime had superseded, so the British regime internalized production costs through a revival of the organizational structures of Iberian imperialism and Genoese cosmopolitan finance capitalism, both of which the Dutch regime had superseded.

By "internalization of production costs" we shall understand the process through which production activities were brought within the organizational domain of capitalist enterprises and subjected to the economizing tendencies typical of these enterprises. To be sure, capitalist enterprises specializing in production activities had existed long before the British cycle of accumulation took off. But this kind of enterprise had played either no role or only a secondary and subordinate role in the formation of the Genoese and Dutch regimes of accumulation. The leading capitalist enterprises of the Genoese and Dutch cycles were typically engaged in long-distance trade and high finance – the activities which Braudel (1982: ch. 4) calls the "home grounds" of capitalism – and as far as possible kept production activities outside their organizational domains. In the British cycle, in contrast, the accumulation of capital came to be based on capitalist enterprises that were heavily involved in the organization and rationalization of production processes.

In assessing the nature and extent of this new "organizational revolution" of the capitalist world-economy, it is important to bear in mind that the distinction between "trade" and "production" is not as clear-cut as it is often assumed to be. The reshuffling of goods in space and time, which is what trade is all about, can involve as much human effort and can add as much use-value ("utility") to the goods so reshuffled as does extracting them from nature and changing their form and substance, which is what we understand by production in a narrow sense. As Abbé Galiani once wrote, "[t]ransport ... is a kind of manufacture" (quoted in Dockés 1969: 321). But so is storage and all other trade-related activities that require human effort and make the goods reshuffled in space and time more useful to potential buyers than they would have been otherwise. Almost no trade activity can be undertaken except in conjunction with some kind of production in this broader sense, or even in the narrower sense mentioned above.

The capitalist organizations that specialized in long-distance trade were always involved in some kind of production activity. Besides storage and transport, they often engaged in some processing of the goods they bought and sold, and in the construction of at least some of the means and facilities required by the storage, transport, and processing of commodities. Shipbuilding was probably the most important of these activities, particularly for capitalist organizations like Venice and the United Provinces which were self-sufficient in "producing" the protection required by their traffics. In addition, capitalist organizations that specialized in long-distance trade engaged in, or closely supervised, the manufacture of goods (such as jewels and coins, high quality textile products and other luxuries, works of art, etc.) which were particularly suitable either as exclusive means of trade or as "stores" of the surplus capital that accrued to their members. But apart from these activities, the leading capitalist organizations of the Genoese and Dutch cycles avoided production as much as they could:

> Venice, Genoa and Amsterdam consumed grain, oil, salt, meat, etc., acquired through foreign trading: they received from the outside world the wood, raw materials and even a number of the manufactured products they used. It was of little concern to them by whom, or by what methods, archaic or modern, these goods were produced: they were content simply to accept them at the end of the trade circuit, wherever agents or local merchants had stocked them on their behalf. Most if not all of the primary sector on which such cities' subsistence and even their luxuries depended lay well outside their walls, and labored on their behalf without their needing to be concerned in the economic and social problems of production. (Braudel 1984: 295)

In partial qualification of this claim, Braudel immediately adds that these cities were often more conscious of the drawbacks than of the advantages of such an externalization of production: "obsessed with their dependence on foreign countries (although in reality such was the power of money that this was reduced to nothing), all leading cities desperately tried to expand their territory and to develop their agriculture and industry." As a result, the Italian city-states, and Holland later, came to be characterized by "1) a very 'modern' relationship between their rural and urban population; 2) an agricultural sector, where it existed, which tended to go in for cash crops and was a natural focus for capitalist investment ... [and] 3) a number of luxury industries, so often the most profitable" (Braudel 1984: 295–6).

There is in fact no need to assume that the Italian city-states or Holland were obsessed with dependence on foreign countries to account for this kind of involvement in domestic production. In the case of luxury industries, their profitability and the lack of social problems associated with their development were in themselves good enough reasons for the involvement. As for cash crops, it was only natural that the massive wealth that accumulated in the capitalist cities would bring into existence in contiguous rural areas a commercial agriculture oriented towards the production of food for the urban population. And it was equally natural that the capitalist centers would sooner or later incorporate these contiguous rural spaces within their political jurisdictions either for strategic or for economic reasons, and so promote their further commercialization and modernization.

Moreover, once a rural space had been incorporated *de facto* or *de jure* within the domains of the capitalist centers, the investment of capital in agriculture came to perform a function analogous to that performed by expenditures in works of art and other durable luxuries – the function, that is, of "storing" the profits that were being made in long-distance trade and high finance but could not be reinvested in these activities without jeopardizing their profitability. Then as now, a significant portion of this surplus capital tended to flow into speculation and into conspicuous consumption; and then as now, investment in real estate within the capitalist cities themselves were the most important means of combining speculation with conspicuous consumption. But investment in the commercialization and "gentrification" of the rural spaces that had been or were in the process of being annexed by the capitalist cities, could and did play an analogous role as complements or as substitutes of investment in urban real estate.

The shipbuilding, luxury, construction, and "modern" agriculture industries were not the only exceptions to the tendency of capitalist city-states to externalize as much as possible the economic and social costs of production. In certain periods, even long periods, some of the city-states engaged in one kind or another of manufacturing. Thus Braudel himself points out that after 1450 Venice began to develop an extensive and diversified manufacturing apparatus, and he goes on to suggest that it was probably inevitable for major commercial entrepôts to become converted to manufacturing. Having said this, however, he hastens to add that this tendency did not seriously challenge the "primacy of commercial capitalism over industrial capitalism until at least the eighteenth century." As far as Venice was concerned, real industrial expansion did not come until between 1580 and 1620. "All in all, industry seems to have contributed to Venetian prosperity only rather late in the day, as a makeweight, a compensation when the climate was unfavorable, a state of affairs very similar ... to that of Antwerp from about 1558–9" (Braudel 1984: 136).

As we shall see, there are good reasons for sharing this view of Venetian industrialization. Nevertheless, "industry" understood quite simply as involvement in non-agricultural extractive and processing activities contributed to the prosperity of other city-states very early rather than late in the day; and was not at all the result of the tendency of major commercial entrepôts to become converted to manufacturing, since these other city-states were not major commercial entrepôts to begin with. This was the case with Milan and Florence, whose fortunes during the pan-Eurasian trade expansion of the late thirteenth and early fourteenth centuries was largely built on specialization in industrial production – Milan in the production of metal goods and Florence in the production of textile goods. And while metal production in Milan was mostly artisanal in structure and orientation, textile production in Florence was thoroughly capitalist, being undertaken with a view to making a profit and through the massive employment of wage labor.

It follows that Braudel's thesis of the tendency towards the externalization of production costs by the leading centers of capital accumulation became operative only at the end of the pan-Eurasian trade expansion of the latter thirteenth and early fourteenth centuries. Before and during that expansion, the most advanced forms of capitalist enterprise – whether industrial, commercial, or financial – all developed in centers directly involved in production processes, most notably in Florence and other Tuscan city-states. But as soon as the expansion tapered off, this association of capitalism with industry gave way to a disassociation; and it was in Florence, where all the most advanced forms of capitalist enterprise were present, that in the fourteenth century the disengagement from industrial production proceeded most expeditiously.

The resulting curtailment of working-class incomes led to intense and protracted waves of class struggle, which culminated in the *Ciompi* seizure of governmental power in 1378. But working-class rebellion and revolution could not and did not stop the transfer of Florentine capital from industry to finance. If anything, by heightening the social problems involved in the marriage of industry and capitalism, it hastened their divorce and paved the way for the rise of finance capital to the dominant structure of governance of the Florentine city-state and of the European world-economy at large. Historical capitalism as world system was thus born of a divorce rather than of a marriage with industry.

Braudel's thesis must be qualified further to account for the fact that the disengagement from production which marked the birth of historical capitalism as a world system did not involve every center of capital accumulation or every sphere of activity of these centers. The financial expansion of the late fourteenth and early fifteenth centuries occurred in a state of generalized warfare both in the Italian sub-system of city-states and in the wider European political system. This created highly profitable opportunities for the armament and metal industries so that, while Florence deindustrialized, Milan did not and went on to benefit from the production of armor for the whole of Europe.

Moreover, the extent of the disengagement from production in any given city or sphere of activity often depended on the vicissitudes of war-making and state-making activities. The centralization of Levant trade in Venetian hands at the expense of the Genoese after the Peace of Turin (1381), meant that entrepôt-related production experienced a far greater contraction in Genoa than in Venice. At the same time, the incorporation of a rural space within the domains of Milan, Venice, and Florence in the course of the "Italian" Hundred Years War meant that in these city-states agricultural production increased, regardless of what was happening to industrial production. And in the cities in which a growing share of surplus capital was diverted from money-making to state-making, as in Venice and Florence, production in the construction industry expanded. Thus, the reserve army of labor created in Florence by the contraction of the textile industry became the foundation of the "informal," that is, unregulated, building boom of the Renaissance.

When all is said and done, however, the main thrust of the financial expansion of the late fourteenth and early fifteenth centuries was towards a fission of the most advanced forms of capitalist enterprise from production. This tendency was obscured during the financial expansion by the fact that it was not experienced uniformly across the system of city-states, and even more by the fact that it was weakest in Milan and Venice – the two city-states that were emerging as great powers in European politics. But as the trends of the following century and a half revealed, state power and industrialism were unreliable indicators of the self-expansion of capital. Starting in the closing decade of the fifteenth century, and more clearly in the course of the sixteenth century, bourgeoisies organized primarily in city-states – the Venetian included – ceased to play the role of the dominant capitalist class of the European world-economy. Increasingly, this role came to be played by expatriate bourgeoisies organized in cosmopolitan "nations," which specialized in high finance and long-distance trade and let territorialist organizations take care of production. Among these "nations," the Venetian bourgeoisie was conspicuous by its absence, and the Milanese played only a secondary and wholly subordinate role. But the expatriate bourgeoisies of Florence and Genoa, where the tendency towards the fission of capitalism from production had been strongest, emerged as the two most prominent members of the system of "nations" which dominated European high finance and long-distance trade throughout the sixteenth century.

Under these new systemic conditions the rapidly increasing involvement of Venice in industrial production in the late sixteenth century does indeed appear to have been, as Braudel maintains, "a makeweight," a compensation for the city's irremediable commercial decline. It was above all at this time of rapid industrialization that Venice as a business organization, though less as a governmental organization, became the victim of its earlier extraordinary successes. Its victories at sea against Genoa, its conquest of the *Terraferma*, its command over the northern Italian balance of power – all had combined in the late fourteenth and early fifteenth centuries in enabling Venice to absorb the effects of the ongoing world economic contraction without having to reorganize and restructure its governmental and business institutions. And yet, the unreformed institutions of Venetian state monopoly capitalism were ill-suited to cope effectively with the challenges posed by the subsequent rise of powerful capitalist–territorialist complexes formed by the alliance of highly specialized cosmopolitan capitalist classes (the so-called "nations") with equally specialized territorialist states.

The differentiation and exchange between these two kinds of organization were based on a division of labor in which the territorialist states took care of production, including the production of protection, and of short-distance trade, while the capitalist "nations" took care of trans-statal monetary regulation and much of long-distance trade. Within this dominant structure, Venice was neither fish nor fowl: neither a powerful capitalist "nation" nor a powerful territorialist state. It was a remnant of the bygone era of capitalist city-states. By the late sixteenth century, Venice, as a governmental organization, still had considerable clout in European politics; but as a business organization, it had become little more than a cog in the Genoese system of the Piacenza fairs. For this system continually turned the balance of payments surplus generated by Venetian industries into a means through which the Genoese obtained in Antwerp the *asientos* that gave them ever more exclusive control over American silver delivered in Seville. This in turn enabled the Genoese to grasp ever more firmly the surplus of the Venetian balance of payments; and so on, in an endless process of circular and cumulative causation through which the industrial expansion of Venice became more and more a means of the self-expansion of Genoese capital (see chapter 2).

It was in this historical context that the foundations of nineteenth-century British capitalism were first laid in an attempt to free Britain from a deeply frustrating condition which in many ways resembled that faced by Venice. For Britain, like Venice in the sixteenth century, was neither one thing nor the other – neither a territorialist organization powerful enough to compete successfully with Spain and France, nor a capitalist organization powerful enough to compete successfully with the Genoese and Florentine "nations." But to be neither fish nor fowl does not mean to belong to the same species. On the contrary, Venice and England in the sixteenth century were opposite types of organization which were "moving" along radically different paths of development but happened to pass one another briefly on the way to their respective destinations.

Whereas Venice was a capitalist state that had become the victim of its past successes, England was a territorialist organization that had become the victim of its past failures. Past successes had translated into territorial acquisitions and into a metamorphosis of the Venetian bourgeoisie into an aristocracy which made Venice resemble a small territorialist state, such as England was. Past failures had translated into a territorial confinement and into a metamorphosis of the English aristocracy into a bourgeoisie that made England resemble a large capitalist state, such as Venice was. The resemblances between Venice and England were further enhanced by the fact that in the late sixteenth and early seventeenth centuries both states experienced rapid industrial expansion. But all these resemblances were highly deceptive, as witnessed by the fact that over the next three centuries England went on to redraw the map of the world and become simultaneously the most powerful territorialist *and* capitalist state the world had ever seen, while Venice lost all its residual power and influence until it was wiped off the map of Europe, first by Napoleon and then by the Peace of Vienna.

This radical divergence of the trajectories of Venetian and English power in the seventeenth and eighteenth centuries was in part a matter of geography. The shift of the crossroads of world commerce from the eastern Mediterranean to the English Channel, where American and Asian supplies met Baltic supplies, opened up for England, at the same time that it closed down for Venice, unique opportunities of commercial and naval expansion. But as Braudel said (1984: 523), "if geography proposes, history disposes." In order to appropriate the gifts of its privileged geographical position, England had to go through a long historical process in the course of which its ruling groups first learned how to turn a geopolitical handicap into an advantage, and then began to exploit this advantage to wipe out all competitors.

This long historical process began with the bloody feuds known as the Wars of the Roses (1455–85), which ensued from the expulsion of the English from France at the end of the Hundred Years War. "Once a victorious royal authority no longer held the higher nobility together, the late-medieval machinery of war turned inwards, as brutalized retainers and indentured gangs were unleashed across the countryside by magnate feuds, and rival usurpers clawed for the succession" (Anderson 1974: 118). The most important domestic effect of the bloodbath that followed was a fundamental weakening of the landed aristocracy and the consolidation of royal power under the victorious Tudor dynasty (Moore 1966: 6).

But this consolidation was not matched by a corresponding increase in the overall power of the English monarchy. On the contrary, by the time consolidation on the home front was completed, the English monarchy had been irremediably marginalized by developments on the continent:

[By] the early 16th century, the balance of forces between the major Western States had totally altered. Spain and France – each victims of English invasion in the previous epoch – were now dynamic and aggressive monarchies, disputing the conquest of Italy between them. England had been suddenly outdistanced by both. All three monarchies had achieved an approximately comparable internal consolidation but it was just this evening-up which permitted the natural advantages of the two great continental powers of the epoch to become for the first time decisive. The population of France was four to five times that of England. Spain had twice the population of England, not to speak of its American Empire and European possessions. This demographic and economic superiority was heightened by the geographical necessity for both countries to develop modernized armies on a permanent basis, for the perpetual warfare of the time. (Anderson 1974: 122–3)

The English monarchy never resigned itself to this condition of marginality in European politics. Under Henry VII a prudent realism prevailed, which none the less did not prevent him from reviving Lancastrian claims to the French monarchy, from fighting to block the Valois absorption of Brittany, and from attempting to gain the succession in Castile. But as soon as Henry VIII acceded to the throne, a determined and sustained effort to regain the lost ground was launched. Having recruited large numbers of modern troops from Germany, the new king started campaigning against the Scots and intervening militarily in the Valois–Habsburg wars in northern France. When the successive campaigns of 1512–14, 1522–25 and 1528 yielded nothing, partly out of frustration and partly out of miscalculation, he stumbled into the break with Rome. "England had been marginalized by the Franco-Spanish struggle for Italy: an impotent onlooker, its interests had little weight in the Curia. The surprise of the discovery was to propel the Defender of the Faith into the Reformation" (Anderson 1974: 123–4).

The break with Rome further consolidated royal power at home. Politically, the greater clergy, who were privileged landowners and franchise-holders, became royal servants. "The authority of the king over the church became the authority of the king in Parliament" (Hill 1967: 21). Financially, revenues which had previously gone to Rome were diverted to the English crown: firstfruits, tithes, and monastic lands more than doubled net annual royal revenue, and the increment would have been considerably larger if monastic lands had not been alienated (Dietz 1964: 138–40; Hill 1967: 21).

Vast as it was, this windfall was immediately dissipated in a new military adventure. Henry's last major act – the wars against France and Scotland of the 1540s – was a costly affair, amounting to a staggering £2,135,000. To cover them the English crown had to resort to forced loans and massive currency debasement as well as to an acceleration in the alienation of monastic domains at drastically reduced rates (Kennedy 1987: 60; Dietz 1964: chs 7–14). The immediate result was a swift regression in the political stability and authority of Tudor rule during the minority of Edward VI and the brief reign of Mary Tudor. In a rapidly deteriorating social context, characterized by serious rural unrest and repeated religious crises, the struggle for control of the court between territorial lords was renewed and the last English toehold on the continent (Calais) was lost to the French (Anderson 1974: 127–8).

Yet, the regression was only temporary and provided the stimulus needed to complete the process through which England was to recognize, and fully exploit, the advantages of its insular position at the main crossroads of world commerce. In the latter half of the century, the "adventurism" of Henry VIII was superseded by the "realism" of Elizabeth I, who promptly acknowledged the limits of English power. "Since her country was no match for any of the real 'superpowers' of Europe, Elizabeth sought to maintain England's independence by diplomacy and, even when Anglo-Spanish relations worsened, to allow the 'cold war' against Philip II to be conducted at sea, which was at least economical and occasionally profitable" (Kennedy 1987: 61).

Elizabeth's economizing behavior in war-making did not rule out military interventions on the continent. Such interventions continued, but their purpose changed to strictly negative aims such as preventing the Spanish reconquest of the United Provinces, or the installation of the French in the Low Countries, or the victory of the League in France (Anderson 1974: 130). Elizabeth's overwhelming preoccupation was to preserve rather than change the continental balance of power, even if this meant buttressing the power of old enemies like France, because "[w]henever the last day of France comes it would also be the eve of the destruction of England" (quoted in Kennedy 1976: 28).

Nor did Elizabeth's realism and prudent behavior in war-making lessen the territorialist predispositions of the English state. Territorialism was simply redirected closer to home, where it completed the fusion of the several political communities into which the British islands were still divided. Where relationships of forces made military conquest costly and risky, as in Scotland, fusion was pursued through peaceful means – namely, through the personal union which at Elizabeth's death would join England and Scotland. But where relationships of forces were favorable, violent means were resorted to without any restraint:

> [Incapable] of frontal advance against the leading monarchies of the mainland, [Elizabethan expansionism] threw its largest armies against the poor and primitive clan society of Ireland.... The guerrilla tactics adopted by the Irish were met by policies of ruthless extermination. The war lasted nine years before all resistance was pulverized by the English commander Mountjoy. By Elizabeth's death, Ireland was militarily annexed. (Anderson 1974: 130–3)

But English expansionism was also redirected towards the oceans and the extra-European world. England from the start had been in the forefront in the introduction of the large warships equipped with firearms which, around 1500, revolutionized naval power in Europe (Lewis 1960: 61–80; Cipolla 1965: 78–81). But it was Henry VIII's fruitless attempts to become a protagonist in the continental power struggle that turned the English navy into a respectable force (Marcus 1961: 30–1). Elizabeth further expanded and rationalized the royal fleet, just in time to ensure security against the Spanish Armada. By the time the Armada was defeated in 1588, "Elizabeth I was the mistress of the most powerful navy Europe had ever seen" (Mattingly, as quoted in Anderson 1974: 134).

This rapid expansion of English seapower would not have been possible without the contribution of English merchants, pirates, and privateers, who were often the same persons. These private forces "raided the far-flung sea routes to foreign colonial empires, garnered fantastic booty, and attained a superiority in shipbuilding and seamanship that made them the true heirs of the Vikings. Elizabeth, maneuvering cautiously, disavowed them as need arose, while silently furthering their ends" (Dehio 1962: 54–6).

This tacit support for the private use of violence by sea bore its fruits in the decisive Anglo-Spanish confrontation of 1588. In the battle against the Armada, Elizabeth could count for her defenses on experienced private crews almost five times as numerous as her own: "welded together in a hundred actions ... [these private crews] were the vanguard of the new maritime England, at their head Francis Drake, the embodiment of England's transition from the age of the freebooters to that of a great naval power" (Dehio 1962: 56).

Elizabeth actively encouraged this transition, not just by expanding and rationalizing the royal fleet and by tacitly supporting piracy and privateering. Earlier than the Dutch, she revived the Genoese tradition of the *maone* by establishing joint-stock chartered companies, which became the main foundation of the later prodigious overseas expansion of English networks of trade and power. Also in this sphere, the initial contribution of the freebooters was decisive.

As John Maynard Keynes has observed, the proceeds of the booty brought back by Drake in the *Golden Hind* (estimated at £600,000) enabled Elizabeth to pay off the whole of her foreign debt and in addition to invest about £42,000 in the Levant Company. Largely out of the profits of the Levant Company came the initial capital of the East India Company, "the profits of which during the seventeenth and eighteenth century were the main foundation of England's foreign connections" (Keynes 1930: II, 156–7). Assuming an annual rate of return of 6½ per cent and a 50 per cent rate of reinvestment of these returns, notes Keynes, the £42,000 of 1580 were sufficient to generate the entire value of the capital of the East India Company, Royal African Company, and Hudson Bay Company in 1700, and something close to £4,000 million that constituted the entire stock of British foreign investments in 1913 (see also Knapp 1957: 438).

Keynes's observations concerning the origins and "self-expansion" of English foreign investments do not tell how, historically, the domestic and systemic conditions of that expansion were reproduced over the three centuries to which the observations refer. The suggestion of a basic continuity of the process of world-wide expansion of English capital from Elizabeth's times through the nineteenth century is none the less valuable in view of the fact that this process was not the only feature of nineteenth-century British capitalism that originated under Elizabeth. As Keynes himself notes in the passage just cited, less than 10 per cent of Drake's booty was invested in starting the self-expansion of English foreign investment. The largest part was used by Elizabeth to repay her foreign debt. In addition, most of the £4½ million worth of bullion coined in Elizabeth's reign was believed to be plunder seized from Spain (Hill 1967: 59).

This recycling of plunder in buttressing the English government's finances initiated another great tradition of English capitalism – the tradition of "sound money":

[The pound sterling] was a money of account, like countless others. But while every other money of account fluctuated, either being manipulated by the state or upset by economic conditions, the pound sterling, having been stabilized in 1560–1 by Elizabeth I, never therafter varied, maintaining its intrinsic value until 1920 or indeed 1931. This is little short of a miracle.... [The] pound alone among European currencies ploughs its straight furrow through an astonishing three hundred years. (Braudel 1984: 356)

This long-term monetary stability, Braudel (1984: 356) goes on to say, "was a crucial element in England's fortunes. Without a fixed currency, there would have been no easy credit, no security for those lending money to the sovereign, no confidence in any contract, and without credit there would have been no rise to greatness, no financial superiority." Braudel also points out that the story of the long-term stability of the pound sterling "takes its course through a series of crises which could very well have changed it, in 1621, 1695, 1774 and 1797." Needless to say, similar considerations apply to Keynes's parallel story of the self-expansion of English foreign investment. And yet, after every crisis each story resumed its imperturbable course right up to the terminal crisis of Britain's nineteenth-century world order in the 1920s and 1930s.

Like foreign investment and a stable metallic monetary standard, industrialism itself was no nineteenth-century novelty for English capitalism. This is John Nef's well-known but often disregarded thesis that the concept of an "industrial revolution" as an explanation of the triumph of industrialism is "especially inappropriate" in the case of Great Britain, because "[i]t gives the impression that the process was especially sudden, when in all probability it was more continuous than in any other country" (Nef 1934: 24). In Nef's view, the "portentously rapid" expansion of English industry in the late eighteenth and early nineteenth centuries was matched by the equally rapid expansion in at least one earlier period – the century preceding the English Civil War. In this century, and especially in the latter half of Elizabeth's reign and in the reign of James I, the importance of mining and manufacturing in the English domestic economy increased as fast as at any other time in English history (Nef 1934: 3–4).

Moreover, although the expansion of English industry proceeded more slowly in the century following than in the century preceding 1640, the diversification of industrial activities, the changes in industrial technology and the concentration of industrial capital that began in the Elizabethan age were as important a foundation of the later "industrial revolution" as any other:

> The rise of industrialism can be more properly regarded as a long process stretching back to the middle of the sixteenth century and coming down to the final triumph of the industrial state towards the end of the nineteenth, than as a sudden phenomenon associated with the late eighteenth and early nineteenth centuries. It is no longer possible to find a full explanation of "the great inventions" and the new factories of the late eighteenth century in a preceding commercial revolution which increased the size of markets. The commercial revolution, if that is the proper term to apply to a rapid growth in foreign and domestic trade during a period of two centuries, had a continuous influence reaching back to the Reformation upon industrial technology and the scale of mining and manufacturing. But so, in turn, the progress of industry had continually stimulated in a variety of ways the progress of commerce. The former progress was quite as "revolutionary" as the latter, and quite as directly responsible for the "Industrial Revolution." (Nef 1934: 22–3)

Recast in the perspective developed in this study, the theses of Keynes, Braudel, and Nef jointly identify the Elizabethan age as a decisive turning point in the relationship between capitalism and territorialism in the European world-economy. In our scheme of things, the reigns of Elizabeth I (1558–1603) and James I (1603–25) correspond precisely to Braudel's Age of the Genoese (1557–1627), that is, to a phase of financial expansion of the European world-economy and of escalating competitive struggles between the capitalist and territorialist organizations of that economy. This was the period in which the power of the Genoese–Iberian capitalist–territorialist complex reached its height; but it was also a period of transition in systemic processes of capital accumulation from the Genoese to the Dutch regime.

The restructuring and reorganization of the English state which began under Elizabeth was an integral aspect of this transition. Like the formation of the Dutch state, they were an expression and a factor of the contradictions that eventually led to the demise of the Genoese–Iberian complex. And although at this time the English state had neither the predispositions nor the capabilities necessary to challenge the rise of Dutch hegemony, the restructuring and reorganization of the Elizabethan age gave England a head start over all other territorialist states – the "model" nation-state France included – in the struggle for world commercial supremacy that began as soon as the Dutch regime itself began to be weighed down by its own contradictions.

This head start was due first of all to the reorganization of state finances through which Elizabeth I tried to put some order in the monetary chaos left behind by her father. Henry's attempt to procure the means needed to finance the costly wars against France and Scotland of the 1540s through forced loans and massive currency debasement had backfired. While forced loans antagonized capitalist interests, the great debasement which between 1541 and 1551 reduced the silver content of the denominations in circulation from almost 93 per cent to 33 per cent resulted in "unspeakable chaos": the currencies issued by the crown ceased to be accepted as a means of payment and of exchange; trade was disrupted and cloth production drastically curtailed; prices doubled or even tripled in a few years; hard currencies disappeared from circulation and the English rate of exchange in Antwerp deteriorated rapidly (Braudel 1984: 357; Shaw 1896: 120–4). Economic chaos and political instability fed one another, forcing the English crown to transfer to private hands and at bargain prices the great bulk of the agrarian property it had acquired from the monasteries – something like a quarter of the land of the realm – in order to make ends meet, or just to buy time and goodwill. As a consequence of this massive transfer, the English monarchy lost a major source of revenue independent of parliamentary taxation, while the power of the main beneficiary of the transfer – the gentry – increased dramatically (Anderson 1974: 24–5).

Elizabeth thus inherited a situation in which the English crown had to bargain continually with the gentry and other capitalist interests over the ways and means of its power pursuits. In such a situation, Elizabeth's prudence and parsimony in war-making were no doubt a means of relaxing or at least of preventing the further tightening of the constraints imposed on her freedom of action by this process. But they were also an expression of the tightness of these constraints (Mattingly 1959: 189–90).

In order to regain some freedom of action, Elizabeth took more positive steps than simply adjusting to the situation. One such step was the stabilization of the pound in 1560–61, which set its silver content for centuries to come at the "ancient right standard" of 11 ounces 2 pennyweight in every 12 ounces. As Braudel (1984: 355–7) underscores, this was no mere structural adjustment to the commands of the emerging capitalist world-economy. On the contrary, it was an attempt to break loose from the constraints imposed on England's wealth and power by the cosmopolitan cliques that controlled and regulated the European monetary and trading system.

At the very beginning of her reign, Elizabeth had been cautioned by the powerful merchant and financier, Sir Thomas Gresham – who was then operating out of Antwerp and who inspired the monetary stabilization of 1560–61 – that only English merchants could save her from dependence on foreigners because English merchants "must stand by you at all events in your necessity" (Hill 1967: 37). As long as Antwerp functioned effectively as a truly "international" marketplace in which the English "nation" was in control of a special bourse for trade in commodities, Gresham continued to operate out of Antwerp and nothing much came of this advice. But as soon as the relationships between "nations" in Antwerp became intensely competitive following the crash of 1557–62, Gresham began building a bourse in London in imitation of Antwerp's commodity and stock exchanges with the declared intent of making England independent of foreign "nations" both in trade and in credit. Once the building of the bourse was completed, he again expressed the wish, in a letter written in 1569, that "the Q. Majestie in this time shuld not use any *strangers but her own* subiectes wherebie [the Duke of Alva] and all *other princes maie se what a prince of powr she ys*" (Ehrenberg 1985: 238, 254; emphasis in the original). And the following year during a visit to the bourse Elizabeth blessed Gresham's undertaking by naming it the Royal Exchange (Hill 1967: 38).

It took decades before the Royal Exchange could actually satisfy the financial needs of the English government, and it took more than two centuries before London could rival Amsterdam as a central money market of the European world-economy. But the stabilization of the pound in 1560–61 and the subsequent establishment of the Royal Exchange, to paraphrase Max Weber, marked the birth of a new kind of "memorable alliance" between the power of money and the power of the gun. It marked the beginning of nationalism in high finance.

In the late fourteenth and early fifteenth centuries, when high finance was born in the context and under the impact of intensifying inter-state competition for mobile capital, its headquarters were located in select city-states, most notably in Florence, but its clientele and organization were cosmopolitan in structure and orientation. "Alliance" is too strong a word to describe the loose and unstable relationships that existed at this time between the leading organizations of high finance and any particular member of their diversified clientele. But the term describes fairly well the most important of these relationships, the papal connection that made the fortunes of the Medici.

High finance was reborn in the sixteenth century as a system of expatriate cosmopolitan "nations." The power of these organizations still stemmed from the intense competition for mobile capital that set the emergent states against one another. But in order to exploit this competition, and at the same time strengthen their own competitive position, the "nations" were drawn into true alliances with a particular state – the most memorable of these alliances being that of the Genoese with Spain and that of the Florentines with France. The main foundation of high finance at this time was thus an alliance between states that were in the process of becoming nations on the one side, and foreign "nations" which, for all practical purposes, had ceased to be states on the other.

What Gresham proposed to Elizabeth at the onset of the financial expansion of the latter sixteenth century was to forge a new kind of alliance: a truly national bloc between the power of money and the power of the gun, an alliance between the English "nation" which was withdrawing from Antwerp and the English state. The crash of 1557–62 had revealed the fundamental weakness of both the English monarchy and English merchant capital in their respective spheres of action in the face of the overwhelming power of the Genoese–Iberian bloc. Gresham's assessment was that a closer mutual alliance would enable them to beat the competition in both spheres. When he wrote that such an alliance would enable Elizabeth to demonstrate her real power to all the foreign princes, Gresham no doubt also thought, though he did not express it, that the alliance would enable him to demonstrate his real power to all the foreign merchants.

As Braudel (1984: 355–7) points out, Gresham was convinced that the benefits of English trade and workmanship were for the most part appropriated by the Italian and German merchants and financiers who controlled the money and credit market in Antwerp. The trade expansion of the early sixteenth century had integrated England more firmly than ever in the European world-economy. As a major cloth exporter, England "was like a trading vessel moored to Europe; her entire economic life depended on the mooring-rope, the rate of exchange on the Antwerp market." Since rates of exchange were determined in markets controlled

by Italian and German "nations," the most important of which cooperated closely with the rulers of Spain and France, it was natural to
perceive dependence on foreign markets for money and credit as the
source of serious threats to England's sovereignty and security. And it was
in response to threats of this kind – "not wholly imaginary, though often
exaggerated" – that an aggressive economic nationalism came to characterize England's pursuit of power:

> The Italian merchant bankers were driven out [of England] in the sixteenth
> century; the Hanseatic merchants were stripped of their privileges in 1556 and
> deprived of the *Stahlhof* in 1595; it was against Antwerp that Gresham
> founded in 1566–8 what would later become the Royal Exchange; it was
> against Spain and Portugal that the Stock Companies were in fact launched;
> against Holland that the Navigation Act of 1651 was directed; and against
> France that the aggressive colonial policy of the eighteenth century was aimed.
> England as a country was tense, watchful and aggressive, determined to lay
> down the law and enforce it both at home and abroad, as her position grew
> stronger. (Braudel 1984: 355–6)

The long-term stability of the pound sterling and the "self-expansion"
of English foreign investment were integral to this pursuit of national
power both during its initial "nationalist" phase – when the main
objective was to "delink" from the Antwerp-centered networks of high
finance and long-distance trade – and during its later "imperialist" phase
– when the main objective was to eliminate all obstacles to England's
determination to lay down and enforce the law for the whole world. As
Braudel (1984: 365) concludes, after surveying the recurrent crises that
punctuated the long-term stability of the pound in the seventeenth and
eighteenth centuries,

> [perhaps] we should see sterling's history as the repeated result of the
> aggressive tension characteristic of a country fiercely conditioned by its
> insularity (as an island to be defended), by its efforts to break through to world
> status and by its clear identification of the enemy: today Antwerp, tomorrow
> Amsterdam, the next day Paris. The stability of the pound was a weapon in this
> battle.

In this long war of position – which is what this "battle" really was –
the stability of the pound was not the only weapon; industrialism was
also. In this regard let us recall that the rapid expansion of English
industry during the financial expansion of the late sixteenth and early
seventeenth centuries – which Nef describes as an important antecedent
of the later "industrial revolution" – had itself an important if lesser
antecedent in the transplant of the woolen cloth industry on English soil

during the financial expansion of the latter fourteenth and early fifteenth centuries.

As previously argued, this transplant had been the result, on the one hand, of Edward III's use of military force and control over raw materials to internalize within his domains the Flemish cloth industry and, on the other hand, of the spontaneous externalization of cloth production from Florence and other capitalist city-states in response to market signals and labor unrest. As such, this early expansion of English industry was a factor and an expression of an increasing structural differentiation between territorialist organizations, which tended to specialize in production, and capitalist organizations, which tended to specialize in high finance, with trade being undertaken by either kind of organizations depending on its relationship to the other two activities. Nevertheless, not all production was externalized by capitalist organizations or was within the reach of territorialist organizations; nor did the actual expansion of production within the domains of territorialist organizations lessen their dependence on the assistance of capitalist organizations.

Particularly significant in this respect was the retention by the city-states of the industries that had become most profitable in the conjuncture of the latter fourteenth and early fifteenth centuries, namely, the metal and armament industries, which remained centered in Milan, and the luxury industries, which expanded in several city-states. England was still too much in a backwater to compete effectively in these more profitable industries, not just with northern Italy, but even with other regions of the European world-economy such as Flanders and southern Germany. England was thus specializing in the least profitable industries. Worse still, in order to convert the products of the cloth industry into the armaments and other supplies needed to fight the increasingly commercialized war with France, the ruling groups of England had to go through Italian merchant bankers who appropriated as commercial or financial profit a non-negligible share of the market value of English primary and secondary production.

In the late fifteenth and early sixteenth centuries, the revival of the wool trade in the European world-economy and the consolidation of royal power in England jointly imparted a new impulse to English commerce and industry (Cipolla 1980: 276–96; Nef 1968: 10–12, 71–3, 87–8). But on the eve of the financial expansion of the late sixteenth century, industrially, England was still "in a backwater compared with Italy, Spain, the Low-Countries, the South-German states, and even France. Englishmen had almost nothing to teach foreigners in the way of mechanical knowledge, except in connection with the production of tin and the manufacture of pewter" (Nef 1934: 23).

The reversal of this position in the latter half of the sixteenth century is what makes Nef single out the Elizabethan age as the true turning point in the rise of British industrialism. But if we focus on the rise of industrialism not *per se* but as an instrument of capital accumulation, England's catching up with, and forging ahead of, other countries in coalmining, metallurgy, and other large-scale industries is not the really significant trend that emerged in the Elizabethan age. In itself this trend was a reaffirmation in new forms of the same pattern that had already emerged in the previous financial expansion of the European world-economy – the pattern, that is, through which England took over and specialized in low value-added activities while the main centers of capital accumulation retained and specialized in high value-added activities. But in the Elizabethan age this was not all that was happening. The most significant aspect of English industrialism in this age was that it was beginning to take over high value-added activities which then, as in the previous financial expansion, were the luxury and armament industries.

Fear of social disorder made Elizabeth even less inclined than her Tudor predecessors to give indiscriminate encouragement to a process of industrial expansion which already had a considerable momentum of its own because of England's natural endowments (including large coal deposits) combined with a steady inflow of Dutch, French, and German entrepreneurs and personnel seeking refuge from continental religious quarrels or just a profitable investment. If anything, her main preoccupation was to restrain the expansion and to minimize its socially disruptive effects. The Statute of Artificers of 1563, which extended guild regulation to the whole country and effectively confined the expansion of the cloth industry to the towns, was the main instrument of this action. Besides luxury industries, like silk, glass, or the manufacture of fine paper, the only industries that were actively encouraged were those related to armaments with the result that, by the end of Elizabeth's reign, English-made cannon was in demand throughout Europe (Hill 1967: 63, 71–5; Nef 1934: 9).

This kind of industrial policy was far more reasonable than later critics and historians have been willing to acknowledge. For one thing, as Polanyi (1957: 36–8) has argued with specific reference to the regulatory thrust of this period, a slowing down of the *rate* of change may be the best way of keeping change going in a given *direction* without causing social disruptions that would result in chaos rather than change. Equally important for our present purposes, the redirecting of industrial expansion from cloth to the luxury and armament industries shows that Elizabeth and her advisers had a better sense than many of our own contemporaries of the relationship that links industrial expansion to the expansion of national wealth and power in a capitalist world-economy. For in a capitalist world-economy industrial expansion translates into an expansion of national wealth and power only if it is associated with a breakthrough in high value-added activities. Moreover, the breakthrough must be sufficient both to enable capital to accumulate faster in the industrializing than in competing states and to reproduce in the industrializing states social structures supportive of its self- expansion.

The expansion of English industries during the Anglo-French Hundred Years War led to no such breakthrough. English balance of payment problems were aggravated, English servitude to foreign capital deepened, English troops were driven out of France, and the English state was thrown into complete chaos. The expansion of English industries in the century following the dissolution of the monasteries, in contrast, did make significant inroads into high value-added industries. But these inroads were not sufficient to enable capital to accumulate in England faster than in competing states – most notably than in the new-born United Provinces – nor, indeed, to reproduce a supportive social structure. As a result, it took another century before the national union of capitalism and territorialism initiated under Elizabeth began its irresistible rise to world dominance.

The Dialectic of Capitalism and Territorialism (Continued)

The long gestation lag that separates the restructuring and reorganization of the English state in the late sixteenth century and its subsequent rise to dominance in the European world-economy was due primarily to the fact that a critical ingredient was still missing from the synthesis of capitalism and territorialism engineered by Gresham and Elizabeth: commercial world supremacy. Throughout the seventeenth century this remained the prerogative of Dutch capitalism. And as long as it did, no amount of industrial expansion and monetary stability could help England to become the master rather than the servant of systemic processes of capital accumulation. Just as Venice's industrial expansion in this same period was associated with the subordination of the old Venetian city-state to the declining Genoese regime of accumulation, so England's industrial expansion was associated with the subordination of the new-born English nation-state to the rising Dutch regime.

The fundamental subordination of the English state to the rising Dutch regime is best illustrated by the outcome of the Anglo-Dutch trade dispute which erupted in the early 1610s when the English government banned the export of undyed cloth. The aim of this ban was to compel English producers to complete manufacture at home in order to increase the value-added of English textile production and set English trade free from the constraints imposed on its expansion by Dutch commercial intermediation. As Jonathan Israel (1989: 117) explains, "Dutch superiority in dyeing and 'dressing' was ... not only a means of syphoning off a large part of the profits of England's own output (for most of the benefits accrued to those who handled the finishing process and distribution) but also a means of undermining English trade with the Baltic generally."

In Barry Supple's (1959: 34) words, the English prohibition was a "gigantic gamble" – a gamble, moreover, that failed abysmally (Wallerstein 1980: 43). For shortly afterwards Holland retaliated by banning all imports into the United Provinces of foreign dyed and dressed cloth. The effect on England was devastating:

> The collapse of English cloth exports to the Dutch provinces, and a large part of their German hinterland, could only be partially compensated for by increased sales of finished cloth in the Baltic. The inevitable result was a paralyzing slump, and widespread distress at home. By 1616, with the recession deepening, James I's ministers were ready to give in. (Israel 1989: 119)

They actually capitulated a year later without having persuaded the States General to withdraw their ban on English finished cloth. The attempt to move up the value-added hierarchy of textile production and to bypass the Dutch entrepôt thus backfired and the English economy entered a long depression which intensified domestic political instability and social tensions. As we shall see presently, the taproot of this instability and tensions lay elsewhere. But their catastrophic if emancipatory development in the middle decades of the century was deeply conditioned by the continuing primacy of commercial over industrial capitalism in the European world-economy at large.

Dutch capital could appropriate the profits of English workmanship not because of its superiority in industrial productiveness as such but because of its centrality in world commercial intermediation. Dutch superiority in dyeing and "dressing," which played such a critical role in the above dispute, was itself primarily a reflection of Amsterdam's role as central entrepôt of world commerce:

> For the rich trades, and for the finishing industries on which the rich trades depended, the stockpiling of the world's commodities in a central storehouse ... was a factor of decisive importance. Dutch superiority in dyeing, bleaching, grinding, and refining was hard to challenge when it was the Dutch who had the stockpiles of dyestuffs, chemicals, drugs, and rare raw materials on which all these processes depended. Thus, there was a high degree of interdependency between the Dutch commerce in high value commodities and Dutch industry, each continually reinforcing the other. (Israel 1989: 410)

In this relationship of mutual reinforcement, Dutch world commercial supremacy was the decisive ingredient. It was comparatively easy for English manufacturers to finish their cloth with sufficient technical proficiency to be able to sell it directly and competitively in Baltic markets. But once the chips were down and their finished cloth was excluded from the Dutch commercial entrepôt, technical proficiency and competitiveness in manufacturing were to no avail. Conversely, as long as Amsterdam remained the central entrepôt of world commerce – the place, that is, where Baltic, Mediterranean, Atlantic, and Indian Ocean supplies met and turned into one another's demand – it was comparatively easy for Dutch merchants and manufacturers to become technically proficient and economically competitive in whatever industrial activity was critical to the enlarged reproduction of Dutch commercial supremacy. But as soon as Amsterdam's role as the central warehouse of world commerce began to be successfully challenged by the rise of competing entrepôts – as it was in the early eighteenth century – Dutch industrial primacy, such as it was, waned as rapidly as it had waxed.

England was the main protagonist and the eventual victor of the struggle to divert traffic from Amsterdam. The seeds of this victory were sown in the Elizabethan age. But its fruits could be reaped only after appropriate domestic and systemic conditions had come into existence.

Domestically, the main problem left behind by Elizabeth was the fragility of the incorporation of the British islands into a single territorial organization. This greatly hampered the ability of the English monarchy under the Stuarts to pursue with the necessary determination the interests of England's commercial classes at a time of rapidly escalating inter-state conflicts. Quarrels between king and parliament over taxation and over the use of resources eventually came to a head under the impact of a Scottish military invasion of England and a Catholic rebellion in Ireland:

> The struggle to seize control over the English army that now had to be raised to suppress the Irish insurrection, drove Parliament and King into the Civil War. English absolutism was brought to crisis by aristocratic particularism and clannic desperation on its periphery: forces that lay historically behind it. But it was felled at the center by a commercialized gentry, a capitalist city, a commoner artisanate and yeomanry: forces pushing beyond it. (Anderson 1974: 142)

As Anderson (1974: 140) notes, the vagaries of English foreign policy undermined Stuart rule from the start. However, these vagaries were not due just to the subjective limitations of successive court administrations in a fractured and increasingly turbulent domestic environment. They were due also to an objective difficulty involved in identifying England's national interest in a period of transition in the world-economy from one system of rule and accumulation to another. Was Spain's collapsing empire still England's principal enemy or was it Holland and France – England's rivals in the coming struggle to appropriate the spoils of the Iberian empire? In the two decades preceding the English Civil War it was all but impossible to decide whether England's national interest was best served by joining competitors in destroying Iberian power, or by letting them bear the costs alone, and seek instead some advantage in the struggle to come through diplomatic and other means.

By the time the English Civil War had completed the process of nation-state formation left unfinished by Elizabeth I, the neutralization of Iberian power and the establishment of the Westphalia System had eliminated all objective difficulties in the identification of England's national interest. The bitter experience of the trade dispute with Holland of the 1610s was not lost in the collective memory of the commercial classes which were brought to prominence by the revolutionary upheavals of the 1640s. And as soon as domestic circumstances permitted, these classes moved fast to challenge Dutch commercial supremacy:

> In 1651 the Venetian Ambassador [in London] had reported that "merchants and trade were making great strides, as government and trade are ruled by the same persons". These rulers first offered union to the Dutch, on terms which would have given English merchants free access to trade with the Dutch empire and transferred the entrepôt trade from Amsterdam to London. When the Dutch government ... refused, war was declared.... The Dutch wars (1652–74) broke the Dutch hold on trade in tobacco, sugar, furs, slaves and codfish, and laid the foundation for the establishment of English territorial power in India. English trade to China also dates from these years ... [and the] capture of Jamaica in 1655 provided the base for the slave trade on which English merchants were to wax rich. (Hill 1967: 123–4)

In the making of an English commercial empire the deployment of military means was supplemented and complemented by the deployment of diplomatic and contractual means. Protection of the Portuguese against the Dutch and support for their independence from Spain prepared the ground for the Anglo-Portuguese alliance, which would in due course transform Portugal and its empire into a *de facto* British protectorate. Thus, Charles II's marriage to Catherine of Braganza – apparently a condition of his restoration – made important additions to England's possessions and connections. "With Catherine came Bombay, direct trade (slaves) with Portuguese West Africa and with Brazil (sugar, partly for re-export and gold). With her also came Tangier, England's first base in the Mediterranean" (Hill 1967: 129).

The foundations were thus laid of that "Empire of Outposts" out of which came the "continental inland expansion" of the next two centuries (Knowles 1928: 9–15) and the incorporation in the British-centered capitalist world-economy of the continents of America, India, Australia, and Africa. In the short run, however, England's most important gain was the takeover of the so-called triangular Atlantic trade from the Dutch, which soon became for England what Levant trade had been for Venice and Baltic trade for Holland – its "mother trade."

As Eric Williams (1964) argued in his classic study, the circuit of trade through which (1) British manufactures were exchanged for African slaves, (2) African slaves were exchanged for American tropical products, and (3) American tropical products were exchanged for British manufactures, boosted at a critical conjuncture the effective demand and the capital resources required by the take-off of the British "industrial revolution." Although triangular Atlantic trade did indeed provide English manufactures with one of their most protected and most rapidly expanding outlets (Davis 1954; 1962), its most important and specific contribution to the expansion of England's networks of trade, accumulation, and power was to promote the transfer of Europe's entrepôt trade from Amsterdam to English port cities. Once again, entrepôt trade and all the advantages that went with it – including industrial competitiveness – followed control over the most strategic supplies of world commerce. And just as in the late sixteenth century control over Baltic supplies of grain and naval stores had brought entrepôt trade to Holland, so in the early eighteenth century control over Atlantic supplies of tobacco, sugar, cotton, gold, and, above all, of the slaves who produced the bulk of these supplies, was instrumental in diverting traffic from Amsterdam to English entrepôts.

There was none the less a fundamental difference between the establishment of Dutch commercial supremacy in the late sixteenth century and the establishment of English commercial supremacy in the early eighteenth century. Whereas Dutch commercial supremacy was based on a strict adherence to a capitalist logic of power (as signified by the formula MTM'), English commercial supremacy was based on a harmonious synthesis of the territorialist logic of power (TMT') with the capitalist. It is this difference more than anything else that accounts for the fact that, historically, English governmental and business institutions were in a position to carry systemic processes of capital accumulation much further than their Dutch predecessors did or could ever have done.

From the very start, the Dutch commercial empire formed and expanded through the investment of the profits of Baltic trade and of the inverted fiscal squeeze imposed on Imperial Spain through piracy and privateering in highly selective and parsimonious territorial acquisitions.

The conquest and incorporation of territory in the domains of the Dutch state and of its chartered companies were limited to what was absolutely essential to the profitable expansion of Dutch business. Through this strategy of power, the Dutch carved out of the far-flung Iberian territorial empire, first a small and secure homeland in the Netherlands – "a fortified island" as Braudel (1984: 202) has called the United Provinces – and then a highly profitable empire of commercial outposts stretching across the Atlantic and Indian Oceans.

The main advantage of this strategy lay in its flexibility. It kept the ruling groups of the United Provinces free from the responsibility, troubles, and commitments involved in the acquisition, governance, and protection of large territories and populations, and assured them a steady cash flow which they could put to whatever use was most profitable or useful at any given time or place. The obverse side of this freedom of action and superior command over mobile capital was of course dependence on the entrepreneurship and labor of foreign countries endowed with superior territorial and demographic resources.

In commenting on the failure of Dutch corporate business in the New World in comparison with its success in the Indian Ocean, Braudel (1984: 235) reports the malicious claim of a Frenchman according to whom the leaders of the United Provinces had "noticed the extraordinary labors and the considerable expense which the Spanish had been obliged to devote to the establishment of their commerce and government in countries hitherto unknown; they therefore determined to have as little as possible to do with such undertakings" – in other words, Braudel adds, they much preferred "to seek out countries which could be exploited rather than settled and developed." The claim was malicious because colonization of suitable regions was specifically envisaged in the 1621 charter of the Dutch West Indian Company (WIC). Controlled by the territorialist rather than by the capitalist component of the Dutch dominant bloc – that is, by the "party" of Orangists, Calvinists, Zeelanders and Southern Netherlander immigrants, rather than by Amsterdam's merchant elite who controlled the VOC (Wallerstein 1980: 51) – the WIC soon became involved in efforts to conquer all or parts of Brazil. Even the WIC, however, showed little patience with the Brazilian undertaking. As its costs escalated over and above commercial profits, the company abandoned territorial conquest and colonization in the Americas in favor of greater specialization in commercial intermediation (Boxer 1965: 49).

Facing bankruptcy, in 1674 the WIC was reorganized as a slave-trading enterprise with profitable sidelines in contraband trade with Spanish America and in sugar production in Surinam. This combination brought the Dutch back to playing the more congenial role of intermediaries who externalized as much as they could of production costs, while concentrating on acquiring exclusive control of the most strategic supplies of long-distance trade. Just as the most strategic supplies of Baltic trade were grain and naval stores, and those of Indian Ocean trade were fine spices, so the most strategic supply of Atlantic trade were African slaves. By stepping in to rationalize previous Portuguese practices in the procurement, transport, and marketing of African slaves, the WIC thus pioneered the Atlantic triangular trade (Emmer 1981; Postma 1990).

As noted above, however, it was English rather than Dutch enterprise that eventually benefited more from this infamous commercial traffic. In the Atlantic, as in the Indian Ocean, the Dutch had stepped into Iberian shoes. But in contrast to what happened in the Indian Ocean, where it took more than a century for the English East India Company to overshadow the performance of the VOC and even longer to drive it out of business, the Dutch hold on the key supplies of Atlantic trade was never firm and it was comparatively easy for the English to step into Dutch shoes as soon as domestic and systemic circumstances permitted.

This different performance of Dutch relative to English enterprise in the Indian Ocean and in the Atlantic was closely related to a crucial difference between the two arenas of commercial expansion. As Braudel (1984: 496) has observed, the ease with which the merchant capitalism of Europe could lay siege to the markets of the East and "use their own vitality to maneuver them to its own advantage," was due to the fact that these markets already "formed a series of coherent economies linked together in a fully operational world-economy." Braudel's observation echoes Max Weber's (1961: 215) remark that it was one thing to undertake commercial expansion in regions of ancient civilization with a well-developed and rich money economy, as in the East Indies, and an altogether different thing to do so in sparsely populated lands where the development of a money economy had hardly begun, as in the Americas.

Probably well aware of this difference, the Dutch capitalist class concentrated on the Indian Ocean rather than the Atlantic as the most likely arena to replicate their Baltic fortunes, and thus strengthen and enlarge the role of Amsterdam as the central entrepôt of world commerce and finance. As we know, the gamble paid off handsomely. The extraordinary and early success with which the Dutch moved to reorganize the Indian Ocean trading system, in order to seize and enforce their control over the supply of fine spices, centralized in Amsterdam a traffic which in the sixteenth century was still being disputed by several entrepôts: Antwerp, Venice, Lisbon, and Seville. More important, that success made VOC shares the "blue chip" that contributed more than any other to the fortunes of the Amsterdam stock market. The enlarged reproduction of Dutch capitalism was thus based on the vitality of Asian markets. But it was also based on the one-sided determination with which the Dutch capitalist class through the VOC used that vitality to maneuver Asian markets to its own advantage.

The WIC was a different kind of enterprise. It was launched almost twenty years after the VOC, more to attack the power, prestige, and revenues of Spain and Portugal than to bring dividends to its shareholders. Initially, it succeeded in doing both things at the same time. Thus, when Piet Heyn captured the Mexican Silver Fleet in 1628, the WIC could declare one of the very few bumper dividends of its history (Boxer 1965: 49), while dealing a serious blow to the finances of Imperial Spain already strained by the war effort (Kennedy 1987: 48). But as soon as sea war turned into a land war aimed at the conquest of sizeable Portuguese territories in Brazil, the Company ran into trouble. Having regained their independence from Spain, the Portuguese reconquered their Brazilian territories, while the escalation of the costs of colonization and land warfare over and above commercial profits weakened irremediably the economic and financial position of the WIC. On its reorganization in 1674, the WIC was modeled more closely on the image of the VOC. But notwithstanding this reorganization, the WIC never came close to replicating the successes of the VOC (Boxer 1957).

The difficulties encountered by the Dutch in replicating through the WIC in the Atlantic what they had achieved through the VOC in the Indian Ocean were symptomatic of the limits imposed on Dutch commercial expansion by capitalist rationality itself. Under the circumstances of the time, capitalist rationality in state- and war-making meant a relentless subordination of territorial expansion to money-making. Strict adherence to this principle had made the fortunes of the Dutch in both the Baltic and Indian Ocean trade. But it had also set an insurmountable spatio-temporal limit to the expansion of those fortunes. This limit was the absolutely and comparatively narrow territorial and demographic base of Dutch power.

Throughout the first half of the seventeenth century, a narrow territorial and demographic base was no problem at all for Dutch commercial expansion. Superior control over mobile capital could be easily and effectively converted into the means of protection (such as fortifications and weaponry) and into the labor that were necessary to acquire and retain control over a small territorial home base. In what was a freer European market for military labor than had ever existed before, or would ever exist thereafter, the good reputation of the Dutch as solvent employers provided them with practically unlimited supplies of labor. Thus, of the 132 companies that in 1600 constituted the "Dutch" army, only 17 were actually Dutch; the others were English, French, Scots, Walloon, and German (Gush 1975: 106).

In domestic industry and ancillary trades, the labor supply was not just unlimited but almost a free good. The capture and sack of Antwerp by Spanish troops in 1585, the displacement of Antwerp by Amsterdam as the central hub of world commerce, and the transformation of the territories that were in the process of becoming the United Provinces into a secure refuge, jointly contributed to generating a massive migration of traders and artisans from the southern to the northern Netherlands. As a result, the population of Amsterdam grew from 30,000 in 1585 to 105,000 in 1622 and Antwerp's textile industry was transplanted almost *en bloc* to Leiden (Taylor 1992: 11–18; Boxer 1965: 19; Israel 1989: 28, 36).

With the military and industrial domestic requirements of labor power being met abundantly by supplies from neighboring countries and territories, Dutch labor could be mobilized in overseas enterprises. Every year between 1598 and 1605, the Dutch on average sent 25 ships to West Africa, 20 to Brazil, 10 to the East Indies, and 150 to the Caribbean. And between 1605 and 1609, the foundations of the VOC's trade empire in the Indian Ocean were laid through the establishment of colonies, factories, and trading ports (Parker 1977: 249).

During the truce of 1609–21 in the war with Spain, the Dutch further consolidated their naval supremacy in the Atlantic and Indian Oceans. And when hostilities against Spain resumed, the previous outbreak of the Thirty Years War enabled the Dutch to count on their Swedish, French, and German allies to neutralize Spanish military might on land, so that they could continue to concentrate on naval warfare, following the dictum "land war brings hunger, sea war brings plunder" (cf. Dehio 1962: 59).

The capture of the Mexican Silver Fleet by the WIC in 1628 dealt a final blow to the already strained Genoese–Iberian connection and left the Dutch as the only arbiters of European high finance. Iberian dependence on Dutch-controlled trade networks (a permanent if discontinuous feature of the eighty-year Dutch–Spanish confrontation) became greater than ever. By 1640, Dutch ships carried three-quarters of the goods delivered in Spanish ports, and by 1647 or 1648, possibly before the peace of Munster, they carried most of Spain's silver (Braudel 1984: 170).

The triumph of the Dutch capitalist logic of power over the territorialist logic of Spain could not have been more complete. Yet, it was precisely at this moment of triumph that the winning logic began to show its limits. For as soon as its triumph was institutionalized by the Westphalia treaties, the energies and resources of territorialist states were set free from their previous mutual engagement in Europe and could be deployed to challenge the commercial and naval supremacy of the Dutch. And just as in the preceding period of struggle the Dutch had effectively mobilized their superior command over mobile capital to neutralize Iberian territorial supremacy, so now the English, the French, and the Iberians themselves were freer than ever to mobilize their superior command over land and labor to undermine Dutch commercial supremacy.

This supremacy was most vulnerable in the Atlantic, where it could not be reproduced simply by controlling trading ports as it could in the Indian Ocean. In Atlantic trade control over production areas was at least as important as control over trading ports; and in order to establish and retain control over production areas command over a labor surplus mattered more than command over surplus capital. The large supply of young, unmarried males who were still available in the United Provinces at this time – a supply that included Germans, French, Scandinavians, and Baltics – was for the most part absorbed by the navy, the merchant marine, and the VOC. Few were left for the Dutch to compete effectively with the English indenture system and with the French *engagé* system in settling Atlantic production areas. Nor was Holland torn apart by the kind of violent religious and political quarrels which, in the middle of the seventeenth century, were leading to the spontaneous or coerced transplantation across the Atlantic of non-negligible fractions of the English and French populations (Emmer 1991: 25).

The same strict adherence to the capitalist logic of power that had made the Dutch triumph over Iberian territorialism now prevented the Dutch from competing effectively in the struggle for commercial supremacy in the Atlantic. The failure of the Brazilian venture had been an omen of far worse things to come. The worst thing of all came with the Navigation Acts of 1651 and 1660 through which the English parliament tightened its control over English colonies and bestowed on the English fleet the monopoly of trade with those colonies. In the Anglo-Dutch wars that followed, the Dutch reaffirmed their naval superiority but could do nothing to prevent the English from enforcing the Navigation Acts and thereby building up a commercial empire of their own in competition with the Dutch.

Yet the days of Dutch commercial supremacy were far from over. The highest rates of profit were still realized in Asian trade, and the centrality of Amsterdam as commercial and financial entrepôt was only beginning to be eroded. But the wheel was turning. Increasingly, the higher *rates* of profit realized by the VOC in the low-volume, Indian Ocean spice trade were more than compensated by the larger *mass* of profit realized by English enterprise in high-volume lines of business, not just in Atlantic trade, but also in East Indian piece goods trade (Arrighi, Barr, and Hisaeda 1993).

Worse still for the Dutch – whether profitable or not, whether English, French, or Iberian – the expansion of high-volume Atlantic trade and of the settlement and colonization that went with it began bringing into the open the latent labor shortage that threatened the vitality of Dutch enterprise. The number of Dutch seamen who were available for service in the navy and in ocean voyages began to decline in the years following the Treaty of Utrecht. This was no accident. In the course of the War of Spanish Succession, the Treaty of Methuen (1703) had granted England privileged access to the Portuguese domestic and colonial markets and to the rapidly expanding supplies of Brazilian gold, and the Treaty of Utrecht (1713) had granted it exclusive control over the slave trade with Spanish America. The golden age of English Atlantic expansion had begun; and as other territorialist states endeavored to keep up with England, the European demand for seafaring labor started to outpace supply.

The almost thirty years of peace between the European great powers that followed the end of the War of Spanish Succession moderated the ensuing labor shortage somewhat, particularly for the Dutch, who were involved only marginally in the expansion of Atlantic trade and colonization. But when in around 1740 the European inter-state struggle suddenly escalated, the shortage became acute, particularly for the Dutch who had a narrow domestic and colonial demographic base. As Stavorinus deplored,

> ever since the year 1740, the many naval wars, the great increase of trade and navigation, particularly in many countries, where formerly these pursuits were little attended to, and the consequent great and continual demands for able seamen, both for ships of war and for merchantmen, have so considerably diminished the supply of them, that, in our own country, where there formerly used to be a great abundance of mariners, it is now, with great difficulty and expense, that any vessel can procure a proper number of able hands to navigate her. (quoted in Boxer 1965: 109)

Even the VOC came to be affected by this acute shortage of seafaring labor. In the seventeenth century, its commercial successes had attracted a large flow of Dutch immigrants to the East Indies (Braudel 1984: 232). But in the 1740s, the general and open shortage of seamen had negative repercussions on the VOC as on all branches of the Dutch commercial empire. "I am afraid to say how things are with us," wrote VOC's Governor General Baron van Imhoff in 1744, "for it is shameful ... everything is lacking, good ships, men, officers; and thus one of the principal props of the Netherlands' power is trembling in the balance" (Boxer 1965: 108).

Seventeen-forty is of course the year which, following Braudel, we have taken as the point in time in which the (MC) phase of material expansion of the Dutch-centered capitalist world-economy turned into a (CM') phase of financial expansion. Although the flight of Dutch surplus capital from Dutch to English investment became massive only at this time, the transfer had already begun some thirty years earlier towards the end of the War of Spanish Succession. The war had shown beyond a shadow of a doubt that the rise of English power by sea and of French power by land had created conditions under which the Dutch had no competitive edge of their own in the European power struggle. The competition that pitted English and French power against one another left the Dutch with plenty of room for maneuver in preserving their political independence and economic freedom of action. But it also translated into a major inflation of Dutch protection costs and of the Dutch national debt.

By the end of the War of Spanish Succession the national debt of the Dutch Republic was almost five times what it had been in 1688 (Boxer 1965: 118). The outstanding debt of the Province of Holland was 6–8 times what it had been in the 1640s. And since in the meantime tax revenue had at most doubled, the Province was rapidly approaching a situation of financial exhaustion. The costs involved in defending simultaneously a land and a sea frontier had become prohibitive for the small Dutch state (Riley 1980: 77; Brewer 1989: 33).

At the same time, the War of Spanish Succession had sharpened further the competitive edge of the English in the struggle for commercial supremacy in the Atlantic and for control over a greater share of entrepôt trade. There was nothing that Dutch capital could do to stop the English from fully exploiting this competitive advantage at the expense of the Dutch themselves. But it could, and promptly did, lay a claim on a share of the future incomes generated by English commercial and territorial expansion by investing in the English national debt and in English stock.

The tendency of Dutch capital to shift its bets from Dutch to English investment was strengthened by the dynastic connection that was established between England and the United Provinces in 1689 with the accession of William of Orange to the English throne. Under William III, Anglo-Dutch relations had become closer and more friendly than they had been for a long time. Equally important, the "sound money" tradition initiated under Elizabeth was reaffirmed at a time of rampant inflation; private creditors were put in control of the management of the public debt through their incorporation in the Bank of England – pretty much in the same way as they had been in Genoa through their incorporation in the *Casa di San Giorgio*; and the silver standard of the English pound was *de facto* converted into a gold standard taking advantage of the newly acquired privileged access to Brazilian gold supplies.

There was little else that a creditor could ask for, and so in the 1710s

Dutch surplus capital eagerly began jumping off the overcrowded Dutch "boat" to jump on the English one in the hope of a free ride to the expanding Atlantic trade and colonization. Already by 1737 the Dutch were thought to hold as much as £10 million of the English national debt – more than one fifth of the total and an amount large enough to make the English government worry about the possibility that a reduction in the interest rate on the national debt might induce a flight of Dutch capital, with disastrous consequences for English finances (Boxer 1965: 110; Wilson 1966: 71). By then, however, the competitive position of the Dutch was rapidly becoming hopeless even in the spheres in which it had been strongest, as Stavorinus and VOC's Governor General, Baron van Imhoff, were to complain. More than ever, investment in English stock and government securities constituted the best bet for Dutch surplus capital. For returns on investment in Dutch securities were lower, while investment in securities of other states (including France) was much riskier. Far from being diverted from England, after about 1740 the flow of Dutch capital into England suddenly greatly increased. In 1758, Dutch investors were said to hold as much as a third of the Bank of England, English East India Comany, and South Sea stocks. In 1762, a well-informed Rotterdam banker estimated that the Dutch held a quarter of the English debt, which then stood at £12 million (Boxer 1965: 110; Carter 1975).

The moment of greatest expansion of Dutch investment in English securities was during the Seven Years War of 1756–63. Since this war was a decisive turning point in the struggle for world commercial supremacy between England and France, there is some truth in Charles Wilson's contention (1966: 71) that without the contribution of Dutch capital England's eventual victory over France might have been more difficult than it actually was. Yet for the most part, the Dutch simply assisted in the completion of a long historical process which they had neither initiated nor could stop, as much as they might have wanted to in view of the fact that the English victory marked the demise of the Dutch from the commanding heights of the capitalist world-economy.

As we have been arguing, the proximate origins of this long historical process lay in the formation in the latter half of the sixteenth century of a new kind of governmental and business organization. This was the English nation-state as restructured by the alliance of English merchant bankers – who, in the first half of the century, had been a subordinate component of the cosmopolitan ensemble of "nations" that regulated the European monetary and trading system out of Antwerp and other continental marketplaces – and Elizabeth – who, at mid-century, had inherited a government bankrupted by the failed attempts of the Tudor dynasty to regain England's prominence in European politics. This alliance was one of several combinations of capitalism and territorialism that emerged out of the obsolescence of city-states as the main centers of capital accumulation of the European world-economy and of continual inter-state competition for mobile capital.

Throughout the sixteenth century, the most important and powerful among these combinations were the loose alliances between capitalist "nations" and territorialist states that characterized both the Genoese–Iberian and the Florentine–French blocs. Towards the end of the century, however, the power of these loose alliances was increasingly undermined by their mutual competition and hostility, as well as by the emergence of more compact and leaner national blocs formed in antagonistic opposition to the financial and political dominance of the Genoese–Iberian complex. The Dutch and the English were the most important among these. Although both blocs were formed by the union of a capitalist with a territorialist component, the Dutch state was far more capitalist in structure and orientation than the English state, which none the less was from the start and remained through the seventeenth and eighteenth centuries far more capitalist in structure and orientation than any of the other territorialist states of Europe.

In the seventeenth century, the more strictly capitalist structure and orientation of the Dutch state endowed Dutch capital with a decisive competitive advantage in the struggle to appropriate the spoils of the disintegrating Iberian territorial empire. But as soon as the territorialist states themselves followed the Dutch path of development by becoming more capitalist in structure and orientation and by throwing their lot in overseas commercial expansion, as they did from the late seventeenth century onwards, the exceedingly lean structure of the Dutch state was transformed from a decisive competitive advantage into an insurmountable handicap. In the ensuing struggle for world commercial supremacy, competitive advantage shifted to the territorialist states that were in the process of internalizing capitalism. It was at this point that the English state, which had carried this internalization further than any other territorialist state and had redirected but not lost its territorialist predispositions, came out on top.

As Cain and Hopkins (1980: 471) have pointed out, the plunder perpetrated by the East India Company following its military victory at Plassey in 1757 "did not start the Industrial Revolution [as some maintain], but it did help Britain to buy back the National Debt from the Dutch." Our analysis fully supports this contention, but adds a new twist to it.

Plassey could not and did not start the "industrial revolution" for the simple reason that what goes under that name was the third and concluding moment of a historical process that had begun centuries earlier. All three moments of this historical process were periods of rapid industrial expansion in England – at least by the standards of the times in which each of the expansions occurred – and of financial expansion in the capitalist world-economy at large. The first moment consisted of the rapid expansion of the English textile industry that occurred during the Florentine-led financial expansion of the late fourteenth and early fifteenth centuries; the second moment consisted of the rapid expansion of the English metal industries during the Genoese-led financial expansion of the late sixteenth and early seventeenth centuries; and the third moment – the so-called industrial revolution – consisted of the rapid expansion of the English textile *and* metal industries during the Dutch-led financial expansion of the eighteenth century.

As Nef has underscored, this third moment drew on a repertoire of industrial and business techniques which had been built up in the second moment; and in all probability, the same could be said of the second moment in relation to the first. Nevertheless, our thesis has been that the main historical link between the three moments of English industrial expansion were systemic rather than local. That is to say, each moment of industrial expansion in England was integral to an ongoing financial expansion, restructuring, and reorganization of the capitalist world-economy, in which England was incorporated from the very start. Periods of financial expansion were invariably moments of intensifying competitive pressures on the governmental and business institutions of the European trade and accumulation system. Under these pressures, agro-industrial production declined in some locales and rose in others, primarily in response to the positional disadvantages and advantages of the locales in the changing structure of the world-economy. And in all three financial expansions, "gifts" of history and of geography made England a particularly suitable locale for one kind of industrial expansion or another.

The ruling groups of England were not passive recipients of these gifts and of the recurrent spurts of industrial expansion that accompanied them. By forcibly destroying the Flemish cloth industry, Edward III gave a big push to the expansion of English textile production during the first financial expansion, in an attempt to move England up in the value-added hierarchy of the European world-economy. Elizabeth I tried to do the same, but by slowing down expansion in the textile industries and encouraging it in the armaments and luxury industries. Neither Edward's expansive policy, nor Elizabeth's selectively restrictive policy, however, could do much to overcome the fundamental subordination of English industrialism, first to Italian and then to Dutch capitalism.

What eventually enabled England to overcome this subordination and to become the new governor and organizer of the capitalist world-economy was not the new spurt of industrial expansion that took off during the Napoleonic Wars. Rather, it was the previous redirection of English energies and resources from industrialism to overseas commercial and territorial expansion. The century-long pause in English industrial expansion after 1640 (which puzzles Nef) was in part a reflection of the changed conjuncture in the European world-economy after Westphalia. But it also reflected the concentration of English energies and resources on the task of transferring control of entrepôt trade from Dutch to English hands so as to turn a major obstacle to the expansion of English wealth and power into a formidable weapon of that expansion. As long as Amsterdam was the central entrepôt of world trade, it was easy for Dutch business to outcompete in high value-added industries even the producers of more industrialized states like Venice or England. But once England – already the most industrialized state of the European world-economy – turned into the central entrepôt of world trade, and on a scale never seen before, the competitiveness of English business became unbeatable in a much wider range of industries than Dutch business ever was.

It was at this time that, retrospectively, Elizabeth I's investment of plunder seized from Spain in the stabilization of the pound and in the launching of joint-stock companies chartered to promote overseas commercial and territorial expansion appeared as the best investment she could have ever made. Although for almost a century the money so invested seemed to many to have been a waste in the face of insurmountable odds in competing with the Dutch, in the eighteenth century Elizabeth's (or Gresham's) foresight was fully vindicated. The reaffirmation and consolidation under William III of the tradition of sound money established by Elizabeth kept English surplus capital invested in the English national debt and, in addition, brought in Dutch capital in the most decisive moments of the inter-state power struggle. And when the burden on the English budget and balance of payments of the interest paid to domestic and foreign investors might have become excessive in the face of rapidly escalating protection costs, an offspring of the £42,000 of booty invested by Elizabeth in the Levant Company – the English East India Company – started to bring returns in the form of plunder and tribute from India which no other investment of comparable size, industrial or otherwise, could ever have generated.

Here lies the true historical significance of the Plassey plunder. As England replaced Amsterdam as the central entrepôt of world trade, English industries began generating far greater cash flows than they could profitably reabsorb, so that there was neither the need nor the room for the Plassey plunder in their prodigious expansion of the late eighteenth century. But there was plenty of need and room for the Plassey plunder, and for the steady stream of imperial tribute of which it was only an advance, in British high finance. By buttressing Britain's credit rating at a critical juncture of the European power struggle and, in addition by freeing Britain once and for all from its dependence on, and subordination to, foreign capital, imperial tribute from India and other colonial sources finally made Gresham's dream come true. The British state and British capital could show the whole world what kind of power each derived from their union in a cohesive national bloc. That the main foundation of the power of this national bloc was imperial is surely something that would have neither surprised nor indeed displeased Gresham, let alone Elizabeth I.

When at the end of the Napoleonic Wars the President of the Board of Trade, Huskisson, maintained that the re-establishment of the gold standard suspended during the wars would make Britain the Venice of the nineteenth century, he was appealing to a metaphor of unsurpassed governmental and business success. Although the Venetian republic had recently been erased from the map of Europe, its almost millenary history of political stability in good and bad times and of harmonious fusion of governmental and business reason still evoked in the minds of Huskisson's contemporaries an image of success in state-making and money-making at the same time that no city-state – least of all chaotic Genoa – or nation-state – least of all extravagant Spain – could match. To mention Genoa or Spain, or even the Dutch quasi-nation-state, as models for Britain to replicate in the century ahead would have been truly bad publicity for the policies advocated by the Board of Trade.

And yet, by the end of the Napoleonic Wars the British state and British capital had developed features that alongside a Venetian lineage betrayed the less reputable lineages of sixteenth-century Genoa and Spain. For more than a century the Bank of England had replicated the main features of the *Casa di San Giorgio*. But it was above all during the wars with France in the late eighteenth and early nineteenth centuries that the Genoese–Iberian lineage rose to prominence in the strategies and structures of British governmental and business institutions.

For one thing, Britain's tendency "to spend on war out of all proportion to its tax revenue, [so as] to throw into the struggle with France and its allies the decisive margin of ships and men" (Dickson 1967: 9), meant that "the nation was mortgaged to a new class in its society, the rentiers, the fundholders, for an annual sum . . . three times the public revenue before the revolutionary wars" (Jenks 1938: 17). This massive subordination of the state to strictly moneyed interests in itself made Britain resemble a combination of Spain and Genoa much more than Venice. More importantly, massive wartime deficit spending and the geographical distribution of this spending endowed the City with a network of foreign business connections that made it the heir of the sixteenth-century cosmopolitan Genoese "nation."

The rise of funded wealth and the domination of flows of money and goods by contracts and licences issued in London placed a heavy strain on the Bank of England's resources. The inability of the Bank to cope with the situation forced the British government "to turn more confidingly to the private banks and those merchants of London that began to be known as 'merchant bankers'" (Jenks 1938: 18). Merchant bankers in particular became absolutely critical to the management and regulation of Britain's wartime expenditures:

> Nearly the entire cost of war was to be met abroad. In gold or supplies the proceeds of loans or taxes must be at the disposal of Great Britain and her Allies in the field. Only merchants thru their foreign correspondents were able to perform this service. They could meet pay-rolls in Flanders out of Mexican dollars coming in payment for calico delivered in Spain. They could assemble cloths from Yorkshire, sabres and muskets from Sheffield, and horses from Ireland, and deliver them in Trieste for an Austrian campaign. And as they would contract for the employment of the government's money, their aid was invaluable in providing it. With the bankers they made up groups to bid in the public loans, and when successful had the entire proceeds at their disposal. . . . The business of foreign remittance . . . merged in that of domestic. Both became continuous with the movement of merchandise upon contract or commission in a market in which war demand was the decisive factor. And this was knit up with the movement of the exchanges, the circulation of paper money, and all with the rise and fall of the funds. (Jenks 1938: 18–19)

There is much *déjà vu* in this passage. The Genoese merchant bankers whose fairs enabled Philip II to wage his endless wars in the latter half of the sixteenth century would have found themselves perfectly at home in the space-of-flows described here by Leland Jenks. Also in this respect, the structure of British business which emerged from the Napoleonic Wars resembled far more closely the sixteenth-century structure of Genoese business than that of Venetian business at any time in its history.

There were, of course, important differences between the sixteenth-century Genoese and the nineteenth-century British spaces-of-flows. Apart from the greater scale and complexity of the British space, the Genoese space was "external" and the British space was "internal" to the imperial networks of power that each serviced in war and peace. The Genoese space was external to the Spanish empire – at first in the mobile "Bisenzone" fairs, and then in the Piacenza fairs. The center of the British space-of-flows, in contrast, was in London; it coincided with the center of the British empire. This difference reflected the fact that the Genoese regime was based on a relationship of political exchange between two autonomous organizations – the Genoese capitalist "nation" and the

Spanish territorialist "state." The British regime was instead based on a relationship of political exchange between the City and the British government. Both belonged to the same nation-state, the United Kingdom.

There was also a difference of function between the Genoese and the British cosmopolitan business networks. Both were formed in the service of war. But whereas the Genoese network went on to service war throughout its career, the British network went on to service Britain's Hundred Years Peace.

Braudel seems to suggest that the Genoese network might have done the same had Spain succeeded in its imperial ambitions. This much is implied in two of his many rhetorical questions:

> Even supposing that Charles V had had his way (as all the celebrated humanists of his time hoped), would not capitalism which was already established in the key cities of the new Europe ... somehow have managed to escape unhurt? Would the Genoese not have dominated the transactions of the European fairs in just the same way by handling the finances of "Emperor" Philip II, rather than those of King Philip II? (Braudel 1984: 56)

We shall never know what combination of historical circumstances might have propelled and sustained the self-expansion of Genoese business networks under a Pax Hispanica that never was. We do know, however, that in the nineteenth century the change of function of the analogous British networks from the servicing of war to the servicing of peace occurred through a major restructuring of operations. And we also know that in this restructuring, Britain's role as the workshop of the world played a critical role. As Stanley Chapman (1984) recounts, the ascent of the Rothschilds to the dominant business organization in the City did not originate in the City itself through the handling of British public finances. Rather, it originated in the most dynamic of Britain's industrial districts through the handling of the overseas procurement of inputs (most notably, raw cotton) and the overseas disposal of outputs.

Far from being in contradiction with one another, the "workshop" and the "entrepôt" functions exercised by Britain in the nineteenth century were the obverse and mutually reinforcing sides of the same process of world market formation. This process has been the fount and matrix of our times and will constitute the subject-matter of the opening section of chapter 4. Before we proceed, however, let us pause to unveil the logic that seems to underlie the recurrence of systemic cycles of accumulation and the transition from one cycle to another.

Reprise and Preview

Joseph Schumpeter (1954: 163) once remarked that, in matters of capitalist development, a century is a "short run." As it turns out, in matters of development of the capitalist world-economy, a century does not constitute even a "short run." Thus, Immanuel Wallerstein (1974a; 1974b) borrowed Braudel's notion of a "long sixteenth century" (1450–1640) as the proper unit of analysis of what in his scheme of things is the first (formative) stage of the capitalist world-economy. Eric Hobsbawm (1987: 8–9) similarly speaks of a "long nineteenth century" (1776–1914) as the appropriate timeframe for the analysis of what he envisages as the bourgeois-liberal (British) stage of historical capitalism.

In a similar vein, the notion of a long twentieth century is adopted here as the appropriate timeframe for the analysis of the rise, full expansion, and eventual supersession of the agencies and structures of the fourth (US) systemic cycle of accumulation. As such, the long twentieth century is nothing but the latest link in a chain of partly overlapping stages, each encompassed by a long century, through which the European capitalist world-economy has come to incorporate the entire globe in a dense system of exchanges. The stages, and the long centuries that encompass them, overlap because, as a rule, the agency and structures of accumulation typical of each stage have risen to pre-eminence in the capitalist world-economy during the (CM') phase of financial expansion of the preceding stage. From this point of view, the fourth (US) systemic cycle of accumulation is no exception. The process through which the governmental and business institutions typical of this cycle and stage were created was part and parcel of the process through which the governmental and business institutions of the preceding (British) cycle and stage were superseded – a supersession which began during the Great Depression of 1873–96 and the concomitant financial expansion of the British regime of capital accumulation.

Figure 10 makes explicit the dating scheme that we have adopted in our discusssion of the first three systemic cycles of accumulation and expands it to include that portion of the fourth (US) cycle that has materialized to date. The main feature of the temporal profile of historical capitalism sketched here is the similar structure of all long centuries. These constructs all consist of three distinct segments or periods: (1) a first period of financial expansion (stretching from S_{n-1} to T_{n-1}), in the course of which the new regime of accumulation develops within the old, its development being an integral aspect of the full expansion and contradictions of the latter; (2) a period of consolidation and further development of the new regime of accumulation (stretching from T_{n-1} to S_n), in the course of which its leading agencies promote, monitor, and profit from the material expansion of the entire world-economy; (3) a second period of financial expansion (from S_n to T_n), in the course of which the contradictions of the fully developed regime of accumulation create the space for, and are deepened by, the emergence of competing and alternative regimes, one of which will eventually (that is, at time T_n) become the new dominant regime.

Borrowing an expression from Gerhard Mensch (1979: 75), we shall designate the beginning of every financial expansion, and therefore of every long century, the "*signal* crisis" (S_1, S_2, S_3, and S_4 in figure 10) of the dominant regime of accumulation. It is at this time that the leading agency of systemic processes of accumulation begins to switch its capital in increasing quantities from trade and production to financial inter-mediation and speculation. The switch is the expression of a "crisis" in the sense that it marks a "turning point," a "crucial time of decision," when the leading agency of systemic processes of capital accumulation reveals, through the switch, a negative judgement on the possibility of continuing to profit from the reinvestment of surplus capital in the material expansion of the world-economy, as well as a positive judgement on the possibility of prolonging in time and space its leadership/dominance through a greater specialization in high finance. This crisis is the "signal" of a deeper underlying systemic crisis, which the switch to high finance none the less forestalls for the time being. In fact, the switch can do more than that: it may transform the end of material expansion into a "wonderful moment" of renewed wealth and power for its promoters and organizers, as to different extents and in different ways it has done in all four systemic cycles of accumulation.

However wonderful this moment might be for those who benefit most from the end of the material expansion of the world-economy, it has never been the expression of a lasting resolution of the underlying systemic crisis. On the contrary, it has always been the preamble to a deepening of the crisis and to the eventual supersession of the still dominant regime of accumulation by a new one. We call the event, or series of events, that lead to this final supersession the "*terminal* crisis" (T_1, T_2, T_3 in figure 10) of the dominant regime of accumulation, and we take it to mark the end of the long century that encompasses the rise, full expansion, and demise of that regime.

Like all previous long centuries, the long twentieth century consists of three distinct segments. The first starts in the 1870s and goes through the 1930s, that is, from the signal crisis through the terminal crisis of the British regime of accumulation. The second goes from the terminal crisis of the British regime through the signal crisis of the US regime – a crisis which we can locate around 1970. And the third and last segment goes from 1970 through the terminal crisis of the US regime. Since, as far as we can tell, the latter crisis has not yet occurred, to analyze this segment means in fact investigating the present and the future as part of an ongoing historical process which presents elements both of novelty and of recurrence in comparison with the closing (CM') phases of all previous systemic cycles of accumulation.

Our primary concern in this historical investigation of the present and of the future will be to provide some plausible answer(s) to two closely related questions: (1) What forces are in the process of precipitating the terminal crisis of the US regime of accumulation, and how soon should we expect this terminal crisis to occur and the long twentieth century to end? (2) What alternative paths of development will be open to the capitalist world-economy once the long twentieth century has come to an end? In seeking plausible answers to these questions we shall avail ourselves of a second feature of the temporal profile sketched in figure 10. This is the speed-up in the pace of capitalist history already mentioned in the Introduction.

Although all the long centuries depicted in figure 10 consist of three analogous segments and are all longer than a century, over time they have contracted. That is to say, as we move from the earlier to the later stages of capitalist development, it has taken less and less time for systemic regimes of accumulation to rise, develop fully, and be superseded.

There are two ways of measuring this. The first is to measure the duration of the long centuries themselves. What we call the long fifteenth–sixteenth century encompasses almost the entire length of Braudel's and Wallerstein's "long sixteenth century" *plus* the century of the parallel "Italian" and "Anglo-French" Hundred Years Wars, during which the Florentine-led financial expansion reached its apogee and the strategies and structures of the future Genoese regime of accumulation were formed. It goes from the great crash of the early 1340s to the end of the Age of the Genoese some 290 years later.

This is by far the longest of the three full long centuries depicted in figure 10. The long seventeenth century, which goes from the signal crisis of the Genoese regime in around 1560 to the terminal crisis of the Dutch regime in the 1780s, is only about 220 years long. And the long nineteenth century, which goes from the signal crisis of the Dutch regime in around 1740 to the terminal crisis of the British regime in the early 1930s is even shorter – a "mere" 190 years.

Another way of gauging the speed-up in the pace of capitalist history is to compare the periods of time that separate successive signal crises. This method has two advantages. First, the dating of signal crises is far less arbitrary than that of terminal crises. The latter occur in periods of dualism of power and of turbulence in high finance. It is not easy to choose among the successive crises that mark the transition from one regime to another the "true" terminal crisis of the declining regime. Signal crises, in contrast, occur in periods of comparatively stable governance of the capitalist world-economy and as such are easier to identify. A measurement that involves only signal crises is therefore more reliable than one that involves both signal and terminal crises.

Moreover, by comparing the periods of time that separate successive signal crises we do not double-count periods of financial expansion and we gain one observation. Since the long twentieth century has not yet ended, capitalist history thus far spans only *three* long centuries. But since the signal crisis of the US regime of accumulation has already occurred, we have *four* signal crisis to signal crisis periods. These periods measure the time that it has taken successive regimes to become dominant after the signal crisis of the preceding regime and to attain the limits of their own capabilities to go on profiting from the material expansion of the world-economy. As we can see in figure 10, this time has decreased steadily from about 220 years in the case of the Genoese regime, to about 180 years in the case of the Dutch regime, to about 130 years in the case of the British regime, to about 100 years in the case of the US regime.

While the time taken by successive regimes of accumulation to rise to dominance and attain their maturity has been decreasing, the size and organizational complexity of the leading agencies of these successive regimes has been increasing. The latter tendency is most clearly perceived by focusing on the "containers of power" (that is, on the states) that have housed the "headquarters" of the leading capitalist agencies of the successive regimes: the Republic of Genoa, the United Provinces, the United Kingdom, and the United States.

At the time of the rise and full expansion of the Genoese regime, the Republic of Genoa was a city-state small in size and simple in organization, and which held very little power indeed. Deeply divided socially, and poorly dependable militarily, it was by most criteria a weak state in comparison with and in relation to all the great powers of the time, among which its old rival Venice still ranked fairly high. Yet, thanks to its far-flung commercial and financial networks the Genoese capitalist class, organized in a cosmopolitan "nation," could deal on equal terms with the most powerful territorialist rulers of Europe, and turn the relentless competition for mobile capital between these rulers into a powerful engine for the self-expansion of its own capital.

At the time of the rise and full expansion of the Dutch regime of accumulation, the United Provinces was a hybrid kind of organization which combined some of the features of the disappearing city-states with some of the features of the rising nation-states. A larger and far more complex organization than the Republic of Genoa, the United Provinces "contained" sufficient power to win independence from Imperial Spain, to carve out of the latter's sea-borne and territorial empire a highly profitable empire of commercial outposts, and to keep at bay the military challenges of England by sea and France by land. The greater power of the Dutch state relative to the Genoese enabled the Dutch capitalist class to do what the Genoese had already been doing – turn inter-state competition for mobile capital into an engine for the self-expansion of its own capital – but without having to "buy" protection from territorialist states, as the Genoese had to do.

At the time of the rise and full expansion of the British regime of accumulation, Britain was not only a fully developed nation-state and, as such, a larger and more complex organization than the United Provinces had ever been; it was also in the process of conquering a world-encompassing commercial and territorial empire which gave its ruling groups and its capitalist class an unprecedented command over the world's human and natural resources. This enabled the British capitalist class to do what the Dutch had already been able to do – turn to its own advantage inter-state competition for mobile capital and "produce" all the protection required by the self-expansion of its capital, but without having to rely on foreign and often hostile territorialist organizations for most of the agro-industrial production on which the profitability of its commercial activities rested.

Finally, at the time of the rise and full expansion of the US regime of accumulation, the United States was already something more than a fully developed nation-state. It was a continental military–industrial complex with sufficient power to provide a wide range of subordinate and allied governments with effective protection and to make credible threats of economic strangulation or military annihilation towards unfriendly governments anywhere in the world. Combined with the size, insularity, and natural wealth of its own territory, this power enabled the US capitalist class to "internalize" not just protection and production costs, as the British capitalist class had already done, but transaction costs as well, that is to say, the markets on which the self-expansion of its capital depended.

This steady increase in the size, complexity, and power of the leading agencies of capitalist history is somewhat obscured by another feature of the temporal sequence sketched in figure 10. This is the double movement – forward and backward at the same time – that has characterized the sequential development of systemic cycles of accumulation. As we have emphasized in the discussion of the first three cycles, each step forward in the process of internalization of costs by a new regime of accumulation has involved a revival of governmental and business strategies and structures that had been superseded by the preceding regime.

Thus, the internalization of protection costs by the Dutch regime in comparison with, and in relation to, the Genoese regime occurred through a revival of the strategies and structures of Venetian state monopoly capitalism which the Genoese regime had superseded. Similarly, the internalization of production costs by the British regime in comparison with, and in relation to, the Dutch regime occurred through a revival in new, enlarged and more complex forms of the strategies and structures of Genoese cosmopolitan capitalism and Iberian global territorialism, the combination of which had been superseded by the Dutch regime. As anticipated in chapter 1 and argued further in chapter 4, the same pattern recurred with the rise and full expansion of the US regime, which internalized transaction costs by reviving in new, enlarged, and more complex forms the strategies and structures of Dutch corporate capitalism which had been superseded by the British regime.

This recurrent revival of previously superseded strategies and structures of accumulation generates a pendulum-like movement back and forth between "cosmopolitan-imperial" and "corporate-national" organizational structures, the first being typical of "extensive" regimes, as the Genoese and the British were, and the second of "intensive" regimes, as the Dutch and the US were. The Genoese and British "cosmopolitan-imperial" regimes were extensive in the sense that they have been responsible for most of the geographical expansion of the capitalist world-economy. Under the Genoese regime, the world was "discovered," and under the British it was "conquered."

The Dutch and the US "corporate-national" regimes, in contrast, were intensive in the sense that they have been responsible for the geographical consolidation rather than expansion of the capitalist world-economy. Under the Dutch regime, the "discovery" of the world realized primarily by the Iberian partners of the Genoese was consolidated into a system of commercial entrepôts and joint-stock chartered companies centered in Amsterdam. And under the US regime, the "conquest" of the world realized primarily by the British themselves was consolidated into a system of national markets and transnational corporations centered in the United States.

This alternation of extensive and intensive regimes naturally blurs our perception of the underlying, truly long-term tendency of the leading agencies of systemic processes of capital accumulation to increase in size, complexity, and power. When the pendulum swings in the direction of extensive regimes, as in the transition from the Dutch to the British, the underlying trend is magnified. And when it swings in the direction of intensive regimes, as in the transitions from the Genoese to the Dutch and from the British to the US regimes, the underlying trend appears to have been less significant than it really was.

Nevertheless, once we control for these swings by comparing the two intensive and the two extensive regimes with one another – the Genoese with the British, and the Dutch with the US – the underlying trend becomes unmistakable. The development of historical capitalism as a world system has been based on the formation of ever more powerful cosmopolitan-imperial (or corporate-national) blocs of governmental and business organizations endowed with the capability of widening (or deepening) the functional and spatial scope of the capitalist world-economy. And yet, the more powerful these blocs have become, the shorter the lifecycle of the regimes of accumulation that they have brought into being – the shorter, that is, the time that it has taken for these regimes to emerge out of the crisis of the preceding dominant regime, to become themselves dominant, and to attain their limits as signalled by the beginning of a new financial expansion. In the case of the British regime, this time was 130 years, or about 40 per cent less than it had been for the Genoese regime; and in the case of the US regime it was 100 years, or about 45 per cent less than for the Dutch regime.

This pattern of capitalist development whereby an increase in the power of regimes of accumulation is associated with a decrease in their duration, is reminiscent of Marx's contention that "*the real barrier* of capitalist production is *capital itself*" and that capitalist production continually overcomes its immanent barriers "only by means which again place these barriers in its way on a more formidable scale" (Marx 1962: 245; emphasis in the original):

> The contradiction, to put it in a very general way, consists in that the capitalist mode of production involves a tendency towards absolute development of the productive forces ... regardless of the social conditions under which capitalist production takes place; while, on the other hand, its aim is to preserve the value of existing capital and promote its self-expansion (i.e. to promote an ever more rapid growth of this value).... It is that capital and its self-expansion appear as the starting and closing point, the motive and purpose of production; that production is only production for capital and not vice versa.... The means – unconditional development of the productive forces of society – comes continually into conflict with the limited purpose, the self-expansion of capital. [If the] capitalist mode of production is, for this reason, a historical means of developing the material forces of production and creating an appropriate world-market, [it] is, at the same time, a continual conflict between this ... historical task and its own corresponding relations of social production. (Marx 1962: 244–5)

In fact, this contradiction between the self-expansion of capital on the one side, and the development of the material forces of production and of an appropriate world market on the other, can be reformulated in even more general terms. For historical capitalism as a world system of accumulation became a "mode of production" – that is, it internalized production costs – only in its third (British) stage of development. And yet, the principle that the real barrier of capitalist development is capital itself, that the self-expansion of existing capital is in constant tension, and recurrently enters in open contradiction, with the material expansion of the world-economy and the creation of an appropriate world market – all this was clearly at work already in the first two stages of development, notwithstanding the continuing externalization of agro-industrial production by the leading agencies of capital accumulation on a world scale.

In both stages the starting and closing point of the material expansion of the world-economy was the pursuit of profit as an end in itself on the part of a particular capitalist agency. In the first stage, the "Great Discoveries," the organization of long-distance trade within and across the boundaries of the far-flung Iberian empire(s), and the creation of an embryonic "world market" in Antwerp, Lyons, and Seville, were to Genoese capital mere means of its own self-expansion. And when in around 1560 these means no longer served this purpose, Genoese capital promptly pulled out of trade to specialize in high finance. Likewise, the undertaking of carrying trade among separate and often distant political jurisdictions, the centralization of entrepôt trade in Amsterdam and of high value-added industries in Holland, the creation of a world-wide network of commercial outposts and exchanges, and the "production" of whatever protection was required by all these activities, were to Dutch capital mere means of its own self-expansion. And again, when around 1740 these means no longer served this purpose, Dutch capital, like Genoese capital 180 years earlier, abandoned them in favor of a more concentrated specialization in high finance.

From this angle of vision, in the nineteenth century British capital simply repeated a pattern that had been established long before historical capitalism as a mode of accumulation had become also a mode of production. The only difference was that, in addition to carrying, entrepôt, and other kinds of long-distance and short-distance trade and related protection and production activities, in the British cycle extractive and manufacturing activities – that is, what we defined earlier as production in a narrow sense – had become critical means of the self-expansion of capital. But when in around 1870 production and related trade activities no longer served this purpose, British capital moved fast towards specialization in financial speculation and intermediation, just like Dutch capital had done 130 years earlier and Genoese capital 310 years earlier.

As we shall see, the same pattern was repeated 100 years later by US capital. This latest switch from trade and production to financial speculation and intermediation, like the three analogous switches of earlier centuries, can be interpreted as reflecting the same underlying contradiction between the self-expansion of capital and the material expansion of the world-economy, which in our scheme corresponds to Marx's "development of the productive forces of [world] society." The contradiction is that the material expansion of the world-economy was in all instances mere means in endeavors aimed primarily at increasing the value of capital and yet, over time, the expansion of trade and production tended to drive down the rate of profit and thereby curtail the value of capital.

The idea that all expansions of trade and production tend to drive down the rate of profit and, therefore, to undermine their main foundation was not Marx's but Adam Smith's idea. Marx's version of the "law" of the tendency of the rate of profit to fall was in fact aimed at demonstrating that Smith's own version of the "law" was too pessimistic concerning the long-term potential of capitalism to promote the development of the productive forces of society. In Smith's version of the "law," the expansion of trade and production is inseparable from a continual increase in competition among its agencies – an increase which raises real wages and rents and drives down the rate of profit. Marx followed Smith in assuming that the expansion of trade and production is inseparable from a continual increase in the competition among its agencies. Nevertheless, he conceived of this increase in competition as being associated with an increase in the concentration of capital which restrains the growth of real wages and opens up new opportunities for commercial and agro-industrial expansion notwithstanding the fall in the rate of profit. To be sure, in Marx's scheme this tendency then becomes the source of even greater contradictions. But in the meantime capital accumulation has promoted a far greater expansion of trade and production than Smith thought possible. For our present purposes, Smith's version of the "law" is more useful in explaining the inner dynamic of systemic cycles of accumulation, whereas Marx's version is more useful in explaining the transition from one cycle to another.

As Paolo Sylos-Labini (1976: 219) has pointed out, Smith's thesis of the tendency of the rate of profit to fall was sketched in a passage which both Ricardo and Marx accepted in full and which anticipated Schumpeter's thesis on innovations:

> The establishment of any new manufacture, of any new branch of commerce, or of any new practice in agriculture, is always a speculation, from which the projector promises himself extraordinary profits. These profits sometimes are very great, and sometimes, more frequently, perhaps are quite otherwise; but in general they bear no regular proportion to those of other old trades in the neighbourhood. If the project succeeds, they are commonly at first very high.

When the trade or practice becomes thoroughly established and well known, the competition reduces them to the level of other trades. (Smith 1961: I, 128)

The level to which profits are reduced may be high or low depending on whether business enterprises are in a position to restrict entry into their spheres of operation through private agreements or through governmental regulation. If they are not in a position to do so, profits will be as low as is considered "tolerable" in view of the risks involved in the employment of capital in trade and production. But if they can restrict entry and keep the market undersupplied, profits will be significantly higher than their "tolerable" level. In the first case, the expansion of trade and production *comes* to an end because of low profits; in the second case, it is *brought* to an end by the predisposition of capitalist business to keep the level of profits as high as possible (cf. Sylos-Labini 1976: 216-20).

Smith formulated this thesis with specific reference to trade expansions occurring within a given political jurisdiction. But the thesis can be easily reformulated with reference to the expansion of a trading system that encompasses multiple jurisdictions, which is what John Hicks did in his theoretical account of the mercantile expansion of a system of city-states. As Hicks suggests, a profitable trade continually provides the incentive for the routine reinvestment of profits in its further expansion. Nevertheless, in order to extract a greater volume of material inputs from suppliers, the agency of expansion must offer them a better price; and in order to sell more at the other end, it must take a lower price. Hence, as a growing mass of profit seeks reinvestment in trade and production, the gap between the selling and the buying price tends to diminish and the rate at which trade can expand slows down (Hicks 1969: 45).

Historically, major trade expansions have occurred only because an agency or an ensemble of agencies found ways and means of preventing or counterbalancing the curtailment of profit margins that inevitably ensues from the investment of a growing mass of money in the purchase and sale of commodities along established channels of trade. As a rule, the most important has been one kind or another of trade diversification, "the very characteristic endeavor of the merchant," as Hicks (1969: 45) put it, "to look for new objects of trade and new channels of trade, the activity which makes him an innovator." Trade diversification forestalls the narrowing of profit margins because the surpluses that are being reinvested in the further expansion of trade do not go to increase the demand for the same kind of inputs from the same kind of suppliers (and therefore do not exercise an upward pressure on purchase prices) and/or do not result in a larger supply of the same kind of outputs to the same customers (and therefore do not exercise a downward pressure on sale prices). Rather, expansion proceeds by bringing into the trading system new kinds of inputs and outputs and/or new units either as suppliers or as customers, so that a growing mass of profits can be invested in the expansion of trade and production without exercising any downward pressure on profit margins.

As Hicks emphasizes, diversified trade is not just a combination of simple trades. Innovations in the objects and channels of trade transform the very structure of the trading system, so that returns to the reinvestment of profits in the further expansion of trade, instead of diminishing, may well rise. Just as "it is by no means the case that in the settlement of a new country the best land will be the first to be occupied," so "[it] is . . . by no means necessary that the first of the opportunities for trading to be opened up should be those which prove to be the most profitable; there may be more profitable opportunities from going further afield which will not be discovered until the nearer opportunities have been explored" (Hicks 1969: 47).

By pushing further and further in space the boundaries of the trading system, in other words, the agencies of expansion create the conditions for the discovery of the more profitable opportunities that lie further afield. Historically, this spatial widening of the boundaries of the capitalist world-economy occurred primarily under the Genoese and British regimes. Thanks to the geographical expansion experienced by the capitalist world-economy under these two extensive regimes, the number, range, and variety of commodities in which capital could be invested without narrowing profit margins suddenly multiplied, and the conditions were thereby created for the great commercial expansions of the early sixteenth and mid-nineteenth centuries.

The profitability of trade and the urge to plow profits back into the expansion of trade can none the less increase even if the margin between selling and buying prices is narrowing. As the volume of trade grows, new divisions of labor develop among and within trading centers with a consequent reduction in the costs and risks of their operations. Reductions in unit costs tend to keep profits high even if the margin between buying and selling prices is narrowing; and reduction in risks tends to make the centers willing to go on plowing profits back in the expansion of trade even if net returns are falling. Under extensive regimes, the economies that mattered most were "external" to the centers, that is, were due to the advantages they derived from belonging to a larger trading body; under intensive regimes, the economies were mostly "internal" to the centers, that is, were due to the advantages they derived from themselves growing larger. Either way, some combination of external and internal economies is necessary for any major trade expansion to occur for any length of time (cf. Hicks 1969: 47–8).

It follows that all material expansions of the capitalist world-economy have been shaped by two contrasting tendencies. On the one hand, there was the underlying tendency towards the narrowing of profit margins under the impact of the routine reinvestment of a growing mass of profit in a spatial domain limited by the organizational capabilities of the agency of expansion. Whether "visible" or not, this tendency exercised a constant downward pull on profitability and hence on the forces of expansion. On the other hand, there was the tendency of costs and risks of operation to be reduced by the internal and external economies generated by the increasing volume and density of trade. This was the tendency that propelled the expansion forward in space and time by pushing up profitability.

"It is tempting to suppose," remarks Hicks (1969: 56), "that there must be a phase in which one force is dominant, which must be followed by a phase in which the other is dominant – a phase of expansion followed by a phase of stagnation." Hicks is reluctant to yield to the temptation and warns us against "too easy an identification of logical process with temporal sequence." Although a phase of stagnation may indeed follow a phase of expansion, "it may also happen that after a pause new opportunities are discovered, so that expansion is resumed." In his scheme, stagnation is only a possibility. What is inevitable is that there will be "pauses."

According to this conceptualization, the material expansions of the world-economy can be described by means of one or more S-shaped trajectories (so-called logistics), each consisting of an A-phase of increasing returns and a B-phase of decreasing returns, the latter turning into "stagnation" as expansion approaches its upper asymptote K (see figure 11). Hicks's preference is for conceiving of trade expansions as consisting of a series of conjoined S-shaped curves separated by more or less long "pauses" during which expansion slows down or ceases altogether (see figure 12). Whether this series of conjoined trajectories has itself an upper asymptote is a question about which Hicks is agnostic, as indicated by the bracketed question mark in figure 12.

Hicks's hesitation in identifying logical process with temporal sequence is surprising in view of the fact that the world-economy (his mercantile economy) "in its first form, when it [was] embodied in a system of city states," to which his conceptualization refers (Hicks 1969: 56), never again experienced an overall material expansion after the financial expansion of the late fourteenth and early fifteeenth centuries. When the capitalist world-economy entered a new phase of material expansion in the late fifteenth and early sixteenth centuries, it was no longer embodied in a system of city-states, but in a system of "nations" that were no longer states, and of states that were not yet nations. And this system itself began to be superseded by a new organizational structure as soon as the material expansion turned into a financial one.

Generally speaking, our analysis of systemic cycles of accumulation has shown that every material expansion of the capitalist world-economy has been based on a particular organizational structure, the vitality of which was progressively undermined by the expansion itself. This tendency can be traced to the fact that in one way or another all such expansions were constrained by the very forces that generated them, so that the stronger these forces became, the stronger also was the tendency for expansion to cease. More specifically, as the mass of capital that sought reinvestment in trade increased under the impact of rising or high returns, a growing proportion of the economic space needed to keep returns rising or high was being used up – to borrow an expression from David Harvey (1985; 1989: 205), it was "annihilated through time." And as the centers of trade and accumulation attempted to counter diminishing returns through the diversification of their business, they also annihilated the locational and functional distance that had been keeping them out of one another's way in more or less well-protected market niches. As a result of this double tendency, cooperation between the centers was displaced by an increasingly vicious competition, which depressed profits further and eventually destroyed the organizational structures on which the preceding material expansion had been based.

As a rule, the turning point between the A-phase of increasing returns and accelerating expansion, and the B-phase of decreasing returns and decelerating expansion, was due not to a shortage of capital seeking investment in commodities as in Marx's "overproduction crises," but to an overabundance of such capital as in Marx's "overaccumulation crises." There was a surplus or excess of capital invested, or seeking investment, in the purchase and sale of commodities over and above the level of investment that would prevent the rate of profit from falling. And as long as a portion of this surplus capital was not crowded out, the overall rate of profit tended to fall and competition within and between locations and lines of business intensified:

A portion of old capital has to lie unused under all circumstances.... The competitive struggle would decide what part of it would be particularly affected. So long as things go well, competition affects an operating fraternity of the capitalist class ... so that each [capitalist] shares in the common loot in proportion to the size of his respective investment. But as soon as it no longer is a question of sharing profits, but of sharing losses, everyone tries to reduce his own share to a minimum and to shove it off upon another. The class as such must inevitably lose. How much the individual capitalist ... must share in [the loss] at all, is decided by strength and cunning, and competition then becomes a fight among hostile brothers. The antagonism between each individual capitalist's interest and those of the capitalist class as a whole, then comes to the surface, just as previously the identity of those interests operated in practice through competition. (Marx 1962: 248)

For Marx, as for Hicks, there is thus a fundamental difference between the kind of competition that obtains among centers of accumulation when overall returns to capital are rising or, if declining, are still high on the one hand, and the kind of competition that obtains when returns are falling below what has come to be regarded as a "reasonable" or "tolerable" level on the other. Substantively, the first kind of competition is not competition at all. Rather, it is a mode of regulating relationships between autonomous centers which are in fact *cooperating* with one another in sustaining a trade expansion from which they all benefit, and in which the profitability of each center is a condition of the profitability of all the centers. The second kind of competition, in contrast, is competition in the very substantive sense that an overaccumulation of capital leads capitalist organizations to invade one another's spheres of operation; the division of labor that previously defined the terms of their mutual cooperation breaks down; and, increasingly, the losses of one organization are the condition of the profits of another. In short, competition turns from a positive-sum into a zero-sum (or even a negative-sum) game. It becomes cut-throat competition, the primary objective of which is to drive other organizations out of business even if it means sacrificing one's own profits for as long as it takes to attain the objective.

These fratricidal competitive struggles were by no means a novelty of the nineteenth century, as Marx thought or seemed to think. On the contrary, they marked the very beginning of the capitalist era. Following Hicks and Braudel, we have traced their earliest round to the Italian Hundred Years War. In the course of this long conflict, the leading capitalist organizations of the time, the Italian city-states, turned from the operating fraternity they had been during the preceding pan-Eurasian commercial expansion into hostile brothers struggling to offload on one another the losses involved in the disintegration of the wider trading system that had made their fortunes.

The end of every subsequent material expansion of the European world-economy was marked by analogous struggles. By the end of the trade expansion of the early sixteenth century, the city-states had ceased to be leaders in systemic processes of capital accumulation. Their place had been taken by cosmopolitan "nations" of merchant bankers who operated out of market cities such as Antwerp and Lyons. As long as the trade expansion was in its rising phase, these "nations" cooperated like a fraternity in the regulation of pan-European money and commodity markets. But as soon as returns to capital invested in trade turned sharply downwards, competition became antagonistic and the fraternity was dissolved.

By the end of the trade expansion of the late seventeenth and early eighteenth centuries, the protagonists of the capitalist drama had changed once again. They were now nation-states and associated chartered companies. But the script was very much the same as in the earlier rounds of the inter-capitalist struggle. Relationships that had been fairly harmonious in the first half of the eighteenth century deteriorated rapidly in the second half. Even before the Napoleonic Wars were over, Britain had centralized in its hands control over entrepôt trade, and the East India Company had driven out of business all its competitors.

The only novelty of the escalation of inter-capitalist competition that marked the tapering off of the mid-nineteenth-century trade expansion was that for about twenty-five years cut-throat price competition between business enterprises occupied center-stage, while governments remained behind the scenes. By the turn of the century, however, inter-enterprise cut-throat price competition began to be superseded by an inter-governmental armament race of unprecedented scale and scope. And between the outbreak of the First World War and the end of the Second, the old script of the Italian Hundred Years War was played out once again over a much shorter period, but on a scale and with an abundance and frightfulness of means that earlier protagonists could never have imagined.

Braudel's financial expansions were integral aspects of all these escalations in inter-capitalist competitive struggles. In fact they were the main expression and a factor of a deepening contradiction between the self-expansion of capital and the material expansion of the world-economy. This contradiction can be described as a bifurcation in the logistic of trade expansion (see figure 13). In this representation, the curve (M) before the bifurcation and the upper branch (CC') after the bifurcation jointly describe the expansion of the stock of money capital invested in trade under the assumption that *all* the profits of trade are routinely reinvested in the further expansion of trade. Under this assumption of a purely commercial or mercantile logic of expansion – a logic in which the expansion of trade is an end in itself so that profits are routinely reinvested in it – the rate at which the stock of capital increases over time ($\Delta M/\Delta t$, that is, the slope of the logistic) represents also the rate of return on the stock of capital invested in trade – Adam Smith's "rate of profit."

The lower logistic (MM'), which consists of the same curve (M) before the bifurcation and of the lower branch (CM') after the bifurcation, also describes the expansion of the stock of money capital invested in trade. However, it describes the expansion under the assumption that the reinvestment of the profits of trade follows a strictly capitalist logic – a logic, that is, in which the expansion of money capital rather than trade is the purpose of the reinvestment of profits. An agency that reinvests routinely the profits of trade in the further expansion of trade as long as the returns to the capital so invested are positive cannot be defined as "capitalist" by any stretch of the imagination. A capitalist agency, by definition, is primarily if not exclusively concerned with the endless expansion of its stock of money (M) and, to this end, it will continually compare the returns that it can reasonably expect from reinvesting its capital in commodity trade (that is, from appreciation according to the formula MCM') with the returns that it can reasonably expect from holding cash surpluses liquid ready to be invested in some financial deal (that is, from appreciation according to the abridged formula MM').

In this connection it is curious that capitalist agencies should have come to be defined in the conceptualizations of many followers of Marx and Weber as being characterized by non-rational and irrational inclinations to plow back profits into the businesses that generated them, particularly in plant, equipment, and wage labor, in disregard of the most elementary cost–benefit calculations and utilitarian considerations. This curious definition finds practically no correspondence in the actual experience of *successful* profit-making enterprises at any time or place in world history. It probably originates in Marx's (1959: 595) facetious dictum "Accumulate, accumulate! That is Moses and the prophets," or in Weber's (1930: 53) serious contention that the essence of the capitalist spirit is "the earning of more and more money ... so purely as an end in itself, that from the point of view of the happiness of, or utility to, the single individual, it appears entirely transcendental and absolutely irrational." The purpose of these statements in the contexts in which they were formulated does not concern us here. Nevertheless, it must be emphasized that as characterizations of the actual behavior of capitalist agencies of world-historical significance, these statements are as false as Schumpeter's characterization of pre-capitalist territorialist agencies as being driven by non-rational and irrational inclinations towards forcible expansion without definite, utilitarian limits (see chapter 1).

Shortly before he uttered the dictum "Accumulate, accumulate!" Marx (1959: 592) himself pointed out that "the love of power is an element in the desire to get rich." He then went on to observe:

the progress of capitalist production not only creates a world of delights; it lays open, in speculation and the credit system, a thousand sources of sudden enrichment. When a certain stage of development has been reached, a conventional degree of prodigality, which is also an exhibition of wealth, and consequently a source of credit, becomes a business necessity to the "unfortunate" capitalist. Luxury enters into capital's expenses of representation. (Marx 1959: 593-4)

This is no less true of today's US capital as it was of fifteenth-century Florentine capital. An agency of capital accumulation is capitalist precisely because it reaps large and regular profits by investing its stock of money in trade and production or in speculation and the credit system depending on which formula (MCM' or MM') endows that stock with the greatest power of breeding. And as Marx himself notes, the very expansion of capitalist production creates the conditions for the profitable investment of money in speculation and in the credit system.

To the extent that the powers of breeding of the two formulas are continually and widely compared – to the extent, that is, that investment in trade is dominated by a capitalist logic – trade expansions are bound to end with a financial expansion. When returns to capital invested in the trade of commodities, though still positive, fall below some critical rate (Rx), which is what capital can earn in the money trades, an increasing number of capitalist organizations will abstain from reinvesting profits in the further expansion of trade in commodities. Whatever cash surpluses accrue to them will be diverted from the commodity to the money trades. It is at this point in time that the trajectory of world trade expansions "bifurcates" into two ideotypical branches: an upper branch that describes what the expansion of trade in commodities would be were it driven by a strictly mercantile logic, and a lower branch that describes what the expansion of trade would be were it driven by a strictly capitalist logic.

Figure 13 thus tells us that in the A-phase of mercantile expansions capitalist and non-capitalist organizations are both induced by the increasing returns to, and diminishing risks of, investments in trade to plow back the profits of trade into its further expansion. It also tells us that both kinds of organization continue to reinvest the profits of trade in the expansion of trade in the B-phase also, but only as long as returns, though declining, are still high. But as returns continue to decline, the organizations that are better positioned or more inclined to follow a purely capitalist logic of expansion begin to pull surpluses out of trade and to hold them in money form – so that the capital that they invest in trade no longer increases – whereas non-capitalist organizations continue to reinvest profits in the further expansion of trade as long as returns are positive.

In a Smithian–Hicksian reading of this representation of trade expansions, the bifurcation occurs primarily as a result of restrictive arrangements in restraint of competition promoted and enforced by capitalist organizations in defense of profitability. That is to say, the bifurcation is an expression of the tendency of trade expansions to depress profits on the one side, and of the counter-tendency of capitalist organizations to raise profitability above what it would otherwise be by restricting entry and by keeping the market systematically undersupplied on the other. If the first tendency is predominant, the trade expansion *comes* to an end along the upper trajectory (CC') because profits are depressed to a barely "tolerable" level; but if the second tendency is predominant, the trade expansion is *brought* to an end along the lower trajectory (CM') because of the restrictions imposed on it by the successful attempt of capitalist organizations to keep profits higher than their barely "tolerable" level. The latter situation describes Hicks's dictum to which we have referred repeatedly in our historical analysis, that in the closing phases of trade expansions profits can remain high only on condition that they are not reinvested in the further expansion of trade.

It may be plausible to suppose that within some particular political jurisdiction the "classes of people who commonly employ the largest capitals, and who by their wealth draw to themselves the greatest share of the public consideration," as Smith (1961: I, 278) characterized the big business of his day, have sufficient power to establish and enforce the kind of restrictive arrangements that are needed to keep the economy settled on the lower path (CM') of material stagnation. But in a world-economy consisting of multiple political jurisdictions such a supposition is not at all plausible. Historically, no capitalist group has ever had the power to prevent capitalist and non-capitalist organizations operating under other political jurisdictions from raising purchase prices by stepping up world demand for inputs, or from depressing selling prices by stepping up world supply of outputs.

Nevertheless, following Weber's lead, our analysis has shown that it is precisely the division of the world-economy into multiple political jurisdictions competing with one another for mobile capital that has provided capitalist agencies with the greatest opportunities to go on expanding the value of their capital in periods of overall material stagnation of the world-economy as fast as, or even faster than, in periods of material expansion. In fact, were it not for the power pursuits that over the centuries have fed inter-state competition for mobile capital, our hypothesis of a bifurcation in the logistic of capital accumulation would make no sense at all. As in the imaginary world of theoretical economics, the overabundant supply of money capital created by diminishing returns in the buying and selling of commodities would drive down returns in financial markets too, thereby eliminating the incentive to divert cash flows from the commodity to the money trades. But in the real world of capitalism, from the the age of the Medicis to our own day, things work differently.

In every phase of financial expansion of the world-economy, the overabundance of money capital engendered by the diminishing returns and increasing risks of its employment in trade and production has been matched or even surpassed by a roughly synchronous expansion of the demand for money capital by organizations for which power and status, rather than profit, were the guiding principle of action. As a rule, these organizations were not discouraged as capitalist organizations were by the diminishing returns and increasing risks of the employment of capital in trade and production. On the contrary, they struggled against diminishing returns by borrowing all the capital they could and by investing it in the forcible conquest of markets, territories, and populations.

This rough but recurrent coincidence of the supply and demand conditions of financial expansions reflects the simultaneous tendency of returns to capital invested in the expansion of trade to fall and for competitive pressures to intensify on capitalist and territorialist organizations alike. This combination of circumstances leads some (mostly capitalist) agencies to divert their cash flows from the trading to the credit system, thereby increasing the supply of loanable funds, and other (mostly territorialist) agencies to seek through borrowing the additional financial resources needed to survive in the more competitive environment, thereby increasing the demand for loanable funds. It follows that the revenue-maximizing and profit-maximizing branches into which logistics of world economic expansion are assumed to bifurcate do not describe actual trajectories. Rather, they describe a field of forces defined by the coexistence of two alternative and mutually exclusive ideotypical paths of capital accumulation, the unity and opposition of which is the source of turbulence and instability in the world system of trade and accumulation.

A single path means that the profit-maximizing logic of capital accumulation and the revenue-maximizing logic of trade expansions coincide and sustain one another. The world-economy can count for its expansion on the ever-growing volume of money and other means of payments that seeks investment in trade. And capital can count for its own self-expansion on the availability of an ever-increasing number and variety of specialized market niches in which a growing mass of commodities can be bought and sold without depreciating its value. The accumulation of capital along this single path is as firmly embedded in the material expansion of the world-economy as a railway embankment in the earth. Under these circumstances the pace at which the·volume of trade and the value of capital both increase is not just rapid but steady as well.

When the two paths bifurcate, in contrast, the logic of trade expansion and the logic of capital accumulation diverge; the accumulation of capital is no longer embedded in the expansion of the world-economy; and the pace of both processes not only slows down but becomes unstable. The bifurcation creates a field of turbulence within which capital actually invested in trade is subjected to conflicting forces of attraction/repulsion to/from the two alternative paths that it could in principle follow – an upper path along which the value of trade and revenue would be maximized and a lower path along which the mass of profits and the value of capital would be maximized. The predisposition of non-capitalist organizations to break out of the constraints imposed on their pursuit of status and power by the slowdown in the expansion of trade continually tends to push the mass of borrowed capital invested in the purchase of commodities upwards, towards or above the upper path. The profitability of capital invested in trade and production is thereby depressed to a barely or less than "tolerable" level, while returns to capital invested in lending and speculation soar. The predisposition of capitalist organizations to withdraw cash surpluses from trade and production in response to falling profits and increasing risks, in contrast, continually tends to pull the mass of capital invested in commodities downwards, towards or below the lower path, so that the profits of trade and production rise and those of lending and speculation fall.

In short, when capital accumulation enters a (CM') phase of financial expansion its trajectory does not follow a steady path but becomes subject to more or less violent downswings and upswings which recreate and destroy over and over again the profitability of capital invested in trade. This instability of processes of capital accumulation may be merely local and temporary, or it may be systemic and permanent. In the pattern shown in figure 14, the downswings and upswings in the amount of capital invested in trade are confined to the range of values enclosed by the revenue-maximizing and the profit-maximizing paths of expansion, and eventually bring the world-economy back on a path of stable expansion. In the pattern shown in figure 15, in contrast, the downswings and upswings are not confined to the range of values enclosed by the two ideotypical paths and they do not bring the world-economy back on a path of stable expansion. In this second pattern instability is self-reinforcing and brings the expansion of the world-economy, as instituted at that particular time, to a permanent end, even if in principle stable expansion could resume, as shown by the dotted lines in figure 15.

The distinction between these two patterns of instability can be taken as a specification of Hicks's distinction between mere pauses in the process of expansion of the world-economy and an authentic cessation of expansion. In this specification, the pattern of figure 14 corresponds to a pause. Turbulence is merely local, and as soon as it has been weathered, stable expansion can resume. The pattern in figure 15 corresponds instead to an authentic cessation of expansion. Turbulence is "systemic" and the world-economy as instituted at that time is incapable of getting back on the track of stable expansion.

Our investigation has been limited to financial expansions of the latter kind. In so delimiting our subject-matter, we have followed in the footsteps of Braudel's selection of only a few financial expansions as the "sign of autumn" of major capitalist developments. In pointing to this recurrent phenomenon, Braudel focused on the switches from trade to finance of very specific capitalist communities – the "Genoese," the "Dutch," and the "English." This choice can be justified on two grounds: first, at the time of their switch from trade to finance these agencies occupied a commanding position over the most important networks of long-distance trade and high finance – the networks, that is, that mattered most in the reshuffling of commodities and of means of payments across the entire space of the world-economy; and, second, these agencies had been playing a leading role in epoch-making commercial expansions which were beginning to yield diminishing returns. Thanks to this position of command and leadership in the world trading and monetary systems of their respective times, these agencies (or particular cliques within them) knew better than any other agency when the time had come to pull out of trade in order to avoid a catastrophic fall in profits, and also what to do in order to gain rather than lose from the resulting instability in the world-economy. This superior knowledge – rooted in position rather than in "super-normal qualities of intellect and will," as Schumpeter (1963: 82) would have liked us to believe – endows the actions of these communities at the time of their respective switches from trade to finance with a double systemic significance.

For one thing, their switch from trade to finance can be taken as the clearest sign that the time to bring trade expansion to an end in order to prevent it from destroying profitability had *really* come. Moreover, the agencies in question were better positioned than any other to monitor and act on the *overall* tendencies of the capitalist world-economy, that is, to act as intermediaries and regulators of the expanding supply of, and demand for, money capital. Whether "right on time" or not, when these agencies began specializing in high finance they facilitated the encounter of demand and supply. They thereby simultaneously strengthened the tendency of capitalist organizations to divert cash flows from the purchase of commodities to the lending of money and of non-capitalist organizations to obtain through borrowing the money needed for their pursuit of power and status.

In this capacity, the communities of merchant financiers that occupied the commanding heights of the world-economy registered tendencies which they had not created, and simply "serviced" capitalist and non-capitalist organizations in their respective pursuits. At the same time, superior knowledge of world market conditions and superior command over the liquidity of the trading system enabled these communities to turn the instability of the world-economy into a source of considerable and secure speculative profits. They had no interest, therefore, in moderating instability and some of them may have actually tried to exacerbate it.

But whether they did or not, the leading agencies of financial expansions were never the primary cause of the eventual downfall of the system which they both regulated and exploited. Instability was structural and tended to gain a momentum of its own which was beyond the power of the governors of the capitalist engine to control. Over time, this momentum became too much for the existing organizational structures of the world-economy to bear; and when these structures finally collapsed the ground was clear for a new systemic cycle of accumulation to begin.

The recurrence of systemic cycles of accumulation can thus be described as a series of phases of stable expansion of the capitalist world-economy alternating with phases of turbulence in the course of which the conditions of stable expansion along an established developmental path are destroyed and those of expansion along a new path are created (see figure 16). As such, phases of turbulence are moments of retrenchment and increasing disorganization, as well as of redeployment and reorganization of world-scale processes of capital accumulation. The signal crises $(S_1, S_2, S_3,$ and $S_4)$ that announce the attainment of the limits of stable expansion along the old developmental path signal also the emergence of a new developmental path, as shown in figure 16, by the emergence of a lower but rising dotted trajectory.

The emergence of a new developmental path endowed with a greater growth potential than the old one is an integral aspect of the increasing turbulence experienced by the world-economy in phases of financial expansion. It corresponds to Marx's thesis of a recycling of money capital from organizational structures that have attained the limits of their material expansion to organizational structures that are only beginning to realize their growth potential. As we saw in the Introduction, Marx hinted at this recycling in his discussion of primitive accumulation, when he acknowledged the continuing significance of national debts as means of an invisible inter-capitalist cooperation which started capital accumulation over and over again across the space–time of the capitalist world-economy, from Venice in early modern times, through the United Provinces and the United Kingdom, to the United States in the nineteenth century. And he hinted again at a recycling of money capital from one organizational structure to another in his discussion of the increasing concentration of capital which invariably constitutes the outcome and resolution of overaccumulation crises:

> Concentration increases ... because beyond certain limits a large capital with a small rate of profit accumulates faster than a small capital with a large rate of profit. At a certain point this increasing concentration in its turn causes a new fall in the rate of profit. The mass of small dispersed capitals is thereby driven along the adventurous road of speculation, credit frauds, stock swindles and crises. The so-called plethora of capital always applies essentially to a plethora of the capital for which the fall in the rate of profit is not compensated through the mass of profit ... or to a plethora which places capitals incapable of action on their own at the disposal of the managers of large enterprises in the form of credit. (Marx 1962: 245–6)

Marx did not establish a connection between his observation concerning the recycling of money capital across the space–time of the capitalist world-economy and his observation concerning an analogous recycling from the organizational domains of business enterprises "incapable of action on their own" to the domains of more powerful business organizations. Had he ever written the sixth volume of *Capital*, described in the original synopsis as "Volume on the world market and crises," he might have needed to establish precisely this connection. Be that as it may, Marx's two observations are most useful for our purposes when taken in conjunction as identifying the concentration of capital, via a financial expansion, as the key mechanism through which the end of a particular cycle of accumulation on a world scale is transformed into the beginning of a new cycle.

In incorporating this hypothesis into our conceptual apparatus, we must bear in mind the different kinds of "concentration of capital" that have cropped up in our historical investigation of systemic cycles of accumulation. The verb "to concentrate" has two meanings relevant to our concerns: (1) "to come to or towards a common center," and (2) "to increase in strength, density, or intensity" (*Webster's New World Dictionary of the American Language*, Second College Edition, 1970). Various forms of concentration of capital in one or both of these two senses occurred in all the phases of financial expansion of the capitalist world-economy. And yet, only some forms became the basis of a new systemic cycle of accumulation.

In the financial expansion of the late fourteenth and early fifteenth centuries, capital accumulation came to be concentrated in a smaller number of city-states, which grew in strength and density by diverting traffic in the commodity or in the money trades from competitors and by taking over the territories and populations of weaker city-states. This concentration of capital occurred within the organizational structures of the system of city-states. It increased the size and strength of the system's surviving units and, at least in the short run, of the system itself. It was not this first kind of concentration, however, that laid the foundations of the first systemic cycle of accumulation. These foundations were laid instead through a second kind of concentration. They were laid through the formation of a new organizational structure, which combined the strengths of cosmopolitan networks of accumulation (most notably the Genoese) with the strongest available network of power (the Iberian).

Similarly, in the financial expansion of the late sixteenth and early seventeenth centuries the diversion of traffic from the Lyons fairs and the subordination of Antwerp and Seville to the system of the Piacenza fairs, clearly constituted a form of concentration of capital towards and within the organizational domain of the Genoese "nation" at the expense of all other capitalist "nations." And yet, once again, it was not this kind of concentration of capital within pre-existing structures that became the foundation of the second systemic cycle of accumulation. Rather, it was the concentration of capital that put in the hands of the Dutch merchant elite the means to sponsor the formation of a new kind of state (the United Provinces), of a new kind of inter-state system (the Westphalia System), and of a new kind of business organization (joint-stock chartered companies and a stock market in permanent session).

The concentration of capital that occurred during the financial expansion of the latter half of the eighteenth century was a far more complex process than in previous financial expansions, owing to the intrusion of territorialist organizations that had successfully internalized capitalism. An analogous tendency can none the less be observed by focusing on the leading business organizations of the Dutch cycle: the joint-stock chartered companies. By the end of the century the capital invested in such companies had come to be almost entirely concentrated in one of them – the English East India Company – most of the other companies having gone out of business. Although the territorial conquests of the English Company did become a critical component of the foundations of the third systemic cycle of accumulation, the Company itself did not. The organizational structures of Britain's free trade imperialism rested as much on the formation of a British empire in India as on the progressive "deregulation" and eventual liquidation of the activities of the East India Company.

Generally speaking, then, the historical record shows that in phases of financial expansion of the capitalist world-economy two different kinds of concentration of capital have occurred simultaneously. One kind has occurred within the organizational structures of the cycle of accumulation that was drawing to a close. As a rule, this kind of concentration has been associated with a final "wonderful moment" of revival (R_1, R_2, R_3, R_4 in figure 16) of the still dominant but increasingly volatile regime of accumulation. But this wonderful moment has never been the expression of renewed capabilities of that regime to generate a new round of material expansion of the capitalist world-economy. On the contrary, it has always been the expression of an escalating competitive and power struggle that was about to precipitate the terminal crisis of the regime (T_1, T_2, T_3 in figure 16).

The other kind of concentration of capital that has occurred in phases of financial expansions of the capitalist world-economy may or may not have contributed to the revival of the existing regime of accumulation. Either way, its main historical function has been to deepen the crisis of the system by bringing into existence regional structures of accumulation which further destabilized the old regime and foreshadowed the emergence of a new one. Once the old regimes collapsed under the weight of their own contradictions, the ground was cleared for new regimes to become themselves dominant, to reconstitute the world-economy on new organizational foundations, and to promote a new round of material expansion of the capitalist world-economy.

The rising profile of the succession of systemic cycles of accumulation shown in figure 16 designates this second kind of concentration of capital. Often less spectacular than the first kind, this second kind of concentration is the one that has been most significant in propelling the capitalist world-economy from the depths of each and every systemic crisis outward and onward in space and time in a seemingly endless process of self-expansion. To tell the story of the long twentieth century is largely a question of showing how and why the US regime of accumulation: (1) emerged out of the limits, contradictions, and crisis of Britain's free-trade imperialism as the dominant regional structure of the capitalist world-economy; (2) reconstituted the world-economy on foundations that made another round of material expansion possible; and (3) has reached its own maturity and, perhaps, is preparing the ground for the emergence of a new dominant regime.

In chapter 4, we shall focus first on the contradictions of the British regime that created the conditions for the emergence of the US regime of accumulation. We shall then proceed to analyze the formation of the US regime and the systemic cycle of accumulation that ensued from it. In the concluding section of the chapter, we shall examine the process through which the signal crisis of the US cycle of accumulation was transformed into a new *belle époque* in many ways reminiscent of the Edwardian and periwig eras. Finally, in the Epilogue we shall turn to sketch the regional (East Asian) structures of accumulation that have emerged in the course of the crisis of the US regime and have become increasingly dominant in shaping the present and future of the capitalist world-economy.

4

The Long Twentieth Century

The Dialectic of Market and Plan

The strategies and structures of capital accumulation that have shaped our times first came into existence in the last quarter of the nineteenth century. They originated in a new internalization of costs within the economizing logic of capitalist enterprise. Just as the Dutch regime had taken world-scale processes of capital accumulation one step further than the Genoese by internalizing protection costs, and the British regime had taken them a step further than the Dutch by internalizing production costs, so the US regime has done the same in relation to the British by internalizing transaction costs.

The notion of an internalization of transaction costs as the distinguishing feature of the fourth (US) systemic cycle of accumulation is derived from Richard Coase's (1937) pioneering theoretical study of the competitive advantages of vertically integrated business organizations, from Oliver Williamson's (1970) expansion of Coase's analysis, and from Alfred Chandler's historical study of the emergence and swift expansion of modern US corporations in the late nineteenth and early twentieth centuries. As Chandler (1977; 1978) has shown, the internalization within a single organizational domain of activities and transactions previously carried out by separate business units enabled vertically integrated, multi-unit enterprises to reduce and make more calculable transaction costs – costs, that is, associated with the transfer of intermediate inputs through a long chain of separate organizational domains connecting primary production to final consumption.

The economies thus created were "economies of speed" rather than "economies of size":

[Economies] resulted more from speed than from size. It was not the size of [an] ... establishment in terms of the number of workers and the amount and value of productive equipment but the velocity of throughput and the resulting

239

increase in volume that permitted economies that lowered costs and increased output per worker and per machine.... Central to obtaining economies of speed were the development of new machinery, better raw materials, and intensified application of energy, followed by the creation of organizational design and procedures to coordinate and control the new high-volume flows through several processes of production. (Chandler 1977: 244)

The economies of speed afforded by the internalization of transaction costs were not limited to manufacturing enterprises alone; nor indeed did they originate in them. Railway companies had pioneered most of the organizational innovations that were to revolutionize the structure of accumulation in the United States, and along with those innovations went a thorough reorganization of distribution through the rise of mass marketers (the mass retailer, the advertising agency, the mail order house, the chain store), who internalized a high volume of market transactions within a single enterprise:

Whereas the railroads and telegraph coordinated the flow of goods from the train and express company stations of one commercial center to another, the new mass marketers handled the myriad of transactions involved in moving a high-volume flow of goods directly from thousands of producers to hundreds of thousands of consumers. (Chandler 1977: 236)

The integration of the processes of mass production with those of mass distribution within a single organization gave rise to a new kind of capitalist enterprise. Having internalized a whole sequence of sub-processes of production and exchange from the procurement of primary inputs to the disposal of final outputs, this new kind of capitalist enterprise was in a position to subject the costs, risks, and uncertainties involved in moving goods through that sequence to the economizing logic of administrative action and long-term corporate planning:

Such an internalization gave the enlarged enterprise many advantages. By routinizing the transactions between units, the costs of the transactions were lowered. By linking the administration of producing units with buying and distributing units, costs of information on markets and sources of supply were reduced. Of much greater significance, the internalization of many units permitted the flow of goods from one unit to another to be administratively coordinated. More effective scheduling of flows achieved a more intensive use of facilities and personnel employed in the process of production and distribution and so increased productivity and reduced costs. In addition, administrative coordination provided a more certain cash flow and more rapid repayment for services rendered. (Chandler 1977: 7)

As the large and steady cash flows generated by this kind of concentration of business activities were plowed back into the creation of hierarchies of top and middle managers specialized in monitoring and regulating markets and labor processes, the vertically integrated enterprises came to enjoy decisive competitive advantages *vis-à-vis* single-unit enterprises or less specialized multi-unit enterprises. These advantages translated in a strikingly swift growth and diffusion of the new organizational structure. "Almost nonexistent at the end of the 1870s, these integrated enterprises came to dominate many of the [US's] most vital industries within less than three decades" (Chandler 1977: 285).

Growth was not limited to the US domestic market. "US corporations began to move to foreign countries almost as soon as they had completed their continent-wide integration.... In becoming national firms, US corporations learned how to become international" (Hymer 1972: 121). By 1902 Europeans were already speaking of an "American invasion"; and by 1914 US direct investment abroad amounted to 7 per cent of US GNP – the same percentage as in 1966, when Europeans once again felt threatened by an "American challenge" (cf. Wilkins 1970: 71, 201–2).

Expansion abroad further increased the organizational capabilities of US managerial hierarchies, both at home and abroad, to monitor markets and labor processes in the lines and branches of business they targeted for occupation or had already occupied and regulate them to their advantage. Even in industries in which techniques of mass production were crucial to business success, organization rather than technology came to constitute the real barrier to entry:

> The most imposing barrier to entry in these industries was the organization the pioneers had built to market and distribute their newly mass-produced products. A competitor who acquired the technology had to create a national and often global organization of managers, buyers and salesmen if he was to get the business away from the one or two enterprises that already stood astride the major marketing channels. Moreover, where the pioneer could finance the building of the first of these organizations out of cash flow, generated by high volume, the newcomer had to set up a competing network before high-volume output reduced unit costs and created a sizeable cash flow. [And he had to do this while facing] a competitor whose economies of speed permitted him to set prices low and still maintain a margin of profit. (Chandler 1977: 299) ·

The spectacular domestic and trans-statal expansion of US multi-unit, vertically integrated business enterprises, and the organizational barriers to entry which they created, were associated with an equally spectacular growth of managerial hierarchies and bureaucratic structures. Once in place, these hierarchies and structures themselves "became a source of permanence, power and continued growth":

> In Werner Sombart's phrase, the modern business enterprise took on "a life of
> its own." Traditional enterprises were normally short-lived.... On the other
> hand, the hierarchies that came to manage the new multiunit enterprises had
> a permanence beyond that of any individual or group of individuals who
> worked in them.... Men came and went. The institution and its offices
> remained. (Chandler 1977: 8)

In Chandler's view, the development of managerial hierarchies marked
the culmination of an "organizational revolution" that had begun in the
1850s with the railroads and, by the 1910s, had transformed out of all
recognition the methods by which capitalist enterprises were managed
and administered and the ways in which economic activities were
structured. As a consequence of this organizational revolution, "[a]
businessman of today would find himself at home in the business world
of 1910, but the business world of 1840 would be a strange, archaic and
arcane place. So, too, the American businessman of 1840 would find the
environment of fifteenth-century Italy more familiar than that of his own
nation seventy years later" (Chandler 1977: 455).

To this we may add that the top managers of today's multinational
corporations would find themselves more at home among the *Heeren* of
seventeenth-century Dutch joint-stock companies than in the family
businesses that constituted the backbone of nineteenth-century British
capitalism. And so too the middle managers of the VOC of the late
seventeenth century would find it easier to make a living and a career in
today's multinationals than in the business world of nineteenth-century
England. For the emergence of the joint-stock, vertically integrated,
bureaucratically managed capitalist enterprise as the dominant unit of
capital accumulation on a world scale has in more than one respect
brought the business world back to the strategies and structures of the
Dutch regime of accumulation.

As already underscored in chapter 1, analogies between the system of
joint-stock chartered companies of the seventeenth and eighteenth
centuries and that of transnational corporations of the twentieth century
should not be exaggerated. Joint-stock chartered companies were part-
governmental, part-business organizations which specialized territorially
to the exclusion of other similar organizations. As such, they were few in
number and were integral to the consolidation and expansion of the
territorial exclusiveness of the European system of sovereign states. The
transnational corporations that emerged in the late nineteenth and early
twentieth centuries, in contrast, were strictly business organizations
which specialized functionally in a particular line of business across

multiple territories and jurisdictions. As such, they have been incomparably more numerous than joint-stock chartered companies ever were and have progressively undermined the centrality of the inter-state system as the primary locus of world power.

Important as this difference is as a measure of the evolution of the capitalist world-economy over the last three hundred years, it should not be allowed to conceal the fact that this evolution has not proceeded linearly, but through an alternation of opposite kinds of organizational structures, in which the corporate form of business has come, gone, and come back again. A pendulum-like movement of this kind in the evolution of historical capitalism as world system was first noticed eighty years ago by Henri Pirenne. In his survey of the social history of capitalism which has inspired our conceptualization of systemic cycles of accumulation, Pirenne also observed a "surprising regularity" in the alternation of phases of "economic freedom" and "economic regulation." The free expansion of mobile commerce gave way to the regulative spirit characteristic of the urban economy, which in turn was followed by the individualistic ardor of the Renaissance. This reached its height in the second half of the sixteenth century, when the pendulum once again began to swing in the opposite direction. Just as the regulative spirit of the urban economy followed on the freedom of the twelfth century, "so mercantilism imposed itself upon commerce and industry in the seventeenth and eighteenth centuries" (Pirenne 1953: 515).

The tendency towards economic regulation was destined to last only until the moment when, in the late eighteenth and early nineteenth centuries, "the invention of machinery and the application of steam to manufacturing completely disorganized the conditions of economic activity." The phenomena of the sixteenth century were reproduced "but with tenfold intensity." Once again, "the belief is in individualism and liberalism alone." Under the motto *laissez faire, laissez aller* the consequences of economic freedom were carried to an extreme, leading to a new swing in the opposite direction:

> Unrestrained competition sets [capitalists] to struggling with each other and soon arouses resistance ... among the proletariat that they are exploiting. And at the same time that that resistance arises to confront capital, the latter, itself suffering from the abuse of that freedom which had enabled it to rise, compels itself to discipline its affairs. Cartels, trusts, syndicates of producers, are organized, while states, perceiving that it is impossible to leave employers and employees to contend in anarchy, elaborate a social legislation. (Pirenne 1953: 516)

The secular swings through which Pirenne's alternation of phases of "economic freedom" and phases of "economic regulation" has materialized correspond broadly to our succession of systemic cycles of accumulation. The Genoese regime swung the pendulum away from the highly regulative spirit of the capitalist city-states of the late fourteenth and early fifteenth centuries (best epitomized by Venetian state monopoly capitalism) towards the comparative economic freedom of the system of capitalist "nations" which, in the sixteenth century, regulated the expanded European monetary and trading system out of select marketplaces – Antwerp and Lyons first, then the mobile "Bisenzone" fairs until they settled at Piacenza. The Dutch regime, in contrast, swung the pendulum back towards the direct involvement of governments in the promotion and organization of world-scale processes of capital accumulation, either directly or through the formation of joint-stock companies chartered to exercise governmental functions by proxy in the extra-European world.

The new swing engendered by the rise and full expansion of the British regime – which did indeed reproduce the phenomena of the sixteenth century "with tenfold intensity" – bears directly on the subject-matter at hand, since it created the systemic conditions under which US corporate capitalism first came into existence and then became the dominant structure of accumulation of the entire world-economy. Contrary to Pirenne's suggestion, the "industrial revolution" of the late eighteenth century added a new momentum to the swing, but did not initiate it. After all, *The Wealth of Nations*, which later became the manifesto of the nineteenth-century liberal creed, was published when the "industrial revolution" had hardly begun. And the main target of its call for free trade was not so much big government as the big business of the day, that is, primarily joint-stock chartered companies. "These companies," we are told,

> though they may, perhaps, have been useful for the first introduction of some branches of commerce, by making, at their own expence, an experiment which the state might not think prudent to make, have in the long-run proved, universally, either burdensome or useless, and have either mismanaged or confined the trade. (Smith 1961: II, 255)

Ironically, and tragically for the peoples of Africa, the earliest beginnings of the nineteenth-century free trade movement can be traced to the Atlantic slave trade. As previously noted, the WIC pioneered the triangular trade that boosted the slave trade to historically new heights, but could not forestall the entry of competitors as the VOC had been able to do in the East Indies trade in fine spices. By the late seventeenth century, an English company, the Royal African Company (chartered in 1672), had become the most powerful and most effective of all European companies formed exclusively for the African trade. But even this company could not compete effectively with leaner and more flexible business enterprises. "By the beginning of the eighteenth century there were clear indications that the privileged joint-stock company was no longer the best way to conduct the slave trade; in the next thirty years the countries principally concerned switched to competitive trading by private merchants and firms." By allowing the WIC to retain its monopoly the longest (until 1734), the Dutch simply accentuated the tendency of their share of the trade to contract (Davies 1957; 1974: 127).

The main problem for chartered companies was that in the Atlantic trade in general, and in the African trade in particular, it was difficult to enforce their monopolies. The procurement of slaves required the building and maintenance of expensive fortifications on the West African coast, which none the less were ineffective means in policing the coast against competition; the American colonists, whose entrepreneurship was essential to the expansion of Atlantic trade, constantly complained about the price and quantity of supplies, and the debts they owed for slaves bought on credit proved difficult or impossible to collect; interlopers mobilized continually to obtain governmental recognition, which the French and English governments were only too ready to grant; the companies' employees often embezzled goods, traded with interlopers, and neglected the corporate interest; and the competition between the companies chartered by different governments made these problems worse for each one of them (Davies 1974: 117–31):

> Free trade thus showed itself more efficient than monopoly. . . . Yet monopoly had served some purpose in fostering an English slaving tradition and in accumulating the knowledge needed for a trade which more than most demanded skill and experience. At least the English slave companies were more effective than the French, and the English colonists, notwithstanding their complaints, were saved from the "fearful shortage" of labor which afflicted seventeenth-century Martinique and Guadeloupe. (Davies 1974: 118)

This early victory of free trade in the Atlantic prefigured the dynamics that were to bring about the subsequent deregulation and eventual demise of the system of joint-stock chartered companies. In England, though not in Holland, joint-stock chartered companies always walked a tightrope from which they could fall just as easily as a result of their successes as of their failures. If the considerable expenses incurred in opening up a new branch of commerce proved unprofitable, they simply went out of business, and that was it. But if the investments proved profitable, their life could be made miserable and even cut short by the threatened or actual erosion or revocation of their privileges which, as a rule, were vital to their very existence as part-governmental, part-business enterprises.

The top-heavy and oligarchic structure of the Dutch capitalist class sheltered Dutch companies from the dangers of both kinds of fall. No matter how much it protested against the privileges of a successful company like the VOC, Dutch small business never stood a real chance of having those privileges revoked. But even a comparatively unsuccessful company like the WIC could rely on continuing governmental support in moments of need.

The more broadly based and democratic structure of the English capitalist class, in contrast, exposed English joint-stock companies to the constant danger of being deprived of their privileges once they had done the job of opening up a new branch of commerce. Thus, once the Royal African Company had established an English presence in the Atlantic triangular trade, the Glorious Revolution of 1688 emboldened interlopers, who flooded into the company's trade unhindered. Worse still, in 1698 the English parliament recognized their position and entitled them to use the company's forts against a payment of 10 per cent of their exports from England. Empowered to compete on more or less equal terms with corporate big business, private small business easily swept away the contest (Davies 1957: 122–52; 1974: 117–18).

It took much longer for the free-trade movement to catch up with and promote the liquidation of corporate business in the East Indies. For a long time after its formation under Elizabeth I, the East India Company had led a rather precarious existence. The company did make significant early gains in setting up a number of factories and forts, and even capturing some territory from the Portuguese. Yet it barely survived the adverse conjuncture of the second quarter of the seventeenth century, when the majority of its shareholders began doubting whether it could go on trading at all in the face of overwhelming odds suddenly aggravated by an acute shortage of liquidity in the City (Chaudhuri 1965: chs 2 and 3).

This was due primarily to the pre-emptive centralization of the most profitable East Indies trade in the hands of the VOC. Unable to wrest the spice trade from the VOC's control, the English East India Company was forced to specialize in the less profitable homeward and intra-Asian trade in piece goods. This industry was not only less profitable than the spice industry; it was also far more difficult to take over:

> The textile industry was hard to take over for [the] very reason that it was not contained within a single network as in Europe. Different sectors and circuits governed the production and marketing of raw materials; the manufacture of cotton yarn (a long operation especially if the aim was a yarn both fine and

strong, to make muslin for instance); weaving; bleaching and preparation of fabrics; and printing. Processes which in Europe were vertically linked (as in thirteenth-century Florence) were organized in separate compartments.... In fact all India processed silk and cotton, sending an incredible quantity of fabrics, from the most ordinary to the most luxurious, all over the world.... There can be little doubt that until the English industrial revolution, the Indian cotton industry was the foremost in the world, both in quality and quantity of its output and the scale of exports. (Braudel 1984: 508–9)

This highly differentiated, decentralized, and proficient commercial–industrial apparatus was probably the most extensive and complex instance of "flexible specialization" the world had ever seen. In order to turn this apparatus to its own advantage, the East India Company had no choice but to use local business networks. Necessary as it was, this adaptation to the decentralized structure of the Indian textile industry left the company exposed to the competition of other European companies, of European free traders, of Arabian and indigenous traders, and of Armenian and other diaspora merchants. This competition brought a constant downward pressure to bear on profit margins in the piece goods trade. And this downward pressure in turn was responsible for the precariousness of the Company's existence throughout the seventeenth and early eighteenth centuries, as well as for its continual attempts to compensate for low profit margins through the expansion of its operations (Arrighi, Barr, and Hisaeda 1993).

Over time, however, this expansion moved the fulcrum of European business in Asia from spices to piece goods and from the Malay archipelago to the Indian subcontinent, and in so doing reversed the fortunes of the English *vis-à-vis* the Dutch in the East Indies. In the herculean task involved in this reversal of fortunes, the English East India Company received little help from home. The granting of a charter to a rival company in 1698 certainly did not help, although the merger of the two companies in 1709 prepared the ground for the subsequent rise of the new company to the status of dominant European capitalist and territorialist agency in Asia. But throughout the eighteenth century the imposition of increasingly stiff duties on the homeward trade of the company, in protection of English industries still incapable of competing with Indian manufactures, must have been a major drag on the company's endeavors to establish its control over the supply of Indian piece goods.

Be that as it may, what eventually turned the wheel of the company's fortunes was not help from home, but self-help on the battlefields of India. In response to the disintegration of the Mughal empire, the size and scope of the company's military forces began to expand in the 1740s and to be reorganized along European lines. On the eve of Plassey, Indian battalions were formed and the company thus came to combine superior European techniques in the use and control of force with an extensive use of local manpower. It was this combination more than anything else that accounts for the success of the company in defeating all local competition in the struggle for the Mughal succession (McNeill 1984: 135; Wolf 1982: 244–6; Bayly 1988: 85).

Once the company had become a powerful "company state" (Marshall 1987) the road was clear, not just for the massive appropriation of tribute and its transfer – in D.K. Fieldhouse's (1967: 159) words, "to stock-holders in Europe through the medium of unrequited exports"; in addition, the road was clear for the tightening of the company's control over the Indian textile industry. The previous strategy of adaptation to the pre-existing decentralized structures of production and exchange was increasingly replaced by a strategy of forcible subordination of those structures to the centralized control of the company's managerial hierarchies (Wolf 1982: 245–6). Although in the process the Indian textile industry lost much of its flexibility – and with it some of its competitive-ness – the cash flows that accrued to the company from trade in piece goods grew in size and steadiness until about 1780, when expansion began to taper off (Barr forthcoming).

Success as governmental and business organization brought no comfort to the East India Company. On the contrary, success in replacing the Mughal court as the dominant redistributive organization of South Asia and success in driving the VOC out of business was immediately followed by a fiscal crisis and by a strong movement at home to deprive the company of its commercial privileges. A first portent of things to come was the tripling of the company's debt between 1798 and 1806 despite a huge accession of territory (Bayly 1988: 84). Another, more ominous sign came a few years later when Birmingham and other provincial manu-facturers began campaigning for the abolition of the company's monop-oly of the India trade, which was indeed abolished in 1813 (Moss 1976).

For about twenty years after the abolition, the company could compensate for the loss by exploiting more efficiently its continuing monopoly of the China trade. Although the tea trade with China had been a highly profitable subsidiary activity since the early eighteenth century, initially its expansion had been seriously constrained by the lack of demand for European goods in China and the consequent need to ship bullion to purchase tea. The English East India Company had inherited the age-old problem of a structural imbalance in West–East trade. As previously noted, the imbalance could be traced back to Roman times. The Great Discoveries and the European appropriation of American silver did not redress this imbalance; they simply enabled Europe through the intermediary of the Dutch regime of accumulation to run a larger trade deficit so that, in Louis Dermigny's words, China became "the tomb of American treasure" (quoted in Wolf 1982: 255).

When in 1776 "the American Revolution cut England off from the supply of Mexican silver ... [t]he answer to the Company's financial prayers was opium from India" (Wolf 1982: 257). Once the company began pushing sales of opium in China and monopolizing opium production in Bengal, the China trade quickly became far more profitable and dynamic than the trade in piece goods. This tendency was already underway before the abolition of the Company's monopoly of trade with India. But once the Indian monopoly was abolished, the Company's concentration on this line of business led to an explosive growth of shipments and to a reversal of the chronic balance of payments deficit with China (Wakeman 1975: 126; Greenberg 1979: ch. 5 and appendix I; Bagchi 1982: 96–7). "The Europeans," Eric Wolf (1982: 258) comments wryly, "finally had something to sell to the Chinese."

Profitable as it was, this explosive growth did not help the Company for long because it was afflicted by the same kind of contradiction that had undermined the fortunes of the Royal African Company a century earlier. In the early eighteenth century the fostering of an English tradition in the African slave trade exposed the pioneering chartered company to the competition of a multitude of small unregulated businesses, which successfully challenged corporate privileges in the Atlantic marketplace and in the English parliament. So in the early nineteenth century the fostering of an English tradition in the China opium trade exposed the pioneering chartered company to the same kind of competition and to the same kind of challenges. Since the opium trade was under a Chinese imperial ban, the Company had to use private European and Asian traders to smuggle the drug into China, concentrating its efforts on the monopolization of the supply and on the regulation of prices (Bagchi 1982: 96). But as the trade expanded, the "informal" activities of private European traders quickly outgrew the capabilities of the Company to keep them under control, and free trade came to be perceived at home as a more effective means of national aggrandizement than monopoly.

The abolition of the China trade monopoly in 1833 marked the beginning of the end of the English East India Company. Deprived of all its commercial privileges, the company's capabilities to perform its enlarged state- and war-making functions effectively declined further, until it appeared to friends and foes alike as totally incompetent to govern the empire it had conquered. And when in the wake of the Great Rebellion of 1857 parliament stepped in to "nationalize" that empire, few cared about the Company's fate. What everybody in Britain cared about was that the empire in India be managed and exploited effectively and efficiently in the national interest.

In short, joint-stock chartered companies were business organizations empowered by European governments to exercise in the extra-European world state- and war-making functions, both as ends in themselves and as means of commercial expansion. As long as the companies performed these functions more efficiently than the governments themselves could, they were granted trading privileges and protection more or less commensurate to the usefulness of their services. But as soon as they no longer did, the companies were deprived of their privileges, and their state- and war-making functions were taken over by the metropolitan governments themselves.

By so doing, the British government became the imperial government of India. The freeing of trade from corporate privilege and empire-building in the extra-European world were thus obverse sides of the same process of supersession of the system of joint-stock chartered companies. However, the liquidation of these companies was a strictly pragmatic decision which was reversed as soon as systemic conditions created the perception that joint-stock chartered companies had become useful again. Thus towards the end of the nineteenth century the British government and British business launched a whole new breed of joint-stock chartered companies empowered to widen further (mostly in Africa) the spatial scope of their networks of trade, power, and accumulation.

Although a few of these companies did quite well – most notably, the British South Africa Company – the revival could not and did not bring back to life the old corporate system of chartered companies as leading agencies of the commercial and territorial expansion of the capitalist world-economy. The advent of steam and machinofacture – so-called modern industry – had thoroughly reorganized world-scale networks of trade, accumulation, and power. And when the expansion of Britain's free-trade imperialism attained its limits in the course of the late nineteenth-century Great Depression, this reorganization gave rise to new kinds of corporate business in continental Europe and North America which overpowered joint-stock chartered companies as primary agencies of capitalist expansion.

Pirenne's remarks concerning the impact of modern industry on "regulated" economic activity echo Marx's thesis that the advent of steam and machinofacture initiated a seemingly endless chain of inter-related revolutions in the mode of production and exchange across the space–time of the nineteenth-century world-economy:

A radical change in the mode of production in one sphere of industry involves a similar change in other spheres. This happens at first in such branches of industry as are connected together by being separate phases of a process, and yet are isolated by the social division of labour, in such a way, that each of them produces an independent commodity. Thus spinning by machinery made weaving by machinery a necessity, and both together made the mechanical and chemical revolution that took place in bleaching, printing and dyeing, imperative. So too ... the revolution in cotton-spinning called forth the invention of the gin, for separating the seeds from the cotton fibre; it was only by means of this invention, that the production of cotton became possible on the enormous scale at present required. But more especially, the revolution in the modes of production of industry and agriculture made necessary a revolution in the general conditions of the social process of production, i.e., in the means of communication and transport.... [T]he means of communication and transport handed down from the manufacturing period soon became unbearable trammels on Modern Industry, with its feverish haste of production, its enormous extent, its constant flinging of capital and labour from one sphere of production to another, and its newly created connexions with the markets of the whole world. Hence ... the means of communication and transport became gradually adapted to the modes of production of mechanical industry, by the creation of a system of river steamers, railways, ocean steamers, and telegraphs. But the huge masses of iron that had now to be forged, to be welded, to be cut, to be bored, and to be shaped, demanded, on their part, cyclopean machines [which could only be constructed by means of other machines]. (Marx 1959: 383–4)

This passage details the process through which, as Marx stated elsewhere, "Modern Industry has established the world-market, for which the discovery of America paved the way." The "Great Discoveries," the penetration of the East Indies and Chinese markets, the colonization of the Americas and colonial trade, jointly created the conditions for the emergence of modern industry by giving to commerce and industry "an impulse never known before." But once steam and machinery revolutionized industrial technology, industrial expansion itself became the main factor of integration of the markets of the whole world into a single world market (Marx and Engels 1967: 80–1).

The formation of a single world market in its turn reacted on the extension of industry and endowed production and consumption in every country with a "cosmopolitan character":

To the great chagrin of Reactionists, [the bourgeoisie] has drawn from under the feet of industry the national ground on which it stood. All old-established national industries have been destroyed or are daily being destroyed. They are dislodged by new industries, whose introduction becomes a life and death question for all civilized nations, by industries that no longer work up indigenous raw material, but raw material drawn from the remotest zones; industries whose products are consumed, not only at home, but in every quarter of the globe. In place of the old wants, satisfied by the productions of the country, we find new wants, requiring for their satisfaction the products of distant lands and climes. In place of old local and national seclusion and self-sufficiency, we have intercourse in every direction, universal interdependence of nations. (Marx and Engels 1967: 83–4)

The integration of the markets of the whole world into a single world market thus presented governments and businesses with unprecedented opportunities as well as with unprecedented challenges. The opportunities stemmed primarily from the scope of the world-wide social division of labor within which governmental and business activities were being integrated and through which external economies of all kinds could be reaped. Any governmental and business organization that found a secure market niche within this world-wide division of labor could count on the spontaneous cooperation of numerous other organizations in the procurement of a range and variety of affordable supplies which was incomparably wider than those that could be procured through national seclusion and self-sufficiency.

The opportunities that stemmed from cooperation were none the less inseparable from the challenges that stemmed from competition over cash flows and material resources. This competition continually drove each and every organization integrated in the world market to shift its resources from existing input–output combinations to whatever other combinations promised to yield higher returns, as proclaimed by Alfred Marshall's (1949: 284) "principle of substitution." Any organization that fell behind in substituting more for less economical input–output combinations sooner or later would find itself at a disadvantage in competing with other organizations in the procurement of critical inputs and revenues. But as participants in the world market substituted more for less economical input–output combinations, they deprived one another of essential revenues and/or of essential material supplies and disrupted one another's production and consumption schedules. This deprivation and disruption in turn continually threatened to play havoc with the organizational integrity of governments and businesses and thereby moderated their enthusiasm for too close an integration in the networks and circuits of the world market.

Tension between the cooperative and competitive tendencies of processes of world market formation long preceded the emergence of modern industry. Indeed, our investigation has underscored that a tension of this kind has underlain the recurrence since the late Middle Ages of phases of material expansion of the capitalist world-economy in which cooperative tendencies prevailed, and of phases of financial expansion in which competitive tendencies prevailed. But the emergence of modern industry added an entirely new dimension to this tension. The resources of a large number of governmental and business organizations came to be sunk more or less permanently in expensive and specialized industrial and infrastructural facilities, which were owned and managed separately but were none the less linked to one another by a complex chain of interconected technical processes:

> No one of the mechanical processes carried on by the use of a given outfit of appliances is independent of other processes going on elsewhere. Each draws and presupposes the proper working of many other processes of a similar mechanical character. None of the processes ... is self-sufficing. Each follows some and precedes other processes in an endless sequence, into which each must adapt its own working. The whole concert of industrial operations is to be taken as a machine process, made up of interlocking detail processes, rather than as a multiplicity of mechanical appliances each doing its particular work in severalty. This comprehensive industrial process draws into its scope and turns to account all branches of knowledge that have to do with the material sciences, and the whole makes a more or less delicately balanced complex of subprocesses. (Veblen 1978: 7–8)

In short, with the emergence of modern industry, the relationships of complementarity which linked the fate of separate production units to one another became incomparably stronger than before and forced each and every unit to seek the cooperation of other units in order to ensure reliable sources of inputs and reliable outlets for outputs. And yet, this strengthening of complementarities was not associated with a weakening of competitive pressures. On the contrary, as Veblen (1978: 24–5) himself points out, with the development of modern industry the sway of Marshall's principle of substitution became much stronger than it had ever been. The very integration and comprehensiveness of the industrial system magnified the gains and losses experienced by the owners of the sub-processes as a result of any disturbance in the industrial balance. Moreover, disturbances tended to become cumulative, seriously crippling some branches of industry while inducing the overexpansion of others.

Under these circumstances a strong tendency developed within business enterprises to control the conjuncture through an alert redistribution of investments from less to more gainful ventures. Those enterprises that were heavily committed to a particular sub-process and did not have the predispositions or the capabilities to mobilize the surplus capital owned by other units in the system could only endure the conjuncture. But those enterprises that controlled abundant cash flows and were free to dispose of them as they pleased could and did master the conjuncture:

> The economic welfare of the community at large is best served by a facile and uninterrupted interplay of the various processes which make up the industrial system ... but the pecuniary interests of the business men in whose hands lies

the discretion in the matter are not necessarily best served by an unbroken maintenance of the industrial balance. Especially is this true as regards those greater business men whose interests are very extensive. The pecuniary operations of these latter are of large scope, and their fortunes commonly are not permanently bound up with the smooth working of a given sub-process in the industrial system. Their fortunes are rather related to the larger con-junctures of the industrial system as a whole, the interstitial adjustments, or to conjunctures affecting large ramifications of the system. (Veblen 1978: 28)

If this class of "greater businessmen" had no ulterior strategic objective besides profiting from the disturbances of the system, it was a matter of indifference to its members whether these disturbances helped or hin-dered the system at large. But if the purpose of their transactions was to gain control of a large portion of the industrial system, indifference to the effects of disturbances ceased as soon as control was achieved.

When such control has been achieved, it may be to [the investors'] interest to make and maintain business conditions which shall facilitate the smooth and efficient working of what has come under his control ... for, other things equal, the gains from what has come under his hands permanently in the way of industrial plant are greater the higher and the more uninterrupted its industrial efficiency. (Veblen 1978: 30)

This contrast between a strictly pecuniary business logic, which is indifferent to disturbances in the industrial balance, and a technological business logic, which has an interest in uninterrupted industrial efficiency, has been widely held as describing the different responses of the British and of the German business communities to the challenges and opportun-ities posed by the nineteenth-century reconstitution of the world market on industrial foundations. Thus, David Landes has contrasted the "pecuniary rationality" of British business with the "technological rationality" of German business. While British business tended to treat technology as mere means in the pursuit of maximum pecuniary returns to capital, German business tended to make the means the end:

The significance of [the] pecuniary approach [of the British] is best appreciated when it is contrasted with the technological rationality of the Germans. This was a different kind of arithmetic, which maximized, not returns, but technical efficiency. For the German engineer, and the manufacturer and banker who stood behind him, the new was desirable, not so much because it paid, but because it worked better. There were right and wrong ways of doing things, and the right was the scientific, mechanized, capital-intensive way. The means had become the end. (Landes 1969: 354)

We do not need to make any special assumption about psychological differences between German engineers, manufacturers, and bankers on the one side, and their British counterparts on the other, in order to understand the divergence of their business rationalities in the latter half of the nineteenth century. This divergence is perfectly understandable in terms of the different positions of the two business communities and of their respective national governments *vis-à-vis* the ongoing process of world market formation. The pecuniary rationality of British business was primarily a reflection of the control wielded by the British state over the process of world market formation. The technological rationality of German business, in contrast, was primarily a reflection of the serious challenges that that same process posed to the integrity of the newly formed German state.

More specifically, the two rationalities were obverse sides of the "double movement" towards the extension and simultaneous restriction of "self-regulating" market mechanisms which Karl Polanyi has singled out as the "one comprehensive feature" in the history of the late nineteenth and early twentieth centuries. Like Veblen, Polanyi underscores the risks involved in undertaking production in a system of elaborate, specialized, and expensive industrial facilities. The advent of this kind of facilities completely changed the relationship of commerce to industry. "Industrial production ceased to be an accessory of commerce organized by the merchant as a buying and selling proposition; it now involved long-term investment with corresponding risks. Unless the continuance of production was reasonably assured, such a risk was not bearable" (Polanyi 1957: 75).

Such a risk would be bearable only on condition that all the inputs required by industry be readily available in the quantities needed, where and when they were needed. In a commercial society, this meant that all the elements of industry had to be available for purchase. Among these elements, three were of oustanding importance: labor, land, and money. But none of these could be transformed into commodities because they were not produced for sale on the market. "Labor" stands for human activity, an entity inseparable from life itself, which in turn is not produced in order to be sold on the market but for altogether different reasons; "land" stands for the natural environment of human life and activity, a gift of geography and history and, as such, something that present generations inherit rather than produce; and "money" stands for tokens of purchasing power (means of payment), which, as a rule, come into being through the mechanisms of banking and state finance and, as such, are "produced" only metaphorically. In short, the commodity nature of land, labor, and money is purely fictitious. To subject the fate of these fictitious commodities – that is, of human beings, their natural environment, and means of payments – to the vagaries of a self-regulating market, is to invite social disaster:

> For the alleged commodity "labor power" cannot be shoved about, used indiscriminately, or even left unused, without affecting also the human individual who happens to be the bearer of this peculiar commodity.... Robbed of the protective covering of cultural institutions, human beings would perish from the effects of social exposure; they would die as the victims of acute social dislocation through vice, perversion, crime, and starvation. Nature would be reduced to its elements, neighborhoods and landscapes defiled, rivers polluted, military safety jeopardized, the power to produce food and raw materials destroyed. Finally, the market administration of purchasing power would periodically liquidate business enterprise, for shortages and surfeits of money would prove as disastrous to business as floods and droughts in primitive society. Undoubtedly, labor, land, and money *are* essential to a market economy. But no society could stand the effects of such a system of crude fictions even for the shortest stretch of time unless its human and natural substance as well as its business organization was protected against the ravages of this satanic mill. (Polanyi 1957: 73; emphasis in the original)

And protected it was. As soon as the disruptive effects of the self-regulating market began to be felt, a powerful counter-movement aimed at restricting its operations developed. A "double movement" was thus initiated whereby the extension of the self-regulating market in respect of genuine commodities was accompanied by a counter-movement in defense of society which restricted the operation of market mechanisms in respect of fictitious ones:

> While on the one hand markets spread all over the face of the globe and the amount of goods involved grew to unbelievable proportions, on the other hand a network of measures and policies was integrated into powerful institutions designed to check the action of the market relative to labor, land, and money. While the organization of world commodity markets, world capital markets, and world currency markets under the aegis of the gold standard gave an unparalleled momentum to the mechanisms of markets, a deep-seated movement sprang into being to resist the pernicious effects of a market-controlled economy. (Polanyi 1957: 76)

Polanyi traces the origins of this double movement to the rise in Britain, under the influence of David Ricardo, of the utopian belief "in man's salvation through the self-regulating market." Conceived in pre-industrial times as a mere penchant for non-bureaucratic methods of government, this belief assumed evangelical fervor after the industrial revolution in Britain took off, where in the 1820s it came to stand for its three classical tenets: "that labor should find its price on the market; that the creation of money should be subject to an automatic mechanism; that goods should be free to flow from country to country without hindrance or preference; in short, for a labor market, the gold standard, and free trade" (Polanyi 1957: 135).

In the 1830s and 1840s the liberal crusade for free markets resulted in a series of legislative Acts aimed at repealing restrictive regulations. The key measures were the Poor Law Amendment Act of 1834, which subjected the domestic labor supply to the price-setting mechanisms of the market; Peel's Bank Act of 1844, which subjected monetary circulation in the domestic economy to the self-regulating mechanisms of the gold standard more strictly than it already was; and the Anti-Corn Law Bill of 1846, which opened up the British market to the supply of grain from the entire world. These three measures established the core of a self-regulating world market system centered on Britain. They formed a coherent whole:

> Unless the price of labor was dependent upon the cheapest grain available, there was no guarantee that the unprotected industries would not succumb in the grip of the voluntarily accepted task-master, gold. The expansion of the market system in the nineteenth century was synonymous with the simultaneous spreading of international free trade, competitive labor market, and gold standard; they belonged together. (Polanyi 1957: 138–9)

In Polanyi's view, to embark upon such a venture of world market formation required a major act of faith. For the implications of international free trade "were entirely extravagant":

> International free trade ... meant that England would depend for her food supply upon overseas sources; would sacrifice her agriculture, if necessary, and enter on a new form of life under which she would be part and parcel of some vaguely conceived world unity of the future; that this planetary community would have to be a peaceful one, or if not, would have to be made safe for Great Britain by the power of the Navy; and that the English nation would face the prospects of continuous industrial dislocations in the firm belief in its superior inventive and productive ability. However, it was believed that if only the grain of all the world could flow freely to Britain, then her factories would be able to undersell all the world. (Polanyi 1957: 138)

As far as Britain was concerned, there was in fact nothing doctrinaire, let alone extravagant, in the unilateral adoption of free trade. As the leader of the Tory protectionists, Benjamin Disraeli, declared in 1846, even Cobden knew that "there [was] no chance of changing the laws of England with abstract doctrine." Something more substantial than "scientifically" demonstrated truth was required to convert the British parliament to the principles of free trade (Semmel 1970: 146).

The main reason why British foreign and colonial trade was liberalized is that protectionism had become a drag on the effective mobilization of Britain's newly acquired industrial capabilities for the benefit of its ruling classes:

> The Whig grandees (though not so much the lesser Tory country squires) knew quite well that the power of the country, and their own, rested on a readiness to make money militantly and commercially. It so happened that in 1750 not a great deal of money was yet to be made in industry. When it was, they would have no great difficulty in adjusting themselves to the situation. (Hobsbawm 1968: 18)

Neither the Whig grandees nor the lesser Tory country squires ever made a great deal of money *in* industry. But as soon as the opportunity of mobilizing industry as an instrument of national aggrandizement arose, they seized it promptly. For the most part this involved no major departure from well-established traditions. Thus, as previously argued, the nineteenth-century gold standard of the British pound was simply a continuation by other means of a practice established centuries earlier under Elizabeth I. Polanyi underscores the close relationship of interdependence which in the 1840s came to link the fixed metallic standard of the British currency, to unilateral free trade and to the self-regulation of the domestic labor market. But for two and a half centuries before these three elements of Ricardian free trade came to constitute a coherent whole, the fixed metallic standard had formed a coherent whole with something far more fundamental for its smooth functioning than free markets: the successful overseas expansion of the British state and of British capital.

The more successful this expansion became, the greater and the steadier the mass of surplus capital in the form of interest, profit, tribute, and remittances that accrued to British subjects or residents from abroad and that could be mobilized in support of the preservation of the stable metallic standard of the British pound. And conversely, the longer and the more successfully this standard had been preserved, the easier it became for British governmental and business agencies to obtain on the world's financial markets all the credit and liquidity they needed to expand their overseas networks of accumulation and power. Britain's industrial expansion during the Napoleonic Wars did not alter the underlying interest of its ruling classes in the continuation of this virtuous circle between the voluntary submission of the national currency to a metallic taskmaster on the one side, and the overseas expansion of British networks of power and accumulation on the other. On the contrary, it intensified the urge and multiplied the means of this two-pronged pursuit.

The central aspect of wartime industrial expansion was the creation of an autonomous capital goods industry. Prior to that, the capital goods industry in Britain, as anywhere else, had little autonomy from the branches of the economy that used its products. Most enterprises produced or subcontracted the production of the fixtures and equipment they used in their activities. The seat and backbone of the nineteenth-century British capital goods industry – iron and related trades – was still for all practical purposes no more than a subordinate branch of the British army and navy:

> War was pretty certainly the greatest consumer of iron, and firms like Wilkinson, the Walkers, and the Carron Works, owed the size of their undertakings partly to government contracts for cannon, while the South Wales iron industry depended on battle.... Henry Cort, who revolutionized iron manufacture, began in the 1760s as a navy agent, anxious to improve the quality of the British product "in connexion with the supply of iron to the navy".... Henry Maudslay, the pioneer of machine tools, began his career in the Woolwich Arsenal and his fortunes (like those of the great engineer Mark Isambard Brunel, formerly of the French navy) remained closely bound up with naval contracts. (Hobsbawm 1968: 34)

As government expenditures escalated on the eve and during the Napoleonic Wars, the level of production and the pace of product and process innovation in the iron industry increased sharply, and the capital goods industry became a far more autonomous "department" of the British domestic economy than it had ever been or than it still was in any other country. The proliferation of enterprises specializing in the production of means of production quickened the pace of innovation among the users of these means and stimulated British producers, traders, and financiers to find ways and means of profiting from the greater number, range, and variety of capital goods available on the market (see chapter 3).

> Military demands on the British economy thus went far to shape the subsequent phases of the industrial revolution, allowing the improvement of steam engines and making such critical innovations as the iron railway and iron ships possible at a time and under conditions which simply would not have existed without the wartime impetus to iron production. (McNeill 1984: 211–12)

The development of an autonomous capital goods industry presented the ruling class with as many problems as opportunities. For one thing, the advantages gained through this development in the competitive and power struggle that opposed them to the ruling classes of other states were not easily retained. The innovations that were being embodied in the new capital goods technically were rather primitive. They were the result of practical men – "ingenious mechanics, conversant in the practices in use in their time," as Serjeant Adair described them when defending Richard Arkwright in 1785 (Mantoux 1961: 206) – putting their minds to using widespread knowledge to solve practical problems under exceptionally favorable circumstances (Hobsbawm 1968: 43–4; Barrat Brown 1974: 75–6).

A multitude of equally practical and knowledgeable persons in Europe and elsewhere could therefore take over or even improve on these innovations once their usefulness had been demonstrated. And their appropriation became even easier once the innovations came to be embodied in capital goods sold on the market. Fully aware of the difficulties involved in excluding actual or potential competitors from the use of the new techniques, from the mid-1770s through the Napoleonic Wars the British government resorted to the imposition of an increasing number of restrictions on the export of tools and machinery as well as on the emigration of skilled artisans and technicians. But these restrictions were more effective in preventing British producers of capital goods from fully exploiting foreign demand than in attaining the purpose for which they had been enacted (Kindleberger 1975: 28–31).

In addition to being difficult to retain, the advantages of Britain's newly acquired industrial capabilities were a mixed blessing, both domestically and internationally. Domestically, the development of machinofacture was a source of considerable economic and social turbulence. The more autonomous the capital goods industry became from the branches of the economy that used its products, the more its capacity tended to expand beyond what the domestic economy could profitably sustain. Violent upswings in prices, incomes, and employment were followed by equally violent downswings. Combined with the disruptions of established ways of life and work due to the use of the new capital goods, this economic turbulence led to considerable social unrest and to the Chartist challenge to established political institutions.

Internationally, the development of machinofacture made the British domestic economy unprecedentedly dependent not just on exports, on which it had been thoroughly dependent since the fourteenth century, but also on foreign sources for essential supplies. Although still self-sufficient in staple food supplies, for the first time in British history an industry vital to exports and employment came to depend on external sources for an essential input, raw cotton. At the beginning of the Napoleonic Wars the bulk of cotton imports came from British colonies, most notably the West

Indies, but by 1800 most of it came from a foreign country, the United States. Moreover, the reduction in unit costs that sustained the expansion of the British cotton industry depended critically on increasing sales to foreign markets, including and especially the markets of continental Europe and of the United States (Farnie 1979: 83; Cain and Hopkins 1980: 472–4).

In short, the leading branch of the late eighteenth-century British "industrial revolution" was from the very start a global industry dependent for its competitiveness and continuing expansion on the external economies afforded by the procurement of inputs and disposal of outputs on foreign markets. More importantly, under the impact of wartime expenditures, the British capital goods industry had far outgrown what the domestic traffic could bear under normal circumstances; and as these expenditures began to level off and then contracted, the capital goods industry could retain its size and specialization only by itself becoming global in scope. In the closing years of the Napoleonic Wars and during the slump in prices and outputs that followed the end of hostilities, the ruling class of Britain thus faced a situation in which the industrial expansion of the preceding thirty years threatened the internal and external security of the British state unless ways and means could be found to consolidate the global scope of the cotton industry and of widening the market of the capital goods industry. However, if these ways and means were found, then both industries could be turned from actual or potential sources of social and political trouble into engines of further expansion of British wealth and power.

Initially, a concern for domestic and external security was predominant in the ruling class's perception of their interests, and it was this concern that started the movement towards trade liberalization. Thus, a primary objective of the abolition of the East India Company's trade monopoly in India in 1813 was the extension of employment and the preservation of the "tranquillity of the manufacturing population" after the emergence of Luddism (Farnie 1979: 97). Issues of domestic security were, however, indissolubly interwoven with issues of external security. When in 1806/7 the Berlin and Milan Decrees closed much of Europe to British exports, the loss could be compensated by a more concerted penetration of Latin American markets. But when in 1812 war broke out with the United States – Britain's main source of raw cotton as well as a major outlet of British cotton manufactures – the precarious international foundations of British industrial expansion were starkly revealed. The abolition of the East India Company's Indian monopoly, as well as the total separation of the company's territorial and commercial accounts, which prepared the way for a fully imperial administration, must be seen as an attempt simultaneously to solve problems of internal and external security.

Shortly after the liberalization of the India trade, the end of the wars with the United States and with France lessened the urgency of problems of external security. However, problems of domestic security not only remained but were aggravated by the post-war slump in production and employment. To make things worse, the export of British semi-finished manufactures, such as yarn, combined with widening breaches in the wall of prohibitions set up by the British government to prevent the outflow of technicians and machinery, helped the import-substitution efforts of European and American governments and businesses and resulted in widespread losses of foreign markets for the British cotton weaving and finishing industries (Jeremy 1977; Davis 1979: 24–5; Crouzet 1982: 66).

It was in these circumstances that political control over large, captive, and unprotected economic spaces became the main source of external economies for British business. The Indian subcontinent, with its huge textile industry and commercialized agriculture, was by far the most important among these captive and unprotected economic spaces. An insignificant outlet for British cotton goods up to 1813, by 1843 India had become the single biggest market for such goods, taking up to 23 per cent of their exports in 1850 and 31 per cent ten years later (Chapman 1972: 52).

The spread of machinofacture from spinning to weaving dates from this period of the British cotton industry's increasing dependence on the Indian market. In 1813, this industry still employed fewer than 3,000 powerlooms and more than 200,000 handloom weavers. But by around 1860, there were more than 400,000 powerlooms in operation and handloom weavers had become an extinct species (Wood 1910: 593–9; Crouzet 1982: 199).

It is hard to imagine how this great leap forward in the mechanization of the British textile industry could have occurred at a time of stagnant domestic and foreign demand for its output except through the conquest of the Indian market and the consequent destruction of the Indian textile industry. Just as in the latter half of the fourteenth century the initial creation of an English woolen cloth industry had as its counterpart the forcible destruction of the Flemish cloth industry and the spontaneous deindustrialization of Florence, so in the early to mid-nineteenth century the final flourishing of mechanization in the British cotton industry had as its counterpart the parallel destruction of the Indian textile industry. In both instances, industrial expansion in Britain reflected a major spatial transplant of enterprise. The main difference was the incomparably greater scale, speed, and sophistication of means involved in the latter transplant.

As Polanyi (1957: 159–60) has underscored, "[t]he term 'exploitation' describes but ill a situation which became really grave [for the Indian producers] only after the East India Company's ruthless monopoly was abolished and free trade was introduced in India." The Company's monopoly had been an instrument of exploitation of the Indian textile industry, and this exploitation in turn had sapped the industry's vitality and thereby prepared its subsequent destruction by the cheap products of Lancashire. But under the Company's monopoly, "the situation had been fairly kept in hand with the help of the archaic organization of the countryside ... while under free trade and equal exchange Indians perished by the millions." Lancashire did something quite different and worse than exploit the Indian masses: it deprived them of the cash flows essential to their reproduction. "That this was brought about by forces of economic competition, namely the permanent underselling of hand-woven *chaddar* by machine-made piece goods, is doubtless true; but it proves the opposite of economic exploitation, since dumping implies the reverse of surcharge."

The destruction of the foundations of the East India Company's exploitation of South Asian labor, entrepreneurship, and natural resources was none the less only the preamble of their exploitation on new and enlarged foundations. As Marx observed in 1853, "[t]he more the [British] industrial interest became dependent on the Indian market the more it felt the necessity of creating fresh productive powers in India after having ruined her native industry." Railroads, steamships, and the opening of the Suez Canal in 1869 transformed India into a major source of cheap food and raw materials for Europe – tea, wheat, oil seeds, cotton, jute – as well as into a major remunerative outlet protected by administrative action for the products of the British capital goods industry and for British enterprise. What is more, in the late nineteenth and early twentieth centuries the large surplus in the Indian balance of payments became the pivot of the enlarged reproduction of Britain's world-scale processes of capital accumulation and of the City's mastery of world finance (Saul 1960: 62, 188–94; Barrat Brown 1974: 133–6; Tomlinson 1975: 340; Bairoch 1976a: 83; Crouzet 1982: 370; de Cecco 1984: 29–38).

Equally critical was another pivot of the enlarged reproduction of British wealth and power: the Indian surplus of military labor which came to be organized in the British Indian army:

It was not an army intended primarily for domestic defense and police duties in India. Rather, it was the army of British imperialism, formal and informal, which operated worldwide, opening up markets to the products of the industrial revolution, subordinating labor forces to the domination of capital and bringing "benighted" civilizations the enlightened values of Christianity and Rationality. The Indian army was the iron fist in the velvet glove of

Victorian expansionism.... Moreover, because the British Empire was the
principal agency through which the world system functioned in this era, the
Indian army was in a real sense the major coercive force behind the
internationalization of industrial capitalism. (Washbrook 1990: 481)

In the light of this centrality of the Indian surpluses of money and labor
in the formation and expansion of the British regime of rule and
accumulation on a world scale, it is not surprising that, in Hobsbawm's
(1968: 123) words, "not even the free-traders wished to see this gold-
mine escape from British control, and that a great part of British foreign
and military or naval policy was designed essentially to maintain safe
control of it." To this we should add that without political control over
this gold mine the conversion of the ruling classes of Britain to Ricardian
free trade doctrine would have been "entirely extravagant" indeed. But
political control over India made this conversion a quite sensible course
of action in the pursuit of power and profit for two closely related
reasons. First, the disruptive effects of self-regulating markets could be
dumped on India in order to moderate them in Britain. And second,
disruptions in India set free huge surpluses of human, natural, and
pecuniary resources which endowed Britain with an exceptional freedom
of choice in the world-wide procurement of its means of livelihood,
accumulation, and protection.

As free a flow as possible of supplies from all over the world to the
British domestic market was essential to cutting domestic costs of
production, while provisioning foreign customers with the means needed
to buy British products. The assertiveness of provincial industrial interests
and fear of Chartism played a critical role in pushing the ruling groups of
Britain further and faster towards the adoption of unilateral free trade
than they would have done otherwise (Cain and Hopkins 1986: 516). But
a free flow of supplies from all over the world to the British domestic
market was essential not just to the appeasement of industrial interests
and subordinate classes; it was also essential to the effective exercise by
Britain's ruling groups of their exceptional freedom of choice in an
increasingly integrated world market.

Such were the advantages of unilateral free trade for Imperial Britain,
that the protectionist counter-movement never had a chance of becoming
hegemonic among its ruling or even subaltern classes. Britain was and
remained to the bitter end the epicenter of the free trade movement. To
paraphrase Hobsbawm (1968: 207), Britain never actually abandoned
the free trade system it had created; rather, it was the world that
abandoned Britain.

The world began abandoning Britain's free trade system almost as soon
as this system was established:

[T]he increase in the rhythm and volume of international trade as well as the universal mobilization of land, implied in the mass transportation of grain and agricultural raw materials from one part of the planet to another, at a fractional cost ... dislocated the lives of dozens of millions in rural Europe.... The agrarian crisis and the Great Depression of 1873–86 had shaken confidence in economic self-healing. From now onward the typical institution of market economy could usually be introduced only if accompanied by protectionist measures, all the more so because since the late 1870's and early 1880's nations were forming themselves into organized units which were apt to suffer grievously from the dislocations involved in the sudden adjustment to the needs of foreign trade or foreign exchanges. (Polanyi 1957: 213–14)

The epicenter of the protectionist counter-movement was newly created Imperial Germany. When the slump of 1873–79 hit Germany, Chancellor Bismarck believed as strongly as any of his contemporaries in the self-regulating powers of market mechanisms. Initially, he found consolation in the world-wide scope of the depression and waited patiently for the slump to hit its bottom. However, when this occurred in 1876–77, he realized that the verdict of the market on the viability of the German state and of German society was too harsh to take and that, moreover, the slump had created unique opportunities for the continuation of his state-making endeavors by other means.

The spread of unemployment, labor unrest, and socialist agitation; the persistence of the industrial and commercial slumps; plummeting land values; and, above all, a crippling fiscal crisis of the Reich – all combined to induce Bismarck to intervene in protection of German society lest the ravages of the self-regulating market destroy the imperial edifice he had just built. At the same time, the growing convergence of agrarian and industrial interests in pressing for governmental protection from foreign competition made it easy for him to switch suddenly from free trade and laissez faire to a highly protectionist and interventionist stance. Through this switch he was not just yielding to social and economic pressures. He was also consolidating and strengthening the powers of the German Reich (Rosenberg 1943: 67–8).

Bismarck had never liked a system that placed the central authority at the mercy of the Federal States:

In 1872 he told the Reichstag: "An empire that is dependent upon the contributions of individual states lacks the bonds of a strong and common financial institution." And in 1879 he declared that it was degrading that the central authority should have to pass a begging bowl from one federal state to another to secure revenues essential to its requirements. (Henderson 1975: 218–19)

In line with these sentiments, governmental intervention in protection of German society did not surrender to particularistic interests. On the contrary, it was used to strengthen governmental authority and the sovereignty of the *Reich*:

> The political power vested in the *Reich* executive was to be used to help overcome short-term economic contraction and stagnation, but in exchange for its services the state was to make durable political conquests.... Vast schemes loomed before Bismarck's eyes; the establishment ... of the unassailable financial independence of the *Reich* and its military machine, beyond the reach of parliamentary control, by manipulating the producers' demand for tariff protection and by reforming taxation so as to reduce overhead costs. Or the political exploitation of economic and fiscal maladjustments so as to secure a new balance of power between the *Reich* and the states ... and to complete the national unification by cementing it with unbreakable economic ties. (Rosenberg 1943: 68)

An organic relationship of "political exchange" was thus established between the German government and select business enterprises. While the German government did all that was within its powers to assist the expansion of these enterprises, the latter did all they could to assist the German government in cementing the unity of the German domestic economy and in endowing the German state with a powerful military–industrial apparatus. The main partners of the German government in this relationship of political exchange were industrial enterprises involved critically in the ongoing "industrialization of war" and, above all, six large banks.

These *Grossbanken* had emerged out of the personal and interfamilial structure of German banking, still prevalent in the 1850s, primarily through the promotion and financing of railway companies and of heavy industrial enterprises involved in railway construction (Tilly 1967: 174–5, 179–80). Their dominance in German finance increased further during the slump of the 1870s. And in the 1880s, when a large proportion of their entrepreneurial and pecuniary resources were released by the nationalization of the railways, they moved swiftly to take over, integrate, and reorganize German industry in collusion with a small number of powerful industrial firms. "Large concerns and cartels working in close association with the great banks – these were the twin pillars of the German economy in the last quarter of the nineteenth century" (Henderson 1975: 178).

Whereas on the eve of the Great Depression family capitalism was still the norm in Germany as it was in Britain, by the turn of the century a highly centralized corporate structure had taken its place. Over the next two decades centralization increased further, mostly through horizontal integration. To the extent that small and medium-sized enterprises survived, as many did, they lived on as subordinate members of a private command economy controlled by a closely knit group of financiers and industrialists acting through increasingly extensive and complex managerial bureaucracies. The German domestic economy, to paraphrase Engels (1958), was indeed beginning to look like "one big factory."

Hilferding (1981), and generations of Marxist thinkers after him down to present-day theorists of "organized" and "disorganized" capitalism, interpreted this development as the clearest sign that Marx's expectation of an ever-increasing centralization of capital was being fulfilled, and went on to conceptualize it as marking the beginning of a new stage of capitalism characterized by the progressive supersession of the "anarchy" of market regulation by centralized capitalist planning (cf. Auerbach, Desai, and Shamsavari 1988). By fostering the formation of cartels that encompassed entire branches of industry, large banks facilitated the smooth and efficient working of the enterprises which they had come to control. As the profitability of these enterprises increased relative to the enterprises still subject to the vagaries of the market, banks acquired new means with which to extend further their control over the industrial system, and so on until a general cartel controlled the entire national economy:

> The whole capitalist production would then be consciously regulated by a single body which would determine the volume of production in all branches of industry. Price determination would become a purely nominal matter, involving only the distribution of the total product between the cartel magnates on one side and all other members of society on the other. Price would then cease to be the outcome of factual relationships into which people have entered, and would become a mere accounting device by which things were allocated among people.... In its perfected form finance capital is thus uprooted from the soil which nourished its beginnings.... [T]he ceaseless turnover of money has attained its goal in the regulated society. (Hilferding 1981: 234)

By the early twentieth century this process had gone far enough to enable German business to pursue technical efficiency with unprecedented and in many respects unparalleled determination. Here lay the taproot of the "techological rationality" of German business which, following David Landes, we have contrasted with the "pecuniary rationality" of British business. Since this technological rationality of German business was associated with far higher rates of industrial growth and with a more systematic application of science to industry than the pecuniary rationality of British business – two features which made German industry the "wonder of the world" – it was a short step for Marxists to think that the more consciously and centrally planned German system of business enterprise had superseded the British as the paradigm of advanced capitalism.

In reality, the German system was superseding the British only in industrial performance. As far as the generation and appropriation of value-added were concerned, the German system was scarcely reducing the large gap that separated Germany and Britain at the beginning of the Great Depression. As Landes (1969: 329) notes:

> the difference in overall rates of growth between [Germany and Britain] was considerably smaller than the discrepancy in rates of industrial growth would lead one to expect. Where British output of manufactured commodities … slightly more than doubled from 1870 to 1913, against a German increase of almost sixfold, the ratio between the rising incomes of the two countries, whether calculated in aggregate or *per capita*, was of the order of 0.7 or 0.8 to 1.

In other words, the German business community had to expand industrial output almost three times faster than the British in order to make a relatively small gain in value-added. Economically, this performance looks like a minor failure rather than the great success that many still think it was.

It may be objected that value-added does not provide an adequate foundation for assessing the achievements of the German system of business enterprise, because the main purpose of that system was social and political. As we have seen, this is undoubtedly true. But it is precisely on political and social grounds that the German performance relative to the British was most disastrous. The more powerful the German *Reich* became, the more it entered into a collision course with the power and interests of Imperial Britain (see chapter 1). When the two great powers actually clashed in the First World War, all the incremental gains in world power that Imperial Germany had made over the preceding half-century turned suddenly into a huge loss. Imperial Germany did not survive defeat in the war, and the imposition of disarmament and heavy war reparations reduced the successor republic to the status of a tributary "quasi-state" *vis-à-vis* not just Britain but France as well. Moreover, the unprecedented social unrest that ensued from the political and economic collapse of the industrialization effort threw the German ruling classes and business community into complete disarray, propelling them towards the even more disastrous ventures of the following two decades.

Far from superseding Britain's market capitalism, German corporate capitalism was a minor economic failure and a colossal political and social failure. Nevertheless, its development had the effect of precipitating the terminal crisis of the British regime of accumulation, thereby initiating the transition to the US regime. German corporate capitalism was only the antithesis of British free-trade imperialism. The synthesis that eventually transcended both was a kind of corporate capitalism which was as different from the German system of accumulation as it was from the British.

The Fourth (US) Systemic Cycle of Accumulation

The *belle époque* of the Edwardian era marked the high point of Britain's free-trade imperialism. The wealth and power of the propertied classes, not just of Britain but of the entire Western world, had attained unprecedented heights. And yet the systemic crisis of the British regime of accumulation had not been resolved, and within a generation it would bring the entire edifice of nineteenth-century civilization crashing down.

The most serious underlying problem faced by the British regime remained the intensity of inter-capitalist competition. As previously noted, the upturn in prices of the mid-1890s cured the malady of the European bourgeoisie by reversing the squeeze on profits of the preceding quarter-century. Over time, however, the cure proved worse than the disease. For the upturn was based primarily on a further escalation in the armaments race among the Great Powers of Europe. As such, it reflected not a supersession of the intense inter-capitalist competition of the Great Depression of 1873–96 but a change in its primary locus from the sphere of inter-enterprise relations to the sphere of inter-state relations.

Initially, to paraphrase Max Weber once again, control over the supply of mobile capital endowed the capitalist classes of Europe in general and of Great Britain in particular with the capability of dictating to the competing states the conditions under which they would assist them in the power struggle. It was this more than anything else that enabled the European bourgeoisie not just to recover from the Great Depression, but to enjoy for some twenty years a moment of great splendor. The inter-state power struggle, however, tended to raise protection costs over and above their benefits for each and every European state, Britain included, and simultaneously to undermine the capabilities of the bourgeoisie in most countries to externalize the burdens of the struggle. When the struggle came to a head in the First World War, the fate of the British regime of accumulation was sealed:

The scaffolding of multilateral settlements, which before 1914 held together the structure of international trade, rested on two chief bases. The first was that of India's balance of payments deficit to Britain and the surpluses with other countries with which this deficit was financed, the second the trading balances between Britain, Europe and North America. The framework of settlements so gradually constructed was violently disrupted by the First World War, and the Second World War completed its destruction. (Milward 1970: 45)

In the half-century preceding the First World War Britain's overseas empire, and India in particular, had become more essential than ever to the self-expansion of British capital on a world scale. As Marcello de Cecco (1984: 37–8) has pointed out, by bolstering the ability of its empire to earn foreign exchange through the export of primary commodities, Britain "managed to exist without having to restructure [its] industry and was able to invest in the countries where [capital] gave the highest return" (see also Saul 1960: 62–3, 88). The United States happened to be the country that received the largest share of these investments and that provided British investors with the largest claims on foreign assets and future incomes. Thus, between 1850 and 1914, foreign investment and long-term lending to the United States amounted to a total of $3 billion. But during this same period the United States made net payments of interest and dividends, mostly to Britain, amounting to $5.8 billion. The consequence was an increase in the US foreign debt from $200 million in 1843 to $3,700 million in 1914 (Knapp 1957: 433).

British claims on US assets and incomes were of the greatest importance in the economy of British rule, because the United States could provide Britain promptly and efficiently with all the supplies that the latter would need to defend its far-flung territorial empire in a global war. Thus, in 1905 the Royal Commission on the Supply of Food and Raw Materials in Time of War reported that, with sufficient money and ships, supplies in case of war would be guaranteed and that a shortage of money was the least likely to occur. In a similar vein, when the First World War broke out the Chancellor of the Exchequer reckoned that the proceeds of British foreign investments would be enough to pay for five years of war. Massive currency movements into London and an increase of almost 300 per cent in the Bank of England's gold reserves between August and November 1914 seemed to bear out these optimistic expectations (Milward 1970: 44–6).

However, in 1915 Britain's demand for armaments, machines, and raw materials already far surpassed what the Royal Commission of 1905 had projected. Much of the machinery needed could only be supplied by the United States, and their purchase initiated the erosion of British claims on incomes produced in the United States and the building up of US claims on British incomes and assets. British assets in the United States were liquidated on the New York Stock Exchange at heavily discounted prices in the early years of the war. By the time the United States entered the war and lifted restrictions on lending to Britain,

> the British Government, with commitments in the United States running into hundreds of millions of pounds, was at the end of its tether. It had no means whatever of meeting them. Between that date and the Armistice it borrowed from the American Government to pay for "absolute necessities of life and warfare" not far short of £1,000 million. (R.H. Brand, as quoted in Milward 1970: 46)

At the end of the war, therefore, the United States had bought back at bargain prices some of the massive investments which had built up the infrastructure of its domestic economy in the nineteenth century, and in addition, had accumulated huge war credits. Moreover, in the initial years of the war Britain had lent heavily to its poorer allies, most notably Russia, while the still neutral United States had a free hand at speeding up its displacement of Britain as the main foreign investor and financial intermediary in Latin America and parts of Asia. By the end of the war this process had become irreversible. Most of the $9 billion of US net war credits was owed by comparatively solvent Britain and France; but more than 75 per cent of Britain's $3.3 billion of net war credits was owed by bankrupt (and revolutionary) Russia and had to be largely written off (cf. Fishlow 1986: 71; Eichengreen and Portes 1986; Frieden 1987: 27–8).

The extent of this first reversal in the financial fortunes of the United States and Britain was substantial but should not be exaggerated. Gold reserves in London were higher in the 1920s than before the war and seemed to justify the return of sterling to the gold standard in 1926 at its pre-war parity; British claims on foreign incomes, though reduced, were still considerable; German war reparation payments could be counted on to pay at least part of the costs of servicing war debts towards the United States; and, above all, Britain's colonial and semi-colonial empire had further expanded, and constituted a safety net into which metropolitan Britain could fall in case of need, as it did in the 1930s. As for the United States, the end of the war brought its trade surplus roughly back to where it was before 1914. The main difference from the pre-war situation was that US claims on incomes produced abroad now balanced foreign claims on incomes produced at home, so that the trade surplus translated into a significant net current account surplus (see figure 17).

Thanks to this surplus and to its war credits, the United States joined but did not displace Britain in the production and regulation of world money. The US dollar became a full-fledged reserve currency like the British pound. But neither the dollar nor the pound alone accounted for a majority of the foreign exchange holdings of central banks (Eichengreen 1992: 358).

More importantly, US capabilities to manage the world monetary system remained distinctly inferior to Britain's own residual capabilities. From this point of view, as Geoffrey Ingham (1989: 16–17; 1984: 203) has suggested, the thesis that the inter-war world monetary system was rendered unstable by British inability and US unwillingness to assume responsibility for stabilizing it (Kindleberger 1973: 292) must be revised. For control over a substantial share of world liquidity did not endow the United States with the capability to manage the world monetary system. Organizationally, US financial institutions were simply not up to the task. In the 1920s, the Federal Reserve System, established only in 1913, was still a loose and inexperienced body incapable of exercising with minimal effectiveness even its domestic functions. In foreign dealings, only New York among the twelve regional reserve banks had any significant experience.

New York itself remained entirely subordinate to London both organizationally and intellectually. To be sure, the great upward hike in the US share of world liquidity during the war led to an equally significant increase in the power and influence of the New York financial community in general, and of the House of Morgan in particular, *within* the networks of London-based *haute finance*. This redistribution of power and influence, however, did not change the mode of operation of the world monetary system. Wall Street and the Federal Reserve of New York simply joined the City of London and the Bank of England in maintaining and enforcing the international gold standard, whose main beneficiary was and remained Britain. As Jacques Rueff wrote in 1932 in a partisan but none the less accurate characterization of the monetary arrangements of the 1920s:

> [t]he application of the gold-exchange standard had the considerable advantage for Britain of masking its real position for many years. During the entire postwar period, Britain was able to loan to Central European countries funds that kept flowing back to Britain, since the moment they had entered the economy of the borrowing countries, they were again deposited in London. Thus, like soldiers marching across the stage in a musical comedy, they could reemerge indefinitely and enable their owners to continue making loans abroad, while, in fact, the inflow of foreign exchange, which in the past had made such loans possible, had dried up. (Rueff 1964: 30)

Through its support for the international gold standard, the New York financial community thus encouraged and sustained London's ultimately futile attempts to remain at the center of world finance. New York was not alone in supporting London's attempt to return to the world of 1913. Throughout the 1920s most Western governments shared the conviction that only the re-establishment of the pre-1914 world monetary system, "this time on solid foundations," could restore peace and prosperity. Whatever their ideological orientation, national governments adapted their fiscal and monetary policies to the safeguarding of the currency, while innumerable international conferences, from Brussels to Spa and Geneva, from London to Locarno and Lausanne, were held to create the political conditions of the restoration of the gold standard (Polanyi 1957: 26).

Ironically, however, this concerted effort, instead of reviving the pre-1914 world monetary system, precipitated its terminal crisis. Everybody agreed that stable currencies ultimately depended on the freeing of trade. And yet, "the incubus of self-sufficiency haunted the steps taken in protection of the currency." In order to stabilize their currencies, governments resorted to import quotas, moratoria and stand-still agreements, clearing systems and bilateral trade treaties, barter arrangements, embargoes on capital exports, foreign trade control, and exchange equalization funds, the combination of which tended to restrict foreign trade and foreign payments. "While the intent was the freeing of trade, the effect was its strangulation" (Polanyi 1957: 27).

The pursuit of stable currencies under the pressure of "capital flight" eventually turned the stagnation of world trade and production of the 1920s into the slump of the early 1930s. Throughout the 1920s productivity continued to grow faster in the United States than in any of the debtor countries, further increasing the competitive edge of US business and the difficulties of debtor countries to service, let alone repay, their debts. And as the dependence of the world's payments system on the US dollar increased, the United States acquired foreign assets "with a rapidity ... which ... is unparalleled in the experience of any major creditor nation in modern times" (Dobb 1963: 332).

By the end of the 1920s, US foreign loans and direct investments had built up net assets on private account to over $8 billion. Ultimately, however, the growing structural imbalances of world payments were bound to impair the continuation of the process, particularly in view of the generalized attempts of governments to restore the gold standard of their currencies. Capital movements across state boundaries assumed an increasingly short-term, speculative character:

These movements of "hot money", as it came to be called ... darted about between the financial centers of the world in search of temporary security or speculative profit and at frequent intervals exerted a dangerous pressure on the gold and foreign exchange reserves of one country or another. (Arndt 1963: 14)

Under these circumstances, a domestic speculative boom or bust in the United States would result in a halt in foreign lending and in the collapse of the whole complex structure on which the restoration of world trade was based. This is indeed what eventually happened. Towards the end of 1928, the boom on Wall Street began diverting funds from foreign lending to domestic speculation. As US banks recalled their European loans, the net export of capital from the United States – which had risen from less than $200 million in 1926 to over a billion in 1928 – plunged to $200 million again in 1929 (Landes 1969: 372).

The halt in US foreign lending and investment was made permanent by the collapse of the Wall Street boom and the ensuing slump in the US economy. Faced with sudden recalls or flights of short-term funds, one country after another was forced to protect its currency, either by depreciation or exchange control. The suspension of the gold convertibility of the British pound in September 1931 led to the final destruction of the single web of world commercial and financial transactions on which the fortunes of the City of London were based. Protectionism became rampant, the pursuit of stable currencies was abandoned, and "world capitalism retreated into the igloos of its nation-state economies and their associated empires" (Hobsbawm 1991: 132).

This is the "world revolution" that Karl Polanyi traced to the "snapping of the golden thread" (see chapter 3). Its main landmarks were the disappearance of *haute finance* from world politics, the collapse of the League of Nations in favor of autarchist empires, the rise of Nazism in Germany, the Soviet Five Year Plans, and the launching of the US New Deal. "While at the end of the Great War nineteenth century ideals were paramount, and their influence dominated the following decade, by 1940 every vestige of the international system had disappeared and, apart from a few enclaves, the nations were living in an entirely new international setting" (Polanyi 1957: 23, 27).

In fact, the international setting in 1940 was not all that new since the great powers of the inter-state system were in the midst of yet another military confrontation which, except for its unprecedented scale, ferocity, and destructiveness, reproduced a recurrent pattern of the capitalist world-economy. Soon, however, this confrontation was translated into the establishment of a new world order, centered on and organized by the United States, which differed in key respects from the defunct British world order and became the foundation of a new enlarged reproduction of the capitalist world-economy. By the end of the Second World War, the main contours of this new world order had already emerged: at Bretton Woods the foundations of a new world monetary system had been established; at Hiroshima and Nagasaki new means of violence had demonstrated what the military underpinnings of the new world order would be; and at San Francisco new norms and rules for the legitimization of state-making and war-making had been laid out in the UN Charter.

The initial conception under Roosevelt and its subsequent downsized realization under Truman reflected the unprecedented concentration of world power which had occurred as a result of the Second World War. Militarily, even as the war was at its height,

> [f]ormer Great Powers – France, Italy – were already eclipsed. The German bid for mastery in Europe was collapsing, as was Japan's bid in the Far East and the Pacific. Britain, despite Churchill, was fading. The bipolar world, forecast so often in the nineteenth and early twentieth centuries, had at last arrived; the international order, in DePorte's words, now moved "from one system to another." Only the United States and the USSR counted . . . and of the two, the American "superpower" was vastly superior. (Kennedy 1987: 357)

The centralization of world financial power was even greater. As can be seen in figure 17, the impact of the Second World War on the US trade balance reproduced on an enlarged scale the impact of the First World War. The peak is both higher and longer. This reflects the greater extent to which the United States acted as the workshop of the Allied war effort and as the granary and workshop of post-war European reconstruction. Moreover, for the first time in US history, US claims on incomes generated abroad came to exceed by a good margin foreign claims on incomes produced in the United States, so that after the war the current account surplus was much greater than the trade surplus.

As a result of this new and enlarged upward movement of its trade and current account surplus, the United States came to enjoy a virtual monopoly of world liquidity. In 1947, its gold reserves were 70 per cent of the world's total. Moreover, the excess demand for dollars by foreign governments and businesses meant that US control over world liquidity was far greater than implied by this extraordinary concentration of monetary gold.

The concentration and centralization of productive capacity and effective demand was equally impressive. In 1938 US national income was already about the same as the combined national incomes of Britain, France, Germany, Italy, and the Benelux countries, and almost three times that of the USSR. But in 1948 it was more than twice that of the above-mentioned group of Western European countries, and more than six times that of the USSR (calculated from Woytinsky and Woytinsky 1953: tables 185–6).

The final breakdown of the UK-centered world-economy had thus been extremely beneficial for the United States. Less than twenty years after the Great Crash of 1929, the world was in a shambles but the national wealth and power of the United States had attained unprecedented and unparalleled heights. The United States was not the first state to benefit tremendously from the troubles of the world-economy of which it was an integral and major component. Its experience had been prefigured by Venice in the fifteenth century, the United Provinces in the seventeenth century, and the United Kingdom in the eighteenth century. As in all previous instances of prodigious enrichment and empowerment in the midst of increasing systemic chaos, the great leap forward of US wealth and power between 1914 and 1945 was primarily the expression of the protection rent which it enjoyed thanks to a uniquely privileged position in the spatial configuration of the capitalist world-economy. The more turbulent and chaotic the world system became, the greater the benefits that accrued to the United States in virtue of its continental size, its island position, and its direct access to the two major oceans of the world-economy (see chapter 1).

And yet, more than ever, the extent to which the wealth and power of a particular state could benefit from systemic chaos was limited. The more that was redistributed in its favor, the less there was to redistribute and the greater the disruptive effects of chaos in the world at large on its foreign trade and investment. Of more immediate relevance was the fact that the industrialization of warfare had turned global wars into powerful engines of innovations in means of transport, communication, and destruction that "shrank" the globe and threatened the security of even the most secure of states.

If the Second World War had demonstrated that the United States could grow rich and powerful in the midst of increasing systemic chaos, it had also demonstrated that US political isolationism had reached the point of decreasing returns. The isolationist position depended on the belief that US security was inviolable. Once the bombing of Pearl Harbor shattered that belief, President Roosevelt made astute use of the nationalist sentiments aroused by the first foreign attack on US territory since 1812 to graft his vision of one world onto his New Dealism. "Roosevelt's vision of the new world order was an extension of his New Deal philosophy. The core of that philosophy was that only big, benign, and professional government could assure the people order, security, and justice. . . . Just as the New Deal brought 'social security' to America, so 'one world' would bring political security to the entire world" (Schurmann 1974: 40–2).

The essence of the New Deal was the notion that big government must spend liberally in order to achieve security and progress. Thus, postwar security would require liberal outlays by the United States in order to overcome the chaos created by the war. . . . Aid to . . . poor nations would have the same effect as social welfare programs within the United States – it would give them the security to overcome chaos and prevent them from turning into violent revolutionaries. Meanwhile, they would be drawn inextricably into the revived world market system. By being brought into the general system, they would become responsible, just as American unions had during the war. Helping Britain and the remainder of Western Europe would rekindle economic growth, which would stimulate transatlantic trade and, thus, help the American economy in the long run. America had spent enormous sums running up huge deficits in order to sustain the war effort. The result had been astounding and unexpected economic growth. Postwar spending would produce the same effect on a worldwide scale. (Schurmann 1974: 67)

And so it did, but only after Roosevelt's one-world ideology was made operational by Truman's doctrine of two worlds irremediably opposed to one another: an aggressively expansionist Communist world on the one side, and a free world, which only the United States could organize and empower in self-defense on the other. For Roosevelt's one worldism was simply not realistic enough to win the necessary support from the US Congress and US business. The world was too big and too chaotic a place for the United States to reorganize in its image and to its likeness, particularly if this reorganization had to be achieved through organs of world government, as envisaged by Roosevelt, within which the United States would have to compromise continually with the particularistic views of friends and foes alike. The US Congress and the US business community were far too "rational" in their calculations of the financial costs and benefits of US foreign policy to release the means necessary to carry out such an unrealistic plan.

Roosevelt knew that the United States would never adopt free trade unilaterally as Britain had done in the 1840s, and he never proposed such a policy. But even his less radical proposal to create an International Trade Organization (ITO) empowered to reconstruct a system of multi-lateral trade compatible with the objective of promoting and sustaining a global economic expansion, never got past Congress. Congress simply refused to surrender sovereignty on trade issues even to a body that for the foreseeable future was bound to be controlled by US personnel, interests, and ideology. As previously noted, what eventually came into being – the General Agreement on Tariffs and Trade (GATT) created in 1948 – was no more than a forum for the bilateral and multilateral *negotiation* of reductions in tariffs and of other restrictions on inter-national trade. It left the pace of trade liberalization in the hands of national governments. Although the GATT no doubt helped in recon-stituting a multilateral trading system, trade liberalization followed rather than led the world economic expansion of the 1950s and 1960s, in sharp contrast to Britain's unilateral adoption of free trade which preceded and contributed decisively to the mid-nineteenth-century expansion of world trade and production.

Even if international trade had been liberalized more speedily through a unilateral adoption of free trade by the United States or through the action of the stillborn ITO, the extreme centralization of world liquidity, productive capacity, and purchasing power within the jurisdiction of the United States would have constituted a far more serious obstacle to world economic expansion than tariff walls and other governmentally imposed trade restrictions. Unless world liquidity was distributed more evenly, the world could not purchase from the United States the means of production which it needed to supply anything of value to US consumers in whose hands most of the world's *effective* demand was concentrated. But here too, the US Congress was extremely reluctant to relinquish its control over world liquidity as a means to the end of boosting world economic expansion.

In this connection it must be underscored that the world monetary system established at Bretton Woods was far more than a set of technical arrangements aimed at stabilizing parities between select national currencies and at anchoring the ensemble of these parities to production costs via a fixed rate of exchange between the US dollar and gold. Had that been all, the new monetary regime would have simply restored the late nineteenth- and early-twentieth century international gold standard, with the dollar and the Federal Reserve System taking over the role of the pound and of the Bank of England. But that was far from all. Underneath this old technical drapery, a major revolution in the agency and in the mode of "production" of world money occurred (cf. Cohen 1977: 93, 216f).

In all previous world monetary systems – including the British – the circuits and networks of high finance had been firmly in the hands of private bankers and financiers who organized and managed them with a view to making a profit. World money was thus a by-product of profit-making activities. In the world monetary system established at Bretton Woods, in contrast, the "production" of world money was taken over by a network of governmental organizations motivated primarily by considerations of welfare, security, and power – in principle the IMF and the World Bank, in practice the US Federal Reserve System acting in concert with the central banks of the closest and most important of US allies. World money thus became a by-product of state-making activities. As Henry Morgenthau put it in 1945, the security and monetary institutions of the new world order were as complementary as the blades in a pair of scissors (cited in Calleo and Rowland 1973: 87).

Roosevelt and Morgenthau, as the latter once boasted, had indeed succeeded in transferring control over world liquidity from private to public hands and from London and Wall Street to Washington. In this respect, Bretton Woods was a continuation by other means of Roosevelt's earlier break with *haute finance*. In spite of his internationalist pedigree, which included service in the Wilson administration and support for the League of Nations, the main thrust of Roosevelt's New Deal was to free US policies aimed at national economic recovery from subordination to the principles of sound money upheld by London and New York. One of his first decisions as president was the suspension of the dollar's convertibility into gold, which destroyed what was left of the international gold standard. He then mobilized his government in the promotion and management of national economic recovery and overhauled the US banking system. One of the most important reforms – the Glass–Steagall Act of 1933 – separated commercial and investment banking and thereby dealt a fatal blow to the House of Morgan's domination of US financial markets (Frieden 1987: 54–5).

The break with *haute finance* was all but finalized in July 1933 when Roosevelt lashed out at "old fetishes of so-called international bankers" and sabotaged the London Economic Conference, which was attempting to restore some order in the regulation of world money. Wall Street was shocked, as was James Warburg, an influential banker and adviser to the State Department, who submitted his resignation. A few months later, the Roosevelt administration further violated the principles of sound money and international financial cooperation by devaluing the dollar relative to gold in support of US farm prices – a measure that led to the resignation of Acting Treasury Secretary and prominent Wall Street lawyer, Dean Acheson (Frieden 1987: 55).

As the troubles of the US economy eased and the international situation deteriorated further, Roosevelt's internationalist predispositions resurfaced and led to a rapprochement with Wall Street. But in spite of the close cooperation between Washington and Wall Street during the Second World War, at Bretton Woods bankers and financiers were conspicuous by their absence. Washington rather than New York was confirmed as the primary seat of "production" of world money, and security considerations remained paramount in the shaping of the post-war monetary world order.

However, the fact that world liquidity was now centralized in the US banking system enabled the US financial elite to find enough support among economic nationalists in Washington to impose on the Bretton Woods institutions its unshakeable belief in the virtues of sound money in general and of the gold standard in particular (Van Dormael 1978: 97–8, 240–65). As a result, Keynes's and White's original consensus on the need to banish the deflationary bias of the international gold standard and to create a climate of world expansion consistent with the social and economic objectives of the New Deal had little impact on US monetary policies (Gardner 1986: 71–100, 112–14). Although the automaticity of the old gold standard was not restored, the Bretton Woods institutions proved wholly unfit for the task of recycling world liquidity into a renewed expansion of world trade and production (Walter 1991: 152–4).

The only form of redistribution of world liquidity that met with no opposition in Congress was private foreign investment. Indeed, many incentives were created to increase the flow of US capital abroad: tax subsidies, insurance schemes, exchange guarantees, etc. But all these incentives notwithstanding, US capital showed no inclination to break the vicious circle that was constraining its global expansion. Scarce liquidity abroad prevented foreign governments from lifting exchange controls; exchange controls discouraged US capital from going abroad; and small flows of US private foreign investment kept liquidity abroad scarce. As with trade liberalization, US private foreign investment followed rather than led the world economic expansion of the 1950s and 1960s (Block 1977: 114).

As a study group chaired by William Y. Elliott reported in the mid-1950s, the integration of the world economic system could not be achieved again by the same means as in the nineteenth century. "Like nineteenth-century Britain," many claimed, "the United States is a 'mature creditor' and must open its economy freely to imports and must commit itself annually to invest substantial amounts of capital abroad so that it can balance its exports of goods and services at a high level of trade" (Elliott 1955: 43). Plausible as it sounded in principle, in the study group's opinion this prescription overlooked a fundamental difference between the relationship that linked Britain to the nineteenth-century world-economy and the one that linked the United States to the twentieth-century world-economy.

Britain's role was that of a *leading economy*, fully integrated into the world economic system and in large measure making possible its successful functioning owing to Britain's dependence on foreign trade, the pervasive influence of its commercial and financial institutions, and the basic consistency between its national economic policies and those required for world economic integration. In contrast, the United States is a *dominant economy*, only partially integrated into the world economic system, with which it is also partly competitive, and whose accustomed mode and pace of functioning it tends periodically to disturb. No network of American commercial and financial institutions exists to bind together and to manage the day-to-day operations of the world trading system. However essential certain imports may be, foreign trade is in the aggregate not of crucial importance to the American economy. (Elliott 1955: 43; emphasis in the original)

The choice of terms is unfortunate, because the relationships of the British economy to the nineteenth-century world-economy and of the US economy to the twentieth-century world-economy were both relationships of dominance and leadership at the same time. But the gist of the distinction is accurate. It corresponds to the distincion between "extroverted" and "autocentric" national economies introduced for altogether different purposes by Samir Amin. In Amin's scheme of things, the economies of core countries are "autocentric" in the sense that their constituent elements (branches of production, producers and consumers, capital and labor, etc.) are integrated organically into a single national reality, in sharp contrast to the "extroversion" of the constitutent elements of peripheral economies: "in an extroverted economy, [the unity of its constituent elements] is not to be grasped within the national context – this unity is broken, and can be rediscovered only on a world scale" (Amin 1974: 599).

In our scheme of things, the distinction between an extroverted and an autocentric national economy is most useful in the identification of a fundamental structural difference, not between core and peripheral economies, but between the nineteenth-century British regime of accumulation and the successor US regime. In the British regime, the extroversion of the dominant and leading national economy (the British) became the basis of a process of world market formation in which the most important branches of British economic activity developed stronger links of complementarity with the economies of colonial and foreign countries than they did with one another. In the US regime, in contrast, the autocentric nature of the dominant and leading national economy (the US) became the basis of a process of "internalization" of the world market within the organizational domains of giant business corporations, while economic activities in the United States remained organically integrated into a single national reality to a far greater extent than they ever were in nineteenth-century Britain.

This difference between the two regimes was the outcome of a long historical process, in the course of which the US regime came into existence as an integral and subordinate component of the structures of accumulation of the dominant British regime, and then contributed to the destabilization and destruction of these structures, finally to emerge as the new dominant regime. As previously noted, in the half-century following the US Civil War, US business underwent an organizational revolution that gave rise to a large number of vertically integrated, bureaucratically managed corporations, which began expanding transnationally as soon as they had completed their continent-wide integration within the United States. This development constituted a major reversal of the main thrust of the still dominant British regime of accumulation.

Until its terminal crisis, the British regime was and remained primarily a system of small and medium-sized business enterprises. Once large joint-stock chartered companies had done their job of opening up new spheres of overseas trade and investment for British enterprise, they were liquidated. And their revival in the late nineteenth and early twentieth centuries to open up Africa was not accompanied by a corporate reorganization of British business at home comparable to that experienced by German or US business. In the words of P.L. Payne (1974: 20), "there was little movement towards the differentiation of management from ownership, towards the elongation of organizational hierarchies" (see also Chandler 1990: chs 7–9).

In particular, the vertical integration of processes of production and exchange – which became the single most important feature of the US regime of accumulation – played no role in the formation and expansion of the nineteenth-century British regime. On the contrary, the main thrust of the regime was towards the vertical *fission* rather than integration of the sequential sub-processes of production and exchange that linked primary production to final consumption. We have already mentioned the organizational separation of the production and use of capital goods as a central feature of the British "industrial revolution." This separation was accompanied by an analogous tendency in the procurement of raw materials and in the marketing of final products.

From about 1780 to the end of the Napoleonic Wars, leading London and provincial industrialists had ventured into overseas trade, often beginning in the United States and the West Indies where most of the raw cotton of the English textile industry was procured. During the economic depression that followed the end of the war, however, the phenomenon was reduced to insignificance by intensifying competition in overseas trade and increasing specialization in British industry. As export markets became more dispersed and the supplies on which the competitiveness of British industries depended critically came to be procured more economically through volume cash purchases, British manufacturers lost the capability to compete, and indeed interest in competing, in overseas trade. Their capabilities and interests came instead to reside ever more firmly in specialized production in domestic market niches, while the procurement of supplies and the disposal of outputs was left safely and profitably in the hands of equally specialized accepting houses, which promoted the formation and financed the growth of networks of commission agents and small general merchants that spanned the five continents (Chapman 1984: 9–15).

Even in mechanized mass production vertical fission rather than integration was the rule. The rapid spread of machinofacture from spinning to weaving of the second quarter of the nineteenth century was associated with some vertical integration of these sub-processes. But after 1850 the tendency was reversed. Increasingly, spinning, weaving, finishing, and marketing became the separate and specialized domains of different enterprises, often highly localized and specialized even within each branch. As a result, in the last quarter of the nineteenth century the British system of business enterprise was more than ever an ensemble of highly specialized, medium-sized firms held together by a complex web of commercial transactions – a web that was centered on Britain but spanned the entire world (Copeland 1966: 326–9, 371; Hobsbawm 1968: 47–8; Gattrell 1977: 118–20; Crouzet 1982: 204–5, 212).

This highly extroverted, decentralized, and differentiated structure of British business constituted a major obstacle for its corporate reorganization along German or US lines. Not only did it make horizontal combinations in restraint of competition difficult, as already noted by Hilferding (1981: 408), but, in addition, it prevented British business from seizing opportunities to cut unit costs through a closer planning and integration of the sequential activities into which processes of production and exchange were divided:

New assembly techniques, for example, may require new standards of accuracy, hence new equipment, in the plants of subcontractors; more rapid loading facilities may yield far less than their possibilities if carriers do not adjust their methods to the new tempo. In such cases, the allocation of cost and risk poses a serious obstacle, not only because calculation is objectively difficult but even more because human beings are typically suspicious and stubborn in this kind of bargaining situation. (Landes 1969: 335)

In Landes's view, these "burdens of interrelatedness," as he calls them, weighed most heavily on successful early industrializers and were a major reason why in the late nineteenth century British enterprises fell behind both their German and US counterparts in adopting more efficient techniques of production and management. Ironically, the recent rediscovery of the advantages of flexible production systems has led many scholars to detect in the decentralized and differentiated structure of British business a source of competitive advantage, rather than a handicap. Integral here has been a revival of Alfred Marshall's notion of "industrial districts" consisting of spatial clusters of single-unit enterprises which engage in the same line of business but none the less cooperate with one another in drawing from, and continually reconstituting, a local repertoire of technical know-how and business connections. Thanks to this common repertoire, the enterprises operating in an industrial district are the beneficiaries of localized external economies, which enable them to survive and prosper as single-unit undertakings, in spite of continual changes in the demand and supply conditions of the wider domestic and world markets within which they operate (cf. Marshall 1919: 283–8; Becattini 1979; 1990; Sable and Zeitlin 1985).

In Marshall's view the advantages of belonging to local business communities of this kind were such as to account for the persistence of small and medium-sized firms as the representative units of the Lancashire textile industry and the Sheffield metal industry. Our analysis suggests that the entire British regime of accumulation in its domestic, foreign, and colonial ramifications should in fact be conceived of as constituting a world system of flexible specialization, formed through the vertical fission of processes of production and exchange and continually generating for its constituent units external economies that were global in scope. Recast in this wider perspective, the formation and full expansion of the British system of flexible specialization appears to have been the obverse side of the process of consolidation of the entrepôt and imperial functions of the British state.

By becoming the main commercial and financial entrepôt of the world, the British state created unique opportunities for businesses established in its metropolitan domains to specialize in high value-added activities, to obtain inputs from anywhere in the world they happened to be cheapest, and to dispose of outputs anywhere in the world they happened to fetch the highest price. The full exploitation of these opportunities required that the specialization of British business be highly flexible – be such, that is, as to keep the specialized enterprises ready to switch at short notice from one kind of input–output combination to another in response to changes in the value-added hierarchy of economic activities and in the comparative advantages of different locales of the world-economy as sources of inputs or outlets for outputs. This flexibility did, of course, keep the industrial structure in a permanent state of flux, and thereby prevented British business from developing a "technological rationality" comparable to that of German or US business. But British business could not have it both ways, and its strictly "pecuniary rationality" was and remained the best strategy for a business community fortunate enough to be situated at the nerve centre of world trade and finance.

It was also the best strategy for a business community that was positioned at the center of a world-encompassing territorial empire. Privileged access to the supplies, markets, and liquidity of the empire endowed Britain with great flexibility in the investment of capital anywhere in the world it promised to yield the highest return. Flexibility in the world-wide investment of capital, in turn, further consolidated Britain's role as the central entrepôt of world trade and finance. As Britain's industries began to lose out in world markets not just to Germany and the United States, but to a host of other countries –

including India, which began to "re-industrialize" during the Great Depression – "her finance triumphed, her services as shipper, trader and intermediary in the world's system of payments, became more indispensable. Indeed if London ever was the real economic hub of the world, the pound sterling its foundation, it was between 1870 and 1913" (Hobsbawm 1968: 125).

In short, the flexible specialization and pecuniary rationality of British market capitalism were the expression of the world entrepôt and imperial functions of the British state. The profitability of the constituent units of the system depended critically on being supplied by the whole world so as to supply the whole world again and also on political control over a territorial empire that provided the means – the liquidity, the markets, the material supplies, as the case may be – necessary to keep the world tied to the British entrepôt. To the extent that world commercial and financial intermediation, buttressed by imperial tribute, was more profitable than, or as profitable as, industrial production, the emergence of new industrial centers did not in itself pose any threat to the British business community as a whole. And to the extent that these new industrial centers competed with one another for the services of British business in the procurement of their inputs or in the disposal of their outputs – as most did at the turn of the century – their emergence and expansion benefited more than they penalized British business.

In an address to the Institute of Bankers in 1899, geopolitician Halford Mackinder summed up very well the positional advantage of British business in the changing spatial configuration of industrial and commercial activities:

> While it seems that industrial activity and commerce will tend to become decentralized, it will become more and more important that there should be a single clearing house.... It does not follow that there should be, along with decentralization, an actual fall of [industrial] activity in our islands; but it appears to be inevitable that there shoud be a relative fall. But the world's clearing house tends, from its very nature, to remain in the single position, and that clearing house will always be where there is the greatest ownership of capital. This gives the real key to the struggle between our free trade policy and the protection of other countries – we are essentially the people with capital, and those who have capital always share in the activity of brains and muscles of other countries. (Quoted in Hugill 1993: 305)

Like the German variant, the US variant of corporate capitalism developed in response to the world-wide intensification of competitive pressures that ensued from the full expansion of this UK-centered world market economy. It is no historical accident that both variants emerged simultaneously in the course of the Great Depression of 1873–96. As in Germany, so also in the United States the intensification of competitive pressures convinced businessmen, politicians, and intellectuals that a regime of unrestricted competition among atomized units delivered neither social stability nor indeed market efficiency:

> The competitive market, left to itself, yielded not the harmonies of Frédéric Bastiat, not the equilibriums of Jean-Baptiste Say, not the steady accumulation and investment of capital, not the balancing of supply and demand at high levels of employment of labor and resources, but market disorganization, "wastes of competition," business failures, recurrent depressions, strikes and lockouts, social distemper, and political upheaval.... By the mid-1890s, in the midst of the third long depression in three successive decades, a revulsion against the unregulated market spread among the bourgeoisie in all major sectors of the economy. Whatever their programmatic differences, farmers, manufacturers, bankers, and merchants, in addition to already disenchanted railway capitalists, found a common ground in the idea that unregulated competitive market activity resulted in production of goods and services in excess of effective demand at prices that returned reasonable earnings to producers of normal efficiency. (Sklar 1988: 53–4)

As predicted by Adam Smith a century earlier, the intensification of competitive pressures inherent in processes of market formation was driving profits down to a barely "tolerable" level. That the outcome had been predicted was of course of no consolation to US businessmen. Manufacturers in particular, wrote Edward S. Meade in 1900, were "tired of working for the public." In periods of depression even the stronger enterprises hardly attained a tolerable profit margin. Under these circumstances, it was only natural that manufacturers would seek "to stop this worrisome struggle, whose benefits are nearly all of them gained by the consumer in low prices.... They want a larger profit without such a desperate struggle to get it" (quoted in Sklar 1988: 56).

Initially, the attempt to stop the competitive struggle had resulted in a restructuring of business in the United States in the same direction as in Germany, namely, towards the formation of horizontal combinations in restraint of competition and towards an increasing dominance of a small group of private financial institutions which had grown through investments in railway companies and related industrial enterprises. In the United States, however, these nationwide associations of manufacturers largely failed to attain their objectives long before they were declared illegal in 1890 by the Sherman Antitrust Act; and the dominance of financial institutions never went far beyond the construction and operation of railroad systems (Chandler 1977: 317, 335, 187).

Then, in the 1880s and 1890s, the changing structures of German and

US business began to diverge radically. In both countries the centralization of capital gained momentum. In Germany opportunities to pursue
vertical integration – integration, that is, of a firm's operations with those
of its suppliers and customers – were rapidly exhausted and the main
thrust of the centralization of capital became horizontal integration
(Landes 1966: 109–10) – integration, that is, of competing firms. In the
United States, in contrast, the main thrust of the centralization of capital
became vertical integration. As underscored by Chandler (1977; 1978;
1990), ineffectual, unpopular, and eventually illegal horizontal combinations were abandoned, and in branch after branch of the US domestic
economy, ranging from cigarettes and canned meat to office and
agricultural machinery, select business enterprises moved towards integrating within their organizational domains the sequential sub-processes
of production and exchange that linked the procurement of primary
inputs to the disposal of final outputs. The transaction costs, risks, and
uncertainties involved in moving inputs/outputs through the sequence of
these sub-processes were thus internalized within single multi-unit
enterprises and subjected to the economizing logic of administrative
action and long-term corporate planning.

Contrary to widespread opinion, the variant of corporate capitalism
that emerged during the Great Depression of 1873–96 in the United
States constituted a far more effective and radical departure from the
dominant British regime of market capitalism than the variant that
emerged at about the same time in Germany. Both kinds of corporate
capitalism developed in reaction to the "excessive" competition and
disruptions that ensued from the unfolding of the UK-centered process of
world market formation. But whereas the German variant merely
suspended the process, the US variant truly *superseded* it.

The difference between a true supersession and a mere suspension of
the process of world market formation can be elucidated by recasting in
world system perspective John K. Galbraith's discussion of the various
ways in which large-scale, bureaucratically managed, industrial organizations (his "technostructures") can protect themselves from the disruptions of price-making markets. Like Veblen, Galbraith detects a
fundamental contradiction between the pecuniary rationality involved in
profit-maximization in a self-regulating market and the technological
rationality involved in the use of expensive and specialized industrial
facilities and personnel:

> The market has only one message for the business firm. That is the promise of
> more money. If the firm has no influence on its prices ... it has no options as
> to the goals that it pursues. It must try to make money, and, as a practical
> matter, it must try to make as much as possible. Others do. To fail to conform

is to invite loss, failure and extrusion from the business. (Galbraith 1985: 116)

However, modern industry with its specialized technology and companion commitments of capital and time forced business to emancipate itself from the uncertainties of the market. Prices and the amounts to be sold or bought at those prices must somehow be subjected to the authority of corporate planning. If they are not,

> there is risk of loss from uncontrolled price movements, and there is no reliable number by which units of product and input can be multiplied to get projected income and outlay. If these estimates are not available in reliable form, there is a large random element in decisions as to what to produce, and with what and by what means, and there is total uncertainty as to the outcome – whether there will be profit or loss and in what dimension. (Galbraith 1985: 206)

The replacement of the market by the authoritative determination of prices and of the amounts to be sold and bought at these prices so essential to industrial planning can occur in three ways: by "controlling," by "suspending," and by "superseding" the market. The market is controlled when the independence of action of those to whom the planning unit sells or from whom it buys is reduced or eliminated. Formally, the process of buying and selling remains intact, but the large market share of a particular unit or groups of units ensures a highly cooperative posture on the part of suppliers and/or customers. "The option of eliminating a market is an important source of power for controlling it" (Galbraith 1985: 29–30).

The market is suspended when the planning unit enters into contracts specifying prices and amounts to be provided and bought over long periods of time. A matrix of contracts thus comes into existence "by which each firm eliminates market uncertainty for other firms and, in turn, gives them some of its uncertainty." Although at all times and places business enterprises enter into open or tacit agreements of this kind, the main agencies in the suspension of markets have been governments engaged in the procurement and development of means of war- and state-making. "Here the state guarantees a price sufficient, with suitable margin, to cover costs. And it undertakes to buy what is produced or to compensate fully in the case of contract cancellation, technical failure or absence of demand. Thus, effectively, it suspends the market with all its associated uncertainty" (Galbraith 1985: 31–2).

Finally, the market is superseded by vertical integration. "The planning unit takes over the source of supply or the outlet; a transaction that is subject to bargaining over prices and amounts is thus replaced with a transfer within the planning unit." This internalization within the planning unit of transactions previously carried out in the market does not eliminate market uncertainty altogether, because the planning unit still has to compete for the primary inputs that it cannot itself produce and the purchasing power of the final consumers. It does none the less replace the large and unmanageable uncertainty associated with the market regulation of the sequential sub-processes of production with the smaller and more manageable uncertainties associated with the procurement of primary inputs and the disposal of final outputs (Galbraith 1985: 28–9).

In Galbraith's scheme of things, the control, suspension, and supersession of markets strengthen one another in providing the techno-structures of modern corporations with the protection from market uncertainties that is essential to their very existence and enlarged reproduction. As we shall see, a mutual strengthening of this kind has indeed been at the roots of the rise to world dominance of corporate capitalism, US style. Nevertheless, the *differentia specifica* of US corporate capitalism in world system perspective was neither control over nor suspension of the market but its supersession.

Control over the world market was the specificity of British capitalism. The world market of the nineteenth century was a British creation, which British business and the British government jointly controlled from the moment of its making during and immediately after the Napoleonic Wars to the moment of its unmaking during and immediately after the First World War. In the last analysis, the main reason why British capitalism did not undergo a corporate reorganization of the German or US variety is that such a reorganization was neither feasible nor advisable. For the self-expansion of British capital was always embedded in a process of world market formation which made all its most important branches dependent on foreign and colonial supplies and/or outlets. To delink from such supplies and outlets in favor of domestic horizontal or vertical integration, if at all possible, would have deprived British business of the main source of its profitability and the British government of the main source of its power.

Control is not too strong a word to designate Britain's relationship to the world market in the nineteenth century. Indeed, if by market we understand the place where demand and supply meet, then Britain *was* the world market since its governmental and business institutions were the chief intermediaries between the producers and the consumers of the world. The more intensely the producers (consumers) of the world competed for markets (supplies), the greater were the options open to British business to substitute sources of supply (markets) for one another, and hence the greater its power to control the world market. British business never got "tired to work for the public," as US manufacturers did, because the entire world worked for British business.

Needless to say, Britain's power to control the world market was not unlimited. It was limited most immediately by the countervailing power of some states to *suspend* the operation of the world market. A suspension of the world market was indeed the specificity of corporate capitalism, German style. The horizontal integration of Germany's national industries and the active intervention of the central government in support of the cohesion, modernization, and expansion of the resulting technostructure transformed Imperial Germany into the paradigm of centrally planned ("organized") capitalism. But as Hilferding himself was careful to point out, this reorganization of German business merely suspended rather than superseded market competition.

From being "a defensive weapon of the weak," tariffs quickly turned into "an offensive weapon in the hands of the powerful" – means of realizing extra profits on the domestic market with which to subsidize dumping abroad, or means with which to negotiate from a position of strength the opening up of foreign markets. The seeming supersession of competition in the domestic market and its intensification in the world market were two sides of the same coin: "capital ... detests the anarchy of competition and wants organization, though ... only to resume competition on a still higher level" (Hilferding 1981: 310, 334).

This competition on a higher level tended to divide the world market ever more deeply into distinct territorial domains and thus increase the importance of the size of the economic space enclosed by each domain in determining the outcome of the competitive struggle.

> The larger and the more populous the economic territory, [other things being equal] the larger the individual plant can be, the lower the costs of production, and the greater the degree of specialization within the plant, which also reduces costs of production. The larger the economic territory, the more easily can industry be located where the natural conditions are most favorable and the productivity is highest. The more extensive the territory, the more diversified its production and the more probable it is that the various branches of production will complement one another and that transport costs on imports from abroad will be saved. (Hilferding 1981: 311)

In other words, business enterprises operating within the domains of a state that controlled a large and diversified territory had better opportunities than enterprises operating within the domains of a territorially smaller and less diversified state of reaping internal economies – economies, that is, due to the "technical" division of labor within the enterprises themselves – or of compensating lesser internal economies with external economies – economies, that is, due to a "social" division of labor among enterprises. This is indeed the single most important reason why British market capitalism was eventually superseded not by the German but by the US variant of corporate capitalism. No matter how centralized and "organized" German capital became, it could not compensate for the much greater external economies that British capital enjoyed by virtue of the extent and variety of the territorial domains encompassed by Britain's formal and informal empire.

Although the transformation of Germany into "one big factory" could not compensate for the external economies enjoyed by British capital, it did none the less raise tremendously the defense costs of the world empire on which those economies rested. Once Germany mobilized its powerful military–industrial apparatus in its quest for *Lebensraum*, the viability of the British regime of accumulation was undermined irremediably. What the First World War demonstrated above all was that British capital needed a territorial empire more than ever, and yet it could no longer afford it.

US capital, in contrast, did not need such an empire to emerge victorious from the escalating competitive struggle. Between 1803 and 1853 purchases and conquests had more than doubled the territory of the United States, which became continental in scope. Shortly afterward, the civil war (1860–65) settled the dispute between the southern states – which favored the continuation of territorial expansion in the Caribbean and a closer integration of the United States within Britain's world market system – and the northern states – which favored a reorientation of US strategic concerns from outward territorial expansion to the integration of the acquired territories into a cohesive national economy. The victory of the northern states led to a swift move in the latter direction. The main military objective of the government became the wresting of the continent from the native Indian population, following Benjamin Franklin's long-standing prescription, while legislation passed during or immediately after the civil war promoted the centralization of banking, the protection of domestic industries through a sharp increase in tariffs, the settlement and exploitation of land, the formation of transcontinental railway and telegraph systems, and the inflow of immigrants from Europe (cf. Williams 1969: 185–93).

As a result more land was occupied by farmers, cattle-breeders, and speculators in the thirty years that followed the civil war than in the previous three centuries. The ensuing rapid expansion of primary production, in turn, created the supply and demand conditions for the complementary formation of a larger and diversified national industrial apparatus. Although industries producing for the highly protected and rapidly expanding domestic market became the main loci of capital accumulation in the United States, the continuing expansion of this market depended critically on the sale abroad of a large and growing agricultural surplus:

> By 1870 the American economy depended so much upon foreign markets for the agricultural surplus that the ups and downs for the next thirty years can be traced to the success or failure of marketing each year's wheat and cotton crop. No matter how many markets could be found, more always seemed to be needed. (LaFeber 1963: 9–10; see also Williams 1969: 201)

On the eve of the Great Depression of 1873–96 the relationship of the US domestic economy to the British world market system was thus somewhat analogous to that of the German domestic economy, because German economic expansion also had hitherto depended critically on the export of its agricultural surplus. And yet, during the Great Depression the two relationships began to diverge radically. For the US state enclosed an economic space that was not only much larger and more diversified, but also far more malleable than the economic space enclosed by Imperial Germany – a space, that is, that could be depopulated and repopulated to suit the requirements of high-tech agricultural production more easily than the smaller and more densely populated German economic space could. In the course of the Great Depression, this competitive advantage translated into the progressive displacement in the world market of German by US agricultural surpluses so that the already larger US domestic market grew much faster than Germany's.

Other things being equal, the control and suspension of competition in a large and dynamic market are more problematic than in a smaller and less dynamic market. But a large and dynamic market endowed with the full complement of natural resources needed to satisfy the consumers' wants offers greater opportunities to supersede competition through vertical integration than a smaller, less dynamic, and not so well-endowed market. In fact, in some US industries success in superseding the market was a direct result of the difficulties met in controlling or suspending competition. In the words of an annual report of a company formed through a merger of three regional consolidations (The National Biscuit Company),

> when this company started, it was believed that we must control competition, and that to do this we must either fight competition or buy it. The first meant a ruinous war of prices and great loss of profits; the second, constantly increasing capitalization. Experience soon proved to us that, instead of bringing success, either of these courses, if persevered in, must bring disaster. This led us to reflect whether it was necessary to control competition.... We soon satisfied ourselves that within the company itself we must look for success. (quoted in Chandler 1977: 335)

Looking for success within the company itself meant above all taking over from the market the integration and coordination of the physical flow of commodities from the purchase of primary inputs to the sale of final outputs. This was true not just for the undertakings that had arisen out of horizontal combinations, like the National Biscuit Company or the powerful Standard Oil, but also for a large number of individual enterprises operating in industries in which horizontal combinations never went very far. As underscored by Alfred Chandler in the passages quoted at the beginning of this chapter, this internalization within a single organizational domain of the sequential sub-processes of production that linked specific primary inputs to specific final outputs generated considerable "economies of speed," which in turn endowed the pioneering vertically integrated, multi-unit enterprises with abundant and steady cash flows. As these cash flows were plowed back in the formation of specialized hierarchies of top and middle managers, imposing organizational barriers to the entry of new competitors were erected in branch after branch of the US domestic economy. As a result, the enterprises that had pioneered the supersession of the market through vertical integration also acquired the power to control or suspend competition in the procurement of primary inputs and in the disposal of final outputs, that is, in markets that were unprofitable or altogether impossible to internalize.

Contrary to Hilferding's predictions, the emergence of this kind of corporate structure in the United States – rather than the emergence of state monopoly capitalism, German style – became the effective foundation of a new stage of capitalism on a world scale. To be sure, US corporate capitalism's rise to world dominance was an integral aspect of the process of transformation of inter-capitalist competition as theorized by Hilferding. In particular, the US government and US business were from the very start vanguards of the protectionist movement which eventually destroyed the British world market system and led world capitalism to retreat into the "igloos" of its national economies and associated empires. The huge hike of US tariffs passed during the Civil War was followed by further increases in 1883, 1890, 1894, and 1897. Although minor cuts were introduced by President Wilson in 1913, these were tolerated by Congress only as long as the war reduced competition from foreign imports and boosted US exports. But as soon as the war was over and the first indicators of a recession made their appearance, the US protectionist tradition was resumed in earnest. Major increases in tariffs were enacted in the early 1920s in response to commercial adversity, prefiguring the astronomical Smoot–Hawley tariff of 1930. Moreover, as Hilferding theorized, US protectionism in this period became increasingly a means of compensating dumping abroad with extra profit at home and, above all, of negotiating from a position of strength the opening of foreign markets – first and foremost Latin American markets – to US exports and investment.

Contrary to Hilferding's generalizations, however, US finance capital played no role whatsoever in fostering US protectionism. The New York financial community in particular consistently preached the virtues of free trade and did all that was in its power to induce the US government to assume leadership and responsibility in countering the destruction of the world market. "The world has become so interdependent in its economic life that measures adopted by one nation affect the prosperity of others," wrote a Wall Street banker and former Under Secretary of State, Norman Davis, on the eve of the Great Crash of 1929. "The units of the world economy," he added, "must work together, or rot separately" (quoted in Frieden 1987: 50).

Ideally and practically, US finance capital thus stood to the very end in defense of the collapsing British world market system and never became the agency of supersession of that system as Hilferding posited. The leading and dominant agency of that supersession was not finance capitalism as such in any of its variants, but the corporate capitalism that emerged in the United States through the formation of vertically integrated, bureaucratically managed, multi-unit business enterprises. Once these enterprises had consolidated themselves within the large, diversified, self-sufficient, dynamic, and well-protected economic space enclosed by the US state, they came to enjoy decisive competitive advantages in the world-economy at large relative to both market capitalism British style, and corporate capitalism German style.

As a national ensemble, US corporations combined the advantages of extensive "technical" division of labor (internal economies) with the advantages of extensive "social" division (external economies) to a much greater degree than either single-unit British business or horizontally integrated German business. The economic space enclosed by Imperial Germany was not sufficiently large, diversified, or dynamic to enable German business to compensate for the greater external economies enjoyed by British business with greater internal economies. But the economic space enclosed by the United States enabled US business to realize a highly effective synthesis of the advantages of planning and market regulation.

Moreover, by expanding transnationally as soon as they had completed their domestic continental integration, US corporations became so many "Trojan horses" in the domestic markets of other states as to mobilize foreign resources and purchasing power to the benefit of their own bureaucratic expansion. US corporate capital thus benefited in two related and mutually reinforcing ways from the protectionist movement that was ripping apart the British world market. It benefited through its control of the largest, most dynamic, and best protected among the national economies into which the world market was being divided; and it benefited through its superior ability to neutralize and turn to its own advantage the protectionism of other states by means of foreign direct investment.

In the light of all this, it is not surprising that the US government paid little attention to the demands of the New York financial community for a reversal of the United States' protectionist tradition. Norman Davis and other spokesmen for Wall Street were of course highly prescient in foreseeing that the unwillingness of nations to "work together" within the disintegrating world market meant that the nations would soon "rot separately." Nevertheless, it did not follow from this diagnosis that it was in the power or indeed in the national interest of the United States to reverse the final demise of the nineteenth-century world market system and to prevent the nations of the world from rotting separately. The world market system was collapsing under the weight of its own contradictions – including the unwaivering support of the London and New York financial communities for the gold standard. It is highly doubtful whether the US or any other government could have saved the system from its own self-destructiveness. But even assuming that there was something that the US government could have done, it is even more doubtful that the persistence of the old regime of accumulation would have resulted in as great a leap forward in US wealth and power as actually ensued from its final breakdown.

US corporate capitalism thus was and remained a powerful agency of the destruction of the structures of accumulation of British market capitalism and of the centralization in the United States of the liquidity, purchasing power, and productive capacity of the world-economy. But once the destruction and centralization had become as complete as they possibly could, US corporate business was powerless to create the conditions of its own self-expansion in a chaotic world. No tax subsidy, insurance scheme, or exchange guarantee was sufficient to overcome the fundamental asymmetry between the cohesiveness and wealth of the US domestic market and the fragmentation and poverty of foreign markets.

These were the structural roots of the impasse which after the Second World War prevented the recycling of liquidity back into the expansion of world trade and production. Eventually, the impasse was broken by the "invention" of the Cold War. What cost–benefit calculations could not and did not achieve, fear did. As long as surplus capital stagnated within the United States and its regional hinterland (Canada and Latin America), chaos in Eurasia continued to escalate and create a fertile ground for the takeover of state power by revolutionary forces. The genius of Truman and of his advisers was to attribute the outcome of systemic circumstances which no particular agency had created or controlled to the allegedly subversive dispositions of the other military superpower, the USSR. By so doing, Truman reduced Roosevelt's vision of a global New Deal to a very shoddy reality indeed, but at least made it workable.

The building up of Western Europe and of Japan as bastions and showpieces of the free world was a far more concrete and attainable objective than the remaking of the entire world in the American image. Moreover, President Truman and Under Secretary of State Acheson well knew that fear of a global communist menace worked much better than any appeal to *raison d'état* or to cost–benefit calculations in spurring to action legislators better known for fiscal prudence than for interest in world affairs:

> [E]arly drafts of Truman's message, prepared by State Department staffers, candidly stressed economic factors. "Two great wars and an intervening world depression," began the first draft, "have weakened the [capitalist] system almost everywhere except in the United States.... If, by default, we permit free enterprise to disappear in other countries of the world, the very existence of our democracy will be gravely threatened." Both President Truman and Under Secretary of State Acheson remarked that the draft "made the whole thing sound like an investment prospectus." Accordingly, they redrafted the document to provide its more biting tone.... When Secretary of State Marshall was wired a copy of the final message ... even he wondered if the speech might not be "overstating the case a bit." The President's reply spoke reams about crisis-management on the home front: "it was clear that this was the only way in which the measure could be passed." Following the famed advice of Arthur Vandenberg, the President had indeed "scared hell out of the American people." What worked for the Truman Doctrine would prove recyclable for the Marshall Plan as well: (McCormick 1989: 77–8)

The Marshall Plan initiated the remaking of Western Europe in the American image and, directly and indirectly, made a decisive contribution to the "take-off" of the expansion of world trade and production of the 1950s and 1960s. However, its very objective of fostering the formation of a United States of Europe was seriously hampered throughout the late 1940s by the continuing dollar shortage. Balance of payment difficulties compounded national jealousies in preventing progress within the Organization for European Economic Cooperation (OEEC) in general, and in European inter-state monetary cooperation in particular (Bullock 1983: 532–41, 659–61, 705–9, 720–3).

European integration and world economic expansion required a far more comprehensive recycling of world liquidity than that involved in the Marshall Plan and other aid programs. This more comprehensive recycling eventually materialized through the most massive rearmament effort the world had ever seen in peacetime. As its architects, Secretary of State Acheson and Policy Planning Staff chief Paul Nitze, realized, only an effort of this kind could overcome the limits of the Marshall Plan:

[Acheson and Nitze] saw neither European integration nor currency realignments as adequate to maintain a significant export surplus or to continue American–European economic ties after the end of the Marshall Plan. The new line of policy they proposed – massive U.S. and European rearmament – provided a brilliant solution to the major problems of US economic policy. Domestic rearmament would provide a new means to sustain demand so that the economy would no longer be dependent on maintaining an export surplus. Military aid to Europe would provide a means to continue providing aid to Europe after the expiration of the Marshall Plan. And the close integration of European and American military forces would provide a means to prevent Europe as an economic region from closing itself off from the United States. (Block 1977: 103–4)

This new line of policy was proposed to the National Security Council in early 1950, and its position document (NSC-68) was examined and approved in principle by President Truman in April. The document gave no precise data on the costs involved, but estimates by staff were in the order of yearly expenditures three times the amount originally requested by the Pentagon for 1950:

How to get that kind of money from a fiscally conservative Congress, even in the name of anticommunism, presented no small task for the administration. What was required was an international emergency, and since November 1949, Secretary Acheson had been predicting that one would occur sometime in 1950 in the Asian rimlands – in Korea, Vietnam, Taiwan, or all three. Two months after the President examined NSC-68, that crisis happened. Acheson was to say later, "Korea came along and saved us." (McCormick 1989: 98)

Massive rearmament during and after the Korean War solved once and for all the liquidity problems of the post-war world-economy. Military aid to foreign governments and direct US military expenditures abroad – both of which grew constantly between 1950 and 1958 and again between 1964 and 1973 – provided the world-economy with all the liquidity that it needed to expand. And with the US government acting as a highly permissive world central bank, world trade and production did expand at unprecedented rates (cf. Calleo 1970: 86–7; Gilpin 1987: 133–4).

According to McCormick (1989: 99) the 23-year period inaugurated by the Korean War and concluded by the Paris Peace Accords in early 1973, which virtually ended the Vietnam War, was "the most sustained and

profitable period of economic growth in the history of world capitalism."
This is the same period that Stephen Marglin and Juliet Schor (1991),
among others, have called "the Golden Age of Capitalism":

> There is little doubt that the quarter century following post-World War II
> reconstruction was a period of unprecedented prosperity and expansion for
> the world economy. Between 1950 and 1975 income per person in the
> developing countries increased on average by 3 per cent p.a., accelerating from
> 2 per cent in the 1950s to 3.4 per cent in the 1960s. This rate of growth was
> historically unprecedented for these countries and in excess of that achieved by
> the developed countries in their period of industrialization.... In the devel-
> oped countries themselves ... GDP and GDP per head grew almost twice as
> fast as in any previous period since 1820. Labour productivity grew twice as
> fast as ever before, and there was a massive acceleration in the rate of growth
> of the capital stock. The increase in capital stock represented an investment
> boom of historically unprecedented length and vigour. (Glyn et al. 1991:
> 41–2)

There is little doubt that the rate of expansion of the capitalist world-
economy as a whole at this time was exceptional by historical standards.
Whether it was also the best of times for historical capitalism so as to
warrant its designation as *the* golden age of capitalism is another matter.
It is not at all clear, for example, whether it was more of a golden age than
Eric Hobsbawm's "Age of Capital" (1848–75) which late nineteenth-
century observers thought to have had no precedent since the Age of the
Great Discoveries (see chapter 3). If we take average yearly rates of
growth of GDP, or of the more elusive entity "capital stock," over the
25-year period 1950–75 and compare them with those of the 50-year
period 1820–70, as Andrew Glyn and his co-authors do, it would seem
so. But these indicators are biased in favor of production in a narrow
sense and against trade. Were we to choose indicators with opposite
biases and compare the period 1950–75 with the period of equal length,
1848–73, performances in the two "golden ages" may appear to have
been not all that different.

Be that as it may, from the perspective adopted in this study the 1950s
and 1960s, like the 1850s and 1860s, constitute another (MC) phase of
material expansion of the capitalist world-economy – a period, that is,
during which surplus capital was thrown back into commodity trade and
production on a sufficiently massive scale to create the conditions of
renewed cooperation and division of labor within and among the separate
governmental and business organizations of the capitalist world-
economy. To be sure, the speed, scale, and scope of the conversion of
surplus capital into commodities were greater in the US cycle than in any
previous cycle. Nevertheless, the phase of material expansion of the

1950s and 1960s resembled all the others in one key respect: its very unfolding resulted in a major intensification of competitive pressures on each and every governmental and business organization of the capitalist world-economy and in a consequent massive withdrawal of money capital from trade and production.

The switch occurred in the critical years 1968–73. It was during these years that deposits in the so-called Eurodollar or Eurocurrency market experienced a sudden upward jump followed by twenty years of explosive growth. And it was during these same six years that the system of fixed parities between the main national currencies and the US dollar and between the US dollar and gold, which had been in force throughout the phase of material expansion, was abandoned in favor of the system of flexible or floating exchange rates – a system which some (e.g. Aglietta 1979b: 831) regard not as a system at all, but as the form taken by the crisis of the pre-existing system.

These were distinct but mutually reinforcing developments. On the one hand, the accumulation of a growing mass of world liquidity in deposits that no government controlled put increasing pressure on governments to manipulate the exchange rates of their currencies and interest rates in order to attract or repel liquidity held in offshore markets to counter shortages or surfeits in their domestic economies. On the other hand, continuous changes in exchange rates among the main national currencies and in rate of interest differentials multiplied the opportunities for capital held in offshore money markets to expand through trade and speculation in currencies.

As a result of these mutually reinforcing developments, by the mid-1970s the volume of purely monetary transactions carried out in offshore money markets already exceeded the value of world trade many times over. From then on the financial expansion became unstoppable. According to one estimate, by 1979 foreign exchange trading amounted to $17.5 trillion, or more than eleven times the total value of world trade ($1.5 trillion); five years later, foreign exchange trading had ballooned to $35 trillion, or almost twenty times the total value of world trade, which had also increased but only by 20 per cent (Gilpin 1987: 144). According to another estimate, yearly transactions in the London Eurodollar market alone were six times the value of world trade in 1979 but about twenty-five times seven years later (Walter 1991: 196–7).

"Revolution," suggests Robert Gilpin (1987: 144), might not be too strong a term to characterize this change in world economic circumstances. Andrew Walter (1991: 200) has no doubts that this is indeed a most appropriate characterization. In his view,

what is most striking about the last few decades is the liberalization of capital flows between the major countries and the incredible growth of the Euro-markets, which has averaged about 30 per cent per year since the 1960s. This has so far outstripped the growth of global trade and output that financial flows now utterly dominate real flows between countries in quantitative terms.

These changes he calls "the global financial revolution."

The Dynamics of Global Crisis

We are thus back to the seemingly revolutionary transformations undergone by world capitalism since about 1970. Recast in the perspective adopted in this study, the financial expansion of the 1970s and 1980s does indeed appear to be the predominant tendency of processes of capital accumulation on a world scale. But it does not appear to be a "revolutionary" tendency at all. Financial expansions of this kind have recurred since the fourteenth century as the characteristic reaction of capital to the intensification of competitive pressures which have invariably ensued from all major expansions of world trade and production. The scale, scope, and technical sophistication of the current financial expansion are, of course, much greater than those of previous financial expansions. But the greater scale, scope, and technical sophistication are nothing but the continuation of a well-established tendency of the *longue durée* of historical capitalism towards the formation of ever more powerful blocs of governmental and business organizations as leading agencies of capital accumulation on a world scale.

The formation of these more powerful blocs has always been an integral aspect of the crisis and contradictions of the previously dominant bloc. In order to grasp the logic of the ongoing transformation of world capitalism, we must therefore focus on the crisis and contradictions of the disintegrating US regime. This has proceeded much further than the recent triumphs of US capitalism over Soviet communism may seem to imply. Increasingly, these triumphs look like yet another one of those "wonderful moments" that, as a rule, have intervened between the signal and terminal crises of all dominant regimes of accumulation. Faster than under any previous regime, the *belle époque* of the US regime, the Reagan era, has come and gone, having deepened rather than solved the contradictions that underlay the preceding signal crisis.

The coming crisis of the US regime was signalled between 1968 and 1973 in three distinct and closely related spheres. Militarily, the US army got into ever more serious troubles in Vietnam; financially, the US Federal Reserve found it difficult and then impossible to preserve the mode of production and regulation of world money established at Bretton Woods; and ideologically, the US government's anti-communist crusade began losing legitimacy both at home and abroad. The crisis deteriorated quickly, and by 1973 the US government had retreated on all fronts.

For the rest of the 1970s, US strategies of power came to be characterized by a basic neglect of world governmental functions. It was as if the ruling groups within the United States had decided that, since the world could no longer be governed by them, it should be left to govern itself. The result was a further destabilization of what was left of the post-war world order and a steep decline of US power and prestige through the Iranian Revolution and the hostage crisis of 1980.

The take-off of the current phase of financial expansion of the US-centered capitalist world-economy was an integral and early aspect of this crisis. It began in 1968, when the growth of liquid funds held in the London-centered Eurodollar market experienced a sudden and explosive acceleration. As a result of this explosive growth, by 1971 the US government was forced to abandon the fiction of the gold–dollar exchange standard, and by 1973 the US Federal Reserve and associated central banks had to acknowledge defeat in their struggle to stem the tide of mounting speculation against the regime of fixed exhange rates which had dominated high finance during the phase of material expansion of the 1950s and 1960s. From then on the market – that is, primarily, the Eurodollar market – became the master of the process that fixed the prices of national currencies in relation to one another and to gold.

The formation of the Eurodollar or Eurocurrency market was the unintended outcome of the expansion of the US regime of accumulation. An embryonic "dollar deposit-market" first came into existence in the 1950s as a direct result of the Cold War. Communist countries had to keep dollar balances for their trade with the West, but could not risk depositing these balances in the United States lest the US government should freeze them. The balances were thus deposited in European banks, mostly in London, which initially redeposited the funds in US banks. Soon, however, London banks realized the advantages of holding the funds in the form of what came to be known as Eurocurrencies – currencies, that is, "held and used outside the country where they have status of legal tender" (Versluysen 1981: 16, 22).

Communist dollar balances were very small and Eurocurrency markets would never have become a dominant factor in world finance were it not for the massive migration of US corporate capital to Europe in the late 1950s and early 1960s. Large US multinationals were among the most important depositors in the New York money market. It was only natural, therefore, that the largest among New York's banks would promptly enter the Eurodollar market, not just to take advantage of the lower costs and greater freedom of action afforded by offshore banking, but also to avoid major losses in deposits. And so they did, controlling a 50 per cent share of the Eurodollar business by 1961 (de Cecco 1982: 11).

An organizational structure thus developed which for all practical purposes was beyond the control of the system of central banks that regulated the supply of world money in accordance with the regime of fixed exchange rates established at Bretton Woods. As long as this regime was buttressed by large US gold reserves and by a sizeable current surplus in the US balance of payments, the development of the Eurodollar market helped rather than hindered the domestic and foreign power pursuits of the US government. It strengthened the role of the dollar as world money, it eased the global expansion of US corporate capital, and it made this expansion financially self-sufficient through borrowing in Europe.

Sooner or later, however, the joint expansion of US corporate activities abroad and of Eurocurrency markets was bound to enter into contradiction with the national foundations of US power:

> The revitalization of American international banking threatened to undermine the political agreements that had made it possible. Domestic political opposition to international economic integration after World War II had been defused in two ways: first, economic internationalism was presented as crucial to national security; second, economic internationalism was presented as essential to domestic prosperity. In the early 1960s, international financial integration began to come into conflict with both national security and domestic prosperity. (Frieden 1987: 83)

The conflict first emerged in 1963, when the Kennedy administration attempted to counter the pressure that US liabilities to foreign public and private institutions exercised on the declining US gold reserves by putting restrictions on US foreign lending and investment. Total US liabilities to "foreigners" – a non-negligible but unknown share of which no doubt consisted of dollar balances held by US corporations in foreign and offshore banks – was already beginning to exceed US gold reserves in the late 1950s. But around 1963, as figure 18 shows, US gold reserves began falling short even of what was due to foreign monetary authorities and governments – a more serious matter because it impinged directly on intergovernmental power relations.

The Kennedy administration's attempt to deal with the problem through a tighter regulation of US overseas private lending and investment backfired. As Eugene Birnbaum of Chase Manhattan Bank explained,

> the market for international dollar financing shifted from New York to

Europe. Foreign dollar loans that had previously come under the regulatory guidelines of examination of U.S. government agencies simply moved out of their jurisdictional reach. The result has been the amassing of an immense volume of liquid funds and markets – the world of Eurodollar finance – outside the regulatory authority of *any* country or agency. (Quoted in Frieden 1987: 85; emphasis in the original)

As figure 18 shows, this amassing of liquid funds in Eurodollar markets became truly explosive only from 1968 onwards. The question then arises of what provoked this sudden explosion, which quickly became the single most important factor in the destabilization and eventual destruction of the post-war world monetary order. Since at this time US transnational corporations probably were the most important depositors in Eurodollar markets, the explosion must be traced to some change in the conditions of their self-expansion.

Around 1968 these conditions did in fact change quite radically. For more than a decade US foreign direct investment had grown very rapidly, having more than doubled between the mid-1950s and the mid-1960s, while European foreign direct investment had grown in step with it from a modest to a respectable amount (see figure 19). This rapid growth was an expression of the new frontiers that had been opened up for the transnational expansion of US corporate capital by the remaking of Europe in the US image and by the concomitant decolonization of Asia and Africa. But it was also a factor of the progressive closing of these new frontiers.

As long as trade and production in Western European states and in their former colonies were organized by the mixture of familial and state capitalism which had emerged out of the disintegration of the nineteenth-century world market economy, US corporate capital had a decisive competitive advantage in conquering markets for final outputs and sources of primary inputs through direct investment and the vertical integration of the intervening sub-processes of production and exchange. But as an increasing proportion of European and former colonial trade and production was so conquered and reorganized, the further expansion of US corporations came to be constrained ever more tightly by the imposition of organizational barriers to entry that they created for one another. Worse still, European business with active governmental support eagerly responded to the challenges posed by this second "American invasion" (the first, it will be remembered, had occurred half a century earlier) by reorganizing its operations along American lines and by undertaking foreign direct investment on an increasingly massive scale.

Sooner than in all previous phases of material expansion of the capitalist world-economy, the exponential growth of investments in production and trade resulted in an intensification of competitive pressures on the leading business agencies of the expansion. As Alfred Chandler (1990: 615–16) has pointed out, by the time Servan-Schreiber raised the specter of an "American challenge" – a challenge which was neither financial nor technological but organizational, "the extension to Europe of an *organization* that is still a mystery to us" (Servan-Schreiber 1968: 10–11) – a growing number and variety of European firms had found ways and means of effectively meeting the challenge and of themselves becoming effective challengers of the long-established US corporations even in the US domestic market. For the time being, the European challenge to US corporate capital in the US market was still based primarily on commodity exports rather than direct investment. But as figure 19 shows, between 1967 and 1974 the US share of total foreign direct investment declined sharply.

US corporations could not stand idly by and allow European corporations to outcompete them in the world-wide conquest of resources and markets through direct investment. "We can therefore expect," wrote Stephen Hymer and Robert Rowthorn (1970: 81), "a period of intensified multinationalization (almost amounting to capital flight) over the coming decade as both U.S. corporations and non-U.S. corporations try to establish world-wide market positions and protect themselves from the challenges of each other." Hymer and Rowthorn's expectation was fully borne out by actual trends in the 1970s. To be sure, after 1979 the boom in foreign direct investment collapsed – a highly significant event, as we shall see. But the collapse only came after a major resurgence of US foreign direct investment, which temporarily reversed the erosion of the US share of the late 1960s and early 1970s (see figure 19). Overall, between 1970 and 1978 the *accumulated* value of US foreign direct investment more than doubled (from $78 billion to $168 billion), while that of non-US (mostly European) foreign direct investment more than trebled (from $72 billion to $232 billion) raising the non-US share of the total from 48 to 58 per cent (calculated from Kirby 1983: 40).

This intensified transnationalization of US and non-US capital occurred in the context of a strong upward pressure on the purchase prices of primary inputs. Between 1968 and 1973, the main manifestation of this upward pressure was what E.H. Phelps Brown (1975) aptly called the "pay explosion." Real wages in Western Europe and North America had been rising throughout the 1950s and 1960s. But whereas before 1968 they rose more slowly than labor productivity (in Western Europe) or in step with it (in the United States), between 1968 and 1973 they rose much faster, thereby provoking a major contraction in returns to capital invested in trade and production (Itoh 1990: 50–3; Armstrong, Glyn, and

Harrison 1984: 269–76; Armstrong and Glyn 1986).

The pay explosion was still in full swing when at the end of 1973 an equally powerful upward pressure on the purchase price of select primary products materialized in the first "oil shock." Between 1970 and 1973 this upward pressure had already led to a doubling in the price of crude oil imported by OECD countries. But in 1974 alone that same price increased three-fold, deepening further the crisis of profitability (Itoh 1990: 53–4, 60–8, and table 3.3).

After surveying the evidence, Makoto Itoh (1990: 116) concludes that "[o]veraccumulation of capital in relation to the inelastic supply of both the laboring population and primary products ... was more fundamental in launching the current great depression than mismanagement of macro-economic policies." There can indeed be little doubt that the signal crisis of the US regime of accumulation of the late 1960s and early 1970s was due primarily to an overabundance of capital seeking investment in commodities rather than to a failure of national governments – the US government in particular – to compensate for shortfalls in private investment with their own spending. When the crisis broke, both the military and non-military Keynesianism of the US government was in full swing both at home and abroad, creating all the effective demand that was needed to keep the material expansion of the capitalist world-economy going.

Granted all this, it must none the less be emphasized that, starting in 1968 the injection of purchasing power in the world-economy, instead of resulting in the growth of world trade and production as it had done in the 1950s and early 1960s, resulted in world-wide cost inflation and in a massive flight of capital to offshore money markets. This "perverse" effect of the governmental expansion of world purchasing power was due not so much to a mismanagement of macro-economic policies as to the emergence of a fundamental contradiction between the transnational expansion of US corporate capital and the national foundations of US world power.

As previously noted, US corporate capital did not initiate the post-war phase of material expansion of the capitalist world-economy; the global military Keynesianism of the US government did. Nevertheless, the transnational expansion of US corporate capital was both a critical means and a highly significant outcome of the US government's pursuit of world power:

> In conjunction with the international position of the dollar and with nuclear supremacy, the multinational corporation became one of the cornerstones of American hegemony. These three elements of American power interacted with and reinforced one another.... American political and military supremacy

arising out of World War II was a necessary precondition for the predominant position of American multinational corporations in the world economy. But the reciprocal of this is also true: corporate expansionism in turn became a support of America's international political and military position. (Gilpin 1975: 140)

The relationship of complementarity which linked the global expansion of the networks of power of the US government to the transnational expansion of the networks of accumulation of US corporations did not rule out conflicts of interest and contradictions. As Gilpin (1975: 145) notes, the greatest conflict of interest lay in the US government's policy towards Japan throughout the 1950s and 1960s. In the interest of national security, the US government promoted Japanese exports to its domestic market and, what is more, tolerated the exclusion of US investment from Japan – an exclusion which forced US corporations seeking access to the Japanese market to license their technology to Japanese corporations. Only after the withdrawal from Vietnam and the rapprochement with China did the US government become more responsive to the complaints of US corporations about Japanese trade and investment policies.

Ironically, however, the most serious contradiction between the power pursuits of the US government and the transnational expansion of US corporate business developed not where their complementarity was weakest – in East Asia – but where it was strongest – in Western Europe. Here, the US government used the Marshall Plan and rearmament as means of integrating into a single market the separate domestic economies of the European states and insisted that US subsidiaries in the emergent Common Market be treated as "European" corporations. Thanks to these policies, Western Europe quickly became the most fertile ground for the transnational expansion of US corporations and this expansion, in turn, consolidated further the integration of Western Europe within the US regime of rule and accumulation.

In Gilpin's (1975: 141) view, this relationship of complementarity between US governmental and business agencies "is not unlike that between the British government and the mercantile enterprises which dominated the world economy in the seventeenth and eighteenth centuries." In observing this similarity, Gilpin quotes approvingly Kari Levitt's argument that:

the subsidiaries and branch plants of large American-based multinational corporations have replaced the operations of the earlier European-based mercantile venture companies in extracting the staple and organizing the supply of manufactured goods. In the new mercantilism, as in the old, the corporation based in the metropole directly exercises the entrepreneurial function and collects a "venture profit" from its investment. It organizes the collection or extraction of the raw material staple required in the metropolis and supplies the hinterland with manufactured goods, whether produced at home or "onsite" in the host country. (Levitt 1970: 23–4)

As previously argued, the analogy between twentieth-century multinational corporations and the joint-stock chartered companies of earlier centuries is important but should not be exaggerated. For our present purposes, the main difference between the two kinds of business organization is that joint-stock chartered companies were highly malleable instruments of the expansion of state power, whereas twentieth-century transnational corporations are not. Far from being malleable instruments of state power, the latter soon turned into the most fundamental limit of that power.

Nothing illustrates this difference better than a comparison of the incorporation of Western Europe after the Second World War into the US power networks with the late eighteenth and early nineteenth-century incorporation of the Indian subcontinent into the power networks of Britain. The latter incorporation was the work of a single part-governmental, part-business enterprise (the East India Company) chartered by the British government to open up South Asia to British commercial and territorial expansion, in exchange for trading privileges which could be revoked whenever the British government saw fit. The Company did an excellent job in fulfilling its institutional tasks but, as soon as it had done so, its trading privileges were revoked one after another until it was phased out of existence. The British government thus inherited a territorial empire and a source of tribute without which London would never have been in a position to reproduce its world financial supremacy as absolutely and for as long as it did.

The incorporation of Western Europe within the power networks of the US state after the Second World War, in contrast, was undertaken by the US government itself. Once governmental action had prepared the ground for the profitable transplant of US corporations, the latter invaded Europe in large numbers, but their role in consolidating US dominance was limited to internalizing within their technostructures key components of the European market and labor force. Although the US government attempted to retain some control over this transplant of US business on European soil by subjecting foreign subsidiaries of US corporations to US trade laws and by taking steps to regulate the outflow of US capital, almost immediately the transplant developed a dynamic of its own, which the US government, acting alone or even in concert with European governments, could not control. Worse still, the more autonomous this dynamic became, the more Washington's centrality in the regulation and production of world money was undermined.

The transfer of control over world liquidity from private to public hands, and from London and New York to Washington, realized under President Roosevelt and Henry Morgenthau, had been a necessary condition of the subsequent global Keynesianism through which the US government transformed the systemic chaos of the 1930s and 1940s into the orderly US–Soviet condominium of world power of the 1950s and 1960s. But as US corporate capital moved to occupy the new frontiers opened up by this transformation, control over world liquidity began to shift back from public to private hands, and from Washington to London and New York. As Andrew Walter (1991: 182) put it, "London regained its position as the centre for international financial business, but this business was centered on the dollar and the major players were American banks and their clients."

The immediate response of the US government to the resurgence of private high finance in the production and regulation of world money was to reaffirm with a vengeance the centrality of Washington in the supply of world liquidity. Since there was no viable alternative to the dollar as the principal international reserve currency and medium of exchange, the abandonment of the gold–dollar exchange standard resulted in the establishment of a pure dollar standard. Instead of decreasing, the importance of the US dollar as world money increased, and what had previously existed informally was now established formally (Cohen 1977: 232–8).

For about five years, from 1973 to 1978, this pure dollar standard seemed to endow the US government with an unprecedented freedom of action in the production of world money:

> The system of floating exchange rates ... eliminated any need for the United States to control its own balance of payments deficit, no matter what its source, because it was now possible to release unlimited quantities of non-convertible dollars into international circulation. Therefore, while continuing to depreciate the dollar in an attempt to recover competitivity in the production of goods, the United States was no longer saddled with the problem of generating a current account surplus with which to finance its capital-account deficit.... In practical terms, the problem of the settlement of the American balance of payments simply disappeared. (Parboni 1981: 89–90)

The continuing expansion of Eurodollar markets did of course create an additional source of world money, which the US government did not control and which other governments could tap. Nevertheless, borrowing in the Eurodollar market was subject to conditions of creditworthiness which, as a rule, included restraint in running balance of payments deficits and minimal adherence to the principles of sound money. Only the United States was "able to tap the resources of the rest of the world virtually without restriction, simply by issuing its own currency" (Parboni 1981: 47).

As we shall see presently, US seignorage privileges were not as unlimited as they appeared in the mid-1970s. But for a few years these privileges did provide the US government and US business with major competitive advantages in the escalating inter-capitalist struggle over the world's markets and sources of primary inputs. Loose US monetary policies diverted foreign energy resources to the US market and provided outlets for US products at home and abroad at the expense of European and Japanese competitors. In addition, it provided US business with all the liquidity it needed to maintain the momentum of its transnational expansion through direct investment and foreign lending.

The first advantage was closely related to the autocentricity of the US domestic economy relative to the extroversion of the Western European and Japanese economies. The dependence of the latter on foreign trade, as measured by the sum of imports and exports divided by national income, was more than three times greater than that of the United States. Since the United States was itself a major oil producer, whereas Japan and Western European countries (with the later exception of Norway and Britain) were not, differences in the dependence on foreign energy sources were of course much greater. By stimulating a major expansion in net US imports of oil and oil products, from an average of 2.1 million barrels per day in 1960–69 to 6.9 million in 1973–78, loose US monetary policies tended to divert supplies to the US economy and thereby intensify competitive pressures on the Western European and Japanese economies. This tendency was strengthened by the "two-tier pricing" policy, by which the US government imposed a ceiling on the price of domestic oil extracted from wells that were already functioning in 1972. As a result, by the first half of 1979 the average cost of oil in the United States was a good 40 per cent below world market levels (Parboni 1981: 34–5, 53–4).

This cost advantage was compounded by the revenue advantage of the successive depreciations of the dollar created by the liberal expansion of the US money supply. These depreciations boosted US exports and incomes by reducing the price of US products in foreign markets and making foreign products more expensive in the US market. In a more extroverted economy than the US – as the British was in the nineteenth century – the increase in the price of imports implicit in the depreciation of the national currency would have raised domestic costs of production and hence the price of exports, offsetting the decrease implicit in the depreciation. But the autocentricity of the US domestic economy ensured a strong, if temporary, positive effect of the depreciation of the dollar relative to other currencies on US production and value-added. As a result, in the period 1973–79 the comparative performance of the US economy relative to Western Europe, and to a lesser extent Japan, improved considerably (Parboni 1981: chs 3–4; Calleo 1982: 139; Strange and Tooze 1982; Boltho 1993).

This improved performance was not associated with a contraction of the global reach of US networks of accumulation. On the contrary, as previously noted, between 1974 and 1979 the erosion of the US share of total direct foreign investment was reversed. To this we should add that at this time the expansion of US banks in offshore markets, though impossible to quantify, was probably even greater. Supported by the complete elimination in January 1974 of all controls on foreign capital movements, the overabundant supply of dollars released by the US monetary authorities thus provided the means for the self-expansion of US capital not just at home but abroad as well.

The freedom of action of the US government was not unlimited. The switch to a system of flexible exchange rates had released the US government from the balance of payment constraints inherent in its previous commitment to fixed exchange rates. It none the less imposed new constraints, which the US government could not ignore for long without seriously weakening its privileged position in the world monetary system.

For one thing, the breakdown of the regime of fixed exchange rates added a new momentum to the financial expansion by increasing the risks and uncertainty of the commercial–industrial activities of corporate capital. Under the regime of fixed exchange rates, corporate capital was already engaged in currency trade and speculation. "But for the most part the acknowledged responsibility of the central banks for holding the rates fixed relieved corporate finance managers of the need to worry about day-to-day changes" (Strange 1986: 11). Under the regime of flexible exchange rates, in contrast, corporate capital itself had to deal with day-to-day shifts in exchange rates. The coming and going in corporate bank accounts of money in different currencies forced corporations to engage in forward currency trading in order to protect themselves against shortfalls in their accounts due to changes in the exchange rates of the currencies in which their expected receipts and anticipated payments were quoted. Moreover, fluctuations in exchange rates became a major factor in determining variations in corporate cash flow positions, sales, profits, and assets in different countries and currencies. In order to hedge against these variations, corporations had little choice but to resort to the further geopolitical diversification of their operations. A circularity was thus established whereby floating and volatile exchange rates, by increasing risks for multinationals, have made them still more "multinational" in response. But this resulting long-term strategy [tended], in turn, to increase their short-term needs for hedging against exchange rate risks, thus adding still further to the volume of transactions in the financial casino. (Strange 1986: 12–13)

Important as this circular process was in propelling the growth of Eurocurrency markets, under the regime of flexible exchange rates an even more powerful motor came into action. The volatility of exchange rates increased risks and uncertainty not just for the finances of transnational corporations but also for the finances of governments – especially of governments that ruled over highly extroverted domestic economies. Third World governments were more seriously affected than any other by the new monetary regime. As Susan Strange (1986: 13) notes, volatile exchange rates increased risks and uncertainty for them "even more than for the mobile transnational companies. The latter at least have a variety of products, a variety of countries to operate in and an army of highly-paid and well-equipped tax-advisers and financial managers to work on the problem."

The value of Third World countries' receipts from exports, payments for imports, national income, and government revenues have all fluctuated widely with shifts in the exchange rates between the US dollar (in which most of their exports are quoted), other leading currencies (in which many of their imports are quoted), and their own national currencies. In fact, since the early 1970s changes in these exchange rates have been the single most important factor determining the position of Third World countries in the value-added hierarchy of the capitalist world-economy. But most of these countries simply did not command the financial resources needed to hedge against fluctuations. Hence, their main contribution to the growth of the "financial casino" of Eurocurrency markets has been on the demand side rather than on the supply side of the equation; that is, through their demand for funds to offset the devastating effects of financial crises rather than through deposits aimed at forestalling or taking advantage of these same crises.

The intensification of inter-capitalist competition of the 1970s did none the less transform a small number of Third World states not just into depositors but into the main depositors of Eurocurrency markets. As the struggle over the world's energy supplies escalated, surplus capital was transferred ever more massively from the hands of US, Western European, and Japanese governmental and business agencies to states that happened to incorporate within their jurisdictions large and economical reserves of crude oil. Since only a fraction of this huge and growing mass of "oil rent" could be redeployed promptly in productive or useful undertakings by its recipients, a good part of the rent was "parked" or invested in the Eurocurrency market where it enjoyed comparatively high returns and freedom of action. This tendency began to develop in the early 1970s, when the price of crude oil doubled within a few years. But the first oil shock of late 1973, which quadrupled the price of crude oil in a few months,

> not only produced the $80 billion surpluses of "petrodollars" for the banks to recycle, thus swelling the importance of the financial markets and the institutions operating in them, but it also introduced a new, sometimes decisive and usually quite unpredictable factor affecting the balance of payments positions of both the consumer, and eventually the producing, countries. (Strange 1986: 18)

The largest among the oil-consuming countries were, of course, the major capitalist states themselves. Their attempts to protect their domestic economies from the growing uncertainty of energy supplies through deflationary policies aimed at producing a trade surplus in their balance of payments, or through borrowing in the Eurocurrency market, intensified further inter-capitalist competition and added new fuel to the ongoing financial expansion. Moreover, as Marcello de Cecco (1982: 12) has pointed out, the change in the nature of Eurocurrency depositors from the private and public institutions of the major capitalist countries to the private and public institutions of oil-exporting countries was accompanied by a further outward movement of the Eurocurrency market. Once the regime of fixed exchange rates had been displaced by floating rates, the governments and central banks of the Group of Ten (the ten most important capitalist states) attempted to establish some loose control over Eurocurrency markets, or at least to monitor them. To this end, they agreed not to "park" unwanted surpluses in their official currency reserves in the Eurocurrency market, as they had previously done, and entrusted the Bank of England to act with their support as the lender of last resort for banks engaged in the Eurodollar market. For the Bank of England to act in this capacity, some kind of governmental regulation of private banking would have to be introduced. But just as ten years earlier New York banks had responded to the attempts of the Kennedy administration to regulate their foreign operations by moving these operations to the unregulated London-centered Eurodollar market, so in the mid-1970s the US-led confraternity of banks which controlled the enlarged London-based Eurodollar market responded to the much milder regulatory attempts of the Group of Ten by moving business further afield to truly offshore money markets, many of them located in former British colonies.

In other words, the supersession of fixed by flexible exchange rates was associated not with a containment but with an acceleration of the tendency of the governments of the most powerful capitalist states to lose control over the production and regulation of world money. Under these circumstances, the US government's attempt to use the emerging pure dollar standard in support of the self-expansion of US capital at home and abroad did nothing to reinstate the primacy of Washington in high finance. On the contrary, it undermined further the power of the ensemble of national central banks on which that primacy had come to rest.

Thus, the loose US monetary policies of the 1970s, combined with the two-tier pricing of crude oil in the US domestic market and with the complete liberalization of US private lending and investment abroad, strengthened the very tendencies that propelled the explosive growth of offshore money markets. By providing US business with additional pecuniary means and incentives to outbid competitors in the appropriation of the world's energy supplies and in the transnationalization of processes of production and exchange, these policies inflated the oil rents and corporate cash flows that propelled the expansion of the Euro-currency business. And this expansion, in turn, became a new major source of world inflation:

> Formerly, countries other than the United States had to keep their balance of payments in some sort of equilibrium. They had to "earn" the money they wished to spend abroad. Now they could borrow it. With liquidity apparently capable of infinite expansion, countries deemed credit-worthy no longer had any external check on foreign spending.... Under such circumstances, a balance-of-payments deficit no longer provided, in itself, an automatic check to domestic inflation. Countries in deficit could borrow indefinitely from the magic liquidity machine. Many countries ... thus joined the United States in avoiding any real adjustment to higher oil prices. Not surprisingly, world inflation continued accelerating throughout the decade, and fears of collapse in the private banking system grew increasingly vivid. More and more debts were "rescheduled," and a number of poor countries grew flagrantly insolvent. (Calleo 1982: 137–8)

Underneath the accelerating inflation and growing monetary disorder of the 1970s we can detect in new and more complex forms the dynamic typical of the signal crises of all previous systemic cycles of accumulation. As in all such cycles, the rapid expansion of world trade and production had resulted in an intensification of competitive pressures on the leading agencies of the expansion and in a consequent decline of returns to capital. And as in all previous phases of diminishing returns, as Hicks's dictum goes, it is a condition for high returns to be restored or preserved that they should *not* be reinvested in the further expansion of trade and production.

US monetary policies in the 1970s were instead attempting to entice capital to keep the material expansion of the US-centered capitalist world-economy going, notwithstanding the fact that such an expansion had become the primary cause of rising costs, risks, and uncertainty for corporate capital in general and US corporate capital in particular. Not surprisingly, only a fraction of the liquidity created by the US monetary authorities found its way into new trade and production facilities. Most of it turned into petrodollars and Eurodollars, which reproduced themselves many times over through the mechanisms of private interbank money creation and promptly re-emerged in the world economy as competitors of the dollars issued by the US government.

In the last resort, this growing competition between private and public money benefited neither the US government nor US business. On the one hand, the expansion of the private supply of dollars set an increasingly larger group of countries free from balance of payments constraints in the competitive struggle over the world's markets and resources, and thereby undermined the seignorage privileges of the US government. On the other hand, the expansion of the public supply of dollars, fed offshore money markets with more liquidity than could possibly be recycled safely and profitably. It thereby forced the members of the US-led confraternity of banks that controlled the Eurocurrency business to compete fiercely with one another in pushing money on countries deemed creditworthy, and indeed in lowering the standards by which countries were deemed creditworthy. If pushed too far, this competition could easily result in the common financial ruin of the US government and of US business.

By 1978, the US government was faced with the choice of bringing the confrontation with the cosmopolitan financial community that controlled the Eurocurrency market to a showdown by persisting in its loose monetary policies, or seeking instead accommodation through a stricter adherence to the principles and practice of sound money. In the end, capitalist rationality prevailed. Starting in the last year of the Carter presidency, and with greater determination under the Reagan presidency, the US government opted for the second line of action. And as a new "memorable alliance" between the power of state and capital was forged, the looseness of US monetary policies that characterized the entire Cold War era gave way to an unprecedented tightness.

The result was the *belle époque* of the Reagan era. Drawing on Braudel (1984), Hobsbawm (1968), and other sources on which our own investigation has been based, Kevin Phillips (1993: ch. 8) has underscored the striking similarities that can be detected between the cumulative influence of finance on the United States in the 1980s, on Britain in the Edwardian era, on Holland in the periwig era, and on Spain in the Age of the Genoese. "Excessive preoccupation with finance and tolerance of debt are apparently typical of great economic powers in their late stages. They foreshadow economic decline" (Phillips 1993: 194).

Phillips focuses on the costs of "financialization" to the lower and middle social strata of the economic power that has entered the stage of maturity:

> Finance cannot nurture a [large middle] class, because only a small elite portion of any national population – Dutch, British or American – can share in the profits of bourse, merchant bank and countinghouse. Manufacturing, transportation and trade supremacies, by contrast, provide a broader national prosperity in which the ordinary person can man the production lines, mines, mills, wheels, mainsails and nets. Once this stage of economic development yields to the next, with its sharper divisions from capital, skills and education, great middle-class societies lose something vital and unique, just what worriers believe was happening again to the United States in the late twentieth century. (Phillips 1993: 197)

An analogous tendency, Phillips notes, could be observed even earlier in Habsburg Spain. The mortgaging of large chunks of future Spanish revenues to German and Genoese merchant bankers was accompanied and followed by the "financialization" of Spanish society itself. "Narrow monetary wealth, irresponsible finance and an indolent rentier class were important in the decline that was taking hold in Spain one hundred to one hundred and fifty years after Columbus's voyages" (Phillips 1993: 205). Spain, lamented González de Cellorigo in the early 1600s,

> has come to be an extreme contrast of rich and poor, and there is no means of adjusting them one to another. Our condition is one in which we have rich who loll at ease, or poor who beg, and we lack people of the middling sort, whom neither wealth nor poverty prevent from pursuing the rightful kind of business enjoined by natural law. (quoted in Elliott 1970a: 310)

Our investigation has shown that there is an even earlier historical antecedent of social polarization under the cumulative impact of a financial expansion than late sixteenth-century Spain. In fact, the clearest of all antecedents is Renaissance Florence. At no other other time and place have the socially polarizing effects of "financialization" been more in evidence (see chapter 2). From this point of view, all subsequent financial expansions have been variations on a script first played out in the Tuscan city-state.

But our investigation has also shown that domestic social polarizations during financial expansions were integral aspects of ongoing processes of concentration of capital on a world scale in the double sense of coming towards a common center and, also, of growing in strength, density, or intensity. As noted in chapter 3, in all previous phases of financial expansion of the capitalist world-economy two different kinds of concentration of capital have occurred simultaneously. One kind occurred within the organizational structures of the cycle of accumulation that was drawing to a close; and the other kind prefigured the emergence of a new regime and cycle of accumulation.

Leaving aside the issue of whether a concentration of the second kind can be detected in the present conjuncture – an issue to which we shall return in the Epilogue – a concentration of the first kind has indeed been one of the most prominent features of the Reagan era. For the sudden shift from extremely loose to extremely tight monetary policies operated by the US Federal Reserve under Paul Volker in the last year of the Carter administration was only a preamble to a whole series of measures aimed not just at restoring confidence in the US dollar, but at recentralizing within the US privately controlled world money. To this end, the tightening of the US money supply was undertaken in conjunction with four other measures.

First, the US government started to compete aggressively for mobile capital world-wide by raising interest rates well above the current rate of inflation. As figure 20 shows, *nominal* long-term interest rates in the United States had been rising since the mid to late 1960s. Nevertheless, throughout the 1970s inflation had kept *real* interest rates fairly constant at a low level, even depressing them below zero in the mid-1970s. In the early 1980s, in contrast, high nominal interest rates, compounded by the deflationary tendencies generated by tight monetary policies, brought about a major upward jump in real interest rates.

Second, pecuniary incentives for mobile capital to recentralize in the United States were supplemented and complemented by a major "deregulation" drive which provided US and non-US corporations and financial institutions with virtually unrestricted freedom of action in the United States. Particularly significant in this respect was the deregulation of banking in the United States. Having "migrated" from New York to London in the 1960s, and from there to "truly" offshore money markets all over the world in the 1970s, in the 1980s the operations of the New York financial elite could finally be recentralized back home, where they came to enjoy as much freedom of action as any other place could offer and, in addition, a critical advantage that no other place could offer – social and political proximity to what remained the most prominent center of world power.

Third, having won the elections by promising to balance the budget, the Reagan administration initiated one of the most spectacular expansions of state indebtedness in world history. When Reagan entered the White House in 1981 the federal budget deficit stood at $74 billion and the total national debt at $1 trillion. By 1991 the budget deficit had quadrupled to more than $300 billion a year and the national debt had quadrupled to nearly $4 trillion. As a result, in 1992 net federal interest payments amounted to $195 billion a year, and represented 15 per cent of the total budget, up from $17 billion and 7 per cent in 1973 (Phillips 1993: 210; Kennedy 1993: 297). "Formerly the world's leading creditor, the United States had borrowed enough money overseas – shades of 1914–45 Britain – to become the world's leading debtor" (Phillips 1993: 220).

Fourth, this spectacular increase in the US national debt was associated with an escalation of the Cold War with the USSR – primarily, though not exclusively, through the Strategic Defense Initiative (SDI) – and a whole series of punitive shows of military muscle against select unfriendly regimes of the Third World – Grenada in 1983, Libya in 1986, Panama in 1989, and Iraq in 1990–91. As in all previous financial expansions, the mobilization of that "enchanter's wand" that endows barren money with the power of breeding without the necessity of exposing itself to the troubles and risks inseparable from productive undertaking, as Marx described the "alienation of the state" through national debts (see Introduction), was thus associated once again with an escalation in the inter-state power struggle. And it was the competition for mobile capital occasioned by this latest escalation in the inter-state power struggle that once again, to paraphrase Weber, created the greatest opportunities for Western capitalism to enjoy yet another "wonderful moment" of unprecedented wealth and power.

Detractors of the capitalist triumph of the 1980s dwell on its limits and contradictions, as we shall in the Epilogue. Nevertheless, a full appreciation of these limits and contradictions requires a preliminary appreciation of the nature and extent of the triumph itself. And this preliminary appreciation can only begin from a realization of the sorry state of affairs that prompted the US-led capitalist counter-offensive of the late 1970s and early 1980s.

We must first bear in mind how serious the monetary crisis of the 1970s had become. Persistent attempts to reflate the US-centered capitalist world-economy in the face of rapidly decreasing returns to capital were threatening to provoke a major crisis of confidence in the US dollar as viable world money. By 1978 there were clear signs that a crisis of this kind was about to materialize. Had such a crisis gone further than it actually did, whatever competitive advantages the US government and US business had derived from US seignorage privileges would have been nullified. Worse still, it might have destroyed the whole US credit structure and the world-wide networks of capital accumulation on which US wealth and power had become more dependent than ever (cf. Aglietta 1979b: 831f; Aglietta and Orléan 1982: 310–12).

Needless to say, Western European states could afford even less than the United States the ravages of a major crisis of confidence in the US dollar. The greater extroversion and smaller size of their domestic economies made them far more vulnerable than the US to exchange rate fluctuations due to the use of the US dollar as international medium of exchange and means of payment (Cohen 1977: 182; Aglietta 1979b: 833). To limit this vulnerability, the central banks of EC member states had agreed in April 1972 to limit the fluctuation margins of their currencies in relation to one another, thereby creating the so-called Snake. The continuing devaluation of the US dollar over the next six years convinced EC member states of the need to strengthen the arrangement through the resolution of the Council of Europe of December 1978 which created the European Monetary System (EMS) and a European Currency Unit (ECU), both of which became operative the following March. Although the ECU was not a genuine currency but primarily a unit of account, it had the potential to constitute a viable alternative world money should the crisis of confidence in the US dollar deteriorate any further (cf. Parboni 1981: chs 4 and 5).

The threat of the demise of the US dollar as world money (either through a catastrophic collapse of the US domestic and global credit system or through the rise of an alternative reserve currency such as the ECU) was in itself a good enough reason for the US government to show greater respect for the canons of sound money than it had done in the 1970s, or indeed since F.D. Roosevelt had lashed out at the "old fetishes of so-called international bankers." There were none the less other compelling reasons for seeking accommodation with the US-led cosmopolitan community of bankers that controlled the Eurocurrency market.

One was the massive transnationalization of processes of production and exchange that had occurred since the 1950s. In forecasting a period of intensified transnationalization of US and non-US corporate capital for the 1970s, Stephen Hymer and Robert Rowthorn went on to suggest that this tendency did not bode well for the system of nation-states within which the process had thus far been embedded:

Multinational corporations render ineffective many traditional policy instruments, the capacity to tax, to restrict credit, to plan investment, etc., because of their *international flexibility.* ... [T]here is a conflict at a fundamental level between national planning by political units and *international planning* by corporations that will assume major proportions as direct investment grows. ... The propensity of multinational corporations to settle everywhere and establish connections everywhere is giving a new cosmopolitan nature to the economy and policies to deal with it will have to begin from that base. (Hymer and Rowthorn 1970: 88–91; emphasis added)

The explosive growth of the Eurocurrency market since 1968 was an integral aspect of the emergence of this cosmopolitan structure of the capitalist world-economy. It was both an expression and a factor of the flexibility with which corporate capital could move in and out of political jurisdictions to exploit, consolidate, and expand further the global reach of its operations. But it was also an expression and a factor of the inadequacies of national economic policies in coping with an increasingly transnationalized system of business enterprises. In this respect, the inadequacies of US monetary policies were by far the most important.

The attempts of the US government to retain control over transnationalized US capital through legal means and loose monetary policies were at best ineffective and at worst counterproductive. At the same time, the continuing dominance of US business in the financial and non-financial branches of transnationalized capital presented the US government with a unique opportunity to turn the "self-regulating" Eurocurrency market into an "invisible" but formidable weapon of its domestic and global pursuit of power. If ways and means could be found of working hand in hand rather than at cross-purposes with the transnationalized powers of US capital, there would be nothing more for the US government to ask.

The problem, of course, was that finding these ways and means involved much more than a mere change in monetary policies. US neglect of the principles of sound money since Roosevelt and Truman had a social purpose – at first the domestic, and then the international New Deal. Working hand in hand with private high finance meant abandoning almost everything the US government had stood for, for almost half a century not just in monetary matters but in social matters as well.

A break with tradition of this kind was no easy step to take. If it was taken as speedily and determinedly as it was between 1978 and 1982, the reason is not simply that a major crisis of confidence in the US dollar was in the making and that an alliance with private high finance promised to add to the US armory a formidable new means of world power. In all likelihood, the most compelling reason of all was that the US government's pursuit of power by other means was yielding rapidly decreasing returns.

When, on 6 October 1979, Paul Volker began taking forceful measures to restrict the supply of dollars and to bid up interest rates in world financial markets, he was responding primarily to a crisis of confidence in the dollar.

The core of the problem was that for the second time in a year corporations, banks, central banks, and other investors ... had stopped accepting dollars as the universal currency. . . . [I]t became obvious to Volker that a collapse of the dollar was a very real possibility perhaps leading to a financial crisis and pressure to remonetize gold, which the United States had fought doggedly for over a decade. (Moffitt 1983: 196)

But when five months later he resorted to even harsher measures to stop the growth of the US and world money supply, he was responding primarily to the "flight of hot Arab money into gold" in the wake of the Iranian hostage crisis and of the Soviet invasion of Afghanistan. "After Iran and Afghanistan, gold prices took off again. . . . On January 21, gold reached an all-time high of $875. . . . *Business Week* stated flatly that Arab fears over Afghanistan and Iran were behind the surge in prices" (Moffitt 1983: 178).

As previously mentioned, the crisis of the post-war US world monetary order had developed right from the start in step with the crisis of US world hegemony in the military and ideological spheres. The breakdown of the regime of fixed exchange rates coincided with the growing troubles of the US army in Vietnam from the Tet offensive of early 1968 to the beginning of the withdrawal of the US army after the peace accords of 1973. At the same time, the increasing tribute in blood and money exacted to fight a losing war which had no clear direct bearing on US national security precipitated a major crisis of legitimacy of Cold War ideology. According to T.R. Gurr (1989: II, 109), it is hard to tell whether the 1960s was "the most tumultuous in American history." In all likelihood, it was not. Nevertheless, not since the civil war did the US government experience a more severe crisis of legitimacy than during the escalation of its involvement in Vietnam in the late 1960s and early 1970s.

The military and legitimacy crises of US world power were two sides of the same coin. In part, they were the expression of the very success of US rearmament and Cold War ideology in turning the systemic chaos of the 1930s and 1940s into a new world order based on a US–Soviet condominium of world power – a condominium within which the US government clearly had the upper hand, as the Cuban missile crisis demonstrated. By the mid-1960s success in this direction was as complete as it possibly could be. But the very extent of the success made it more difficult for the US government to scare the American people into pouring money, let alone spilling blood, in the anti-communist crusade, or to convince foreign allies that their national interest was best served by the consolidation and further expansion of US world power.

In part, however, the joint military and legitimacy crises of US world power were the expression of the failure of the US military–industrial apparatus to cope with the problems posed by world-wide decolonization. The accommodation of dozens of newly independent states into the rigid power structures of the Cold War world order had proved problematic right from the start. The emergence of a movement of non-aligned states at Bandung in 1955 did nothing but reaffirm the right to self-determination codified in the US-sponsored UN Charter. And yet, the US government perceived the Bandung spirit as a threat to the Cold War world order or, worse still, as nothing but a "communist smokescreen" (cf. Schurmann 1974: 296; McCormick 1989: 118–19).

These difficulties in coping with the formation of a Third World, instead of lessening, increased with the taming of Soviet power and the cooling off of anti-communist passions. The main reason was that the full sovereignty of Third World states constituted a latent and growing challenge to US world power, potentially far more serious than Soviet power itself. This challenge was both economic and political. Economically, the remaking of Western Europe and Japan in the US image – that is, primarily, the extension to their working classes of Rostow's (1960) "high mass consumption" or Aglietta's (1979a) "Fordist consumption norm" – combined with the permanent US–USSR armaments race, put tremendous pressure on the world supplies of primary inputs. This combination also enhanced the strategic importance of the Third World as a reservoir of natural and human resources for the satisfaction of the present and projected needs of First World economies. The expansion and consolidation of the activities of US and Western European transnational corporations in the Third World created highly effective and efficient organizational links between Third World primary inputs and First World purchasing power. But it also created an additional powerful vested interest – the interest of the corporations themselves – in preserving maximum present and future flexibility in the use of Third World resources for the benefit of First World states.

The exercise of full sovereignty rights by Third World states was bound to reduce this flexibility, and eventually eliminate it completely. Should these states feel free to use their natural and human resources as they saw fit – including hoarding or mobilizing them in the pursuit of domestic, regional or world power, as sovereign states had always felt free to do – the pressure on supplies generated by the expansion of the US regime of accumulation would inevitably implode in the form of "excessive" competition within and among First World states.

This is indeed what happened in the 1970s. After the Vietnam War had demonstrated that the most expensive, technologically advanced, and destructive military apparatus the world had ever seen was quite powerless in curbing the will of one of the poorest people on earth, the US government temporarily lost most, if not all of its credibility as the policeman of the free world. The result was a power vacuum which local forces, in open or tacit collusion with the USSR and its allies, promptly exploited in various ways: to complete the process of national liberation from the last residues of European colonialism (as in Portugal's African colonies and in Zimbabwe); to wage war on one another in an attempt to reorganize the political space of surrounding regions (as in East Africa, South Asia, and Indochina); and to oust US client-states from power (as in Nicaragua and Iran). Riding this rising tide of turbulence, which they neither created nor controlled but from which they gained in prestige and power as the designated antagonists of the Cold War order, the ruling groups of the USSR lost sight of the underlying configuration of power and dispatched their army to Afghanistan to do what the more powerful US army had failed to do in Vietnam.

This sudden reversal of relationships of power in the world system in favor of the Third and Second Worlds – the "South" and the "East" – was in itself a highly depressing experience for the bourgeoisie of the West in general and of the United States in particular. But the reversal was all the more depressing because of its association with an equally sudden escalation of inter-capitalist competition that reduced real returns to capital to "unreasonable" levels. The association was not accidental. The price of crude oil had already begun to rise prior to the "shock" of 1973. But it was the virtual acknowledgement of defeat by the US government in Vietnam, followed immediately by the shattering of the myth of Israeli invincibility during the Yom Kippur War, that energized OPEC into effectively protecting its members from the depreciation of the dollar and in imposing on the First World a substantial oil rent.

Combined with the preceding pay explosion, the explosion of oil prices forced First World enterprises to compete even more intensely than they already were for the Third World's supplies of labor and energy, as well as for the purchasing power that was trickling down to some Third World countries in the form of higher real prices for crude oil and other raw materials. Soon, the unregulated recycling of petrodollars into practically unlimited loans for select Third (and Second) World countries turned this trickle-down into a flood. For a few years it seemed that capital had become so abundant as to be almost a free good. Control over the world's purchasing power – the beginning and end of the capitalist accumulation of capital – was slipping from First World states, directly or indirectly assisting the power pursuits of Third and Second World states.

The attempt of the US government to cope with the situation by relying on the manipulation of regional balances of power perhaps helped in some directions but ended in disaster where success mattered most – in the Middle East. Massive investments of money and prestige in building up Iran as the main lever of US power in the region went up in smoke when the friendly regime of the shah was displaced by the unfriendly regime of the ayatollahs. This new setback for US world power – which not accidentally brought in its train the crisis of confidence in the US dollar, the second oil shock, and the Soviet invasion of Afghanistan – finally convinced the US government that the time had come to abandon the New Deal tradition of confrontation with private high finance, and to seek instead by all available means the latter's assistance in regaining the upper hand in the global power struggle.

The resulting "alliance" yielded returns that went beyond the rosiest expectations. The recentralization of purchasing power within the United States achieved almost instantly what US military might acting alone could not. The devastating effects of US restrictive monetary policies, high real interest rates, and deregulation on Third World states quickly brought them to their knees.

The tightening of US monetary policies drastically curtailed the demand for Third World supplies. As a result, between 1980 and 1988 the real prices of the South's commodity exports declined by some 40 per cent and oil prices by 50 per cent (United Nations 1990). And as the London Interbank Offering Rate (LIBOR) for Eurodollars shot up from less than 11 per cent in mid-1977 to over 20 per cent in early 1981, payments to service debts soared. Latin American service payments, for example, increased from less than a third of its exports in 1977 to almost two-thirds in 1982. The ensuing generalized state of de facto bankruptcy completed the reversal of the fortunes of Third World states in world financial markets (Frieden 1987: 142–3).

In recounting a visit to a Mexican funding manager, Jeffry Frieden (1987: 143) gives us a graphic portrayal of the reversal. "When I visited [him] in September 1982, he showed me his empty anteroom in despair. 'Six months ago,' he said, 'there were so many bankers in here you couldn't walk across the room. Now they don't even answer my telephone calls.'"

As if by magic, the wheel had turned. From then on, it would no longer be First World bankers begging Third World states to borrow their overabundant capital; it would be Third World states begging First World governments and bankers to grant them the credit needed to stay afloat in an increasingly integrated, competitive, and shrinking world market. To make things worse for the South and better for the West, Third World states were soon joined in their cut-throat competition for mobile capital by Second World states.

In taking advantage of the overabundance of capital of the 1970s, some of these states had moved quickly to hook up to the global circuits of capital by assuming financial obligations among the heaviest in the world (Zloch-Christy 1987). When capital became scarce again, the Soviet bloc as a whole suddenly felt the cold winds of competition blowing. Bogged down in its own Vietnam and challenged by a new escalation of the armament race with the United States, the atrophied structures of the Soviet state began to crumble.

Thus, while the party for the Third and Second Worlds were over, the bourgeoisie of the West came to enjoy a *belle époque* in many ways reminiscent of the "wonderful moment" of the European bourgeoisie eighty years earlier. The most striking similarity between the two *belles époques* has been the almost complete lack of realization on the part of their beneficiaries that the sudden and unprecedented prosperity that they had come to enjoy did not rest on a resolution of the crisis of accumulation that had preceded the beautiful times. On the contrary, the newly found prosperity rested on a shift of the crisis from one set of relations to another set of relations. It was only a question of time before the crisis would re-emerge in more troublesome forms.

Epilogue:
Can Capitalism Survive Success?

Some fifty years ago Joseph Schumpeter advanced the double thesis that "the actual and prospective performance of the capitalist system is such as to negative the idea of its breaking down under the weight of economic failure," but that "its very success undermines the social institutions which protect it, and 'inevitably' creates conditions in which it will not be able to live" (Schumpeter 1954: 61). Strange as it may seem today, when this double thesis was advanced, the least plausible of the two contentions was the first rather than the second. Capitalism as a world system was then in the midst of one of the most serious crises of its history, and the most relevant question seemed to be not whether capitalism would survive, but by what combination of reforms and revolutions it would die (Arrighi 1990b: 72).

In any event, few were prepared to bet on the chances that capitalism had sufficient residual vitality to generate for another half a century or so the same rates of overall economic growth it had generated in the half a century preceding 1928 – a distinct historical possibility, in Schumpeter's view. The underlying thesis of this study is that history may prove Schumpeter right not once but twice. His contention that another successful run was well within the reach of historical capitalism has of course been proved right. But the chances are that over the next half-century or so, history will also prove right his contention that every successful run creates conditions under which it becomes more and more difficult for capitalism to survive.

The main target of Schumpeter's argument was the view dominant at the time that the displacement of "perfect competition" by the "monopolistic practices" of big business – or of "competitive" by "monopoly" capitalism, as Marxists put it – involved a fundamental weakening of capitalism's earlier capacity to overcome its recurrent crises and to generate over time large increases in total and per capita incomes. Against this view, Schumpeter argued that, historically, "perfect competition" had hardly ever existed and, in any event, it had no title to being set up as a model of efficiency in the promotion of long-term economic growth. On the contrary, a system of business enterprise consisting of large and powerful units of control had all the alleged advantages of "perfect competition" without its disadvantages.

On the one hand, the competition that really mattered in the promotion of long-term growth – the competition, that is, which arises "from the new commodity, the new technology, the new source of supply, the new type of organization" – had been more intense in the presence of large business units than in their absence. On the other hand, the restrictive practices to which big business could and did resort with greater ease and frequency than small business were in the nature of devices needed to secure a "space ... for long-range planning" and to protect business "against temporary disorganization of the market." Hence, "'restraints of trade' ... may in the end produce not only steadier but also greater expansion of total output than could be secured by an entirely uncontrolled onward rush that cannot fail to be studded with catastrophes" (Schumpeter 1954: 84–95; 98–103).

In other words, for Schumpeter "competitive" and "restrictive" practices were not mutually exclusive features of opposite market structures but obverse sides of the same process of creative destruction, which in his scheme of things was the essential fact about capitalism:

> There is no more of a paradox in this than there is in saying that motorcars are travelling faster than they otherwise would *because* they are provided with brakes. . . . [Concerns] that introduce new commodities or processes . . . or else reorganize a part or the whole of an industry . . . . are aggressors by nature and wield the really effective weapon of competition. Their intrusion can only in the rarest of cases fail to improve total output in quantity or quality, both through the new method·itself – even if at no time used to full advantage – and through the pressure it exerts on the preexisting firms. But these aggressors are so circumstanced as to require, for purposes of attack and defense, also pieces of armor other than price and quality of their product which, moreover, must be strategically manipulated all along so that at any point of time they seem to be doing nothing but restricting their output and keeping prices high. (Schumpeter 1954: 88–9; emphasis in the original)

Schumpeter's point in underscoring the growth potential inherent in the capitalism of big business was not to maintain that such potential would necessarily be realized. "The thirties," he wrote, "may well turn out to have been the last gasp of capitalism." In his view, the Second World War, during which he was writing, greatly increased the chances that this possibility would actually materialize in a transition to socialism; or that humanity, as he put it, before it "choke[d] (or baske[d]) in the dungeon (or paradise) of socialism," would "burn up in the horrors (or glories) of imperialist wars." All Schumpeter wished to establish was that there were "no *purely economic* reasons why capitalism should not have another successful run" (Schumpeter 1954: 163; emphasis in the original).

Whether we agree or not with the details or even the main thrust of Schumpeter's argument, there can be little doubt that big business capitalism, for all its restrictive practices, has had over the last fifty years as successful a run as any other kind of previously existing capitalism. Contrary to Schumpeter's expectation, however, big business capitalism was given a chance to demonstrate all its growth potential precisely because of the horrors and glories of the Second World War. Big business seized the chance, but the chance itself was created by (US) big government, which had grown big through and because of the war, and grew even bigger in response to the challenges posed by communist revolution in Eurasia.

Writing at the same time as Schumpeter, Karl Polanyi focused more on government than on business and advanced a thesis which nicely complements Schumpeter's. While Schumpeter's target was the alleged superiority of a mythical competitive age of capitalism, Polanyi's target was the nineteenth-century idea of a self-regulating market. This idea, he maintained, implied a "stark utopia":

> Such an institution could not exist for any length of time without annihilating the human and natural substance of society; it would have physically destroyed man and transformed his surroundings into wilderness. Inevitably, society took measures to protect itself, but whatever measures it took impaired the self-regulation of the market, disorganized industrial life, and thus endangered society in yet another way. It was this dilemma which forced the development of the market system into a definite groove and finally disrupted the social organization based upon it. (Polanyi 1957: 3–4)

Commenting on the social catastrophes that accompanied the final liquidation in the 1930s of the nineteenth-century world order, Polanyi (1957: 22) went on to assert that

> [t]he only alternative to this disastrous condition of affairs was the establishment of an international order endowed with an organized power which would transcend national sovereignty. Such a course, however, was entirely beyond the horizon of the time. No country in Europe, not to mention the United States, would have submitted to such a system.

As Polanyi was writing, the Roosevelt administration was already sponsoring the formation of the inter-statal organizations which foreshadowed such an order. As it turned out, neither the Bretton Woods nor the UN organizations established in the mid-1940s were actually empowered to exercise the world governmental functions they were supposed to in Roosevelt's vision of the post-war world order. Nevertheless, the exceptional world power of the United States at the end of the Second World War enabled the US government itself to exercise those functions effectively for about twenty years.

Throughout this period the idea of a self-regulating market was rejected in principle and in practice by the US government, whose power strategies came instead to be based on radically different premisses. One such premiss was that world markets could be re-established and expanded only through their conscious administration by governments and large business organizations. In addition, US action was premissed on a clear understanding that this re-establishment and expansion of world markets, as well as the national security and prosperity of the United States, required a massive redistribution of liquidity from the US domestic economy to the rest of the world. This redistribution was originally envisaged by Roosevelt as an extension to the entire world of his domestic New Deal. Such an idea turned out to be beyond the horizon of the time. The redistribution did none the less materialize under the Truman and successive administrations through the invention and skilful management of the Cold War as a highly effective means of winning the consensus of the US Congress for the exercise of world governmental functions in both the monetary and military spheres.

The prodigious expansion of trade and production experienced by the capitalist world-economy as a whole from about 1950 to about 1970, during which Truman's Cold War world order remained firmly in place, provides strong evidence in support of Schumpeter's contention that the growth potential of big business capitalism was second to none. But it also provides strong counterfactual evidence in support of Polanyi's contention that world markets can yield positive rather than disastrously negative results only if they are governed, and that the very existence of world markets for any length of time requires some kind of world governance. In the light of this strong evidence, the sudden revival in the 1980s of nineteenth-century beliefs in a self-regulating market and the contemporaneous rediscovery of the virtues of small business by theorists of "flexible specialization" and "informalization" may seem surprising. This tendency, however, is not as bizarre or as anachronistic as it appears at first sight. As a matter of fact, it fits well in the long-established pattern, first observed by Henri Pirenne, of alternating phases of "economic freedom" and of "economic regulation" (see chapter 4).

It is entirely possible that the revival of previously superseded beliefs in free markets and individualism typical of the 1980s is the harbinger of yet another long swing in Pirenne's pendulum towards "economic freedom."

The very success of administered markets in promoting economic expansion in the 1950s and 1960s has disorganized the conditions of "economic regulation" and has simultaneously created the conditions for the enlarged reproduction of the "informal" capitalism typical of the sixteenth and nineteenth centuries. As in all previous swings, an organizational thrust in one direction has called forth an organizational thrust in the opposite direction.

As Larissa Lomnitz has argued with reference to national economies, "[t]he more a social system is bureaucratically formalized, regulated, planned, and yet unable to fully satisfy social requirements, the more it tends to create informal mechanisms that escape the control of the system." These informal mechanisms "grow in the interstices of the formal system, thrive on its inefficiencies, and tend to perpetuate them by compensating for shortcomings and by generating factions and interest groups within the system." Formal economies create their own informality primarily because, in Richard Adams's (1975: 60) words, "[t]he more we organize society, the more resistant it becomes to our abilities to organize it" (Lomnitz 1988: 43, 54).

What is true of national economies is true *a fortiori* of world-economies which, by definition, encompass multiple political jurisdictions and are therefore more difficult to organize, regulate, and plan bureaucratically. Yet, attempts to do so have played as critical a role in the formation and expansion of the capitalist world-economy as the opposite tendency towards "informalization." The successful development of formally organized and regulated Venetian capitalism called forth as a counter-tendency the formation of informally organized and regulated Genoese diaspora capitalism. The full expansion of Genoese capitalism, in its turn, called forth the Dutch revival of formally organized and regulated capitalism through the formation of powerful joint-stock chartered companies. And as the expansion of these companies attained its limits, informal capitalism triumphed once again under British free-trade imperialism, only to be superseded in its turn by the formal capitalism of US big government and big business.

Each swing in the pendulum originated in the dysfunctions of whatever organizational thrust – formal or informal – happened to be dominant at the beginning of the swing. The "regulatory" thrust of the US regime developed in response to the dysfunctions of the "deregulatory" thrust of the British regime. And so today's "deregulatory" thrust may well be indicative of a new swing of the capitalist world-economy towards "economic freedom," as implicitly predicted by Pirenne eighty years ago.

It is also possible, however, that this new swing towards "economic freedom" will be nipped in the bud by the countervailing tendencies that its very scale, intensity, and speed are calling forth. As our investigation has shown, each swing in Pirenne's pendulum did not bring the organizational structures of the capitalist world-economy back to where they were before the preceding swing. Rather, the structures that have emerged out of the successive swings were larger and more complex than earlier ones. Each one of them combined features of the structures which it superseded with features of the structures which it revived. Moreover, the speed of each swing, as measured by the period of time that it has taken each regime to form, become dominant, and attain its limits, has increased steadily with the scale and scope of the leading agencies of systemic processes of capital accumulation.

In the concluding section of chapter 3, we traced this pattern to the tendency of the capitalist accumulation of capital to overcome its immanent organizational barriers by means, in Marx's words, "which again place these barriers in its way on a more formidable scale." Historically, the crises of overaccumulation that marked the transition from one organizational structure to another also created the conditions for the emergence of ever more powerful governmental and business agencies capable of solving the crises through a reconstitution of the capitalist world-economy on larger and more comprehensive foundations. As anticipated in the Introduction, however, this process is necessarily limited in time. Sooner or later, it must reach a stage at which the crisis of overaccumulation cannot bring into existence an agency powerful enough to reconstitute the system on larger and more comprehensive foundations. Or, if it does, the agency that emerges out of the crisis may be so powerful as to bring to an end the inter-state competition for mobile capital which since the fifteenth century, in Weber's words, "created the largest opportunities for modern western capitalism."

There are indeed signs that we may have entered such a stage. Partial as the current revival of a self-regulating world market has actually been, it has already issued unbearable verdicts. Entire communities, countries, even continents, as in the case of sub-Saharan Africa, have been declared "redundant," superfluous to the changing economy of capital accumulation on a world scale. Combined with the collapse of the world power and territorial empire of the USSR, the unplugging of these "redundant" communities and locales from the world supply system has triggered innumerable, mostly violent feuds over "who is more superfluous than whom," or, more simply, over the appropriation of resources that were made absolutely scarce by the unplugging. Generally speaking, these feuds have been diagnosed and treated not as expressions of the self-protection of society against the disruption of established ways of life under the impact of intensifying world market competition – which for the most part is what they are. Rather, they have been diagnosed and treated as the expression of atavistic hatreds or of power struggles among local "bullies," both of which have played at best only a secondary role. As long as this kind of diagnosis and treatment prevails, the chances are that violence in the world system at large will get even more out of control than it already has, thereby creating unmanageable law and order problems for capital accumulation on a world scale, as in Samir Amin's (1992) *Empire of Chaos*.

The uncontainability of violence in the contemporary world is closely associated with the withering away of the modern system of territorial states as the primary locus of world power. As argued in chapter 1, the granting of rights of self-determination to the peoples of Asia and Africa has been accompanied by the imposition of unprecedented restrictions on the actual sovereignty rights of nation-states and by the formation of equally unprecedented expectations about the domestic and foreign duties attached to sovereignty. Combined with the internalization of world-scale processes of production and exchange within the organizational domains of transnational corporations and with the resurgence of suprastatal world financial markets, these unprecedented restrictions and expectations have translated into strong pressures to relocate the authority of nation-states both upward and downward.

In recent years, the most significant pressure to relocate authority upward has been the tendency to counter escalating systemic chaos with a process of world government formation. In a wholly unplanned fashion, and under the pressure of events, the dormant suprastatal organizations established by the Roosevelt administration in the closing years of the Second World War have been hurriedly revitalized to perform the most urgent functions of world governance which the US state could neither neglect nor perform single-handed. Already during the second Reagan administration, and against its original intentions, the IMF was empowered to act in the role of Ministry of World Finance. Under the Bush administration, this role was strengthened and, more importantly, the UN Security Council was empowered to act in the role of Ministry of World Police. And under both administrations, the regular meetings of the Group of Seven made this body look more and more like a committee for managing the common affairs of the world bourgeoisie.

As these suprastatal organizations of world governance were being revitalized, the Bush administration spoke ever more insistently of the need to create a new world order to replace the defunct post-war US order. World orders, however, are more easily destroyed than they are created. As it turned out, the Bush administration's seemingly unflinching belief in self-regulating markets, and its consequent neglect of the US domestic economy in the face of a persistent recession, led to its defeat in the 1992 presidential election. But the problems that had driven it to seek inter-statal forms of world governance remained. The chances are that they will continue to drive the US government in the same direction regardless of the political orientation of the present and future administrations.

Whether this drive will succeed in its objectives is an altogether different question. The very extent and severity of the current crisis of overaccumulation, and the high speed at which it is unfolding, may easily bring about a situation in which the task of creating minimally effective structures of world government surpasses the limited capabilities of the United States and its allies. This outcome is all the more likely in view of the fact that the crisis has been accompanied by a fundamental spatial shift in the epicenter of systemic processes of capital accumulation. Shifts of this kind have occurred in all the crises and financial expansions that have marked the transition from one systemic cycle of accumulation to another. As Pirenne suggested, each transition to a new stage of capitalist development has involved a change in leadership in world-scale processes of capital accumulation. And as Braudel suggested, each change of guard at the commanding heights of the capitalist world-economy reflected the "victory" of a "new" region over an "old" region. Whether we are about to witness a change of guard at the commanding heights of the capitalist world-economy and the beginning of a new stage of capitalist development is still unclear. But the displacement of an "old" region (North America) by a "new" region (East Asia) as the most dynamic center of processes of capital accumulation on a world scale is already a reality.

As a first approximation, the extent of the East Asian great leap forward in processes of capital accumulation can be gauged from the trends depicted in figure 21. The figure shows the most conspicuous instances of "catching up" since the Second World War with the level of per capita income of the "organic core" of the capitalist world-economy. As defined elsewhere, the organic core consists of all the states that over the last half-century or so have consistently occupied the top positions of the global value-added hierarchy and, in virtue of that position, have set (individually and collectively) the standards of wealth which all their governments have sought to maintain and all other governments have sought to attain. Broadly speaking, the members of the organic core during the US cycle have been North America, Western Europe, and Australia (Arrighi 1990a; Arrighi 1991: 41–2).

Japan's "catching up" is clearly the most sustained and spectacular. To be sure, the Japanese trajectory in the 1940s and 1950s is strikingly similar to the German and Italian trajectories – they all more or less recover in the 1950s what they had lost in the 1940s. Nevertheless, starting in the 1960s, the Japanese catching up proceeds much faster than that of its former Axis allies. By 1970, Japanese per capita GNP had overtaken the Italian; by 1985, it had overtaken the German; and soon afterwards it overtook that of the organic core as a whole.

Figure 21 also shows that the regional (East Asian) "economic miracle" did not really begin until the 1970s, that is, until after the signal crisis of the US regime of accumulation. In the 1960s South Korea was still a "basket case" among low-income countries, as people at the Agency for International Development used to call it through the mid-1960s (Cumings 1993: 24). And although in the latter half of the 1960s South Korean per capita GNP increased rapidly, it did not recoup the losses (relative to the organic core) of the preceding five years. The two city-states of Hong Kong and Singapore fared better, but no better than much bigger middle-income non-East Asian states, such as Spain. Among the future Four Tigers or Gang of Four, in the 1960s Taiwan did best, but remained well within the boundaries of the low-income stratum of the world-economy. All in all, through the 1960s only Japan's performance was exceptional by world standards. As in Kaname Akamatsu's "flying geese" model (Kojima 1977: 150–1), the take-off of the Japanese great leap forward preceded and led the regional take-off. It is only in the 1970s, and above all in the 1980s, with the crisis of developmental efforts everywhere else in the world, that the "exceptionalism" of East Asia began to emerge in all its starkness (Arrighi 1991; Arrighi, Ikeda, and Irwan 1993).

As Bruce Cumings (1987: 46) has underscored, the economic miracles of Japan, South Korea, and Taiwan can be understood only by paying due attention to "the fundamental unity and integrity of the regional effort in this century." Focusing on industrial expansion, Cumings sees the post-1955 "long swing" of Japanese industrial growth as being only marginally more successful than the earlier "long swing" of the 1930s, which first promoted the massive industrialization of Japan's colonies:

> Japan is among the very few imperial powers to have located modern heavy industry in its colonies: steel, chemicals, hydroelectric facilities in Korea and Manchuria, and automobile production for a time in the latter.... By 1941, factory employment, including mining, stood at 181,000 in Taiwan. Manufacturing grew at an annual average rate of about 8 percent during the 1930s. Industrial development was much greater in Korea.... By 1940, 213,000 Koreans were working in industry, excluding miners, and not counting the hundreds of thousands of Koreans who migrated to factory or mine work in Japan proper and in Manchuria. Net value of mining and manufacturing grew by 266 percent between 1929 and 1941. By 1945 Korea had an industrial infrastructure that, although sharply skewed toward metropolitan interests, was among the best developed in the Third World. (Cumings 1987: 55–6)

As we have been arguing throughout this study, rates of industrial expansion, or for that matter of production in a narrow sense, are highly unreliable indicators of the success or failure of states in the struggle for competitive advantage in a capitalist world-economy. From Edward III's England to Bismarck's Germany, or indeed Stalin's Russia, no matter how rapid, industrial expansion as such never helped much in moving up the value-added hierarchy of the capitalist world-economy. Historically, in the absence of other, more essential ingredients, rapid industrialization has not translated into a commensurate narrowing of existing value-added gaps. Worse still, it has translated more than once into unmitigated national disasters.

This has been the case, we have argued, with the spectacular industrial expansion of Imperial Germany of the late nineteenth and early twentieth centuries; and this has been the case, we may now add, with the less spectacular but none the less quite significant industrial expansion of Japan and of its colonial hinterland in the 1930s. For all its industrialization, at the outbreak of the Second World War Japan remained a middle-income state with a per capita GNP about one-fifth that of the organic core – in an economic position not all that different from the one it had already attained before the industrialization effort of the 1930s. From what the scanty data available can tell us, Korea and Taiwan did no better, and possibly worse. Rapid industrialization and greater exploitation left both colonies stranded in the low-income stratum, with a per capita GNP well below 10 per cent that of the organic core (assessments based on data provided in Zimmerman 1962; Bairoch 1976b; Maddison 1983).

Rapid industrialization did, of course, turn Japan into a more than respectable military power, which was the real purpose of the industrialization drive. But again, as in the case of Imperial and then Nazi Germany, all the incremental gains in world military and political power that accrued to Japan in virtue of rapid industrialization turned into a huge loss as soon as they began to interfere with the power pursuits of the declining (British) and rising (US) hegemons. As Cumings (1987: 82) himself remarks, in the inter-war period Japan's "striving toward core-power status resembled less flying geese than a moth toward a flame."

What has made the economic expansion of East Asia over the last 20–30 years a true capitalist success, in contrast with the catastrophic failure of pre-war and wartime expansion, is not rapid industrialization as such. A narrowing of the gap in the degree of industrialization between high-income countries (our "organic core") on the one side, and of low-and middle-income countries on the other, has been a feature of the capitalist world-economy at large since the 1960s. But as figure 22 shows, this narrowing of the industrialization gap – and its closing in so far as the middle-income group is concerned – has not been associated with a narrowing of the income gap. On the contrary, the race to industrialize ended in the early 1980s with a sharp increase in the income gap, particularly for the middle-income group.

If we speak at all of an East Asian economic miracle or great leap forward, it is precisely because of the extent to which several of the region's political jurisdictions have escaped this trap. In these few cases rapid industrial expansion has been accompanied by upward mobility in the value-added and in the surplus capital hierarchies of the capitalist world-economy. From both points of view, the Japanese exploit stands head and shoulders above all others within or outside East Asia. The speed and extent of the Japanese acquisition of a larger share of the world's income and liquidity have no parallel in the contemporary world-economy. They put the Japanese capitalist class in a category of its own as the true heir of the Genoese, the Dutch, the British, and the US capitalist classes at the time of their respective great leaps forward as new leaders of systemic processes of capital accumulation.

As we shall see, it is not at all clear whether the emergent Japanese leadership can actually translate into a fifth systemic cycle of accumulation. But whether it will or not, the extent of the Japanese advance in systemic processes of capital accumulation since the signal crisis of the US regime is far greater than the trajectories depicted in figure 21 already imply. For one thing, the trajectories show per capita data. But Japan, on average, had about twice the population of former West Germany (to which the German trend refers) or Italy, 3–4 times the population of Spain or South Korea, and about 10 times the population of Taiwan or of Singapore and Hong Kong combined. In comparison with other upwardly mobile states, therefore, the increase in the Japanese share of world value-added has been more massive than the steeper ascent of its relative per capita income already indicates.

More importantly, this spectacular upgrading of a sizeable demographic mass in the stratified structure of the capitalist world-economy was accompanied by an equally spectacular advance in the world of high finance. Suffice it to say that already in 1970 11 of *Fortune*'s top 50 banks in the world were Japanese. By 1980, their number had increased to 14; and by 1990 to 22. Even more spectacular was the increase in the Japanese share of the total assets of the same top 50 banks: from 18 per cent in 1970, to 27 per cent in 1980, to 48 per cent in 1990 (Ikeda 1993: tables 12 and 13). In addition, by the late 1980s the four largest Japanese security houses had turned into the top Eurobond underwriters, while Tokyo's bond, foreign exchange, and equities markets had all begun to match in size their New York counterparts (Helleiner 1992: 426–7).

Although less dramatic than the Japanese advance, the ascent of South Korea and Taiwan and of the city-states of Singapore and Hong Kong is in itself quite impressive by the standards of the contemporary world-economy. South Korea and Taiwan are the only two states that under the

US regime of accumulation have succeeded in moving from the low-income to the middle-income group of states. And Singapore and Hong Kong are the only ones with Spain to have moved in a stable fashion from the lower to the upper reaches of the middle-income group (Arrighi, Ikeda, and Irwan 1993; and figure 21 this volume).

To repeat, this was not a question of "industrialization" as such. In the 1980s, other states in the region have experienced rapid industrialization, but no upward mobility in the value-added hierarchy of the capitalist world-economy. Thus, rates of growth of manufacturing in Southeast Asia have been among the highest in the world – the average annual rate of growth between 1980 and 1988 being 6.8 per cent in Thailand, 7.3 per cent in Malaysia, and 13.1 per cent in Indonesia, as against an average annual rate of growth of 3.8 per cent for all countries reporting to the World Bank and of 3.2 per cent for all high-income countries (World Bank 1990: 180–1). Yet, World Bank data show that in the same period all three countries lost ground relative to the organic core (let alone Japan and the Four Tigers) as far as per capita incomes are concerned – the ratio of their per capita GNP to the per capita GNP of the organic core showing a *decrease* of 7 per cent in the case of Thailand, 23 per cent in the case of Malaysia, and 34 per cent in the case of Indonesia (Arrighi, Ikeda, and Irwan 1993: 65 and table 3.1).

Moreover, also in the case of the Four Tigers, what is most impressive about their economic expansion since 1970 is the extent to which they have managed to become active participants and major beneficiaries of the financial expansion. Since the late 1960s, Singapore has been closely involved in the creation of the Asian dollar market and in providing an offshore base of operations for the Eurocurrency network of banks. Hong Kong followed soon afterwards, and in 1982 became the third largest financial center in the world after London and New York in terms of foreign banks represented (Thrift 1986; Haggard and Cheng 1987: 121–2). Taiwan for its part "specialized" in accumulating foreign cash reserves. By March 1992, it held $82.5 billion in official reserves, topping the international ranking by a good margin over Japan, which came second with $70.9 billion (*The Washington Post*, 29 June 1992: A1). South Korea – the only one of the four to become indebted in the 1970s – has continued to enjoy abundant credit in the 1980s (Haggard and Cheng 1987: 94); and it has even experienced an explosive growth in the inflow of direct foreign investment, from a yearly average of about $100 million in the 1970s, to $170 million in 1984, and to $625 million in 1987 (Ogle 1990: 37). Moreover, like the three smaller "Tigers", South Korea has itself become one of the largest direct foreign investors in the East and Southeast Asian region. By the late 1980s, the Four Tigers as a group surpassed both the United States and Japan as the leading investors in ASEAN countries, accounting for 35.6 per cent of the total flow of foreign direct investment in 1988 and 26.3 per cent in 1989 (Ozawa 1993: 130).

In short, Japanese and East Asian "exceptionalism" in the midst of the crisis and financial expansion of the US regime of accumulation is not adequately or reliably gauged by the continuing sustained industrial expansion of the region. The most important sign of the rise of East Asia to a new epicenter of systemic processes of capital accumulation is that several of its jurisdictions have made major advances in the value-added and world money hierarchy of the capitalist world-economy. To be sure, the share of value-added of the East Asian capitalist "archipelago" is still considerably less than that of the traditional seats of capitalist power (North America and Western Europe); and the private and public financial institutions of these traditional seats are still in control of the production and regulation of world money. As the 6:1 representation in the Group of Seven shows, North American and Western European states collectively still rule the roost at the commanding heights of the capitalist world-economy.

And yet, for what concerns the *material* expansion of the capitalist world-economy, East Asian capitalism has already come to occupy a leading position. In 1980, trans-Pacific trade began to surpass trans-Atlantic trade in value. By the end of the decade, it was 1½ times greater. At the same time, trade between countries on the Asian side of the Pacific Rim was on the point of surpassing in value trade across the Pacific (Ozawa 1993: 129–30).

This shift in the primary seat of the material expansion of capital from North America to East Asia constitutes an additional powerful stimulus for the US-sponsored tendency towards the formation of suprastatal structures of world government. But it also constitutes a formidable obstacle to the actual realization of that same tendency. It constitutes a powerful stimulus, because the formation of suprastatal structures of world government provides the United States and its European allies with an opportunity to harness the vitality of East Asian capitalism to the goal of prolonging Western hegemony in the contemporary world. But it constitutes a formidable obstacle, because the vitality of East Asian capitalism has become a major limitation and factor of instability for the collapsing structures of US hegemony.

A contradictory relationship between the vitality of an emergent capitalist agency and a still dominant capitalist order has been character-istic of all the transitions from one systemic cycle of accumulation to another. In the past, the contradiction was resolved through the collapse of the dominant order and a change of guard at the commanding heights of the capitalist world-economy. In order to assess the chances that this is what we are once again about to witness, we must briefly investigate the sources of the vitality of the emergent capitalism as an integral aspect of the contradictions of the old (US) regime.

The rise of the Japanese capitalist phoenix from the ashes of Japanese imperialism after the Second World War originated in the establishment of a relationship of political exchange between the US government and the ruling groups of Japan. Thanks to this relationship, the Japanese capitalist class, like the Genoese capitalist class four centuries earlier, has been in a position to externalize protection costs and specialize one-sidedly in the pursuit of profit. As Franz Schurmann (1974: 142) remarked in the heyday of the Liberal Democratic Party (LDP) regime, "[a]s in Coolidge's America of the 1920s, the business of the LDP-dominated government of Japan is business."

By dealing a fatal blow to Japanese nationalism, militarism, and imperialism, defeat in the Second World War and US occupation were the essential ingredients of the extraordinary post-war triumph of capitalism in Japan, as in different ways they were in West Germany. Defeat in the Second World War *ipso facto* translated into the collapse of Japanese imperialism, and US occupation completed the job by destroying the organizational structures of nationalism and militarism. These were prerequisites for the new post-war Japanese political system, "but the context which finally allowed it to achieve its full triumph was the restoration of the world economy by the United States" (Schurmann 1974: 142–5):

> Freed from the burden of defense spending, Japanese governments have funneled all their resources and energies into an economic expansionism that has brought affluence to Japan and taken its business to the farthest reaches of the globe. War has been an issue only in that the people and the conservative government have resisted involvement in foreign wars like Korea and Vietnam. Making what concessions were necessary under the Security Treaty with the Americans, the government has sought only involvement that would bring economic profit to Japanese enterprise. (Schurmann 1974: 143)

US patronage itself was initially the primary source of the profits of Japanese enterprise. When "Korea came along and saved us," as Acheson's famous remark went (see chapter 4), "the *us* included Japan" (Cumings 1987: 63). "The Korean War drew the Northeast boundaries of Pacific capitalism until the 1980s, while functioning as 'Japan's Marshall Plan' ... war procurements propelled Japan along its world-beating industrial path" (Cumings 1993: 31; see also Cohen 1958: 85–91; Itoh 1990: 142).

Before the onset of the Cold War, the main objective pursued by the

United States in Japan was the dismantling of military capabilities without much concern for the revival of the Japanese economy. Reconstruction was perceived as an urgent need both of Japan and of the countries against which Japan had committed aggression. Nevertheless, as a 1946 US report on reparations stated bluntly, "[i]n the overall comparison of needs, Japan should have last priority" (Calleo and Rowland 1973: 198–9). Within less than one year, however, the launching of the Cold War brought in its wake a complete reversal of this confrontational thrust:

> George Kennan's policy of containment was always limited and parsimonious, based on the idea that four or five industrial structures existed in the world: the Soviets had one and the United States had four, and things should be kept that way. In Asia, only Japan held his interest. The rest were incontinent regimes, and how could one have containment with incontinence? Kennan and his Policy Planning Staff played the key role in pushing through the "reverse course" in Japan. (Cumings 1987: 60)

With "hot" war breaking out in Korea and the Cold War gathering pace through US and Western European rearmament, soon the most "incontinent" of all regimes became the US regime itself. By 1964 in Japan alone, the US government had spent $7.2 billion in offshore procurements and other military expenditures. Altogether, in the 20-year period 1950–70 US aid to Japan averaged $500 million a year (Borden 1984: 220). Military and economic aid to South Korea and Taiwan combined was even more massive. In the period 1946–78, aid to South Korea amounted to $13 billion ($600 per capita) and to Taiwan $5.6 billion ($425 per capita) (Cumings 1987: 67).

US "incontinence," far from weakening, strengthened US interest in buttressing Japanese regional economic power as a means of US world political power. Already in 1949, the US government had shown some awareness of the virtues of a "triangular" trade between the United States, Japan, and Southeast Asia, giving "certain advantages in production costs of various commodities" (first draft of NSC 48/1; as quoted in Cumings 1987: 62). Nevertheless, throughout the 1950s the US government had more pressing priorities than containing costs. One such priority was to revive Japan's industrial capabilities, even at the cost of re-establishing a reformed version of the centralized governmental and business structures of the 1930s including the big banks that had occupied their commanding heights (Allen 1980: 108–9; Johnson 1982: 305–24). Another priority was to force on its reluctant European partners, and Britain in particular, admittance of Japan to the GATT (Calleo and Rowland 1973: 200–4).

But once the recovery of the Japanese domestic economy had been consolidated and US financial largesse began to attain its limits, the containment of costs did become a consideration and Japan's role in the East Asian regional economy was thoroughly redefined. One of Walt W. Rostow's first projects, when he joined the Kennedy administration in 1961, was

> to get South Korea and Taiwan moving toward export-led policies and to reintegrate them with the booming Japanese economy. Facing America's first trade deficits, the Kennedy administration sought to move away from the expensive and draining security programs of the Eisenhower years and toward regional pump-priming that would bring an end to the bulk grant aid of the 1950s and make allies like Korea and Taiwan more self-sufficient. (Cumings 1993: 25)

In the 1950s, the US had promoted the *separate* integration of Japan and of its former colonies within its own networks of trade, power, and patronage. In the 1960s, under the impact of tightening financial constraints, it began promoting their *mutual* integration in regional trade networks centered on Japan. To this end, the US government actively encouraged South Korea and Taiwan to overcome their nationalist resentment against Japan's colonialist past and to open their doors to Japanese trade and investment. Under US hegemony, Japan thus gained costlessly that economic hinterland it had fought so hard to obtain through territorial expansion in the first half of the twentieth century and had eventually lost in the catastrophe of the Second World War.

Japan actually won much more than an East Asian economic hinterland. Through the intervention of the US government, it obtained admission to the GATT and privileged access to the US market and to US overseas military expenditures. Moreover, the US government tolerated an administrative closure of the Japanese economy to foreign private enterprise which would have resulted in almost any other government being placed among the free world's foes in the Cold War crusade.

It goes without saying that the US government was not motivated by benevolence. Logistics as much as politics required that the US government buttress – if necessary through protection from the competition of US big business – the several foreign centers of industrial production and capital accumulation on which the superior capabilities of the free world *vis-à-vis* the communist world rested. And it so happened that Japan was both the weakest among these centers and the one of greatest strategic value owing to its proximity to the theater of operations of the continuing US war with Asia – first in Korea, then in Vietnam, and throughout in the "containment" of China.

Japan also happened to be a highly effective and efficient "servant" of what James O'Connor (1973: ch. 6) has called the US "warfare–welfare state." The cost advantages of incorporating Japanese business as an intermediary between US purchasing power and cheap Asian labor, as adumbrated in the first draft of NSC 48/1, became particularly useful in the 1960s when the tightening of financial constraints began threatening a fiscal crisis in the United States. It was this impending crisis more than anything else that shaped the context in which the growth of US imports from Japan became explosive, tripling between 1964 and 1970 with a consequent transformation of the previous US trade surplus with Japan into a $1.4 billion deficit.

This explosive growth of Japanese exports to the wealthy US market as well as its trade surplus, was a critical ingredient in the simultaneous take-off of Japan's great leap forward in world-scale processes of capital accumulation. Nevertheless, it was not due in any measure to an aggressive Japanese neo-mercantilist stance. Rather, it was due to the growing need of the US government to *cheapen* supplies essential to its power pursuits, both at home and abroad. Were it not for the massive procurement of means of war and livelihood from Japanese sources at much lower costs than they could be obtained in the United States or anywhere else, the simultaneous escalation of US welfare expenditures at home and of warfare expenditures abroad of the 1960s would have been far more crippling financially than it already was. Japanese trade surpluses were not the cause of the financial troubles of the US government. The increasing fiscal extravagance of the US warfare–welfare state was. The Japanese capitalist class promptly seized the chance to profit from US needs to economize in the procurement of means of war and livelihood. But by so doing, it was servicing the power pursuits of the US government as effectively as any other capitalist class of the free world.

In short, up to the signal crisis of the US regime of accumulation Japan remained a US-invited guest in the exclusive club of the rich and powerful nations of the West. It was a perfect example of what Immanuel Wallerstein (1979: ch. 4) has called "development by invitation." By and large, Japan was also a very discreet guest. The expansion of its exports to the United States had been administratively regulated from the start, so much so that in 1971 an estimated 34 per cent of its trade with the United States was covered by restrictive "voluntary" agreements (Calleo and Rowland 1973: 209–10). Equally important, as figure 19 (this volume) shows, the intensifying competitive struggle through escalating foreign direct investment remained right up to the early 1970s a strictly US–European business.

The overaccumulation crisis of the late 1960s and early 1970s changed all that. The US government stopped twisting the arm of its European partners and East Asian clients to make room for the capitalist expansion of Japan. It began instead twisting the arm of the Japanese government to revalue the yen and to open up the Japanese economy to foreign capital and trade. As the rapprochement with China and the Paris peace accords of 1973 brought the US war with Asia to a close, US pressures on Japan to redistribute the benefits of its economic expansion intensified. The US government turned to close the stable door, but the horse had already bolted. Or, rather, the geese were flying. The overaccumulation crisis propelled Japanese capital on a path of transnational expansion which would soon revolutionize the entire East Asian region and, perhaps, foreshadow the eventual supersession of the US regime of accumulation.

The central fact about this expansion is that it consisted primarily of the enlarged reproduction of the Japanese multilayered subcontracting system of business enterprise. As underscored by theorists of "informal-ization" and "flexible specialization," subcontracting systems of various kinds have flourished all over the world since about 1970. Nevertheless, as argued at greater length elsewhere (Arrighi, Ikeda, and Irwan 1993), the Japanese subcontracting system, which has expanded transnationally in the 1970s and 1980s, differs in key respects from all other kinds of subcontracting systems.

First, the Japanese system relies on, and tends to reproduce, a more decentralized structure of productive activities than do the subcontracting practices of big business of other core capitalist states. It is highly stratified into multiple layers consisting of primary subcontractors (who subcontract directly from the top layer), secondary subcontractors (who subcontract from secondary subcontractors), tertiary subcontractors, and so on, until the chain reaches the bottom layer which is formed by a large mass of households that subcontract simple operations. Without the assistance of all these subordinate layers of formally independent subcon-tractors – notes JETRO (Japan's External Trade Organization), "Jap-anese big business would flounder and sink" (Okimoto and Rohlen 1988: 83–8). This external sourcing by Japanese big business is far greater than that undertaken by its US and Western European counterparts. For example, in 1973 among big car manufacturers the gross value-added to finished vehicles was 18 per cent in Japan, 43 per cent for the "big three" in the United States, and 44 per cent for Volkswagen and Benz in Germany (Odaka 1985: 391). Greater reliance on external sourcing, in turn, was the single most important factor enabling Toyota Motor Corporation to turn out 3.22 million four-wheel cars in 1981 with only 48,000 employees, while General Motors needed 758,000 employees to produce 4.62 million cars (Aoki 1984: 27).

Second, Japanese subcontracting networks are far more stable and effective instruments of vertical and horizontal inter-enterprise cooperation than subcontracting networks in the United States and Western Europe, where subcontractors have to renegotiate more often and under greater competitive pressure from other subcontractors than do those in Japan. As a consequence, cooperation across the organizational jurisdictions of the enterprises integrated in the subcontracting network aimed at the attainment of a common goal, such as the high quality or the low price of the final output of the subcontracting chain, is more problematic than in Japan. Idealized as a "family" relation between "parent companies" and "child subcontractors," cooperation between small and large firms in the Japanese system is so close that "the hard and fast distinction between firms becomes very blurred [as] we find some supplier companies located within the plant of the parent firm, [as] the smaller company is managed by ex-employees of the larger one or [as] the bulk of the small firm machinery is handed down in second-hand sales from their principal buyer." These cooperative arrangements between parent companies and subcontractors are buttressed by cooperative arrangements between the parent companies themselves in the form of semi-permanent trade agreements and inter-group stockholding. This horizontal cooperation at the top eases the procurement of inputs and the disposal of outputs within each subcontracting network; it prevents unwanted takeover bids; and it allows management to concentrate on long-term performance rather than short-term profitability. "This longer run perspective is a feature of Japanese business and is greatly helped by the existence of lead banks within affiliated groups that ensure access to loans even in periods when bank credit is restricted" (Eccleston 1989: 31–4; see also Smitka 1991).

Long-term cooperative arrangements between large, medium, and small businesses have been further enhanced by the activities of powerful trading companies, the *sogo shosha*. In developing outlets for the growing output of such flow-process industries as steel, chemicals, petrochemicals, and synthetic fibers, the *sogo shosha* have built networks of their own of small and medium firms, to which they supply materials for downstream processing and distribution and to which they also extend financial, managerial, and marketing assistance. Like the upstream networks controlled by the large manufacturers, these downstream networks combine the market and financial power of a large enterprise with the flexibility, specific knowledge, and lower wages of small and medium enterprises (Yoshino and Lifson 1986: 29).

Third, and closely related to the above, the Japanese multilayered subcontracting system has endowed Japanese big business with superior capabilites to take advantage of and reproduce wage and other differentials in rewards for effort between different segments and strata of the labor force. From this point of view, the Japanese multilayered subcontracting system is but one aspect of a more general managerial strategy of inter-enterprise cooperation aimed at minimizing competition between small and large enterprises in the labor market. Another closely related aspect has been the practice of discriminating against the employment of women in the top layers of the subcontracting system – a practice that has been instrumental in reproducing a large pool of female workers who are available for the super-exploitation of the lower layers of the system. This practice is, of course, quite widespread in North America and Western Europe too. But nowhere have subcontracting, restraint in bidding employees away from other companies, and discrimination against women been pursued as coherently and systematically as in Japan. In Richard Hill's (1989: 466) words, almost as a rule, "the higher up the value-added chain, the bigger the firm, the larger the business profits, the more privileged the conditions of work and pay, and the more male-dominated the workforce."

Finally, and most importantly for our purposes, the Japanese multi-layered subcontracting system has developed domestically and expanded transnationally in a close symbiotic relation with the abundant and highly competitive supply of labor of the East and Southeast Asian region. It is hardly conceivable that in the absence of such a symbiotic relation capital accumulation in Japan could have proceeded as fast as it has since the 1960s without undermining and eventually disrupting the cooperative arrangements between enterprises, on which the domestic viability and world competitiveness of the Japanese multilayered subcontracting system rests. Inevitably, the reinvestment of an ever-growing mass of profits in the expansion of trade and production within the Japanese domestic economy would have driven individual enterprises or families of enterprises (the *keiretsu*) to invade one another's networks and market niches in an attempt to counter downward pressures in sale prices and/or upward pressures in purchase prices. This mutual invasion, in turn, would have dissolved the cooperating confraternity of Japanese business into a chaotic ensemble of intensely competing factions.

A tendency of this kind actually seemed to be emerging in the mid-1960s in the form of a revival of what was popularly called "excessive competition" – interestingly enough, the same expression that was popular in US business circles at the turn of the century (cf. Veblen 1978: 216). This revival was associated with growing shortages of land and labor, the prices of which – particularly the wages of young factory workers – began to rise both absolutely and relative to the selling prices of the industrial groups engaged in the competition. Initially, the decline of profit margins was more than compensated by large and increasing productivity gains. By the end of the 1960s, however, productivity gains ceased to be large enough to counter the tendency of the rate of profit to fall (Ozawa 1979: 66–7).

Still, the crisis of profitability that ensued from the intensification of competitive pressures did not disrupt the cooperative arrangements on which the multilayered subcontracting system was based. Nor did it end Japanese economic expansion. On the contrary, the multilayered subcontracting system continued to increase in scale and scope through a spillover into select East Asian locations. The spillover contributed decisively to the take-off of the *regional* economic miracle. But it contributed even more decisively to the tendency of the Japanese multilayered subcontracting system, not just to overcome the over-accumulation crisis, but to strengthen its competitiveness in the world-economy at large through the incorporation of the labor and entrepreneurial resources of the surrounding region within its networks (Arrighi, Ikeda, and Irwan 1993: 55ff).

Accumulated Japanese direct foreign investment had begun to grow rapidly since the mid-1960s. But after 1967, and above all after the revaluation of the yen in 1971, the growth became truly explosive (see figure 23). This explosive growth was due primarily to the trans-border expansion of the multilayered subcontracting system aimed at recouping the cost advantages lost with the tightening of labor markets in Japan and the revaluation of the yen. It was a massive transplant of the lower value-added end of the Japanese production apparatus. The transplant involved primarily labor-intensive industries like textile, metal products, and electrical machinery; it was undertaken by large and small enterprises alike; and it was overwhelmingly directed towards Asia and, within Asia, towards the emerging Four Tigers (Yoshihara 1978: 18; Woronoff 1984: 56–8; Ozawa 1985: 166–7; Steven 1990: table III.3).

Large "parent" manufacturing companies were followed abroad by at least some members of their subcontracting "families." But the most critical role in leading small Japanese business abroad was played by the *sogo shosha*. They advanced some of the funds needed; they arranged joint ventures with local partners; and they acted as agents for the import of raw materials and machinery and for the export of final outputs. They frequently secured a continuing role for themselves in the joint venture by taking a small share of the equity (Woronoff 1984: 56–8). Generally speaking, the foreign expansion of Japanese business was far less insistent and reliant on majority ownership than US or Western European business. Thus, in 1971, minority ownership and joint ventures accounted for about 80 per cent of the foreign manufacturing subsidiaries of Japanese firms, as against 47 per cent for French firms, 35 per cent for Italian firms, about 30 per cent for Belgian and German firms, and about 20 per cent for US, UK, Dutch, Swedish, and Swiss firms (Franko 1976: 121).

The foreign expansion of Japanese trade and production networks, in other words, is grossly underestimated by data on foreign direct

investment because Japanese business sunk far less capital in the takeover
or establishment of facilities abroad than US or Western European
business did. And yet, it was precisely the "informal" and "flexible"
nature of the trans-border expansion of Japanese capital in the surrounding low-income region that boosted its world competitiveness at a time of
generalized world cost-inflation. The competitive advantages of these
strategies and structures of capital accumulation were overshadowed
through the mid-1970s by escalating US and Western European direct
foreign investment. The Japanese share of direct foreign investment from
so-called developed market economies, after jumping from less than 3 per
cent in 1970–71 to more than 8 per cent in 1973–74, fell to less than 6
per cent in 1979–80 (calculated from United Nations Center on Transnational Corporations 1983). Moreover, the escalating prices and growing uncertainty of supplies of oil and other raw materials made the
securing of such supplies the top priority of the overseas expansion of
Japanese enterprise. To this end, Japanese capital hedged its bets on
multiple sources as a makeweight for poor connections with the producing countries. This strategy enabled Japan to weather the oil crisis. But on
this terrain the looser vertical integration of Japanese business presented
greater competitive disadvantages than advantages (cf. Hill and Johns
1985: 377–8; Bunker and O'Hearn 1993).

Under these circumstances, the organizational and locational peculiarities of Japanese direct foreign investment appeared to be – and to a large
extent actually were – "weapons of the weak" rather than the source of
a fundamental competitive advantage. Thus, in sketching the main
features of what he called "multinationalism, Japanese style," Terutomo
Ozawa (1979: 225–9) pointed out how the majority of Japanese
manufacturers who were investing overseas were "immature" by Western
standards; how the outward expansion of Japanese business was the
result of necessity rather than choice – that is, the result of a struggle to
escape the trap of rapid industrialization within a narrow domestic
economic space; and how the willingness of Japanese multinationals to
work out compromises with the demands of host countries (such as
accepting minority ownership) was in part due to a weak bargaining
position both *vis-à-vis* host governments and relative to North American
and Western European competitors.

And yet, in the 1980s these weapons of the weak turned out to be the
source of a fundamental competitive advantage in the ongoing struggle
for control over the world's resources and markets. The Japanese ascent
in the value-added and surplus capital hierarchies of the world-economy
continued unabated. But even Japan's share of foreign direct investment
– which grossly underestimates the transnational expansion of Japanese
business networks – more than tripled between 1979–80 and 1987–88

(Arrighi, Ikeda, and Irwan 1993: 62). By 1989, this extraordinary expansion culminated in Japan's topping the international ranking of direct foreign investors in terms of investment flows ($44.1 billion), surpassing the United States ($31.7 billion) by a good margin (Ozawa 1993: 130).

As previously noted, by the late 1980s the recipients of the first round of Japanese outward industrial expansion – the Four Tigers or Gang of Four – had themselves become, as a group, the major direct foreign investors in ASEAN countries. As rising wages undermined the comparative advantages of the Four Tigers in the lower value-added end of industrial production, enterprises from these states joined Japanese business in tapping the still abundant and cheap labor resources of a poorer and more populous group of neighboring, mostly ASEAN, countries. The result was a second round of outward regional industrial expansion through which a larger mass of cheap labor was incorporated. This enlarged incorporation of cheap labor bolstered the vitality of the East Asian capitalist archipelago. But it also undermined the competitiveness of the labor resources on which it was based. As soon as this happened, as it did very recently, a third round took off. Japanese and Gang of Four enterprises were joined by enterprises of second-round recipients of regional industrial expansion (most notably Thailand) in transplanting lower-end, labor-intensive activities to even poorer and more populous countries (most notably, China and Vietnam), which are still endowed with large and competitive reserves of cheap labor (cf. Ozawa 1993: 142–3).

Ozawa sums up this "snowballing" phenomenon of concatenated, labor-seeking rounds of investment flows in the East and Southeast Asian region by means of a chart (reproduced as figure 24, with some changes in vocabulary). Recast in the world historical perspective adopted in this study, the space-of-flows depicted in figure 24 can be interpreted as constituting an emergent regime of accumulation. Like all the emergent regimes of accumulation that eventually generated a new material expansion of the capitalist world-economy, this latest emergent regime is an outgrowth of the preceding regime.

As Ozawa (1993: 130–1) puts it, the East Asian space of labor-seeking investment and labor-intensive exports originated in "the 'magnanimous' ... early postwar ... trade regime of Pax Americana." It was this "magnanimous" regime that made possible "the phenomenal structural transformation and upgrading of the Japanese economy ... since the end of World War II." And it was this phenomenal upgrading of the Japanese economy that became the main factor of the industrial expansion and economic integration of the entire East Asian region.

The continuing dependence of the East Asian capitalist archipelago on the old US regime is shown in figure 24 by the "ascending" flows of labor-intensive exports which connect the locales of the successive rounds of regional industrial expansion to the markets of the organic core – the US market in particular. The upgrading of Japan in the value-added hierarchy of the capitalist world-economy has turned Japan itself into a significant core market for the outputs of the regional industrial expansion. And the lesser upgrading of the Four Tigers has turned them into a remunerative, if less significant, outlet. Nevertheless, the whole process of regional industrial expansion, as well as the prosperity of its capitalist "islands," continue to be based on access to the purchasing power of the wealthy markets of the "old" core. The pattern that the expansion of the Japanese "national" economy established in the 1950s and 1960s is reproduced in the 1970s and 1980s on an enlarged (regional) scale. The main structural feature of the emergent regime remains the provisioning of wealthy markets with products that embody the cheap labor of poor countries.

And yet, this very structural feature constitutes a negation of the old regime, in the interstices of which the emergent regime formed, and on the inefficiencies of which it has thrived. This aspect of the emergent regime is shown in figure 24 by the "descending" flows of labor-seeking investment that connect the locales of each round of regional industrial expansion to the locales of subsequent rounds. Labor-seeking investment from wealthier to poorer countries is of course nothing new, and it is also a feature of US and Western European foreign direct investment, especially since the signal crisis of the US regime. Nevertheless, the "informality" and "flexibility" of the Japanese multilayered subcontracting system, combined with the abundance of parsimonious and industrious labor in the East Asian region, endow Japanese and East Asian capital with a distinctive advantage in the escalating global race to cut labor costs. It is precisely in this sense that the emerging East Asian regime of accumulation is a negation of the old US regime.

For the US regime became dominant through an inflation of the "consumption norm" of the US labor force and an internalization of world purchasing power within the organizational domains of US governmental and business organizations. It promoted a world trade expansion through the redistribution of this purchasing power to a select group of allied and client states and through the adoption by these same states of the inflated US consumption norm. It sustained the expansion through a speed-up of the transfer of primary inputs (oil in particular) from Third to First World countries by multinational corporations. And it attained its limits in the great inflation of protection and production costs of the late 1960s and early 1970s.

It was this that led to the rise of the East Asian capitalist archipelago and to the proliferation of the labor-seeking investment flows that link the main "island" of the archipelago to the lesser "islands," and all "islands" to the "submerged" laboring masses of the entire region. These masses were, and for the most part remain, excluded from the extravagant consumption norm of the US regime – a norm that became unsustainable as soon as it was generalized to 10–15 per cent of the world's labor force. The parsimony and industriousness of these laboring masses constitute the single most important foundation of the emergent East Asian regime of accumulation. Whereas the US regime rose to prominence through a fundamental inflation of reproduction costs, the East Asian regime has emerged through a fundamental deflation of these same costs.

Under the US regime, protection costs have been a major component of reproduction costs. Here lies another strength of the East Asian regime. Historically, we have argued, the upward mobility of the Japanese economy in the value-added hierarchy of the capitalist world-economy was based on a relationship of political exchange that enabled the Japanese capitalist class to externalize protection costs and to specialize in the pursuit of profit through the provisioning of the US welfare–warfare state with cheap manufactures. The terms at which the United States enabled Japan to externalize protection costs at home and to have privileged access to US purchasing power remained "magnanimous" only as long as the US war with Asia lasted. As soon as the United States decided to pull out of Vietnam and to seek a rapprochement with China, the supply "price" of US protection for Japan began to rise and then escalate.

Through most of the Reagan era, Japan by and large complied with US requests. Thus, during the Second Cold War of the early and mid-1980s it deployed an enormous amount of capital to support the US external account deficits and the internal fiscal imbalance. In addition, it gave large amounts of its growing bilateral aid to countries, such as Turkey, Pakistan, Sudan, and Egypt, deemed important for US strategic needs. At the same time, Japan did nothing to upset US dominance in high finance. When US competition for loanable funds in world financial markets provoked the near-bankruptcy of several Latin American countries, Japanese banks followed US guidelines for handling the ensuing debt crisis, in B. Stallings's (1990: 19) words, "even more closely than the US banks themselves." And when the US government decided to bolster the IMF and the World Bank to handle the crisis, Japan readily agreed to increase its contributions to these organizations in ways that did not significantly alter their voting structure (Helleiner 1992: 425, 432–4).

Japan's compliance with US requests is fully understandable in the light of its still fundamental dependence, not so much on US military protection – the limits of which had been laid bare in Vietnam – as on US and other core markets for the profitability of its business. Should the old regime collapse for lack of Japanese financial support, Japanese business might be the first to suffer. These fears were vented by Suzuki Yoshio of the Bank of Japan in an article published on the eve of the crash of 1987. The sentiments expressed are in many ways reminiscent of the internationalist exhortations of Norman Davis on the eve of the crash of 1929 (see chapter 4).

> History teaches us that whenever a newly risen, asset-rich nation refuses to open its markets to other countries or fails to effectively channel its financial resources to the development of the world economy, the result is growing conflict between the old order and the new. In the past, these conflicts have led to war, and to the division of the world economy into blocks demarcated by protectionism. Today's intensifying international economic frictions and the mounting protectionism in the United States are both warning signs that the world is once again faced with just such a crisis. (quoted in Johnson 1988: 90)

Fears of setting off a crisis of historic proportion, however, worked only up to a point in ensuring Japanese support for the US regime. As anticipated in the Introduction, in 1987, before and after the October crash, the huge losses inflicted on Japanese capital by the sharp devaluation of the US dollar led to a reversal of the flow of Japanese investment to the United States. In 1988, the reversal was followed by an increasingly acrimonious US–Japanese dispute over the issue of Third World debt. More importantly, in 1989 the new Governor of the Bank of Japan, Yashushi Mieno, reversed the loose monetary policies pursued since 1985, thereby strengthening the ongoing tendency of Japanese capital to withdraw from the United States both directly by raising interest rates in Japan, and indirectly by bursting Japan's own financial bubble and thus forcing Japanese financial institutions to cover their domestic reserve positions. The following year Japan pushed successfully against initial US opposition to raise to second place its voting share in the IMF. And whereas in the early 1980s Japan had yielded to US pressure to channel its bilateral aid to countries deemed important for US strategic needs, in 1991 it took a strong public stance against US-sponsored strategic debt writedowns for countries such as Poland and Egypt (Helleiner 1992: 435–7).

The US response to Japanese criticisms was a resentful dismissal followed by increasingly extravagant requests that Japan put up the money needed to sort out the global mess left behind by the *belle époque* of the Reagan era. Whereas under Reagan the assistance of Japanese capital for the power pursuits of the US government was sought through borrowing and the alienation of US assets and future incomes, under Bush it was sought through outright donations (true "protection payments") as during and after the Gulf War. At the same time, no longer content with Japanese "voluntary" restrictions on exports to the United States – and in glaring contradiction of the free trade, *laissez faire* doctrine it preached to the rest of the world – the Bush administration began to press the Japanese government to promote administratively a reduction of its trade surplus with the United States.

And yet, even under the US-friendly LDP regime, Japan found fewer and fewer reasons to comply with US commands. Even when it did comply, the substance of the Japanese–US relationship after 1987 was that Japanese investment was progressively redirected from the United States to Asia. Having lost enormous amounts of money in the United States, Japanese capital finally discovered that the largest profits were not to be made in a futile attempt to take over US technology and culture or in financing the US's increasingly irresponsible military Keynesianism. Rather, they were to be made in pursuing more thoroughly and extensively the exploitation of Asian labor resources. The revaluation of the yen relative to the US dollar forced on Japan at the 1985 Plaza meeting of the Group of Seven had inflicted heavy losses on Japanese capital invested in US dollars. Unwittingly, however, it also boosted the power of Japanese capital to thrust its roots more deeply and widely in East and Southeast Asia. As figures 23 and 24 show, it was after 1985 that Japanese direct foreign investment experienced a new acceleration and the second round of regional industrial expansion began.

The more Japanese capital moved in this direction, the more it freed itself from addiction to US protection and purchasing power. As previously noted, the East Asian market became the most dynamic zone of expansion in an overall stagnant and increasingly depressed world-economy. More importantly, the two new rounds of regional industrial expansion generated by the redirection closer to home of the transnational expansion of Japanese capital, have spun old enemies of the Cold War era into a dense and extensive commercial web of mutual interdependence. As a result, protection costs in the region have decreased sharply, and the competitive advantages of East Asia as the new workshop of the world have increased correspondingly.

It is still too early to tell what the final outcome of this process of emancipation of the emergent East Asian regime of accumulation from the old (US) regime is going to be. The withdrawal of Japanese financial support for US deficit spending has accentuated the tendency for the overaccumulation crisis of the 1970s to turn into an overproduction crisis. In the 1970s, profits were driven down primarily by the growing mass of surplus capital that sought reinvestment in trade and production. In the 1980s, they have been driven down primarily by world-wide cuts in governmental and business expenditures. These cuts make an increasing number and variety of production and trade facilities redundant relative to purchasing power in circulation, and thereby provoke new rounds of cuts in expenditures in an "endless" downward spiral. By 1993, this downward spiral seemed to have caught up with Japan too. Nevertheless, there has been as yet little evidence of an escalation of great power conflicts or of a division of the world-economy into protectionist blocs as envisaged by Suzuki Yoshio on the eve of the crash of 1987.

Hot wars have indeed proliferated since 1987. But they have done so mostly in the form of local feuds over increasing material or pecuniary scarcities. Moreover, this escalation of violence has tended to unite militarily the dominant capitalist states in joint police or punitive actions rather than divide them in antagonistic blocs. As for protectionist sentiments, their rise both in the United States and in Western Europe has been strikingly ineffective in stopping the ongoing march of governments towards the further liberalization of their foreign trade, as witnessed by the ratification of the North American Free Trade Agreement by the US Congress and the successful conclusion of the Uruguay Round of GATT negotiations.

The main reason why the scenario envisaged by Suzuki Yoshio has not, and in all likelihood will not, materialize is that the lessons of history to which he referred are those of the transition from the British to the US regime of accumulation, from a regime based primarily on the opening up of the domestic market of the asset-rich nation (the United Kingdom) to a regime based primarily on the channeling of the financial resources of the newly risen asset-rich nation (the United States) to the upgrading of select national economies. Today, however, it is the US regime itself that is being superseded and the relationship between the newly risen, asset-rich nation (Japan) and the dominant nation of the old order (the United States) is radically different from the US–UK relationship in the first half of the twentieth century. As Fred Bergsten (1987: 771) asked: "Can the world's largest debtor nation remain the world's leading power? Can a small island nation that is now militarily insignificant and far removed from the traditional power centers provide at least some of the needed global leadership?"

These two questions point to the peculiar configuration of world power that has emerged at the end of the US systemic cycle of accumulation. On the one hand, the United States retains a near-monopoly of the legitimate use of violence on a world scale – a near-monopoly which has tightened since 1987 with the collapse of the USSR. But its financial indebtedness is such that it can continue to do so only with the consent of the organizations that control world liquidity. On the other hand, Japan and lesser "islands" of the East Asian capitalist archipelago have gained a near-monopoly of world liquidity – a near-monopoly which has also tightened since 1987 with the waning of West Germany's financial power after the takeover of East Germany. But their military defenselessness is such that they can continue to exercise that near-monopoly only with the consent of the organizations that control the legitimate use of violence on a world scale.

This peculiar configuration of world power seems to be eminently suited to the formation of yet another of those "memorable alliances" between the power of the gun and the power of money that have propelled forward in space and time the capitalist world-economy since the latter fifteenth century. All these memorable alliances except the first – the Genoese–Iberian – were alliances between governmental and business groups that belonged to the same state – the United Provinces, the United Kingdom, and the United States. As previously noted, throughout the US cycle of accumulation the relationship of political exchange that has linked the Japanese pursuit of profit to the US pursuit of power already resembled the Genoese–Iberian relationship of the sixteenth century. Now that the US regime is approaching or, perhaps, has entered its terminal crisis, what prevents this relationship from being renewed in order to promote and organize a new material expansion of the capitalist world-economy?

The answer to this question depends on what weight we attach to Bergsten's observation that Japan is "far removed from the traditional power centers." This is, indeed, another fundamental difference between the present configuration of world power and that obtaining in previous transitions – not just from the British to the US regime but also from the Genoese to the Dutch and from the Dutch to the British. For the first time since the earliest origins of the capitalist world-economy, the power of money seems to be slipping or to have slipped from Western hands.

To be sure, Japan has long been an "honorary member" of the West. But this honorary membership has always been conditional on a subordinate role in the power pursuits of "truly" Western states. As Cumings remarks, at the turn of the twentieth century Japan was a *Wunderkind* to the British but a "yellow peril" to the Germans; in the 1930s, it was a *Wunderkind* to the Germans and Italians but an industrial monster to the British; and in the 1980s, it became a *Wunderkind* to US internationalists but a monster to US protectionists. Generally speaking, Japan has been invited by Westerners to do well but not so well as to threaten them, "because at that point you move from miracle to menace" (Cumings 1993: 32).

What is new in the present configuration of power is that Japan has done so well by specializing in the pursuit of profit in the East Asian region and letting the United States specialize in the pursuit of world power (in cooperation and competition with other states that "happened" to be on the winning side of the Second World War) as to wrest from the West one of the two most important ingredients of its fortunes over the preceding five hundred years: control over surplus capital. For each of the successive systemic cycles of accumulation that made the fortunes of the West has been premissed on the formation of ever-more powerful territorialist–capitalist blocs of governmental and business organizations endowed with greater capabilities than the preceding bloc to widen or deepen the spatial and functional scope of the capitalist world-economy. The situation today seems to be such that this evolutionary process has reached, or is about to reach, its limits.

On the one hand, the state- and war-making capabilities of the traditional power centers of the capitalist West have gone so far that they can increase further only through the formation of a truly global world empire. With the collapse of the USSR and the revitalization of the UN Security Council as global "monopolist" of the legitimate use of violence in response to increasing systemic chaos, it is possible that over the next half-century or so such a world empire will actually be realized. What the substantive nature of this world empire will be – saving the planet from ecological self-destruction; regulating the poor of the world so as to keep them in their place; creating the conditions of a more equitable use of the world's resources; and so on – is a question to which the research agenda of this study cannot give any meaningful answer. But whatever the substantive nature of the world empire, its realization requires control over the most prolific sources of world surplus capital – sources which are now located in East Asia.

On the other hand, it is not at all clear by what means the traditional power centers of the West can acquire and retain this control. They may, of course, attempt to re-establish control over surplus capital by following in the path of development of East Asian capitalism. This they have already done, both by stepping up their own investments in East Asia and by seeking to incorporate more thoroughly and extensively reserves of cheap labor closer at home, as the United States and Canada are trying to do with NAFTA. Nevertheless, these attempts escalate further the global intercapitalist struggle at a time when the West's previous gifts of geography and history have turned into handicaps both absolutely and, above all, relative to East Asia. At best, this further escalation of global competitive pressures will undermine the profitability and liquidity of East Asian capital without enhancing those of North American (let alone Western European) capital. At worst, by disrupting the social cohesion on which the state- and war-making capabilities of the traditional power centers of the West have come to rest, it may well destroy the greatest residual source of strength of these centers.

Why not seek a way out of this self-destructive competitive struggle through a renegotiation of the terms of the political exchange that has linked East Asian capitalism to the global military Keynesianism of the United States throughout the Cold War era? Why not acknowledge the fundamental limits that the shift of the epicenter of systemic processes of capital accumulation to East Asia puts on the state- and war-making capabilities of the West, regardless of how unprecedented and unparalleled these capabilities may seem and actually are? Why not, in other words, let East Asian capital dictate the conditions under which it would assist the West to power? Is not this kind of deal what historical capitalism has been all about?

Again, the limited research agenda of this study enables us to raise these questions but not answer them meaningfully. Such answers must be sought primarily at the level of the underlying structures of market economy and material life which have been excluded from our investigation. We can none the less bring our story to a conclusion by pointing to the implications for capitalism as a world system of the three possible outcomes of the ongoing crisis of the US regime of accumulation.

First, the old centers may succeed in halting the course of capitalist history. The course of capitalist history over the last five hundred years has been a succession of financial expansions during which there occurred a change of guard at the commanding heights of the capitalist world-economy. This outcome is also present at the level of tendency in the current financial expansion. But this tendency is countered by the very extent of the state- and war-making capabilities of the old guard, which may well be in a position to appropriate through force, cunning, or persuasion the surplus capital that accumulates in the new centers and thereby terminate capitalist history through the formation of a truly global world empire.

Second, the old guard may fail to stop the course of capitalist history, and East Asian capital may come to occupy a commanding position in systemic processes of capital accumulation. Capitalist history would then continue, but under conditions that depart radically from what they have been since the formation of the modern inter-state system. The new guard at the commanding heights of the capitalist world-economy would lack the state- and war-making capabilities that, historically, have been associated with the enlarged reproduction of a capitalist layer on top of the market layer of the world-economy. If Adam Smith and Fernand Braudel were right in their contentions that capitalism would not survive such a disassociation, then capitalist history would not *be brought to an end* by the conscious actions of a particular agency as in the first outcome, but it would *come to an end* as a result of the unintended consequences of processes of world market formation. Capitalism (the "anti- market") would wither away with the state power that has made its fortunes in the modern era, and the underlying layer of the market economy would revert to some kind of anarchic order.

Finally, to paraphrase Schumpeter, before humanity chokes (or basks) in the dungeon (or paradise) of a post-capitalist world empire or of a post-capitalist world market society, it may well burn up in the horrors (or glories) of the escalating violence that has accompanied the liquidation of the Cold War world order. In this case, capitalist history would also come to an end but by reverting permanently to the systemic chaos from which it began six hundred years ago and which has been reproduced on an ever-increasing scale with each transition. Whether this would mean the end just of capitalist history or of all human history, it is impossible to tell.

Figures

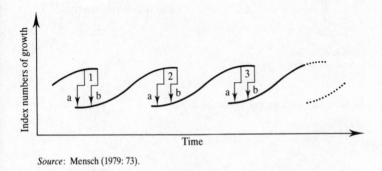

Source: Mensch (1979: 73).

Figure 1 Mensch's Metamorphosis Model

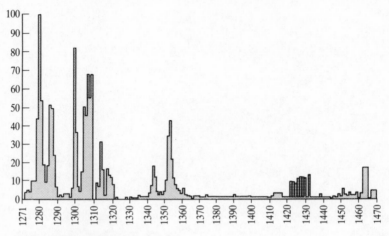

Source: Miskimim (1969: 140).
Note: Checkered bars indicate coinage of Calais.

Figure 2 Total Silver Coinage in England, 1273–1470 (1280 = 100)

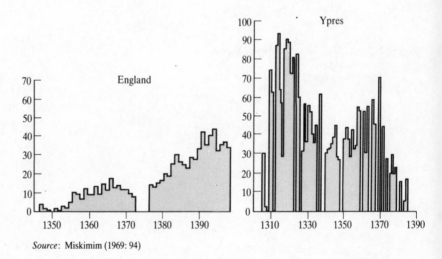

Source: Miskimim (1969: 94)

Figure 3 Trends in the Cloth Trade: Shipments from England and Production at Ypres (thousands of cloths)

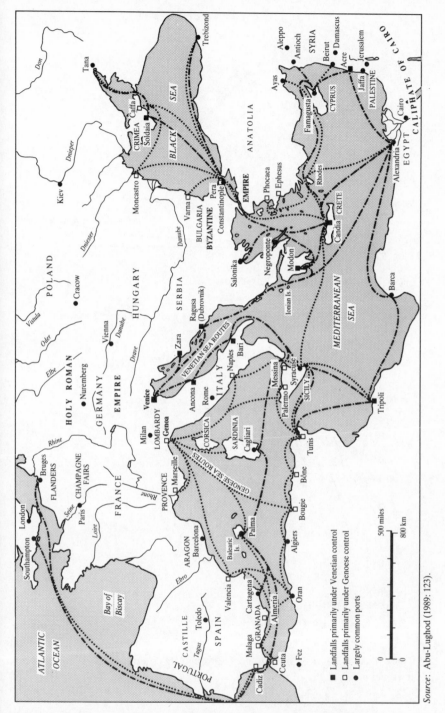

Figure 4 Mediterranean Routes of Genoa and Venice in the Middle Ages

Source: Abu-Lughod (1989: 123).

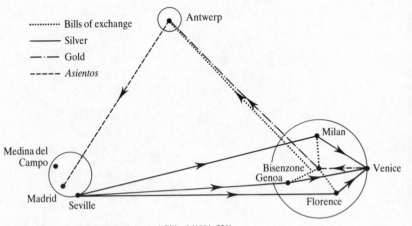

Source: Boyer-Xambeau, Deleplace, and Gillard (1991: 328).

Figure 5 The Genoese Space-of-Flows, Late Sixteenth and Early Seventeenth Centuries

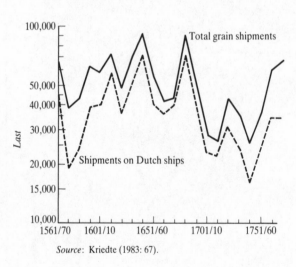

Source: Kriedte (1983: 67).

Figure 6 Volume of Grain Shipments through the Sound, 1562–1780 (ten-year averages in *Last*)

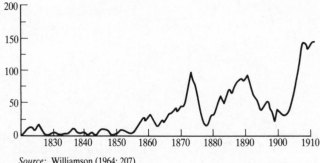

Source: Williamson (1964: 207).

Figure 7 British Capital Exports, 1820–1915 (millions of pounds sterling)

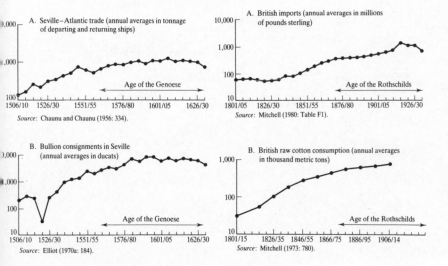

Figure 8 The Sixteenth-century Trade Expansion

Figure 9 The Nineteenth-century Trade Expansion

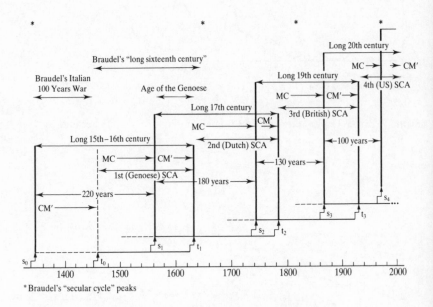

Figure 10 Long Centuries and Systemic Cycles of Accumulation

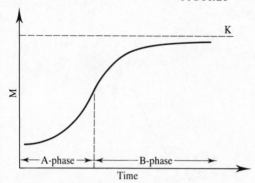

Figure 11 Ideotypical Trajectory of Mercantile Expansions

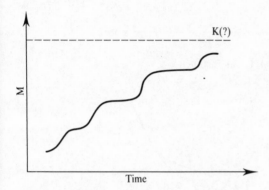

Figure 12 Hicks's Model of Successive Mercantile Expansions

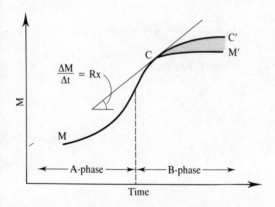

Figure 13 Bifurcation in the Trajectory of Mercantile Expansions

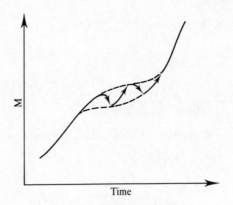

Figure 14 Local Turbulence

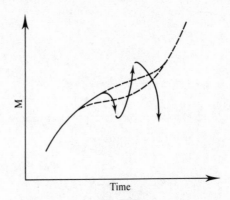

Figure 15 Systemic Turbulence

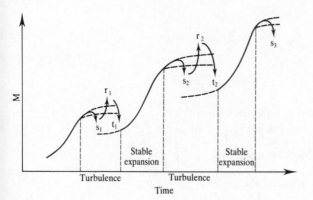

Figure 16 Metamorphosis Model of Systemic Cycles of Accumulation

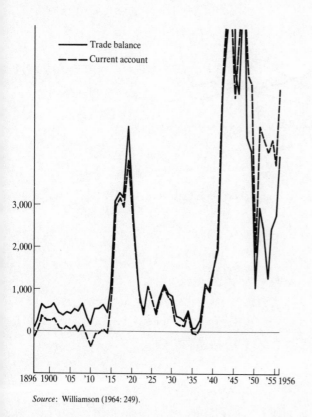

Source: Williamson (1964: 249).

Figure 17 US Trade Balance and Current Account, 1896–1956 (millions of dollars)

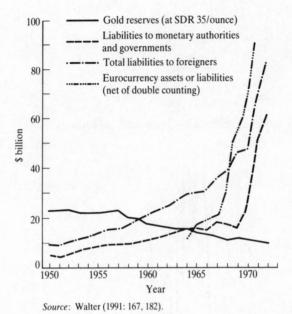

Source: Walter (1991: 167, 182).

Figure 18 US Gold Reserves and Short-term Liabilities, 1950–72

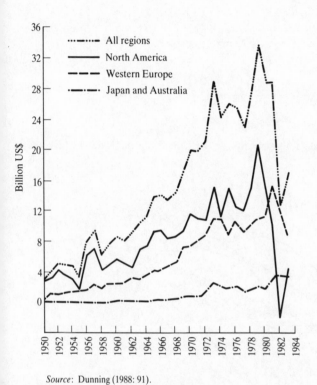

Source: Dunning (1988: 91).

Figure 19 Outflow of Foreign Direct Investments of Developed Market Economy Countries Distributed by Geographical Regions of Origin, 1950–83 (billion US$ at 1975 prices and US$ exchange rates)

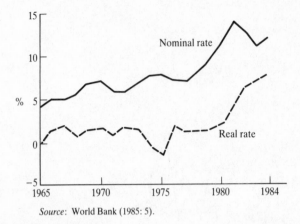

Source: World Bank (1985: 5).

Figure 20 Long-term Interest Rates in the United States, 1965–84 (average of quarterly data)

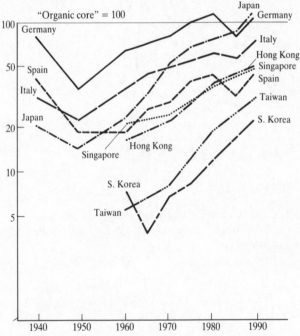

Source: Woytinsky and Woytinsky (1953); World Bank (various years);
Economic Planning Council (1977, 1982, 1988).

Figure 21 The Rise of East Asia in Comparative Perspective (per capita GNP, "organic core" = 100)

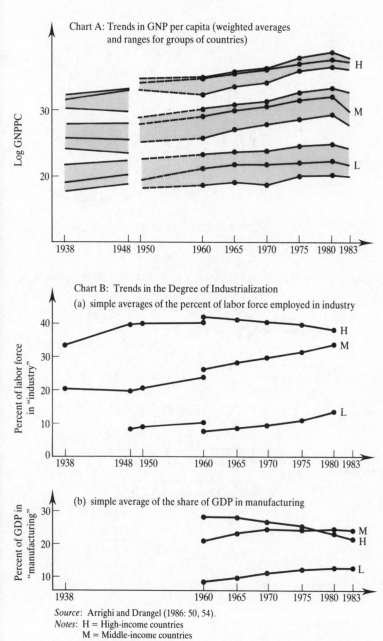

Chart A: Trends in GNP per capita (weighted averages and ranges for groups of countries)

Chart B: Trends in the Degree of Industrialization

(a) simple averages of the percent of labor force employed in industry

(b) simple average of the share of GDP in manufacturing

Source: Arrighi and Drangel (1986: 50, 54).
Notes: H = High-income countries
       M = Middle-income countries
       L = Low-income countries

Figure 22 Income Gaps versus Industrialization Gaps

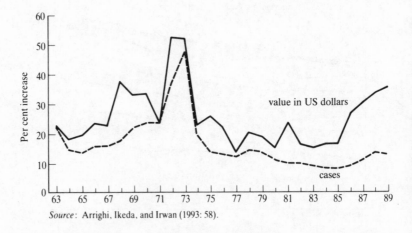

Source: Arrighi, Ikeda, and Irwan (1993: 58).

Figure 23 Rate of Increase of Accumulated Japanese Direct Foreign Investment

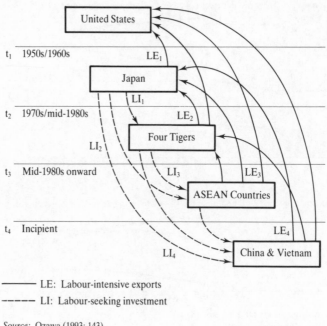

———— LE: Labour-intensive exports

– – – – LI: Labour-seeking investment

Source: Ozawa (1993: 143).

Figure 24 The East Asian Space-of-Flows, Late Twentieth Century

References

Abu-Lughod, Janet, *Before European Hegemony: The World System A.D. 1250–1350*, New York: Oxford University Press 1989.

Adams, Richard, "Harnessing Technological Development," in J. Poggie and R.N. Lynch, eds., *Rethinking Modernization: Anthropological Perspectives*, Westport, CT: Greenwood Press 1975, pp. 37–68.

Aglietta, Michel, *A Theory of Capitalist Regulation: The US Experience*, London: New Left Books 1979a.

—— "La notion de monnaie internationale et les problèmes monétaires européens dans une perspective historique," *Revue Economique*, 30, 5, 1979b, pp. 808–44.

Aglietta, Michel and André Orléan, *La Violence de la monnaie*, Paris: Presses Universitaires de France 1982.

Aguilar, Alonso, *Pan-Americanism from Monroe to the Present: A View from the Other Side*, New York: Monthly Review Press 1968.

Allen, G.C., *Japan's Economic Policy*, London: Macmillan 1980.

Amin, Samir, *The Accumulation of Capital on a World Scale*, New York: Monthly Review Press 1974.

—— *Empire of Chaos*, New York: Monthly Review Press 1992.

Anderson, Perry, *Lineages of the Absolutist State*, London: New Left Books 1974.

—— "The Figures of Descent," *New Left Review*, 161, 1987, pp. 20–77.

Aoki, Masahiko, "Aspects of the Japanese Firm," in M. Aoki, ed., *The Economic Analysis of the Japanese Firm*, Amsterdam: North-Holland 1984, pp. 3–43.

Armstrong, Philip and Andrew Glyn, *Accumulation, Profits, State Spending: Data for Advanced Capitalist Countries 1952–1983*, Oxford: Oxford Institute of Economics and Statistics 1986.

Armstrong, Philip, Andrew Glyn, and John Harrison, *Capitalism since World War II. The Making and Breakup of the Great Boom*, London: Fontana 1984.

Arndt, H.W., *The Economic Lessons of the Nineteen-Thirties*, London: Frank Cass 1963.

Arrighi, Giovanni, "Imperialismo," *Enciclopedia*, VII, Turin: Einaudi 1979, pp. 157–98.

—— "A Crisis of Hegemony," in S. Amin, G. Arrighi, A.G. Frank, and I. Wallerstein, *Dynamics of Global Crisis*, New York: Monthly Review Press 1982, pp. 55–108.

—— *The Geometry of Imperialism*, London: Verso 1983.

373

—— "The Developmentalist Illusion: A Reconceptualization of the Semi-periphery," in W.G. Martin, ed., *Semiperipheral States in the World-Economy*, Westport, CT: Greenwood Press 1990a, pp. 11–47.

—— "Marxist Century–American Century: The Making and Remaking of the World Labor Movement," in S. Amin, G. Arrighi, A.G. Frank, and I. Wallerstein, *Transforming the Revolution: Social Movements and the World System*, New York: Monthly Review Press 1990b, pp. 54–95.

—— "World Income Inequalities and the Future of Socialism," *New Left Review*, 189, 1991, pp. 39–64.

Arrighi, Giovanni, Kenneth Barr, and Shuji Hisaeda, "The Transformation of Business Enterprise," Binghamton, NY: Fernand Braudel Center, State University of New York 1993.

Arrighi, Giovanni and Jessica Drangel, "The Stratification of the World-Economy: An Exploration of the Semiperipheral Zone," *Review*, 10, 1, 1986, pp. 9–74.

Arrighi, Giovanni, Satoshi Ikeda, and Alex Irwan, "The Rise of East Asia: One Miracle or Many?" in R.A. Palat, ed., *Pacific-Asia and the Future of the World-System*, Westport, CT: Greenwood Press 1993, pp. 41–65.

Auerbach, Paul, Meghnad Desai, and Ali Shamsavari, "The Transition from Actually Existing Capitalism," *New Left Review*, 170, 1988, pp. 61–78.

Bagchi, Amiya Kumar, *The Political Economy of Underdevelopment*, Cambridge: Cambridge University Press 1982.

Bairoch, Paul, *Commerce extérieur et développement économique de l'Europe au XIXe siècle*, Paris and The Hague: Mouton 1976a.

—— "Europe's Gross National Product: 1800–1975," *Journal of Economic History*, 5, 2, 1976b, pp. 273–340.

Balibar, Etienne, "The Nation Form: History and Ideology," *Review*, 13, 3, 1990, pp. 329–61.

Barbour, Violet, *Capitalism in Amsterdam in the Seventeenth Century*, Baltimore, MD: Johns Hopkins University Press 1950.

Barfield, Thomas J., *The Perilous Frontier: Nomadic Empires and China*, Oxford: Oxford University Press 1989.

Barnet, Richard J. and Ronald E. Müller, *Global Reach. The Power of the Multinational Corporations*, New York: Simon & Schuster 1974.

Baron, H., *The Crisis of the Early Italian Renaissance*, Princeton, NJ: Princeton University Press 1955.

Barr, Kenneth, "Long Waves: A Selective Annotated Bibliography," *Review*, 2, 4, 1979, pp. 675–718.

—— "Business Enterprise in the World-Economy in the Late Eighteenth and Early Nineteenth Centuries," PhD dissertation, Department of Sociology, State University of New York at Binghamton forthcoming.

Barraclough, Geoffrey, *An Introduction to Contemporary History*, Harmondsworth: Penguin Books 1967.

Barrat Brown, Michael, *The Economics of Imperialism*, Harmondsworth: Penguin Books 1974.

—— "Away with all the Great Arches: Anderson's History of British Capitalism," *New Left Review*, 167, 1988, pp. 22–51.

Bayly, C.A., *Indian Society and the Making of the British Empire*, Cambridge: Cambridge University Press 1988.

Becattini, Giacomo, "Dal 'settore' industriale al 'distretto' industriale: alcune considerazioni sull'unità di indagine dell'economia industriale," *Rivista di economia e politica industriale*, 1, 1979, pp. 7–21.

—— "The Marshallian Industrial District as a Socio-Economic Notion," in F. Pyke, ed., *Industrial Districts and Inter-Firm Cooperation in Italy*, 1990, pp. 37–51.

Bergesen, Albert, "Modeling Long Waves of Crises in the World-System," in A. Bergesen, ed., *Crises in the World-System*, Beverly Hills, CA: Sage 1983, pp. 73–92.

Bergesen, Albert and Ronald Schoenberg, "Long Waves of Colonial Expansion and Contraction, 1415–1969," in A. Bergesen, ed., *Studies of the Modern World-System*, New York: Academic Press 1980.

Bergsten, Fred C., "Economic Imbalances and World Politics," *Foreign Affairs*, 65, 4, 1987, pp. 770–94.

Blackburn, Robin, *The Overthrow of Colonial Slavery, 1776–1848*, London: Verso 1988.

Bloch, Marc, *Esquisse d'une histoire monétaire de l'Europe*, Paris: Cahier des Annales, No. 9 1955.

Block, Fred, *The Origins of International Economic Disorder. A Study of United States Monetary Policy from World War II to the Present*, Berkeley, CA: University of California Press 1977.

Bluestone, Barry and Bennett Harrison, *The Deindustrialization of America: Plant Closings, Community Abandonment, and the Dismantling of Basic Industry*, New York: Basic Books 1982.

Boli, John, "Sovereignty from a World Polity Perspective," paper presented at the Annual Meeting of the American Sociological Association, Miami, FL 1993.

Boltho, Andrea, "Western Europe's Economic Stagnation," *New Left Review*, 201, 1993, pp. 60–75.

Borden, William S., *The Pacific Alliance: United States Foreign Economic Policy and Japanese Trade Recovery 1947–1955*, Madison, WI: University of Wisconsin Press 1984.

Bousquet, Nicole, "Esquisse d'une théorie de l'alternance de périodes de concurrence et d'hégémonie au centre de l'économie-monde capitaliste," *Review*, 2, 4, 1979, pp. 501–18.

—— "From Hegemony to Competition: Cycles of the Core?" in T.K. Hopkins and I. Wallerstein, eds., *Processes of the World-System*, Beverly Hills, CA: Sage, 1980, pp. 46–83.

Boxer, Charles R., *The Dutch in Brazil 1624–1654*, Oxford: Clarendon Press 1957.

—— *The Dutch Seaborne Empire 1600–1800*, New York: Knopf 1965.

—— *The Portuguese Seaborne Empire 1415–1825*, Harmondsworth: Penguin Books 1973.

Boyer, Robert, *The Regulation School: A Critical Introduction*, New York: Columbia University Press 1990.

Boyer-Xambeau, M.T., G. Deleplace, and L. Gillard, *Banchieri e Principi. Moneta e Credito nell'Europa del Cinquecento*, Turin: Einaudi 1991.

Braudel, Fernand, *The Mediterranean and the Mediterranean World in the Age of Philip II*, 2 vols, New York: Harper & Row 1976.

—— *Afterthoughts on Material Civilization and Capitalism*, Baltimore, MD: Johns Hopkins University Press 1977.

—— *The Structures of Everyday Life*, New York: Harper & Row 1981.

—— *The Wheels of Commerce*, New York: Harper & Row 1982.

—— *The Perspective of the World*, New York: Harper & Row 1984.

Braudel, Fernand and Frank Spooner, "Prices in Europe from 1450 to 1750," in E.E. Rich and C.H. Wilson, eds., *The Cambridge Economic History of*

Europe, IV, London: Cambridge University Press, 1967, pp. 374–486.

Brewer, John, *The Sinews of Power. War, Money and the English State, 1688–1783*, London: Unwin 1989.

Bullock, Alan, *Ernst Bevin: Foreign Secretary*, Oxford: Oxford University Press 1983.

Bunker, Stephen G. and Denis O'Hearn, "Strategies of Economic Ascendants for Access to Raw Materials: A Comparison of the United States and Japan," in R.A. Palat, ed., *Pacific-Asia and the Future of the World-System*, Westport, CT: Greenwood Press 1993, pp. 83–102.

Burckhardt, Jacob, *The Civilization of the Renaissance in Italy*, Oxford: Phaidon Press 1945.

Burke, Peter, *The Italian Renaissance. Culture and Society in Italy*, Princeton, NJ: Princeton University Press 1986.

Cain, P.J. and A.G. Hopkins, "The Political Economy of British Expansion Overseas, 1750–1914," *Economic History Review*, 2nd ser., 33, 4, 1980, pp. 463–90.

—— "Gentlemanly Capitalism and British Expansion Overseas. I. The Old Colonial System, 1688–1850," *Economic History Review*, 2nd ser., 39, 4, 1986, pp. 501–25.

Calleo, David P., *The Atlantic Fantasy*, Baltimore, MD: Johns Hopkins University Press 1970.

—— *The Imperious Economy*, Cambridge, MA: Harvard University Press 1982.

Calleo, David P. and Benjamin M. Rowland, *America and the World Political Economy. Atlantic Dreams and National Realities*, Bloomington and London: Indiana University Press 1973.

Cameron, Rondo, "England, 1750–1844," in R. Cameron, ed., *Banking in the Early Stages of Industrialization: A Study in Comparative Economic History*, New York: Oxford University Press 1967, pp. 15–59.

Carr, Edward, *Nationalism and After*, London: Macmillan 1945.

Carter, Alice C., *Getting, Spending, and Investing in Early Modern Times*, Assen: Van Gorcum 1975.

Chandler, Alfred, *The Visible Hand: The Managerial Revolution in American Business*, Cambridge, MA: The Belknap Press 1977.

—— "The United States: Evolution of Enterprise," in P. Mathias and M.M. Postan, eds., *The Cambridge Economic History of Europe*, vol. VII, part 2, Cambridge: Cambridge University Press 1978.

—— *Scale and Scope. The Dynamics of Industrial Capitalism*, Cambridge, MA: The Belknap Press 1990.

Chapman, Stanley, *The Cotton Industry in the Industrial Revolution*, London: Macmillan 1972.

—— *The Rise of Merchant Banking*, London: Unwin Hyman 1984.

Chase-Dunn, Christopher, *Global Formation. Structures of the World-Economy*, Oxford: Basil Blackwell 1989.

Chaudhuri, K.N., *The English East India Company: The Study of an Early Joint-Stock Company 1600–1640*, London: Frank Cass 1965.

Chaunu, Huguette and Pierre Chaunu, *Seville et l'Atlantique 1504–1650*, vol. 6, Paris: Armand Colin 1956.

Cipolla, Carlo M., "The Decline of Italy," *Economic History Review*, 5, 2, 1952, pp. 178–87.

—— *Guns and Sails in the Early Phase of European Expansion 1400–1700*, London: Collins 1965.

—— *Before the Industrial Revolution. European Society and Economy,*

1000–1700, New York: Norton 1980.

Coase, Richard, "The Nature of the Firm," *Economica* (n.s.) 4, 15, 1937, pp. 386–405.

Cohen, Benjamin J., *Organizing the World's Money*, New York: Basic Books 1977.

Cohen, Jerome B., *Japan's Postwar Economy*, Bloomington, IN: Indiana University Press 1958.

Copeland, Melvin Thomas, *The Cotton Manufacturing Industry of the United States*, New York: Augustus M. Kelley 1966.

Coplin, W.D., "International Law and Assumptions about the State System," in R.A. Falk and W.F. Henreider, eds., *International Law and Organization*, Philadelphia: Lippincott 1968.

Cox, Oliver, *Foundations of Capitalism*, New York: Philosophical Library 1959.

Cox, Robert, "Gramsci, Hegemony, and International Relations: An Essay in Method," *Millennium. Journal of International Studies*, 12, 2, 1983, pp. 162–75.

—— *Production, Power, and World Order: Social Forces in the Making of History*, New York: Columbia University Press 1987.

Crouzet, François, *The Victorian Economy*, London: Methuen 1982.

Cumings, Bruce, "The Origins and Development of the Northeast Asian Political Economy: Industrial Sectors, Product Cycles, and Political Consequences," in F.C. Deyo, ed., *The Political Economy of New Asian Industrialism*, Ithaca, NY: Cornell University Press 1987, pp. 44–83.

—— "The Political Economy of the Pacific Rim," in R.A. Palat, ed., *Pacific-Asia and the Future of the World-System*, Westport, CT: Greenwood Press 1993, pp. 21–37.

Davies, K.G., *The Royal African Company*, London: Longmans 1957.

—— *The North Atlantic World in the Seventeenth Century*, Minneapolis: University of Minnesota Press 1974.

Davis, Ralph, "English Foreign Trade, 1660–1700," *Economic History Review*, 7, 2, 1954, pp. 150–66.

—— "English Foreign Trade, 1700–1774," *Economic History Review*, 15, 2, 1962, pp. 285–303.

—— *The Industrial Revolution and British Overseas Trade*, Leicester: Leicester University Press 1979.

de Cecco, Marcello, "Inflation and Structural Change in the Euro-dollar Market," *EUI Working Papers*, 23, Florence: European University Institute 1982.

—— *The International Gold Standard: Money and Empire*, New York: St Martin's Press 1984.

Dehio, Ludwig, *The Precarious Balance: Four Centuries of the European Power Struggle*, New York: Vintage 1962.

de Roover, Raymond, *The Rise and Decline of the Medici Bank, 1397–1494*, Cambridge, MA: Harvard University Press 1963.

De Vroey, Michel, "A Regulation Approach Interpretation of the Contemporary Crisis," *Capital and Class*, 23, 1984, pp. 45–66.

Dickson, P.G.M., *The Financial Revolution in England: A Study in the Development of Public Credit*, London: Macmillan 1967.

Dietz, F., *English Government Finance 1485–1558*, New York: Barnes & Noble 1964.

Dobb, Maurice, *Studies in the Development of Capitalism*, London: Routledge & Kegan Paul 1963.

Dockés, Pierre, *L'Espace dans la pensée économique du XVIe au XVIIIe siècle*, Paris: Flammarion 1969.

Drucker, Peter F., *Post-Capitalist Society*, New York: Harper & Row 1993.

Dunning, John H., "International Business, the Recession and Economic Restructuring," in N. Hood and J.-E. Vahlne, eds., *Strategies in Global Competition*, London: Croom Helm 1988, pp. 84–103.

Eccleston, Bernard, *State and Society in Post-War Japan*, Cambridge: Polity Press 1989.

Economic Planning Council, *Taiwan Statistical Yearbook*, Taipei: Economic Planning Council 1977; 1982; 1988.

Ehrenberg, Richard, *Capital & Finance in the Age of the Renaissance. A Study of the Fuggers and Their Connections*, Fairfield, NJ: Augustus M. Kelly 1985.

Eichengreen, Barry, "International Monetary Instability Between the Wars: Structural Flaws or Misguided Policies?" in B. Eichengreen, ed., *Monetary Regime Transformation*, Aldershot: Edward Elgar 1992, pp. 355–400.

Eichengreen, Barry and Richard Portes, "Debt and Default in the 1930s. Causes and Consequences," *European Economic Review*, 30, 1986, pp. 599–640.

Elliott, J.H., *Imperial Spain. 1469–1716*, Harmondsworth: Penguin Books 1970a.

—— *The Old World and the New 1492–1650*, Cambridge: Cambridge University Press 1970b.

Elliott, William Y., ed., *The Political Economy of American Foreign Policy. Its Concepts, Strategy, and Limits*, New York: Henry Holt & Co. 1955.

Emmer, P.C., "The West India Company, 1621–1791: Dutch or Atlantic?" in L. Blussé and F. Gastra, eds., *Companies and Trade*, Leiden: Leiden University Press 1981, pp. 71–95.

—— "The Two Expansion Systems in the Atlantic," *Itinerario*, 15, 1, 1991, pp. 21–7.

Emmott, Bill, *Japanophobia. The Myth of the Invincible Japanese*, New York: Random House 1993.

Engels, Frederic, *Socialism: Utopian and Scientific*, Moscow: Foreign Languages Publishing House 1958.

Evans-Pritchard, Edward, *The Nuer: A Description of the Modes of Livelihood and Political Institutions of the Nilotic People*, Oxford: Clarendon Press 1940.

Farnie, D.A., *The English Cotton Industry and the World Market, 1815–1896*, Oxford: Clarendon Press 1979.

Favier, Jean, *Les Finances pontificales à l'époque du grand schisme d'Occident, 1378–1409*, Paris: Boccard 1966.

Feige, Edgar, "Defining and Estimating Underground and Informal Economies: The New Institutional Economic Approach," *World Development*, 18, 7, 1990, pp. 989–1002.

Fieldhouse, D.K., *The Colonial Empires: A Comparative Survey from the Eighteenth Century*, New York: Delacorte 1967.

Fishlow, Albert, "Lessons from the Past: Capital Markets During the 19th Century and the Interwar Period," in M. Kahler, ed., *The Politics of International Debt*, Ithaca NY: Cornell University Press 1986, pp. 37–93.

Franko, Lawrence G., *The European Multinationals*, New York: Harper & Row 1976.

Frieden, Jeffry A., *Banking on the World. The Politics of American International Finance*, New York: Harper & Row 1987.

Fröbel, Folker, Jürgen Heinrichs, and Otto Kreye, *The New International*

Division of Labour: Structural Unemployment in Industrialized Countries and Industrialization in Developing Countries, Cambridge: Cambridge University Press 1980.

Galbraith, John, *The New Industrial State*, Boston, MA: Houghton Mifflin 1985.

Gallagher, John and Ronald Robinson, "The Imperialism of Free Trade," *Economic History Review*, 6, 1, 1953, pp. 1–15.

Gardner, Edmund G., *Florence and its History*, London: Dent & Sons 1953.

Gardner, Richard, *Sterling–Dollar Diplomacy in Current Perspective*, New York: Columbia University Press 1986.

Gattrell, V.A.C., "Labour, Power, and The Size of Firms in Lancashire Cotton in the Second Quarter of the Nineteenth Century," *Economic History Review*, 2nd ser., 30, 1, 1977, pp. 95–139.

Giddens, Anthony, *The Nation-State and Violence*, Berkeley, CA: California University Press 1987.

Gilbert, Felix, *The Pope, his Bankers, and Venice*, Cambridge, MA: Harvard University Press 1980.

Gill, Stephen, "Hegemony, Consensus and Trilateralism," *Review of International Studies*, 12, 1986, pp. 205–21.

——, ed., *Gramsci, Historical Materialism and International Relations*, Cambridge: Cambridge University Press 1993.

Gill, Stephen and David Law, *The Global Political Economy: Perspectives, Problems and Policies*, Baltimore, MD: The Johns Hopkins University Press 1988.

Gills, Barry and André G. Frank, "World System Cycles, Crises, and Hegemonic Shifts, 1700 BC to 1700 AD," *Review*, 15, 4, 1992, pp. 621–87.

Gilpin, Robert, *U.S. Power and the Multinational Corporation*, New York: Basic Books 1975.

—— *The Political Economy of International Relations*, Princeton, NJ: Princeton University Press 1987.

Gluckman, Max, *Custom and Conflict in Africa*, Oxford: Basil Blackwell 1963.

Glyn, Andrew, Alan Hughes, Alain Lipietz, and Ajit Singh, "The Rise and Fall of the Golden Age," in S.A. Marglin and J.B. Schor, eds., *The Golden Age of Capitalism. Reinterpreting the Postwar Experience*, Oxford: Clarendon Press 1991, pp. 39–125.

Goldstein, Joshua S., *Long Cycles: Prosperity and War in the Modern Age*, New Haven, CT: Yale University Press 1988.

Goldstein, Joshua S. and David P. Rapkin, "After Insularity. Hegemony and the Future World Order," *Futures*, 23, 1991, pp. 935–59.

Goldstone, Jack A., *Revolution and Rebellion in the Early Modern World*, Berkeley, CA: University of California Press 1991.

Gordon, David, "Stages of Accumulation and Long Economic Swings," in T. Hopkins and I. Wallerstein, eds., *Processes of the World System*, Beverly Hills, CA: Sage 1980, pp. 9–45.

—— "The Global Economy: New Edifice or Crumbling Foundations?" *New Left Review*, 168, 1988, pp. 24–64.

Gramsci, Antonio, *Selections from the Prison Notebooks*, New York: International Publishers 1971.

Greenberg, Michael, *British Trade and the Opening of China 1800–1842*, New York: Monthly Review Press 1979.

Gross, Leo, "The Peace of Westphalia, 1648–1948," in R.A. Falk and W.H. Hanrieder, eds., *International Law and Organization*, Philadelphia: Lippincott 1968, pp. 45–67.

Gurr, T.R., "Historical Trends in Violent Crime: Europe and the United States," in T.R. Gurr, ed., *Violence in America*, vol. II, Beverly Hills, CA: Sage 1989, pp. 21–54.

Gush, G., *Renaissance Armies 1480–1650*, Cambridge: Stephens 1975.

Haggard, Stephan and Tun-jen Cheng, "State and Foreign Capital in the East Asian NICs," in F.C. Deyo, ed., *The Political Economy of New Asian Industrialism*, Ithaca, NY: Cornell University Press 1987, pp. 84–135.

Halliday, Fred, *The Making of the Second Cold War*, London: Verso 1986.

Harrod, Roy, *Money*, London: Macmillan 1969.

Hartwell, R.M., "Demographic, Political and Social Transformations of China 750–1550," *Harvard Journal of Asiatic Studies*, 42, 2, 1982, pp. 365–422.

Harvey, David, "The Geopolitics of Capitalism," in D. Gregory and J. Urry, eds., *Social Relations and Spatial Structures*, New York: St Martin's Press 1985.

—— *The Condition of Postmodernity: An Enquiry into the Origins of Cultural Change*, Oxford: Basil Blackwell 1989.

Heers, Jacques, *Gênes au XVe Siècle*, Paris: SEVPEN, 1961.

—— *Société et économie à Gênes (XIVe–XVe siècles)*, London: Variorum Reprints 1979.

Helleiner, Eric, "Japan and the Changing Global Financial Order," *International Journal*, 47, 1992, pp. 420–44.

Henderson, W.O., *The Rise of German Industrial Power 1834–1914*, Berkeley, CA: California University Press 1975.

Herz, J.H., *International Politics in the Atomic Age*, New York: Columbia University Press 1959.

Hicks, John, *A Theory of Economic History*, Oxford: Clarendon Press 1969.

Hilferding, Rudolf, *Finance Capital. A Study of the Latest Phase of Capitalist Development*, London: Routledge & Kegan Paul 1981.

Hill, Christopher, *Puritanism and Revolution*, New York: Schocken Books 1958.

—— *Reformation to Industrial Revolution. A Social and Economic History of Britain, 1530–1780*, London: Weidenfeld & Nicolson 1967.

Hill, Hal and Brian Johns, "The Role of Direct Foreign Investment in Developing East Asian Countries," *Weltwirtshaftliches Archiv*, 129, 1985, pp. 355–81.

Hill, Richard C., "Comparing Transnational Production Systems: The Automobile Industry in the USA and Japan," *International Journal of Urban and Regional Research*, 13, 2, 1989, pp. 462–80.

Hirschman, Albert, *The Strategy of Economic Development*, New Haven, CT: Yale University Press 1958.

Hirst, Paul and Jonathan Zeitlin, "Flexible Specialization versus Post-Fordism: Theory, Evidence and Policy Implications," *Economy and Society*, 20, 1, 1991, pp. 1–56.

Hobsbawm, Eric, *The Age of Revolution 1789–1848*, New York: New American Library 1962.

—— *Industry and Empire: An Economic History of Britain since 1750*, London: Weidenfeld & Nicolson 1968.

—— *The Age of Capital 1848–1875*, New York: New American Library 1979.

—— *The Age of Empire 1875–1914*, New York: Pantheon Books 1987.

—— *Nations and Nationalism since 1780: Programme, Myth, Reality*, Cambridge: Cambridge University Press 1991.

Hobson, John, *Imperialism. A Study*, London: George Allen & Unwin 1938.

Hopkins, Terence K., "Note on the Concept of Hegemony," *Review*, 13, 3, 1990, pp. 409–11.

Hopkins, Terence and Immanuel Wallerstein (with the Research Working Group on Cyclical Rhythms and Secular Trends), "Cyclical Rhythms and Secular Trends of the Capitalist World-Economy: Some Premises, Hypotheses and Questions," *Review*, 2, 4, 1979, pp. 483–500.

Hugill, Peter J., *World Trade since 1431. Geography, Technology, and Capitalism*, Baltimore, MD: The Johns Hopkins University Press 1993.

Hymer, Stephen, "The Multinational Corporation and the Law of Uneven Development," in J.N. Bhagwati, ed., *Economics and World Order*, New York: Macmillan 1972, pp. 113–40.

Hymer, Stephen and Robert Rowthorn, "Multinational Corporations and International Oligopoly: The Non-American Challenge," in C.P. Kindelberger, ed., *The International Corporation: A Symposium*, Cambridge, MA: The MIT Press 1970, pp. 57–91.

Ikeda, Satoshi, "Structure of the World-Economy 1945–1990," Binghamton, NY: Fernand Braudel Center, State University of New York 1993.

Ikenberry, John G., "Rethinking the Origins of American Hegemony," *Political Science Quarterly*, 104, 3, 1989, pp. 375–400.

Ingham, Geoffrey, *Capitalism Divided? The City and Industry in British Social Development*, London: Macmillan 1984.

—— "Commercial Capital and British Development," *New Left Review*, 172, 1988, pp. 45–65.

—— "The Production of World Money: A Comparison of Sterling and the Dollar," paper presented at the Second ESRC Conference on Structural Change in the West, Emmanuel College, Cambridge 1989.

Israel, Jonathan, *Dutch Primacy in World Trade, 1585–1740*, Oxford: Clarendon Press 1989.

Itoh, Makoto, *The World Economic Crisis and Japanese Capitalism*, New York: St Martin's Press 1990.

Jackson, Robert, *Quasi-States: Sovereignty, International Relations and the Third World*, Cambridge: Cambridge University Press 1990.

Jameson, Fredric, "Postmodernism, or the Cultural Logic of Late Capitalism," *New Left Review*, 146, 1984, pp. 53–92.

Jenkins, Brian, *New Modes of Conflict*, Santa Monica, CA: RAND Corporation 1983.

Jenks, Leland H., *The Migration of British Capital to 1875*, New York and London: Knopf 1938.

Jeremy, David J., "Damming the Flood: British Government Efforts to Check the Outflow of Technicians and Machinery, 1780–1843," *Business History Review*, 51, 1, 1977, pp. 1–34.

Jessop, Bob, "Regulation Theories in Retrospect and Prospect," *Economy and Society*, 19, 2, 1990, pp. 153–216.

Johnson, Chalmers, *MITI and the Japanese Miracle*, Stanford, CA: Stanford University Press 1982.

—— "The Japanese Political Economy: A Crisis in Theory," *Ethics and International Affairs*, 2, 1988, pp. 79–97.

Kasaba, Reşat, "'By Compass and Sword!' The Meaning of 1492," *Middle East Report*, Sept.–Oct. 1992, pp. 6–10.

Kennedy, Paul, *The Rise and Fall of British Naval Mastery*, London: Scribner 1976.

—— *The Rise and Fall of the Great Powers: Economic Change and Military Conflict from 1500 to 2000*, New York: Random House 1987.

—— *Preparing for the Twenty-First Century*, New York: Random House 1993.

Keohane, Robert, *After Hegemony: Cooperation and Discord in the World*

Political Economy, Princeton, NJ: Princeton University Press 1984a.

—— "The World Political Economy and the Crisis of Political Liberalism," in J.H. Goldthorpe, ed., *Order and Conflict in Contemporary Capitalism,* New York: Oxford University Press 1984b, pp. 15–38.

Keynes, John Maynard, *A Treatise on Money,* vol. II, London: Macmillan 1930.

Kindleberger, Charles, *The World in Depression 1929–1939,* Berkeley, CA: University of California Press 1973.

—— "The Rise of Free Trade in Western Europe, 1820 to 1875," *Journal of Economic History,* 35, 1, 1975, pp. 20–55.

—— *Economic Response. Comparative Studies in Trade, Finance, and Growth,* Cambridge: Cambridge University Press 1978.

Kirby, S., *Towards the Pacific Century. Economic Development in the Pacific Basin,* Economist Intelligence Unit Special Report 137, London: The Economist Intelligence Unit 1983.

Knapp, J.A., "Capital Exports and Growth," *Economic Journal,* 67, 267, 1957, pp. 432–44.

Knowles, L.C.A., *Economic Development of the Overseas Empire,* vol. I, London: Routledge & Kegan Paul 1928.

Kojima, Kiyoshi, *Japan and a New World Economic Order,* Boulder, CO: Westview 1977.

Kotkin, Joel and Yoriko Kishimoto, *The Third Century. America's Resurgence in the Asian Era,* New York: Ivy Books 1988.

Krasner, Stephen, "The Tokyo Round: Particularistic Interests and Prospects for Stability in the Global Trading System," *International Studies Quarterly,* 23, 4, 1979, pp. 491–531.

—— "A Trade Strategy for the United States," *Ethics and International Affairs,* 2, 1988, pp. 17–35.

Kriedte, Peter, *Peasants, Landlords, amd Merchant Capitalists. Europe and the World Economy, 1500–1800,* Cambridge: Cambridge University Press 1983.

LaFeber, Walter, *The New Empire. An Interpretation of American Expansion, 1860–1898,* Ithaca, NY: Cornell University Press 1963.

Landes, David S., "The Structure of Enterprise in the Ninenteenth Century," in D. Landes, ed., *The Rise of Capitalism,* New York: Macmillan 1966.

—— *The Unbound Prometheus. Technological Change and Industrial Development in Western Europe from 1750 to the Present,* Cambridge: Cambridge University Press 1969.

Lane, Frederic, *Venice and History,* Baltimore, MD: The Johns Hopkins University Press 1966.

—— *Profits from Power. Readings in Protection Rent and Violence-Controlling Enterprises,* Albany, NY: State University of New York Press 1979.

Lash, Scott, and John Urry, *The End of Organized Capitalism,* Madison: University of Wisconsin Press 1987.

Lenin, Vladimir, "Imperialism, the Highest Stage of Capitalism," in *Selected Works,* vol. I, Moscow: Foreign Languages Publishing House 1952.

Levitt, Kari, *Silent Surrender: The American Economic Empire in Canada,* New York: Liveright Press 1970.

Lewis, M., *The Spanish Armada,* London: Batsford 1960.

Lichteim, George, *Imperialism,* Harmondsworth: Penguin Books 1974.

Lipietz, Alain, *Mirages and Miracles: The Crisis of Global Fordism,* London: Verso 1987.

—— "Reflection on a Tale: The Marxist Foundations of the Concepts of Regulation and Accumulation," *Studies in Political Economy,* 26, 1988, pp. 7–36.

Lipson, Charles, "The Transformation of Trade," *International Organization*, 36, 2, 1982, pp. 417–55.

Lomnitz, Larissa Adler, "Informal Exchange Networks in Formal Systems: A Theoretical Model," *American Anthropologist*, 90, 1, 1988, pp. 42–55.

Lopez, Robert S., "Hard Times and Investment in Culture," in W.K. Ferguson *et al.*, *The Renaissance*, New York: Harper & Row 1962, pp. 29–54.

—— "Quattrocento genovese," *Rivista Storica Italiana*, 75, 1963, pp. 709–27.

—— *The Commercial Revolution of the Middle Ages, 950–1350*, Cambridge: Cambridge University Press 1976.

Lopez, Robert S. and Irving Raymond, eds., *Medieval Trade in the Mediterranean World: Illustrative Documents*, New York: Columbia Univeristy Press 1955.

Luzzatto, Gino, *An Economic History of Italy; from the Fall of the Roman Empire to the Beginning of the Sixteenth Century*, New York: Barnes & Noble 1961.

McCormick, Thomas J., *America's Half Century. United States Foreign Policy in the Cold War*, Baltimore, MD: Johns Hopkins University Press 1989.

McIver, R.M., *The Modern State*, London: Oxford University Press 1932.

McMichael, Philip, "Incorporating Comparison within a World-Historical Perspective: An Alternative Comparative Method," *American Sociological Review*, 55, 1990, pp. 385–97.

McNeill, William, *The Pursuit of Power: Technology, Armed Force, and Society since A.D. 1000*, Chicago: University of Chicago Press 1984.

Maddison, Angus, "A Comparison of the Levels of GDP per capita in Developed and Developing Countries," *Journal of Economic History*, 43, 1, 1983, pp. 277–41.

Magdoff, Harry, *Imperialism. From the Colonial Age to the Present*, New York: Monthly Review 1978.

Maland, D., *Europe in the Seventeenth Century*, London: Macmillan 1966.

Mann, Michael, *The Sources of Social Power. Vol. I. A History of Power from the Beginning to A.D. 1760*, Cambridge: Cambridge University Press 1986.

Mantoux, Paul, *The Industrial Revolution in the Eighteenth Century*, London: Methuen 1961.

Marcus, G.J., *A Naval History of England. Vol. I. The Formative Centuries*, Boston: Little Brown 1961.

Marglin, Stephen A. and Juliet B. Schor, eds., *The Golden Age of Capitalism. Reinterpreting the Postwar Experience*, Oxford: Clarendon Press 1991.

Marshall, Alfred, *Industry and Trade*, London: Macmillan 1919.

—— *Principles of Economics*, London: Macmillan 1949.

Marshall, P.J., *Bengal: The British Bridgehead. Eastern India 1740–1828*, Cambridge: Cambridge University Press 1987.

Martines, Lauro, *Power and Imagination. City-States in Renaissance Italy*, Baltimore, MD: The Johns Hopkins University Press 1988.

Marx, Karl, *Capital*, Vol.I, Moscow: Foreign Languages Publishing House 1959.

—— *Capital*, Vol. III, Moscow: Foreign Languages Publishing House 1962.

Marx, Karl and Friedrich Engels, *The Communist Manifesto*, Harmondsworth: Penguin Books 1967.

Massey, Doreen, *Spatial Divisions of Labour: Social Structures and the Geography of Production*, London: Macmillan 1984.

Mathias, Peter, *The First Industrial Nation: An Economic History of Britain 1700–1914*, London: Methuen 1969.

Mattingly, Garrett, *The Armada*, Boston, MA: Houghton Mifflin 1959.

—— *Renaissance Diplomacy*, New York: Dover 1988.

Mayer, Arno, *Political Origins of the New Diplomacy, 1917–1918*, New Haven, CT: Yale University Press 1959.
—— *Dynamics of Couterrevolution in Europe, 1870–1956. An Analytic Framework*, New York: Harper & Row 1971.
—— *The Persistence of the Old Regime. Europe to the Great War*, New York: Pantheon 1981.
Mensch, Gerhard, *Stalemate in Technology*, Cambridge, MA: Ballinger 1979.
Milward, Alan S., *The Economic Effects of the Two World Wars on Britain*, London: Macmillan 1970.
Miskimin, Harry A., *The Economy of Early Renaissance Europe 1300–1460*, Englewood Cliffs, NJ: Prentice-Hall 1969.
Mitchell, B.R., "Statistical Appendix 1700–1914," in C.M. Cipolla, ed., *The Fontana Economic History of Europe*. Vol. IV, Part 2. *The Emergence of Industrial Societies*, London: Collins/Fontana 1973, pp. 738–820.
—— *European Historical Statistics 1750–1975*, London: Macmillan 1980.
Mjoset, Lars, "The Turn of Two Centuries: A Comparison of British and US Hegemonies," in D.P. Rapkin, ed., *World Leadership and Hegemony*, Boulder, CO: Lynne Reiner 1990, pp. 21–47.
Modelski, George, "The Long Cycle of Global Politics and the Nation-State," *Comparative Studies in Society and History*, 20, 2, 1978, pp. 214–38.
—— "Long Cycles, Kondratieffs and Alternating Innovations: Implications for U.S. Foreign Policy," in C.W. Kegley and P. McGowan, eds., *The Political Economy of Foreign Policy Behavior*, Beverly Hills, CA: Sage 1981, pp. 63–83.
—— *Long Cycles in World Politics*, Seattle, WA: University of Washington Press 1987.
Modelski, George and Sylvia Modelski, eds., *Documenting Global Leadership*, Seattle, WA: University of Washington Press 1988.
Modelski, George and William R. Thompson, *Seapower and Global Politics, 1494–1993*, Seattle, WA: University of Washington Press 1988.
Moffitt, Michael, *The World's Money. International Banking from Bretton Woods to the Brink of Insolvency*, New York: Simon & Schuster 1983.
Moore, Barrington, *Social Origins of Dictatorhip and Democracy. Lord and Peasant in the Making of the Modern World*, Boston: Beacon Press 1966.
Moss, D.J., "Birmingham and the Campaigns against the Orders-in-Council and East India Company Charter, 1812–13," *Canadian Journal of History. Annales Canadiennes d'Histoire*, 11, 2, 1976, pp. 173–88.
Nadel, George and Perry Curtis, eds., *Imperialism and Colonialism*, New York: Macmillan 1964.
Nef, John U., "The Progress of Technology and the Growth of Large-Scale Industry in Great Britain, 1540–1640," *The Economic History Review*, 5, 1, 1934, pp. 3–24.
—— *War and Human Progress*, New York: Norton 1968.
Neumann, Franz, *Behemoth: The Structure and Practice of National Socialism*, London: Gollancz 1942.
Nussbaum, Arthur, *A Concise History of the Law of Nations*, New York: Macmillan 1950.
O'Connor, James, *The Fiscal Crisis of the State*, New York: St Martin's Press 1973.
Odaka, Konosuke, "Is the Division of Labor Limited by the Extent of the Market? A Study of Automobile Parts Production in East and Southeast Asia," in K. Ohkawa, G. Ranis, and L. Meissner, eds., *Japan and the Developing*

Countries: A Comparative Analysis, Oxford: Basil Blackwell 1985, pp. 389–425.

Offe, Claus, *Disorganized Capitalism. Contemporary Transformations of Work and Politics*, Cambridge, MA: MIT University Press 1985.

Ogle, George E., *South Korea: Dissent within the Economic Miracle*, London: Zed Books 1990.

Okimoto, Daniel I. and Thomas P. Rohlen, *Inside the Japanese System: Readings on Contemporary Society and Political Economy*, Stanford, CA: Stanford University Press 1988.

Ozawa, Terutomo, *Multinationalism, Japanese Style: The Political Economy of Outward Dependency*, Princeton, NJ: Princeton University Press 1979.

—— "Japan," in J.H. Dunning, ed., *Multinational Enterprises, Economic Structure and International Competitiveness*, Chichester: John Wiley 1985, pp. 155–85.

—— "Foreign Direct Investment and Structural Transformation: Japan as a Recycler of Market and Industry," *Business & the Contemporary World*, 5, 2, 1993, pp. 129–50.

Palat, Ravi, *From World-Empire to World-Economy: Southeastern India and the Emergence of the Indian Ocean World-Economy, 1350–1650*, Ann Arbor, MI: UMI 1988.

Pannikar, Kavalam M., *Asia and Western Dominance. A Survey of the Vasco Da Gama Epoch of Asian History 1498–1945*, London: Allen & Unwin 1953.

Parboni, Riccardo, *The Dollar and its Rivals*, London: Verso 1981.

Parker, Geoffrey, *The Dutch Revolt*, Ithaca, NY: Cornell University Press 1977.

Parker, Geoffrey and Lesley Smith, eds., *The General Crisis of the Seventeenth Century*, London: Routledge & Kegan Paul 1985.

Parry, J.H., *The Age of the Reconnaissance. Discovery, Exploration and Settlement*, Berkeley, CA: California University Press 1981.

Payne, P.L., *British Entrepreneurship in the Nineteenth Century*, London: Macmillan 1974.

Perez, Carlota, "Structural Change and the Assimilation of New Technologies in the Economic and Social Systems," *Futures*, 15, 5, 1983, pp. 357–75.

Phelps Brown, E.H., "A Non-Monetarist View of the Pay Explosion," *Three Banks Review*, 105, 1975, pp. 3–24.

Phillips, Kevin, *Boiling Point. Republicans, Democrats, and the Decline of Middle-class Prosperity*, New York: Random House 1993.

Piore, Michael J. and Charles F. Sable, *The Second Industrial Divide: Possibilities for Prosperity*, New York: Basic Books 1984.

Pirenne, Henri, "Stages in the Social History of Capitalism," in R. Bendix and S. Lipset, eds., *Class, Status and Power: A Reader in Social Stratification*, Glencoe, IL: The Free Press 1953, pp. 501–17.

Platt, D.C.M., "British Portfolio Investment Overseas before 1820: Some Doubts," *Economic History Review*, 33, 1, 1980, pp. 1–16.

Polanyi, Karl, *The Great Transformation: The Political and Economic Origins of Our Time*, Boston, MA: Beacon Press 1957.

Pollard, Sidney, "Fixed Capital and the Industrial Revolution in Britain," *Journal of Economic History*, 24, 1964, pp. 299–314.

—— "Capital Exports, 1870–1914: Harmful or Beneficial?" *Economic History Review*, 2nd ser., 38, 1985, pp. 489–514.

Portes, Alejandro, "Paradoxes of the Informal Economy: The Social Basis of Unregulated Entrepreneurship," in N.J. Smelser and R. Swedberg, eds.,

Handbook of Economic Sociology, Princeton, NJ: Princeton University Press 1994, in press.

Portes, Alejandro, Manuel Castells, and Lauren A. Benton, eds., *The Informal Economy. Studies in Advanced and Less Developed Countries*, Baltimore, MD: The Johns Hopkins University Press 1989.

Postma, Johannes Menne, *The Dutch in the Atlantic Slave Trade, 1600–1815*, Cambridge: Cambridge University Press 1990.

Rapkin, David P., "The Contested Concept of Hegemonic Leadership," in D.P. Rapkin, ed., *World Leadership and Hegemony*, Boulder, CO: Lynne Reiner 1990, pp. 1–19.

Reich, Robert, *The Work of Nations. Preparing Ourselves for 21st-Century Capitalism*, New York: Random House 1992.

Riley, James C., *International Government Finance and the Amsterdam Capital Market 1740–1815*, Cambridge: Cambridge University Press 1980.

Romano, Ruggiero, "Between the Sixteenth and the Seventeenth Centuries: The Economic Crisis of 1619–22," in G. Parker and L.M. Smith, eds., *The General Crisis of the Seventeenth Century*, London: Routledge & Kegan Paul 1985, pp. 165–225.

Rosenau, James N., *Turbulence in World Politics: A Theory of Change and Continuity*, Princeton, NJ: Princeton University Press 1990.

Rosenberg, Hans, "Political and Social Consequences of the Great Depression of 1873–1896 in Central Europe," *Economic History Review*, 13, 1943, pp. 58–73.

Rostow, Walt W., *The Stages of Economic Growth. A Non-Communist Manifesto*, Cambridge: Cambridge University Press 1960.

Rubinstein, W.D., "Wealth, Elites, and the Class Structure of Modern Britain," *Past and Present*, 76, 1977, pp. 99–126.

Rueff, Jacques, *The Age of Inflation*, Chicago: Regenery 1964.

Ruggie, John G., "International Regimes, Transactions, and Change: Embedded Liberalism in the Postwar Economic Order," *International Organization*, 36, 2, 1982, pp. 379–415.

—— "Continuity and Transformation in the World Polity: Toward a Neorealist Synthesis," *World Politics*, 35, 2, 1983, pp. 261–85.

—— "Territoriality and Beyond: Problematizing Modernity in International Relations," *International Organization*, 47, 1, 1993, pp. 139–74.

Sable, Charles and Jonathan Zeitlin, "Historical Alternatives to Mass Production: Politics, Markets and Technology in Nineteenth-Century Industrialization," *Past and Present*, 108, 1985, pp. 133–76.

Said, Edward W., *Orientalism*, New York: Pantheon 1978.

—— *Culture and Imperialism*, New York: Knopf 1993.

Sassen, Saskia, *The Mobility of Labor and Capital: A Study in International Investment and Labor Flow*, Cambridge: Cambridge University Press 1988.

Saul, S.B., *Studies in British Overseas Trade, 1870–1914*, Liverpool: Liverpool University Press 1960.

—— "The Engineering Industry," in D.H. Aldcroft, ed., *The Development of British Industry and Foreign Competition, 1875–1914: Studies in Industrial Enterprise*, London: Allen & Unwin 1968, pp. 186–237.

—— *The Myth of the Great Depression, 1873–1896*, London: Macmillan 1969.

Sayers, R.S., *Lloyds Bank in the History of English Banking*, Oxford: Clarendon Press 1957.

Schama, Simon, *The Embarrassment of Riches. An Interpretation of Dutch*

Culture in the Golden Age, Berkeley, CA: University of California Press 1988.

—— *Citizens: A Chronicle of the French Revolution*, New York: Knopf 1989.

Schevill, Ferdinand, *History of Florence: from the Founding of the City through the Renaissance*, New York: Harcourt, Brace & Co. 1936.

Schumpeter, Joseph, *Capitalism, Socialism, and Democracy*, London: George Allen & Unwin 1954.

—— *Imperialism – Social Classes*, New York: Meridian 1955.

—— *The Theory of Economic Development*, New York: Oxford University Press 1963.

Schurmann, Franz, *The Logic of World Power. An Inquiry into the Origins, Currents, and Contradictions of World Politics*, New York: Pantheon 1974.

Scott, A.J., *New Industrial Spaces: Flexible Production Organization and Regional Development in North America and Western Europe*, London: Pion 1988.

Semmel, Bernard, *The Rise of Free Trade Imperialism*, Cambridge: Cambridge University Press 1970.

Sereni, A.P., *The Italian Conception of International Law*, New York: Columbia University Press 1943.

Servan-Schreiber, J.-J., *The American Challenge*, New York: Athaeneum 1968.

Shaw, W.A., *The History of Currency 1252 to 1894*, New York: Putnam's 1896.

Silver, Beverly J., "Class Struggle and Kondratieff Waves, 1870 to the Present," in A. Kleinknecht, E. Mandel, and I. Wallerstein, eds., *New Findings in Long Wave Research*, New York: St Martin's Press 1992, pp. 279–96.

—— "World-Scale Patterns of Labor–Capital Conflict: Labor Unrest, Long Waves and Cycles of Hegemony," *Review*, 18, 1, 1995, in press.

Skinner, W.G., "The Structure of Chinese History," *Journal of Asian Studies*, 44, 2, 1985, pp. 271–92.

Sklar, Martin J., *The Corporate Reconstruction of American Capitalism, 1890–1916. The Market, the Law, and Politics*, Cambridge: Cambridge University Press 1988.

Smith, Adam, *An Inquiry into the Nature and Causes of the Wealth of Nations*, 2 vols, London: Methuen 1961.

Smitka, Michael J., *Competitive Ties. Subcontracting in the Japanese Automotive Industry*, New York: Columbia University Press 1991.

Stallings, B., "The Reluctant Giant: Japan and the Latin American Debt Crisis," *Journal of Latin American Studies*, 22, 1990, pp. 1–30.

Stedman Jones, Gareth, "The History of US Imperialism," in R. Blackburn, ed., *Ideology in Social Science*, New York: Vintage 1972, pp. 207–37.

Steensgaard, Niels, *The Asian Trade Revolution of the Seventeenth Century. The East Indian Companies and the Decline of the Caravan Trade*, Chicago: The University of Chicago Press 1974.

—— "Violence and the Rise of Capitalism: Frederic C. Lane's Theory of Protection and Tribute," *Review*, 5, 2, 1981, pp. 247–73.

—— "The Seventeenth-century Crisis," in G. Parker and L.M. Smith, eds., *The General Crisis of the Seventeenth Century*, London: Routledge & Kegan Paul, 1985, pp. 26–56.

Steven, Rob, *Japan's New Imperialism*, Armonk, NY: Sharpe 1990.

Stopford, John M. and John H. Dunning, *Multinationals: Company Performance and Global Trends*, London: Macmillan 1983.

Storper, Michael and Richard Walker, *The Capitalist Imperative: Territory, Technology, and Industrial Growth*, Oxford: Basil Blackwell 1989.

Strange, Susan, "The Management of Surplus Capacity: How Does Theory Stand up to Protectionism 1970s Style?" *International Organization*, 33, 3, 1979, pp. 303–34.

——— *Casino Capitalism*, Oxford: Basil Blackwell 1986.

Strange, Susan and R. Tooze, eds., *The International Management of Surplus Capacity*, London: Allen & Unwin 1982.

Supple, Barry E., *Commercial Crisis and Change in England 1600–42*, Cambridge: Cambridge University Press 1959.

Sylos-Labini, Paolo, "Competition: The Product Markets," in T. Wilson and A.S. Skinner, eds., *The Market and the State: Essays in Honor of Adam Smith*, Oxford: Clarendon Press 1976, pp. 200–32.

Taylor, Peter, "Territoriality and Hegemony, Spatiality and the Modern World-System," Newcastle upon Tyne: Department of Geography, University of Newcastle upon Tyne 1991.

——— "'Ten Years That Shook the World'? The United Provinces as the First Hegemonic State," Newcastle upon Tyne: Department of Geography, University of Newcastle upon Tyne 1992.

Thompson, William R., *On Global War: Historical-Structural Approaches to World Politics*, Columbia, SC: University of South Carolina Press 1988.

——— "Dehio, Long Cycles, and the Geohistorical Context of Structural Transition," *World Politics*, 45, 1992, pp. 127–52.

Thrift, Nigel, "The Internationalization of Producer Services and the Integration of the Pacific Basin Property Market," in M. Taylor and N. Thrift, eds., *Multinationals and the Restructuring of the World Economy: The Geography of Multinationals*, Vol. 2, London: Croom Helm 1986, pp. 142–92.

Tickell, Adam and Jamie A. Peck, "Accumulation, Regulation and the Geographies of Post-Fordism: Missing Links in Regulationist Research," *Progress in Human Geography*, 16, 2, 1992, pp. 190–218.

Tilly, Charles, "Reflections on the History of European State Making," in C. Tilly, ed., *The Formation of National States in Western Europe*, Princeton, NJ: Princeton University Press 1975, pp. 3–83.

——— *Big Structures, Large Processes, Huge Comparisons*, New York: Russell Sage 1984.

——— *Coercion, Capital, and European States, AD 990–1990*, Oxford: Basil Blackwell 1990.

Tilly, Richard, "Germany, 1815–1870," in R. Cameron, ed., *Banking in the Early Stages of Industrialization: A Study in Comparative Economic History*, New York: Oxford University Press 1967, pp. 151–82.

Tomlinson, B.R., "India and the British Empire, 1880–1935," *The Indian Economic and Social History Review*, 12, 4, 1975, pp. 337–80.

Tracy, James D., *A Financial Revolution in the Habsburg Netherlands. Renten and Rentiers in the Country of Holland*, Berkeley, CA: University of California Press 1985.

Trevor-Roper, H.R., "The General Crisis of the Seventeenth Century," in T. Aston, ed., *Crisis in Europe, 1560–1660*, Garden City, NY: Doubleday Anchor 1967.

United Nations, *World Economic Survey*, New York: United Nations 1990.

United Nations Center on Transnational Corporations, *Transnational Corporations in World Development. Third Survey*, New York: United Nations 1983.

Van Alstyne, Richard W., *The Rising American Empire*, New York: Norton 1960.

——— "Woodrow Wilson and the Idea of the Nation State," *International Affairs*, 37, 1961, pp. 293–308.

vanDoorn, Jacques, ed., *Armed Forces and Society*, The Hague: Mouton 1975.
Van Dormael, Armand, *Bretton Woods: Birth of a Monetary System*, London: Macmillan 1978.
van Leur, Jacob C., *Indonesian Trade and Society: Essays in Asian Social and Economic History*, The Hague and Bandung: W. van Hoewe 1955.
Veblen, Thorstein, *The Theory of Business Enterprise*, New Brunswick, NJ: Transaction Books 1978.
Versluysen, Eugène L., *The Political Economy of International Finance*, New York: St Martin's Press 1981.
Vilar, Pierre, *A History of Gold and Money 1450–1920*, London: Verso 1976.
Wakeman, Frederic, *The Fall of Imperial China*, New York: Free Press 1975.
Wallerstein, Immanuel, *The Modern World System I. Capitalist Agriculture and the Origins of the European World-Economy in the Sixteenth Century*, New York: Academic Press 1974a.
—— "The Rise and Future Demise of the World Capitalist System: Concepts for Comparative Analysis," *Comparative Studies in Society and History*, 16, 4, 1974b, pp. 387–415.
—— *The Capitalist World-Economy*, Cambridge: Cambridge University Press 1979.
—— *The Modern World System II: Mercantilism and the Consolidation of the European World-Economy, 1600–1750*, New York: Academic Press 1980.
—— *Historical Capitalism*, London: Verso 1983.
—— "The Three Instances of Hegemony in the History of the Capitalist World-Economy," *International Journal of Comparative Sociology*, 24, 1–2, 1984, pp. 100–8.
—— *The Modern World-System III. The Second Era of Great Expansion of the Capitalist World-Economy, 1730–1840s*, New York: Academic Press 1988.
—— *Unthinking Social Science: The Limits of Nineteenth-Century Paradigms*, Cambridge: Polity Press 1991.
Walter, Andrew, *World Power and World Money. The Role of Hegemony and International Monetary Order*, New York: St Martin's Press 1991.
Walton, John, "The Third 'New' International Division of Labor," in J. Walton, ed., *Capital and Labor in the Urbanized World*, Beverly Hills, CA: Sage 1985, pp. 3–16.
Waltz, Kenneth N., *The Theory of International Politics*, Reading, MA: Addison-Wesley 1979.
Washbrook, David, "South Asia, the World System, and World Capitalism," *The Journal of Asian Studies*, 49, 3, 1990, pp. 479–508.
Weber, Max, *The Protestant Ethic and the Spirit of Capitalism*, London: Unwin 1930.
—— *General Economic History*, New York: Collier 1961.
—— *Economy and Society*, Berkeley, CA: California University Press 1978.
Wilkins, Mira, *The Emergence of Multinational Enterprise*, Cambridge: Cambridge University Press 1970.
Williams, Eric, *Capitalism and Slavery*, London: André Deutsch 1964.
Williams, William A., *The Roots of the Modern American Empire: A Study of the Growth and Shaping of Social Consciousness in a Marketplace Society*, New York: Random House 1969.
Williamson, Jeffrey G., *American Growth and the Balance of Payments 1820–1913. A Study of the Long Swing*, Chapel Hill, NC: The University of North Carolina Press 1964.
Williamson, Oliver, *Corporate Control and Business Behavior*, Englewood Cliffs,

NJ: Prentice Hall 1970.

Wilson, Charles, *Mercantilism*, London: Routledge & Kegan Paul 1958.

—— *Anglo-Dutch Commerce and Finance in the Eighteenth Century*, Cambridge: Cambridge University Press 1966.

—— *The Dutch Republic and the Civilization of the Seventeenth Century*, New York: McGraw-Hill 1968.

Wolf, Eric, *Europe and the People without History*, Berkeley, CA: University of California Press 1982.

Wood, George Henry, "The Statistics of Wages in the Nineteenth Century. Part XIX. The Cotton Industry," *Journal of the Royal Statistical Society*, n.s., 73, part 6, 1910, pp. 585–626.

World Bank, *World Developement Report*, New York: Oxford University Press, various years.

Woronoff, Jon, *Japan's Commercial Empire*, Armonk, NY: M.E. Sharp 1984.

Woytinsky, W.S. and E.S. Woytinsky, *World Population and Production. Trends and Outlook*, New York: The Twentieth Century Fund 1953.

Yoshihara, Kunio, *Japanese Investment in Southeast Asia*, Honolulu: University of Hawaii Press 1978.

Yoshino, M.Y. and Thomas B. Lifson, *The Invisible Link: Sogo Shosha and the Organization of Trade*, Cambridge, MA: MIT Press 1986.

Zimmerman, L.J., "The Distribution of World Income 1860–1960," in E. de Vries, ed., *Essays in Unbalanced Growth*, The Hague: Mouton 1962, pp. 28–55.

Zloch-Christy, Iliana, *Debt Problems of Eastern Europe*, New York: Cambridge University Press 1987.

Index